Yugoslavia
at the Paris Peace Conference

A Study in Frontiermaking

Yugoslavia at the Paris Peace Conference

A STUDY IN FRONTIERMAKING

by Ivo J. Lederer

New Haven and London, Yale University Press, 1963

Library of Congress catalog card number: 63-13966
Published with assistance from the foundation
established in memory of Philip Hamilton McMillan
of the Class of 1894, Yale College.

FOR MICHAEL AND PHILIP

Contents

Preface

YUGOSLAVIA has led a troubled existence since its inception in 1918. A mosaic of nationalities, religions, cultural heritages, and levels of socio-economic advancement, it has not enjoyed much internal stability. Nor has it enjoyed notable security in the international sphere. Both phenomena are closely related to the forces that produced the Serbo-Croat-Slovene state at the end of World War I.

This study is concerned with one aspect of Yugoslavia's formative history, the making of its frontiers in 1918–20. The young state was without firmly set frontiers for nearly two years, a circumstance that affected adversely every facet of its national life. Yet once the frontiers were set, the problem was far from resolved. Ringed by seven neighboring states—Albania, Greece, Bulgaria, Rumania, Hungary, Austria, and Italy—Yugoslavia faced territorial disputes with all save Greece. This reality dominated Yugoslav foreign relations between the two world wars and considerably influenced its internal life. Even today, despite a foreign policy in which factors of communist ideology appear to be given precedence, it continues to affect Yugoslavia's relations with the outside world. Some borderland disputes have by now been resolved and some are presently inert. But the possibility that at a future point some issues may be revived can certainly not be excluded.

It would be an exaggeration to suggest that all this is a legacy of the Paris peace settlement. Territorial conflicts throughout Southeast Europe are also rooted in the distant past, in the entangled pattern of nationality movements and in the complex history of the region as a whole. Indeed, the disputed and changing frontier has been—particularly since the mid-nineteenth century—a dominant theme of Balkan history, an intoxicant for nationalist movements, and an unfailing catalyst of conflict. The peacemakers of Paris rearranged Balkan frontiers in 1919. Their handiwork, perhaps inevitably, did not bring stability to the region. Nevertheless, it signified a crucial step forward for Yugoslavia. It provided the new nation with viable frontiers which, in a world system based on a confrontation of nation-states, was considered essential to the full exercise of its creative energies.

A fair amount has been written about Yugoslav problems at the time of World War I. Much of the literature, however, reflects highly partisan points of view—Serb, Croat, Yugoslav irredentist, pro-Italian, anti-Versailles revisionist—or, in the case of interwar historians mainly interested in the peace conference, a singular preoccupation with the so-called "Adriatic question," to the exclusion of Yugoslavia's other territorial issues. Most of the literature, moreover, was necessarily based on limited documentation. It thus concentrated on the central stage of wartime councils and the peace conference, while underplaying the formation of national policies as they evolved in the *coulisses* and the records of individual statesmen. This is particularly true of Yugoslav policies and statesmen at the peace conference.

This monograph seeks to analyze Yugoslav territorial issues at the end of World War I in a comprehensive frame, focusing not only on the labors of the peace conference but also on national, especially Yugoslav, policies. It makes extensive use of recently available Yugoslav archival sources. These sources, complemented by Italian, American, and peace conference materials, permit a deeper exploration of the subject than has heretofore been possible. For the student of general Yugoslav history, the vicissitudes of Yugoslav peace conference diplomacy will also reveal symptoms of the political malaise that plagued the country from its inception to the brutal civil war of 1941–45. But in addition to elucidating an important chapter of Yugoslav history, this study is also intended to fill one of the remaining gaps in the historiography of the Paris Peace Conference.

Of the various problems encountered in the preparation of this work, the reader should be alerted to at least two. One pertains to nonterritorial issues, the other to the rendition of geographical names. The issues of economic reconstruction, reparations, the League of Nations Covenant, war guilt, war crimes, and Yugoslav participation in special (nonterritorial) commissions established by the peace conference lie outside the scope of this study. They are referred to only in connection with the main theme of frontier making. Thus, for example, the disposition of the former Austro-Hungarian maritime fleet receives considerable attention, because it became a major political factor in Italo-Yugoslav territorial negotiations.

As to the rendition of geographical names, the problem of uniformity has proved difficult to resolve. In 1918–20 most disputed localities were known under a Slav as well as an Italian, German, Magyar, Rumanian, or Albanian name. Under the circumstances, the Serbo-Croat version has been adopted as the standard. Yet a number of exceptions appear in the text. For example, Rijeka is rendered as Fiume, Zadar as Zara, Celovec as Klagenfurt. In deciding on this matter the author was guided by the following criterion: main localities *not* assigned to Yugoslavia by the peace settlements are rendered in their non-Slav version, while the others are given in Serbo-Croat (as in the case of Maribor rather than Marburg, Split rather than Spalato). This method corresponds to the prevailing usage of the time and has no other significance. Wherever appropriate, usually on the first mention, both names are given in the text, as for example Fiume (Rijeka). However, this practice could not be carried through the entire text.

It is gratifying to be able to record my indebtedness to those who so generously helped me in this enterprise. I am, first of all, grateful to Professor Cyril E. Black of Princeton University for his constant support and encouragement. I owe a special debt to the late Professor Slobodan Jovanović for the many discussions in London in which he let me draw on his vast knowledge of Serbian and Yugoslav history. My work benefited greatly from discussions with Dr. Ivan Soubbotitch of New York and the late H. Wickham Steed. Dr. Bogdan Krizman of Zagreb, whose researches and articles on Yugoslav affairs at the end of World War I were in themselves of immense help, gave me valued criticism and counsel.

In the course of my work I received much appreciated cooperation from the staffs of the Library of the School of Slavonic and East European Studies of the University of London and the British Museum, London; the Bibliothèque de Documentation Internationale Contemporaine, Paris; the Library of Congress and the National Archives, Washington, D.C.; the Archive of the Serbian Academy, Belgrade; the Archive of the Historical Institute of the

Yugoslav Academy, Zagreb; the Archive of the Italian Ministry of Foreign Affairs, Rome; the Princeton University Library; and the Yale University Library. For special assistance and cooperation I am particularly indebted to Dr. Howard B. Gotlieb, Librarian of Historical Manuscripts and the Edward M. House Collection at the Yale University Library; to Dr. Matko Rojnić, Director of the Library of the University of Zagreb; and to Professor Rodolfo Mosca of the University of Florence and the Commissione per la Pubblicazione dei Documenti Diplomatici Italiani in Rome. I should also like to record my debt to Mr. Reinhold Krallert of Vienna and Mr. Robert L. Williams of Yale University for preparing the maps; to Mrs. Carole Parsons for preparing the index; and to Mr. William E. Gould, Yale '64, for valuable clerical assistance.

I am grateful for the financial support of the Ford Foundation; the Slavic and East European Grants Committee of the American Council of Learned Societies and the Social Science Research Council; the Faculty Research Fund at Princeton University; and the Morse and Stimson Funds at Yale University.

New Haven, Conn.
January 1963   I.J.L.

Abbreviations

Arch. Gab., or Gab.	Archivio di Gabinetto, or Gabinetto.
BDIC	Bibliothèque de Documentation Internationale Contemporaine, Paris.
CRYA-PV	"Committee on Rumanian and Yugoslav Affairs," *Procès Verbal*. Papers of the American Commission to Negotiate the Peace, 1919–20, Department of State, Washington, D.C.
DBFP	*Documents on British Foreign Policy, 1919–1939*, E. L. Woodward and R. Butler, eds., Vol. 4, 1st Ser. London, 1952.
DDI	*I Documenti diplomatici italiani*, R. Mosca, ed., Vol. I, 6th Ser. Rome, 1956.
Délibérations	*Les Délibérations du Conseil des Quatre (24 Mars–28 Juin, 1919)*, P. Mantoux, ed., 2 vols. Paris, 1955.
FRUS	*Papers Relating to the Foreign Relations of the United States, 1918–1919*, 4 vols. Washington, 1930–34.
FRUS-PPC	*Papers Relating to the Foreign Relations of the United States. The Paris Peace Conference, 1919*, 13 vols. Washington, 1942–47.
House Papers	C. Seymour, *The Intimate Papers of Colonel House*, 4 vols. Boston, 1926–28.
Int. Bez.	*Die Internationale Beziehungen im Zeitalter des Imperialismus*, O. Hoetzsch, ed., 8 vols. Berlin, 1931–36.

K&H

B. Krizman and B. Hrabak, eds., *Zapisnici sa Sednica Delegacije Kraljevine SHS na Mirovnoj Konferenciji u Parizu 1919–1920,* Belgrade, 1960.

MFA

Archives of the Ministry of Foreign Affairs, Rome.

Miller *Diary*

D. H. Miller, *My Diary at the Conference of Paris,* 20 vols., privately printed, 1928.

Question Adriatique

P. H. Michel, ed., *La Question de l'Adriatique (1914–1918)—recueil de documents,* Paris, 1938.

Résolutions

Actes du Conseil Suprême. Recueil des résolutions (Paris, 1934–35). Printed for official use.

Sten. Bel.

Stenografske Beleške Privremenog Narodnog Pretstavništva Srba, Hrvata i Slovenaca, 1919–1920, 5 fascs. Belgrade, 1920.

TP, F

The Trumbić Papers, Fascicle. Arhiv. Istorijski Institut Jugoslavenske Akademije Znanosti i Nauka, Zagreb.

Tel. Arr. and Tel. Part.

Telegrammi in Arrivo and Telegrammi in Partenza, MFA.

Wilson Letters

R. S. Baker, *Woodrow Wilson: Life and Letters,* 8 vols. Garden City, N.Y., 1927–39.

Zap.

"Zapisnik Delegacije S.H.S. na Mirovnoj Konferenciji u Parizu, 1919–1920," Manuscript Division, Library of the University of Zagreb.

Guide to Pronunciation

c—ts as in Keats.

č—ch as in chess.

ć—also ch but softer than č.

dj—j as in jest.

j—y as in yes.

š—sh as in short.

ž—as the French j in *jour*.

PART I

War and Armistice

1. World War I and the Yugoslav Movement

WORLD WAR I revolutionized the political configuration of Europe. Nowhere was this more evident than in the Balkans, where Southern Slav nationalism and Allied victory combined to bring into being the Kingdom of Serbs, Croats, and Slovenes on December 1, 1918.[1] The emergence of the Yugoslav state—through the union of the Kingdom of Serbia, the Croat and Slovene provinces of Austria-Hungary, and the Kingdom of Montenegro—was not foreseen when the war began. Yet when the new state emerged, it testified to the revolutionary consequences of the war. A pivotal force in the Balkans, Yugoslavia immediately commanded a strategic position as the gateway between Central Europe and the Middle East, and played a notable role in the maintenance of the political order established at Versailles.

Allied victory was a precondition to the founding of the new state, but by no means its cause. The ideological roots of the Yugoslav union extend back into the nineteenth century and are closely linked to the struggles for emancipation from Ottoman and Habsburg rule. As elsewhere in Central and Eastern Europe, initial nationalist manifestations appeared in the form of a literary and intellectual agitation that presently led to political action. By the turn of the twentieth century the notion of Serbo-Croat-Slovene kinship was firmly implanted in Southern Slav society. *Yugoslavism* came to represent a practical platform for political cooperation between Serbs, Croats, and Slovenes. The years of turbulence following the Bosnian Crisis of 1908 served to galvanize Southern Slav nationalism. Finally, the outbreak in August 1914 of war on a con-

1. This was the official name of the new state until 1929, when the term "Yugoslavia" was adopted. For the sake of convenience, and because the terms were already commonly used during World War I and at the Paris Peace Conference, "Yugoslavia," the "Kingdom of Serbs, Croats, and Slovenes," and the "Serbo-Croat-Slovene State" will be used interchangeably throughout this study. The term "Southern Slavs," as used in this study, is intended to include only the peoples of Yugoslavia, not the Bulgarians.

tinental scale offered the first practical possibility of creating a
Yugoslav state. Only such a war could lead to the disintegration of
Austria-Hungary and pave the way for the union of Serbs, Croats,
and Slovenes.

The wartime leaders of the Yugoslav movement, however, faced
a formidable struggle. First of all, their objectives were not shared
by the Entente. The Allies were primarily interested in crushing
the might of Imperial Germany, not in the dismemberment of
Austria-Hungary. Had the fortunes of war in 1918 not dictated
a change of Allied policy toward the Habsburg empire, the Yugoslavs might not so readily have gained their way. Second, one
major Allied power, Italy, was intrinsically opposed to Yugoslav
unification and did much to obstruct its realization. Hoping to
replace Austria-Hungary as the dominant power in the Balkans,
the Italians entered the war in 1915 on the promise—given by
Great Britain, France, and tsarist Russia—that they would gain
key territories on the eastern shores of the Adriatic and a commanding position in Albania. The secret Treaty of London,
through which Italy's intervention was obtained, was long to
plague Yugoslav and Allied statesmanship alike.

Finally, Yugoslav leadership was split into two competing wings.
The Serbian government, headed by Nikola Pašić and his Radical
Party, took for granted the right to represent the interests of all
the Southern Slavs before the Allied world. Pašić, whose philosophy was bound to traditional concepts of territorial compensation,[2] expected Allied victory to result in an enlarged Serbian
kingdom that would include adjacent Serb-inhabited territories
and, possibly, the Croat and Slovene provinces of Austria-Hungary.
He accepted the view—expressed by his government and the
Skupština in November 1914—that Serbia's war aims included
the "liberation and unification" of all the Serbs, Croats, and
Slovenes. However, he envisaged this process within a Serbian

2. For the development of Pašić's ideas see Charles Jelavich, "Nikola P. Pasić:
Greater Serbia or Jugoslavia?" *Journal of Central European Affairs, 11* (1951), pp.
133–52; M. Djordjević, *Srbija i Jugosloveni za Vreme Rata, 1914–1918* (Belgrade,
1922); Oscar Randi, *Nicola P. Pašić* (Rome, 1927); Carlo Sforza, *Nikola Pašić* (Belgrade, 1937); Slobodan Jovanović, *Moji Savremenici: Nikola Pašić* (Windsor, Canada,
1962).

national framework, not one calling for the abdication of Serbia's sovereignty.

Pašić's approach came into conflict with the ideas of the scores of Croat and Slovene political leaders who made their way to Western Europe when the war broke out. Organized into a Yugoslav Committee by Frano Supilo and Ante Trumbić, the emigrés envisaged an eventual Yugoslav state as an organic union and equal partnership of Serbs, Croats, and Slovenes, not an enlarged Serbia.[3] Supported mainly by contributions from Yugoslavs living in America and aided by a group of influential British and French sympathizers, the Yugoslav Committee, after a brief sojourn in Rome, established itself in London and Paris. There, like the Czechoslovak and Polish National Committees, it began to lobby in official Allied circles for its own political program. Throughout most of the war the Yugoslav Committee and the Serbian government did little to coordinate their efforts. In mid-1917 they agreed upon a joint program, yet often continued to work at cross-purposes. Time and exigency failed to mend the breach. The road was thus full of pitfalls and the outcome by no means clear.

The war, everyone thought, would not last very long. Both the Allied and the Central Powers hoped for an early and decisive end. But victory proved elusive and by late 1914 military stalemate was at hand. This development had a profound effect on the fortunes of the Southern Slavs.

In their search to change the military balance, the Allies and the Central Powers turned to neutral Italy. Though bound to Germany and Austria-Hungary through the Triple Alliance, Italy had remained on the sidelines, because the alliance was formally defensive and Austria-Hungary had attacked Serbia. But when the military stalemate began to draw Italy toward war, the government in Rome started to negotiate with both sides in order to

3. On the history of the Yugoslav Committee see M. Paulova, *Jugoslavenski Odbor* (Zagreb, 1925); N. Stojanović, *Jugoslovenski Odbor: Članci i Dokumenti* (Zagreb, 1927); F. Potočnjak, *Kobne Smjernice Naše Politike Spram Italije* (Zagreb, 1925), and *Iz Emigracije* (2 vols. Zagreb, 1919); A. Mandić, *Fragmenti Za Historiju Ujedinjenja* (Zagreb, 1956); D. Šepić, *Supilo Diplomat. Rad Frana Supila u Emigraciji, 1914–1917 godina* (Zagreb, 1961).

obtain the highest price for its intervention. In March 1915, negotiations began in earnest. Within six weeks Rome, London, Paris, and Petrograd came to terms, and on April 26, 1915, signed the Treaty of London which brought Italy into the war on the Allied side.[4] Allied Serbia was not consulted or informed of the treaty's terms. The secrecy was motivated by practical considerations. Allied statesmen were about to grant Italy the Dalmatian littoral and key concessions in Albania, to which Serbia was not likely to agree. Also, by maintaining secrecy, they hoped to maximize the psychological and military impact of Italy's entry into the war.

Total secrecy, however, could hardly be maintained in negotiations involving four capitals. Members of the Yugoslav Committee and the Serbian ministers in Rome, Paris, London, and Petrograd inevitably learned that a momentous transaction involving Yugoslav interests was in the making. But they knew none of the details. Thus they did not know that Italian demands, formulated by Foreign Minister Baron Sidney Sonnino and transmitted on March 4 in London by his ambassador, the Marquis Guglielmo di Francavilla Imperiali, were readily accepted by Great Britain and France.[5] Nor did they know during the next few weeks that inter-Allied discussions centered on Russia's opposition to assigning Dalmatia to Italy.

The Russian qualms were logical. The tsarist government had good strategic and political reason to protect Serbian interests. The two countries were also dynastically and culturally linked. After 1903, Serbia had become the main outpost of Russian influence in the Balkans, a fact that greatly influenced the tsarist decision to go to war in 1914. Thus in the spring of 1915 Foreign Minister Sergei D. Sazonov could not lightly abandon Serbian interests and risk forfeiting Russia's future position in the Balkans. Great Britain and France, however, were moved mainly by military

4. For detailed treatments of these negotiations see M. Marjanović, *Londonski Ugovor iz Godine 1915* (Zagreb, 1960); F. Šišić, *Predratna Politika Italije i Postanak Londonskog Pakta* (Split, 1933); M. Toscano, *Il Patto di Londra* (Bologna, 1934) and *La Serbia e l'intervento in guerra dell'Italia* (Milano, 1939); A. Salandra, *La Neutralità italiana* (Milano, 1928), and *L'Intervento* (Milano, 1931); R. Albrecht-Carrié, *Italy at the Paris Peace Conference* (New York, 1938).

5. Salandra, *L'Intervento*, pp. 149, 155.

considerations. The fighting was inconclusive and only Italy, it seemed, could swing the balance in their favor. Under heavy pressure from London, Paris, and his own military colleagues, Sazonov gradually gave in. On April 21 the Russian ambassador in London, Count Aleksandr Konstantinovich Benckendorff, was authorized to sign.[6]

By the terms of the secret treaty Italy was promised the Austrian-held Trentino, the Southern Tyrol, Trieste, the counties of Gorizia-Gradisca, the Istrian peninsula as far as the Quarnero, including Volosca and the islands of Cherso and Lussin. Fiume (Rijeka) was conspicuously excluded. Parts of Albania were reserved for Serbia, Montenegro, and Greece, while Italy would receive the strategic port of Valona and a protectorate over the rest of the country. Italy was also promised the Dodecanese archipelago, part of the Anatolian littoral—if the Turkish empire were partitioned —possibly territories in Libya, Eritrea, and Somaliland, a just share of the war indemnity, an immediate loan of fifty million sterling, British and French naval assistance against the Austrian fleet, Russian military assistance through intensified pressure on the eastern Austrian front, the exclusion of the Vatican from the peace conference, and a pledge that the terms of the London treaty would not be revealed to nonsignatory powers, including Italy's new ally, Serbia. The main reason for this pledge lay in Article 5, which assigned to Italy the province of Dalmatia, from Lisarica and Tribanj in the north to Cape Planka in the south, the islands facing that portion of the coast, as well as Lagosta, Pelagosa, and Lissa.

Sonnino insisted on obtaining Dalmatia for reasons of security, geopolitics, and historical sentimentality. The eastern Adriatic coast, providing through its islands and inlets incomparable cover for naval operations and unique facilities for naval bases, contrasts sharply with the barren western coast. Control of Dalmatia, therefore, would not only ensure the safety of the western littoral

---

6. *Die Internationale Beziehungen im Zeitalter des Imperialismus,* trans. and ed. O. Hoetzsch (8 vols. Berlin, 1931–36), II, 7, ii, pp. 575–76. (This collection contains official tsarist documents, published after the Bolshevik Revolution by the Soviet Commission for the Publication of Documents in the Age of Imperialism. Hereafter it is cited as *Int. Bez.*)

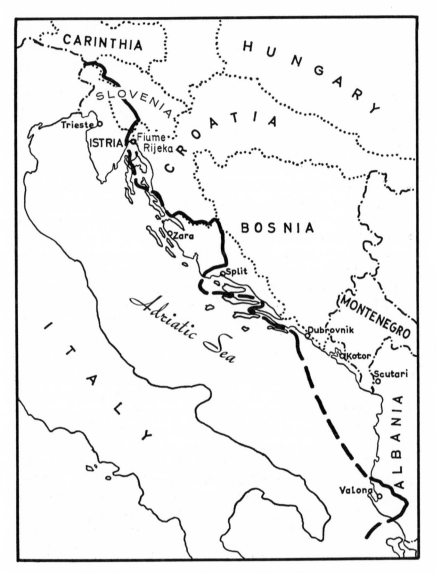

The Line of the Treaty of London, 1915

but also enhance Italian naval mastery over the whole Adriatic.[7] Combined with a protectorate over Albania and possession of Valona, it would also serve as a bridgehead for furthering Italy's political dominance in the Balkans. As an historical outpost of Italian culture (Dalmatia was long ruled by Venice until it fell to Austria by the Treaty of Campo Formio in 1797 [8]), its acquisition catered to the nationalist imagination.

In 1915 Sonnino believed that after the war Italy would still face a hostile power to the east. He counted on the survival of a much weakened Austria-Hungary, feared an increase of Russian power in the Balkans, particularly if Serbia were unduly enlarged, and did not anticipate the creation of a Yugoslav state. The security argument, though sound when applied to Austria's might as of 1914, was basically geopolitical rather than military. In 1915 even General Luigi Cadorna, Chief of the Italian General Staff, questioned the military importance of Dalmatia.[9] As to the historico-cultural argument, the Italian case was not convincing. Venetian sway came to an end in 1797, and by 1900 the Italian population component was diminutive compared to the Slav. In the nineteenth century Dalmatia became the cradle of Yugoslav nationalism, the center of the Illyrian Movement, and subsequently the fountainhead of Serbo-Croat cooperation. Modern Dalmatian civilization embodied both Slav and Italian contributions, but the latter had long been on the wane. Moreover, by the turn of the twentieth century Italians showed little *political* interest in Dalmatia, and *Italia Irredenta* was not presumed to extend beyond Trieste and Istria.[10] Despite the activities of the circle of *Pro Dalmazia Italiana,* Italian political figures of the late nineteenth

7. For the clearest exposition of the Italian strategic argument see G. Roncagli, *Il Problema militare adriatico spiegato a tutti* (Rome, 1918).

8. On the history of Dalmatia see L. Vojnović, *Histoire de la Dalmatie* (2 vols. Paris, 1934), and *La Dalmatie, l'Italie et l'unité yougoslave, 1797–1917* (Geneva, 1917); P. Digović, *La Dalmatie et les problèmes de l'Adriatique* (Lausanne, 1944); G. Prezzolini, *La Dalmatie* (Paris, 1917).

9. Carlo Sforza, *Jugoslavia, storia e ricordi* (Milano, 1948), p. 109, and *L'Italia dal 1914 al 1944 quale io la vidi* (Rome, 1946), p. 49.

10. This was so much the case that the Yugoslavs, as well as their friends in Italy and elsewhere, frequently cited Dante's famous dictum: "Pola, presso del Quarnaro/che Italia chiude e i suoi termini bagna" (*La Divina Commedia,* "Inferno," IX. 113–14).

century, including Crispi and even Sonnino, never contemplated
the acquisition of Dalmatia. Their ambitions stopped at the
Quarnero, heeding as it were Mazzini's pleas for Slav-Italian amity
and his dictum that "Istria is Italian and as necessary to Italians
as Dalmatia is to the Slavs." [11]

In 1915 the Yugoslavs did all they could to forestall Allied concessions to Italy, as soon as rumors about the negotiations began
to spread. Pašić first learned that the talks were under way in mid-
March, when Ljuba Mihajlović, the Serbian minister in Rome,
hastily traveled to see him in Niš. Pašić immediately inquired of
the Russians, who responded with uncomfortable silence. The Serbian ministers in London (Mata Bošković) and Petrograd (Miro-
slav Spalajković) kept an anxious vigil, but they too failed to
learn anything concrete. The first definite confirmation that Allied-
Italian negotiations had reached an advanced state came, ironically,
not from official Serbian sources but from the Croat emigré Supilo.

With the concurrence of the Yugoslav Committee, Supilo journeyed to Russia in February 1915 to press the cause of Yugoslav
unification. His prominence in prewar Croatian politics and his
stirring defense as a defendant at the Zagreb High Treason Trial
of 1909 had made him well known abroad. In London both Prime
Minister Herbert Asquith and Foreign Secretary Sir Edward Grey
had received him privately. In Petrograd, too, Supilo met with a
friendly reception.

The heavy atmosphere prevailing at the Russian Foreign Ministry and a chance remark concerning Italian demands alerted
him to the mounting danger. In mid-March he began sending a
series of cables to Trumbić and Pašić, asking for quick action in
all Allied capitals. He urged Trumbić to enlist the aid of R. W.
Seton-Watson and H. Wickham Steed, Foreign Editor of the London *Times,* both ardent partisans of the Yugoslav cause. But the
British Foreign Office remained unmoved. On March 26 Supilo
cabled Pašić, urging the Premier and Regent Alexander to issue
direct appeals to the Allied Powers. As for himself, Supilo made
the rounds of Petrograd officialdom, and even sought audiences
with the Tsar, with Rasputin, and with the British ambassador,

11. *Scritti editi e inediti di Guiseppe Mazzini, 14* (3d. ed. Rome, 1885), 215.

Sir George Buchanan. All was to no avail. On Sazonov's urging, Tsar Nicholas refused to receive him, for Russian policy was by now set.

During the week of April 4 Supilo accidentally stumbled on the truth. In a conversation with Sazonov in which the latter tried to reassure him of Russia's interest and sympathy, the Croat spoke as though he had already learned everything. Sazonov became embarrassed and revealed the current state of negotiations with Rome. Frightened by the extent of Allied concessions, Supilo intensified his efforts to bolster Russian resistance to Italian demands. Unable to thwart Allied designs, he at least succeeded in inducing Sazonov to fight, albeit temporarily, for Dalmatia.

In response to Supilo's frantic calls, Pašić and Alexander began to act. The Regent personally called on Prince Grigorii Fedorovich Trubetskoi, the tsarist minister in Niš, appealing to Russia to prevent the transfer of "Slav population from Austrian to Italian domination which would inevitably provoke a new war in the near future." [12] Pašić proposed to travel immediately to Russia, a plan Sazonov quickly vetoed. Pašić accordingly changed his tactics, instructing Spalajković to protest against the proposed concessions to Italy. "It is evident," Pašić cabled Spalajković, for transmittal to Sazonov, "that the Southern Slavs could not enjoy friendly and close relations with the Italians, except in the event of their receiving, together with liberty, their part of the Adriatic coast. United, the Serbs, Croats and Slovenes who inhabit Serbia, Montenegro, Hercegovina, Bosnia, Croatia, Slavonia, Dalmatia, Istria, Carinthia and Carniola, will constitute for Italy a powerful rampart against German assault." [13] But despite his high standing in Petrograd, Pašić too was unable to stay the course of events. In the face of military realities and Anglo-French pressure, Sazonov agreed to Sonnino's demands.

The Yugoslavs were unaware that the Treaty of London was signed on April 26. On that very day Trumbić visited Mikhail

12. Trubetskoi to Sazonov, March 31, 1915, in P. H. Michel, ed., *La Question de l'Adriatique (1914–1918)—recueil de documents* (Paris, 1938), p. 65 (hereafter cited as *Question Adriatique*).
13. Pašić to Spalajković, April 6, 1915 (ibid., p. 70).

Nikolaevich Giers, the Russian minister in Rome, to argue that the Allies were sowing the seeds of a future war.[14] Simultaneously, Pašić met with Trubetskoi and charged that Serbia was being abandoned.[15] Next day he sent an emotional cable to Spalajković, instructing him to tell Sazonov that the Southern Slavs "would prefer to remain under Austro-Hungarian domination than to be annexed to Italy" and that they would resist any intrusion on Slav territory.[16] The issue even broke into public debate in Niš. On April 28 the Skupština debated Serbian-Italian relations in a mood of great bitterness. But for Sazonov the issue was now closed and on April 29 he wrote to Trubetskoi: "Neither the Heir Apparent nor the Serbian government can doubt our ardent desire to defend Slav interests within limits of the possible. If we do not find it possible to fulfill in large measure all the wishes of the Slavs, this must be attributed to special circumstances. . . . Our rejection of his visit can be used by Pašić for his own justification in Serbian political circles." [17]

Realizing that the die had been cast, Pašić on May 4 informed the Russian, French, and British ministers that territorial concessions to Italy should still be treated as an open question, while the Skupština passed a resolution calling on the powers to keep the secret treaty from coming into effect.[18] Next day Prince Alexander addressed a lengthy letter to his great-uncle, the Grand Prince Nikolai Nikolaievich, warning that Serbia would send troops to Montenegro to prevent the landing of *Allied* Italian forces there and protesting the decision abandoning the Slavs of Istria and Dalmatia to Italy.[19]

In the west, meanwhile, the Yugoslav emigrés were preparing a dramatic move of their own. On May 12 the Yugoslav Committee

14. Giers to Sazonov, April 27, 1915 (ibid., pp. 95–96).

15. *Int. Bez.*, II, 7, ii, pp. 615–616. Jovan Jovanović, then a high official in the Serbian Ministry of Foreign Affairs, asserts that Pašić had already discovered on April 27 that the treaty had been signed. See J. Jovanović, *Borba za Narodno Ujedinjenje, 1914–1918* (Belgrade, 1934), p. 106.

16. *Question Adriatique*, p. 96.

17. *Int. Bez.*, II, 7, ii, p. 629.

18. *Question Adriatique*, pp. 102–03; F. Šišić, *Dokumenti o Postanku Kraljevine Srba, Hrvata i Slovenaca, 1914–1919* (Zagreb, 1920), p. 24.

19. See *Int. Bez.*, II, 7, ii, pp. 669–670. See also *Question Adriatique*, pp. 103–05, and Šišić, *Predratna Politika Italije*, pp. 127–28.

published a manifesto calling for the liberation and unification of all Southern Slavs and submitted a memorandum to this effect to the foreign ministers of Great Britain, France, and Russia.[20] With the aid of British friends, the Committee also issued an appeal for support to the British nation and to Parliament, an appeal that received much publicity and attention. The Committee's action fell on deaf ears in official quarters, but it marked the beginning of an intensive campaign in Western Europe and the United States that was to continue until the end of the war.

Allied grand strategy prevailed and Italy entered the war. But the Treaty of London led to unexpected results. The Italian military factor failed to tip the scales of war. The treaty nearly wrecked Italo-Serbian relations and had a bad effect on military operations in the Balkans. The Austrians adopted the slogan "Defend yourselves against Italian imperialism!" and induced many Croats and Slovenes, fighting under Habsburg colors, to fight with new vigor on the Italian front.[21] Serbia at first reacted with military passivity against the Austrians, which greatly exasperated Sonnino, and then began to move its army in the direction of Albania. Sonnino tried desperately to change Serbian tactics and urged London, Paris, and Petrograd to force the Serbs into activity on their western front. Pašić and the General Staff, however, would not budge. On June 8, Serbian units advanced into Albania, prompting the following reaction from Sonnino: "I do not regard it opportune to inform the Serbian Government of the particulars of the Treaty of London; but it is necessary that the British, French and Russian Governments convey energetic words at Niš to make Serbia respect the decision of the Powers concerning Albania and to ensure that Serbia does not disperse her forces which are now needed against Austria-Hungary." [22] Within a week his words became even sharper: "If Serbia were allied with Austria she would not have acted differently . . . As soon as she has seen us involved against the Austrians, even though our action was all to her favor,

20. Šišić, *Dokumenti*, pp. 36–37. See also *The Southern Slav Programme* (London, 1915).

21. *New York Times* (Dec. 15, 1918), Sec. IV, pp. 7–8.

22. Sonnino to Bonin, Imperiali, and Carlotti, June 8, 1915 (Tel. Part. No. 547, Archives of the Italian Ministry of Foreign Affairs, Rome [hereafter cited as MFA, Rome]).

instead of intensifying hostilities in that direction, as she was bound to do, she creates for us new embarrassments and gravely infringes upon our interests in Albania." [23]

Italy's new allies agreed to make representations at Niš, but the British government proposed at the same time to reassure the Serbs that the London treaty left Fiume, Split, Dubrovnik, and Kotor in Slav hands and that the powers would protect Serbia's rights to the Slav portion of the Banat. Sonnino, however, refused,[24] and at his continued insistence the terms of the treaty were never communicated to the Serbs. Before long, Niš was forced to change Serbian military strategy, but not as a result of Italian intercessions. Its relations with Rome were to take over a year to heal.

The Treaty of London did much to infuse new energy into the Yugoslav movement. It prompted the emergence of the Yugoslav Committee as spokesman for the Southern Slavs of Austria-Hungary, jolted the Serbian government into pressing its cause on the Allies, and dramatized the need for cooperation between the two groups. And since a central premise of the Entente's action was the political survival of Austria-Hungary, the treaty sharpened the Yugoslavs' determination to work for the complete dismemberment of the Habsburg empire.

During the summer of 1915 the Allies decided to bring Bulgaria into the war, in an effort to open a new southern front and break the continuing military deadlock. The strategic gamble of the Gallipoli campaign had failed and the Allies now groped for ways of tipping the scales of war to their side. The negotiations that ensued again involved vital Yugoslav, mainly Serbian, interests.

When the war first began, the Allies—particularly the Russians —were interested mainly in ensuring the neutrality of Bulgaria, an outpost of German and Austro-Hungarian influence in the Balkans. But as the need for an Allied military base in Salonika became more pressing, Bulgaria's position became critically im-

23. Sonnino to Bonin, Imperiali, Carlotti, and Squitti, June 15, 1915 (Tel. Part. 394, MFA, Rome).
24. Sonnino to Bonin, Imperiali, Carlotti, and Squitti, June 15, 1915 (Tel. Part. 395, MFA, Rome).

portant. Bulgaria, like Italy, could negotiate with both sides and opt for the highest bidder. Its territorial demands involved the interests of Rumania, Turkey, and Greece, as well as of Serbia, in the Dobruja, Thrace, and Macedonia. With regard to Serbia, Sofia sought much of the Macedonian area won by the Serbs in the Second Balkan War. That war had resulted from a Bulgarian attack on the Serbs, but now, nevertheless, the Allies were ready to trade Serbian territory for Bulgarian cooperation.

As early as August 1914 Sazonov, who ultimately hoped to bring Bulgaria into the Allied camp, began to prepare Pašić for the need for Serbian concessions in Macedonia. In return, he promised, Serbia would gain considerable compensations in the west.[25] But the Serbs were not prepared to nullify the results of the Balkan wars or to accept vague promises in return for painful territorial sacrifices. Pašić refused. Sazonov, however, pressed on, and on August 19, 1914 presented Niš with a joint Entente note calling for Serbian concessions in Macedonia.[26] Under such pressure, Pašić gave in and declared Serbia ready to cede parts of Macedonia "at the end of the war" in return for gaining access to the Adriatic Sea.[27] When the Bulgarians suddenly raised a demand for the *immediate* cession of all Macedonia assigned to Serbia in 1912, the flirtations between Sofia and the Entente came to a temporary end. But the episode greatly embittered the Serbs. Some months later, in fact, Pašić informed Sir Edward Grey that, given the state of Serbian public opinion, making peace with Austria might be preferable to ceding an inch of ground to Bulgaria.[28]

Italy, too, had begun to show an interest in the position of Bulgaria, long before the Treaty of London was signed. By January 1915 Sonnino was keeping close track of Macedonian affairs. After Italy's entry into the war and the ensuing dispute with Serbia, he hoped to obtain Pašić's military cooperation by offering support of Serbian interests in the east. On May 8 he even au-

25. *Int. Bez.*, II, 6, i, p. 2.
26. Ibid., pp. 155–58.
27. Ibid.
28. On Feb. 1, 1915. See Sir Edward Grey, *Twenty-five Years, 1892–1916,* 2 (2 vols. New York, 1925), 193.

thorized Baron Squitti, the Italian minister in Niš, to disclaim the anti-Yugoslav propaganda carried on by the society Pro Dalmazia Italiana. A fortnight later, however, Sonnino began to pave the way for ultimate Serbian sacrifices. On May 25 he assured the Bulgarian government, through Cucchi, the Italian minister in Sofia, that "as we hope and desire, Serbia will acquire Bosnia and Hercegovina and gain access to the Adriatic at the end of the war; we will have absolutely no objections to the cession of Macedonia to Bulgaria as a means of pacification between the two Kingdoms." [29]

As the summer of 1915 wore on and the Allies became increasingly anxious to win Bulgaria over to their side, the British proposed to lure them with extensive territorial concessions. At the same time, however, Sir Edward Grey proposed to inform the Serbs that they could expect substantial gains in the west in return for Macedonia. He was supported by Sazonov, who specified that Serbia should also receive the coast between Split and Dubrovnik, while the issue of Fiume and Croatia would be taken up at the end of the war. Toward the end of July, Sonnino agreed in principle to granting Serbia part of the Adriatic coast, but he would not agree to any mention of Fiume or Croatia.

On August 2 Grey urged that "the only means to insure the alliance of Bulgaria without risking the definitive estrangement of Serbia is to give M. Pašić a precise guarantee concerning the territories to be assigned to Serbia at the end of a victorious war." [30] The Allies all agreed and began to formulate a joint note. In the end, the note—transmitted to the Serbs on August 4—remained vague, since Sonnino persisted in his view that "the problem of Croatia must be left unresolved." [31] In return for ceding the 1912 uncontested zone of Macedonia to Bulgaria, the Serbs were promised "ample compensations on the Adriatic, in Bosnia-Hercegovina and elsewhere which have already been reserved for her, which

29. Sonnino to Cucchi (copies to Bonin, Imperiali, Carlotti, Fasciotti), May 25, 1915 (Tel. Part. 326 MFA, Rome). The writer failed to find any indication in the Italian archives that Sonnino, at this point, informed Pašić of his position. It is interesting to note that a copy of this communication was not sent to Baron Squitti.

30. Grey to Rodd, Aug. 2, 1915 (*Question Adriatique*, pp. 145–46).

31. Sonnino to Bonin, Imperiali, Carlotti, and Fasciotti, July 11, 1915 (Tel. Gab. Part. 697, MFA, Rome).

will realize and satisfy her most important political and economic aspirations." [32] Pašić immediately asked for clarification—hoping apparently to gain immediate agreement concerning all future frontiers—and the Allies devoted the next ten days to formulating a joint reply. The British, French, and Russians were in agreement on what to offer Serbia, but could not agree on how to deal with the Italians. Sazonov proposed to ignore them; Grey, however, wanted to persuade them to disclose the London treaty terms to Pašić. Sonnino flatly refused.[33] Already displeased with the concessions his Allies were prepared to offer—all of Syrmia, the Bačka, and Slavonia, in addition to the coastal strip—Sonnino continued to insist on the minimum possible—Bosnia-Hercegovina plus the coastal strip—and on avoiding all mention of Croatia and Fiume.[34] Furthermore, he emphatically refused to reveal the London treaty terms.[35]

In view of Sonnino's stand, on August 15 Great Britain, France, and Russia acted on their own and informed Pašić that he could count on compensation in Syrmia, Bačka, Slavonia, a strip along the Adriatic, and on "as large as possible" a frontier with Greece in Albania.[36] With his hand thus forced, two days later Sonnino instructed Squitti to submit a similar program to Pašić, except that the Italian version made no mention of Slavonia and stressed the right of Montenegro to the coastline south of Cavtat.[37] At the same time, however, he twice protested in London, Paris, and Petrograd against the promise of Slavonia, a large Greco-Serbian frontier, and the disregard of Montenegro's rights south of Cavtat.[38]

The Serbs considered the Allied "offer" for two weeks. Mace-

32. Squitti to Sonnino, Aug. 6, 1915 (No. 1210/111, MFA, Rome).

33. Sonnino to Bonin, Imperiali, and Carlotti, Aug. 6, 1915 (Tel. Part. 603, MFA, Rome).

34. Sonnino to Bonin, Imperiali, and Carlotti, Aug. 9, 1915 (Tel. Part. 626, MFA, Rome).

35. See *Int. Bez.*, II, 8, ii, pp. 470–71.

36. Ibid., pp. 477–78. Several days earlier Squitti told Trubetskoi that continued Allied pressure might force Sonnino to accept a compromise. This indiscretion later caused him much difficulty with Sonnino.

37. Ibid.

38. Sonnino to Bonin, Imperiali, Carlotti, and Squitti, Aug. 15, 1915 (Tel. Part. 684); Sonnino to Bonin, Imperiali, Carlotti, and Squitti, Aug. 16, 1915 (Tel. Part. 697); Sonnino to Bonin, Imperiali, Carlotti, and Squitti, Aug. 18, 1915 (Tel. Part. 712; MFA, Rome).

donia, long the motive force of Serbian irredentism, lay close to
their hearts. Now, as the Russian Tsar appealed to King Peter
and the Serbs to accept their fate "in a spirit of abnegation," [39]
they faced a great dilemma. Most Serbs were truly opposed to
ceding an inch of Macedonia. Sensing this trend of thought, the
Allies pressed on. Trubetskoi brought an offer of support for
Serbian claims in the Banat—*if* Rumania remained neutral
throughout the war.[40] The French supported this move.[41] On
August 30 Grey summoned Supilo in London and offered self-
determination for Bosnia-Hercegovina, Dalmatia, Slavonia, and
Croatia at the end of the war, hoping the Yugoslav Committee
would urge Pašić to tow the Allied line.[42] But the final decision
could only be made in Niš.

Pašić was captivated by the prospect of access to the sea and the
territorial gains in the north and the west, but equally unhappy
at the prospect of renouncing any part of Macedonia. He consulted
with the military, and obtained parliamentary approval for his
overall policy vis-à-vis the Allies.[43] On September 1 he gave his
formal reply, a characteristically skillful and equivocal document
that in effect agreed to the Allied program, but made it practically
inoperable. Pašić agreed to the cession of Macedonia, but with so
many qualifications and reservations as to make the gesture almost
empty.[44] The Allies were both furious and uncertain how to
proceed. They temporized at first and then thought of asking Pašić

39. Squitti to Sonnino, Aug. 18, 1915 (No. 1287/117, MFA, Rome).

40. *Int. Bez.*, II, 8, ii, pp. 491–92.

41. Ibid., p. 497.

42. Paulova, *Jugoslavenski Odbor*, pp. 123–24. Also D. Lloyd George, *The Truth about the Peace Treaties*, *1* (2 vols. London, 1938), 39. By choosing Supilo as an intermediary, Grey hoped to use the Yugoslav Committee as an additional instrument of pressure. The episode, however, led to a misunderstanding between the Committee and the Serbian government, and Grey failed to achieve the desired effect.

43. See Paulova, p. 125.

44. The Serbian note demanded adequate strategic protection for Skoplje and insisted on keeping Prilep in Serbia, again on strategic grounds. It stressed Serbia's sacrifices, made in the interests of the common Allied war effort, gave no recognition to Bulgaria's rights, and demanded a pledge that Croatia would be united with Serbia and that Slovenia would be allowed to determine its own future at the end of the war. For the Macedonian settlements of 1912 and 1913 see E. C. Helmreich, *The Diplomacy of the Balkan Wars, 1912–1913* (Cambridge, Mass., 1938).

to Paris for a clarification of Serbian opposition and a thorough review of the entire issue. This plan, however, could not be carried out, for unforeseen events suddenly eclipsed the whole diplomatic venture.

Bulgaria had of course been negotiating with the Central Powers as well as with the Allies all along. All along, too, Vienna and Berlin actually held the upper hand since they could make greater offers at Serbia's expense than could the Entente. However, the Central Powers expected Bulgaria to enter the war right away. In the spring of 1915 King Ferdinand was reluctant to oblige. But as spring gave way to summer and the prospect of Allied victory began to wane, the element of choice, for Sofia, became increasingly unreal. The Allies' Gallipoli campaign had misfired and their position in Flanders became precarious. By contrast, German and Austro-Hungarian military fortunes had dramatically improved, to the point of nearly pushing the Russians out of Poland and Bukovina. For the Bulgarians these developments were singularly telling. They at no point assigned less than maximum priority to their claims in Macedonia; those affecting Rumania, Greece, and Turkey, while important, took second place. Logically, the diplomacy of the Central Powers took this fully into account. In return for entering the war and launching an offensive against Serbia, the Bulgarian government was promised maximum gains in the west that assured Bulgaria most of Macedonia, proximity to the Adriatic, and, in effect, the status of dominant Balkan state after the war. Convinced by the unfolding military successes of the Central Powers that Vienna and Berlin would be able to deliver on their promises while the Allies would not, Ferdinand resolutely ceased to hesitate. On September 6, induced by considerably greater territorial (at the last minute Turkey granted to Bulgaria a favorable rectification of their common frontier along the river Marica) and financial offers, Sofia joined the Central Powers.[45] Twenty-nine days later, without a declaration of war, the Bul-

---

45. For further details see K. Kratchounov, *La Politique extérieure de la Bulgarie, 1880–1920* (Sofia, 1932), p. 67 and passim; G. C. Logio, *Bulgaria Past and Present* (Manchester, Eng., 1936), pp. 401 ff.; I. Slivensky, *La Bulgarie depuis le Traité de Berlin et la paix dans les Balkans* (Paris, 1927), pp. 130–36; B. Auerbach, *L'Autriche et la Hongrie pendant la guerre* (Paris, 1925), pp. 95–102.

garian attack on Serbia began. Coordinated with an Austrian offensive in the north, it radically changed the tide of war throughout Southeast Europe.

Serbia collapsed. Belgrade fell on October 9, Skoplje on October
28, and Niš on November 5. Seven days later the Serbian army
began to move south, across Montenegro and Albania toward
the Adriatic coast.[46] During January and February 1916 the sur-
vivors of the long winter trek made their way to the island of
Corfu. There, Pašić, the cabinet, and those members of the Skupština who managed to escape, had taken refuge in December 1915.
Corfu remained the seat of the Serbian government and, until
the end of the war, the center of Serbian political and diplomatic
activity.

Military defeat, of course, did little to improve Serbia's prestige
in inter-Allied councils. Nevertheless, the damage was not too
great, partly because of French and Russian determination to
preserve and increase their influence with the Serbs, partly because of Pašić's prompt action. In March 1916 the aged premier,
together with Prince Alexander, left Corfu for Rome, Paris, and
London to persuade the Allied governments that Serbia could
still make important contributions to the Allied war effort. Serbian
army elements that had reached Corfu could be reconstituted into
a fighting corps and placed at the disposal of the Allied command
at Salonika, while the now exiled government had much to contribute in the way of propaganda, intelligence activity, and special
operations in Serbia, Montenegro, and northern Albania. Moreover, with the expected extension of the Southeast European
theater of war, the liberation of Serbia would be a primary inter-
Allied objective. The Allies agreed and on March 11 authorized
the transfer of Serbian contingents from Corfu to the Greek mainland, in preparation for the Salonika offensive that was to be
launched in August. From London, Pašić proceeded alone to
Petrograd, where he was warmly received by the Tsar in mid-May
and given assurances of Russia's continuing support for Serbian
interests.

46. For the military operations see Milan Zelenica, *Rat Srbije i Crne Gore 1915*
(Belgrade, 1954). For a stirring account of the famous retreat see John Clinton
Adams, *Flight in Winter* (Princeton, 1942).

That support, however, proved to be more chimerical than real. For within weeks after Pašić's "success" in Western Europe and Petrograd, the Allies transacted another secret agreement at the expense, in part, of Serbian interests. Neutral Rumania, courted like Italy and Bulgaria by both sides since the start of the war, decided to join the Allies in the summer of 1916. This decision climaxed two years of Rumanian vacillation and protracted negotiations with the Entente. In contrast to the Bulgarian case, the Central powers never had a chance. Rumanian interests in the main involved Transylvania, Bukovina, the Dobruja, and the Banat—all territories belonging to the Central Powers. The real issue, therefore, was not which side to join but how much the Allies would offer and when the Rumanian intervention should take place. The existence of some traditional Germanophile and Russophobe strains in Rumanian political thinking caused various complications. But these were overshadowed by the willingness of the Allies to bid high for Rumania's favors by promises of territory, military assistance, and financial aid. In 1915, when the Allied cause had suffered, the Rumanian Premier, Ion I. C. Bratianu, could not decide on intervention, though that did not keep him from raising the price to the Allies. The Allies, more than ever anxious to redress the military balance, were on the whole prepared to accede to his demands. These included the whole of the Banat, but at this demand Sazonov balked, fearing the international consequences for Russia entailed in a further sacrifice of Serbian interests. The Serbs claimed at least half of the Banat and would not voluntarily accept additional compensation in Bosnia-Hercegovina, Dalmatia, or elsewhere in the west. But Bratianu persisted and so the talks dragged on and then lapsed. In 1916, however, the tide of war on the eastern front seemed to favor the Entente, and in the summer the great Brusilov offensive even raised briefly the prospect of an Austrian defeat. In such an eventuality, the ambitions of a neutral Rumania would surely remain unfulfilled. Bucharest, therefore, renewed the talks, and in July and early August the issue was distinctly moving to a head. Bratianu shrewdly held fast to his demands, and the Allies, freshly frustrated in the west by the failure of their great effort on the Somme, now met his terms. The details were set on paper on

August 17. By the secret Treaty of Bucharest, the Allies pledged Bukovina and Transylvania, as well as the Banat of Temesvar which, due to the large Serbian component, the Serbs had long hoped to absorb. Like the Treaty of London, the Bucharest convention was not communicated to the Serbian government. Yet despite the secrecy, its terms became known to the Serbs, adding to their bitterness and frustration.

The Allies, of course, had acted in the conviction that they had had no choice. The past year had brought mainly disappointments —the Gallipoli fiasco, Italy's failure to swing the military balance, Bulgaria's intervention on the side of the Central Powers, Serbia's collapse, the eventual failure of the Russian offensive in June 1916 as well as failures at Verdun, the Somme, and in Mesopotamia —and Rumania's intervention loomed as a master stroke, no matter what the price. Yet the master stroke missed the mark, for the Rumanians had temporized too long. Had they intervened at the height of the Russian offensive, the impact could have been immense. By August it was too late. The Central Powers rallied, struck against Rumania with a might and fury that took the Allied world by surprise, and by December 1916 occupied Bucharest, literally knocking the Allies' newest partner out of the war. The secret Treaty of Bucharest, however, was to remain in force, and when Rumania re-entered the war in 1918, its signatories were to pledge anew to carry it into effect.

1916 was a significant year for the Yugoslav cause in other respects as well. In Western Europe, for one, interest was mounting in the idea of a large Southern Slav state that would serve as a rampart against future German expansion and at the same time fulfill what was thought to be historic justice. The Yugoslav Committee, like the Polish and the Czechoslovak National Councils, enlisted the support of influential friends—Steed, Seton-Watson, Sir Arthur Evans in England; Ernest Denis, Emile Haumant, Victor Bérard, Louis Léger in France—to agitate for the dismemberment of Austria-Hungary and the union of all Southern Slavs. Bulgaria's aggression and Serbia's collapse dramatized the issue and produced much public discussion and sympathetic publicity in the Allied press. Allied chancelleries became increasingly aware of a concerted campaign for the dissolution of Austria-Hungary.

British official circles were the first to take up the problem of postwar Central and Eastern Europe and to consider a major policy change. Thus in the autumn of 1916 the Foreign Office began the task of reviewing past and current British policy and recommending guidelines for the future. The results were drawn up in a confidential memorandum that began with the premise that England should "ensure that all the states of Europe, great and small, shall in the future be in a position to achieve their national development in freedom and security." [47] As applied to Serbia, however, great obstacles were seen in the way of fulfilling this noble goal. The Treaty of London, the Foreign Office admitted, "unfortunately constitutes a very distinct violation of the principle of nationalities, and there is consequently no doubt that it involves the risk of producing the usual results, namely, irredentism, and the lack of stability and peace." As a solemn obligation, the treaty could not be abandoned, but the Foreign Office hoped the parties involved would reach a mutually acceptable solution. How, was not suggested. But significantly, the memorandum urged the British government "in every way [to] encourage and promote the union of Serbia, Montenegro, and the Southern Slavs into one strong federation of States with the view to its forming a barrier to any German advance towards the East." [48]

In Italy, by contrast, official thinking remained firmly predicated on the concepts of Sonnino. An improvement in relations with the Pašić government, already facilitated by Serbia's collapse and Pašić's consequent dependence on Allied good will, was furthered by the replacement of Baron Squitti as minister to Corfu by Count Carlo Sforza. Initially a supporter of Sonnino's conceptions, Sforza modified his position within several months of his arrival in mid-1916. He was deeply impressed with Pašić—the two men formed an enduring friendship—and soon came to believe in the necessity of Slav-Italian amity. Like Sonnino, Sforza wanted to increase Italian influence in the Balkans; but what the one sought to achieve through imposition, the other proposed to achieve through cooperation. Sforza had no intention of renouncing Istria and Dalmatia, or encouraging the development of a vast

47. Lloyd George, *1,* 32.
48. Ibid., p. 39.

Yugoslav state that might endanger Italian interests. Rather, he
sought to persuade Sonnino that Italy's best interests lay in encouraging Serbia's expansion to the east to keep her from ex-
panding to the west. For two years he was to press this view in
Rome, urging a policy of conciliation and concession toward the
Serbs. At one point—in October 1916—he even proposed to effect
a "radical division of the Serbo-Croat lands, the Catholic in Europe,
the Orthodox in the East," by corrupting the Serbs with lavish
offerings in Macedonia and Albania.[49] Sonnino, however, would
have none of it, particularly in regard to Albania, and insisted
instead on standing by the Treaty of London.

Both Pašić and the Yugoslav Committee sensed a gradual change
in British and French attitudes, even if not in official policies. In
London and Paris, after Rumania's collapse, the atmosphere was
becoming increasingly favorable. Privately, officials were sympathetic and receptive, though unwilling to offer undue encouragement. In Rome, however, Yugoslav suppliants continued to encounter disinterest.

At the same time, a gradual change became noticeable in the
relations between the Yugoslav Committee and the Serbian government. The two groups had pursued their aims independently
of each other and had maintained relatively little contact. Pašić,
whose policy was primarily based on the objective of gaining
Bosnia-Hercegovina, the Banat, an outlet to the Adriatic, and
further concessions in Macedonia for Serbia, was unhappy about
the Yugoslav Committee's agitation for an organic Yugoslav union
in which Serbia would become but one of several equal units,
thus greatly reducing the Serbian-Orthodox influence in the state.
The disaffection was entirely reciprocal and the Yugoslav Committee was equally unhappy with Pašić's efforts to win the Allies
to his point of view. A meeting between Trumbić and Prince
Alexander in Paris in April 1916 failed to resolve the conflicting
points of view. Before long, however, both sides felt the need to
begin exploring their differences, to coordinate their efforts and,
above all, to present a solid front before the Allied world. By
November 1916 Pašić concluded, somewhat reluctantly, that it

49. Sforza to Sonnino, Oct. 24, 1916 (Archivio Gabinetto [hereafter cited as Arch.
Gab.] No. 336/68, MFA, Rome).

would be wise to station a member of the Yugoslav Committee at Corfu. He wrote to Trumbić about the need for improving their contact and organization: "I am entertaining the thought of asking you to send me one of your trusted men, for him to stay with me, and of letting you take one of my trusted men . . ." [50] Trumbić, Supilo, and the Yugoslav Committee were more than willing, yet because of a variety of mutual disagreements, the plan was not carried through.

Half a year elapsed before concrete results were obtained, and then mainly because the tide of events and a group of Serbian opposition leaders forced Pašić to reconsider his position in the spring of 1917. The fall of the tsarist regime, Pašić's principal supporter in the past, came as an immense shock. More than anything else, this event caused Pašić to realize that unless his policies were more closely aligned to the principles that animated liberal Western opinion, Serbia would become politically isolated. The intervention in April 1917 of the United States, which was generally sympathetic to the idea of self-determination for all oppressed peoples, only reinforced this realization. On May 30 the Southern Slav members of the Parliament in Vienna, constituted into a "Yugoslav Club," issued a dramatic and far-reaching public declaration that called for the unification of all the Serbs, Croats, and Slovenes living in the Monarchy into an independent entity under Habsburg aegis.[51]

Shortly thereafter, Pašić and the Radicals decided they had little choice. They invited the Yugoslav Committee to Corfu, where the two sides negotiated a common program. On July 20 they

50. Pašić to Trumbić, Corfu, Nov. 12, 1916, in Trumbić Papers, Fasc. 10 (Istorijski Institut Jugoslavenske Akademije Znanosti i Nauka, Zagreb). (Hereafter cited as TP, F.)

51. Šišić, *Dokumenti*, p. 94. This declaration has at times been cited as evidence of pro-Habsburg feelings on the part of Croats and Slovenes. Yet in wartime Vienna, Southern Slav deputies could hardly call for the dissolution of the Habsburg empire and unification with "enemy" Serbia. In the circumstances of May 1917, the Declaration represented a courageous act, understood in all quarters as a call to arms in behalf of Yugoslavism. See also B. Auerbach, *L'Autriche et la Hongrie*, pp. 239 ff.; Edmund von Glaise-Horstenau, *The Collapse of the Austro-Hungarian Empire* (London, 1930), pp. 30 ff.; J. Redlich, *Austrian War Government* (New Haven, 1929), p. 148; and Z. A. B. Zeman, *The Break-up of the Habsburg Empire, 1914–1918* (London, 1961), p. 128.

issued the so-called Declaration of Corfu, a document calling for
the union of all Southern Slavs into a single, independent, democratic state, a constitutional monarchy under the House of Karadjordjević, to be known as the Kingdom of Serbs, Croats, and
Slovenes, in which freedom of religion would be guaranteed and
the Cyrillic and Latinic alphabets equally maintained.[52] This
program was immediately accepted by the Montenegrin National
Committee in Paris. The negotiations leading to the Declaration
were difficult and marked by profound differences of approach.[53]
The delegates could not agree on the crucial issue of the internal
political system, on adopting the federal principle sought by Trumbić and his associates, or on the Serb-oriented centralized system
demanded by Pašić. On this subject the document was left deliberately vague—a compromise that was to cause untold difficulties
later on—but in all other respects the Declaration marked a moment of immense significance. It became the foundation on which
the Yugoslav state was ultimately built. At the same time, it
presented the Allies, especially the Italians, with a united Yugoslav
front. The cause of Yugoslav unity now became the official policy
of Serbia. From this point on, the Allies were given notice that
no future arrangement for Southeast Europe would be accepted
unless it embodied the principles enunciated at Corfu.

Allied policies were not quick to respond to the Yugoslav program issued at Corfu. But the Allies were far from oblivious to
its implications for the future. 1917 was a year of trial and up-
heaval for their cause. The downfall of the Tsar, followed late in
the year by the Bolshevik Revolution and the practical elimina-
tion of Russia from the war, changed the whole complexion of
the war. The damage was partly offset by the intervention of the
United States in April 1917, but the full impact of America's
enormous might was not to be felt militarily until the following
year. On the political front, too, America's participation in the

52. For the full program see Šišić, *Dokumenti*, pp. 96–100. See also Paulova,
Jugoslavenski Odbor, pp. 325–79; H. Hinković, *Iz Velikog Doba* (Zagreb, 1927),
passim; F. Potočnjak, *Iz Emigracije* (Zagreb, 1919), Pt. II; Marjanović, *Londonski
Ugovor*, pp. 407 ff.

53. See Ante Smith Pavelić, *Dr. Ante Trumbić: Problemi Hrvatsko-Srpskih
Odnosa* (Munich, 1959), pp. 73-91; Šišić, *Dokumenti*, pp. 306–14.

war was to cause major changes within the Allied camp. The ideas of Woodrow Wilson clashed with the traditional precepts of European politics and diplomacy. Before long they were to become the dominant factor in Allied war policies.

The first full expositions of Wilsonian principles—the President's Annual Address to Congress on December 4, 1917 (recommending, *inter alia,* a declaration of war on Austria-Hungary) and the Fourteen Points speech of January 8, 1918—were favorable to the cause of Yugoslavism only in a limited way. In calling for "open covenants openly arrived at," Wilson implicitly attacked the secret treaties of the past, presumably also those of London and Bucharest. The exponents of Yugoslavism were disappointed that the President made no specific reference to the secret pacts that stood in the way of their program. The Italians, however, interpreted the "open covenants" phrase as an attack on the Treaty of London, and Prime Minister Vittorio Emanuele Orlando hastened to London to demand reassurances that this was not the case.

The Yugoslavs were apprehensive, however, because three days prior to Wilson's Fourteen Points speech, Prime Minister Lloyd George, in his famous Trade Unions Address, asserted that the *dissolution* of Austria-Hungary was not part of Allied war aims. His position was based on the President's Annual Address to Congress of December 4. Then came Wilson's reference to the peoples of Austria-Hungary whose "place among nations" he wished to see safeguarded through *autonomous* development. Point XI of Wilson's speech referred to Serbia, with a promise of free and secure access to the sea. The broader program of Yugoslav unification was mentioned not at all.[54]

Wilson's and Lloyd George's motivations soon became quite

54. Part of the blame for this must be attributed to Milenko Vesnić, Serbian minister in Paris, who in December 1917 headed a special mission to Washington. The only non-American consulted by Wilson on Point XI, Vesnić apparently did not press hard for recognition of the Yugoslav national program. He did indicate opposition to the preservation of the Habsburg Empire and to any attempt to conclude a separate peace, which disappointed Wilson. See Charles Seymour, *The Intimate Papers of Colonel House, 3* (4 vols. Boston, 1926–28), 132–33 (hereafter cited as *House Papers*). Also, Jelavich, in *Journal of Central European Affairs, 11,* 142. For a detailed discussion of the Fourteen Points, the Vesnić mission, and the Yugoslav cause, see Victor Mamatey, *The United States and East Central Europe, 1914–1918: A Study in Wilsonian Diplomacy and Propaganda* (Princeton, 1957), pp. 181–83, 185–87.

clear. Through the winter of 1917–18 the Allies were in under-
cover contact with representatives of the Habsburg Monarchy, exploring the possibilities for a separate peace to hasten the end of
the war. So long as such a possibility existed, the Allies were determined not to spoil matters by calling for the dismemberment of
Austria-Hungary. The British and American speeches were, in part,
even designed to assure Vienna that the Monarchy would be allowed to survive the war, albeit only through major concessions to
its dependent nationalities, mainly the Southern Slavs and the
Czechoslovaks. In part, however, the Allied action—particularly
Woodrow Wilson's—reflected lack of appreciation of probable
effects on Yugoslav and Czechoslovak opinion. As applied to the
Slavic world, Wilson's ideas at the time of the Fourteen Points
speech were doubtless far from crystallized. Rather than come to
grips with all the issues at this particular time, the President simply
preferred to remain vague and undogmatic in his *territorial* formulas.

The Yugoslavs, nevertheless, reacted swiftly and sharply. In
Allied capitals, the Committee began agitating for a general review
of Allied policy, at the same time urging Pašić to start a Serbian
diplomatic offensive toward the same end. At Corfu, the United
States minister, H. Percival Dodge, sensed a general disappointment in Serbian political ranks which he reported to Secretary of
State Robert Lansing in Washington. After much discussion within
Serbian and Yugoslav circles, Pašić in early March finally asked
Washington for authorization to interpret Wilson's speech of January 8 as a "brief summary" of Allied war aims that otherwise included the intention of fulfilling "Serbo-Croat national aspirations
as far as possible." [55] On March 14 Lansing agreed to such a formula,
though soon, he realized, a fuller statement of American intentions
would be called for.

The Italians, too, decided not to mark time. Deeply troubled by
Wilson's reference in Point IX to the need of adjusting Italy's
frontiers along 'clearly recognizable lines of nationality,' Orlando
rushed to London in late January to protect the Treaty of London.

55. *Papers Relating to the Foreign Relations of the United States, 1918–1919,*
1918, Supp. I, *1* (4 vols. Washington, 1930–34), 793–94 (hereafter cited as *FRUS*). On
the Yugoslav reaction to the Fourteen Points see Mamatey, *United States,* pp. 209–13.

The British government assured him it would stand by its commitment. Reassured, Orlando returned to Rome. But within several weeks Italy's leaders began to feel uneasy. Italian opinion became increasingly divided over the question of how to deal with the Slavs. Following America's intervention and, particularly, the humiliating Italian defeat at Caporetto, there developed a strong current of opinion favoring an understanding with the Yugoslavs. Luigi Albertini, G. A. Borgese, Giovanni Amendola, and such newspapers as the *Corriere della Sera* and *Secolo* all urged that Italy assume the moral leadership in the movement for the liberation of the Austro-Hungarian oppressed nationalities.[56] Within the government, too, various elements—including, to all appearances, Orlando—began to question the wisdom of Sonnino's unbending anti-Yugoslav policy. Cooperation with the Yugoslavs, or even a friendly gesture toward their national program, might influence the Croat and Slovene units in the Austrian army, which were fighting with particular zest on the Italian front. It would also align Italian policy more closely with that of the other Allies. A significant experiment was thus now launched.

Initial Italian overtures toward the Yugoslavs began in London in December 1917, partly through the good offices of Wickham Steed. During his trip to London in January 1918, Orlando met with Trumbić for a general exchange of views and invited him to visit Rome. To safeguard his own position, he told the Yugoslav that Sonnino might oppose any modification of Italian policy.[57] Nonetheless, his purpose was clear. The Yugoslavs in London, in fact, rejoiced. In Rome, soon thereafter, Dr. Andrea Torre was appointed chairman of a new parliamentary committee for cooperation with the subject peoples of the Habsburg empire. In late February, Torre traveled to London to meet with the Yugoslavs, Czechs, and representatives of other nationalities to prepare for a general congress, under Italian sponsorship, in Rome.

The Torre-Trumbić meetings laid the foundations for the so-

56. See L. Albertini, *Venti Anni di vita politica, 3* (5 vols. Bologna, 1950–53), Bk. II, 233–77; H. Wickham Steed, *Through Thirty Years, 1892–1922, 2* (2 vols. New York, 1925), 164–221; Pietro Silva, "Italian Public Opinion and the Southern Slav Problem," *New Europe, 6* (1918), 401–06. See also Paulova, pp. 404 ff., and G. A. Borgese, *Goliath: The March of Fascism* (New York, 1937), passim.

57. Steed, 2, 184.

called Pact of Rome, signed in conjunction with the Congress of
Oppressed Nationalities that met in Rome on April 8–10, recognizing the legitimacy of Yugoslav aspirations for national and territorial integrity. The Pact marked a new phase in Italo-Yugoslav
relations—for the time being at least. Sanctioned by Orlando—
for Sonnino, opposed as ever to any departure from the Treaty
of London line, temporarily withdrew into the background—it
was everywhere interpreted as signifying a fundamental change
in official Italian policy, even as the "coup de grâce to the secret
convention concluded at London in April 1915." [58] It was bitterly
resented by Italian Irredentists [59] and to some extent even by
Pašić, because as the brain child of the Yugoslav Committee it
placed the Serbian government in a secondary light.

The Congress of Oppressed Nationalities marked a climactic
stage in the struggle of the Habsburg Slavs for liberation and independence. Coming at a time when the prospects for a separate
peace with Austria were quickly waning, the Congress foreshadowed official Allied recognition of the national programs of the
oppressed nationalities. It also presaged an Allied psychological
offensive that would tangibly influence Slav units in the Austrian
army to sabotage the Habsburg cause.[60] News of the Congress
spread rapidly through the Dual Monarchy. On May 16 a great
demonstration took place in Prague with a meeting of representatives of all the nationalities. This occasion, in the words of an
American diplomat, was the first step "in the long-expected revolt
of the oppressed nationalities against Austria." [61] The Prague
demonstration was followed in August by a similar occurrence

58. *Southern Slav Bulletin,* 37 (1918). See also Digović, *La Dalmatie,* pp. 355 ff.;
Albertini, *3,* Bk. II, 274–76. For further details see the works of Paulova, Steed, and
Borgese, as well as E. Beneš, *Souvenirs de guerre et de révolution, 1914–1918,* 2
(2 vols. Paris, 1928), 106 ff.

59. See Attilio Tamaro, *Il Patto di Roma* (Rome, 1923). The Italian Press divided
sharply over the issue. For a review of the conflicting positions see the *New York
Times* (Dec. 15, 1918), Sec. IV, p. 7.

60. "Report on the Work of the Department of Propaganda in Enemy Countries," MS (Crewe House, London, 1918), pp. 4–33. This document was kindly made
available to the author by Dr. Christopher Seton-Watson of Oxford University.
See also F. Barac, *Croats and Slovenes, Friends of the Entente* (Paris, 1919).

61. *FRUS,* 1918, Supp. I, *1,* 806.

in Ljubljana, which served to give the green light for the internal disintegration of the Habsburg empire.[62]

Despite its positive aspect for the Allied war effort, this trend caused some anxiety in Italian circles, particularly on the part of Sonnino. Alarmed by the Pact of Rome and the implications of the April Congress, Sonnino resolved to forestall hasty Allied recognition of the "Yugoslav program." On the occasion of the Congress, Wilson and Lansing expressed their sympathy for Czechoslovak and Yugoslav independence.[63] Within three weeks Sonnino pressed Washington against any specific declaration favoring a Yugoslav union. On May 18, and often thereafter, he repeated the same demand.[64]

American policy, however, began to follow a course of its own. By mid–May a vital reorientation had taken place. Realizing that the chances of concluding a separate peace with Austria were dead following the Clemenceau–Czernin imbroglio over the "Sixtus Letter," and impressed by the quick and positive effects of the Roman congress, Washington policy-makers—principally Secretary of State Lansing—began to reassess the whole Allied approach toward the Habsburg nationalities. The cause of self-determination and justice for the Slavs of the Dual Monarchy corresponded to Wilsonian ideals and would doubtless receive popular support everywhere. American, together with Allied, support for such national programs would cause havoc in Austrian ranks and help to speed Allied victory. The Yugoslavs and Czechoslovaks were already aiding the Allied war effort in vital ways. Their representatives in the west were fomenting mutinies and revolts at home through a massive and skillful propaganda campaign. Slovene, Croat, Czech, and Slovak soldiers in the Austrian army were deserting to the Allies and many were already fighting on the Italian front on the Allied side. On the Salonika front a Yugoslav division,

62. See Jules Chopin (Pichon), *Les Yougoslaves et l'Entente* (Paris, 1918), p. 8.

63. Ray Stannard Baker, *Woodrow Wilson: Life and Letters, 8* (8 vols. Garden City, N.Y., 1927–39), 136 (hereafter cited as *Wilson Letters*); *FRUS*, 1918, Supp. I, *1*, 803.

64. *FRUS*, 1918, Supp. I, *1*, 801–02, 805–06. On Sonnino's efforts to sabotage the Pact of Rome see A. A. Bernardy and V. Falorsi, *La Questione Adriatica vista d'oltre Atlantico, 1917–1919* (Bologna, 1923), pp. 53 ff.

composed of ex-Austrian prisoners of war who were transferred from Russia to Balkan battlefields, was fighting alongside Serbian, French, and other Allied contingents and creating for itself a worthy military record.[65] To stimulate these efforts further, Lansing, with Wilson's approval, issued a statement on May 29 expressing American sympathy for the Yugoslav and Czechoslovak national causes.[66] This action did not involve official recognition of the Czechoslovak National Council or the Yugoslav Committee, but it did much to bolster their status and determination to press on.

Indeed, the Yugoslavs were quite emboldened and interpreted Lansing's statement as the prelude to a general revision of Allied war aims and recognition of their Committee as the legitimate and official agency of the Southern Slavs. The Yugoslav colony in the United States (with the support of the Serbian minister in Washington, Ljuba Mihajlović, who in 1915 had served in Rome) launched a veritable campaign to arouse American public opinion in favor of the Yugoslav cause and to press Washington into official action, through public meetings, symposia, advertisements, and petitions to the White House and members of the Congress.[67] Yet little did the Yugoslavs realize that their efforts, unlike those of the Poles and the Czechs, were destined to generate a bitter diplomatic contest within the Allied camp. For Czechoslovak and (after the October Revolution in Russia) Polish national objectives in no way conflicted with the interests of any Allied power; those of the Yugoslavs, on the other hand, did exactly that.

The outward Italo-Yugoslav cordiality following the Pact of Rome in reality failed to change the course of Italy's foreign policy. Sonnino was determined to prevent Allied recognition of the Yugoslav Committee and to exercise a virtual veto power in all inter-Allied discussions of the subject. He was fighting not only to block a Yugoslav union but also to prevent any modifica-

65. See Vojnoistoriski Institut J.N.A., *Jugoslovenski Dobrovoljački Korpus u Rusiji* (Belgrade, 1954).

66. See Victor S. Mamatey, "The United States and the Dissolution of Austria-Hungary," *Journal of Central European Affairs, 10* (1950), 261, and his *United States and East Central Europe*, pp. 260–61.

67. See *Nova Evropa* (March 21, 1921), pp. 10–23; Paulova, *Jugoslavenski Obdor*, pp. 450–52.

tion of the Treaty of London. Unknown to the Yugoslavs, the Italian government on April 21, 1918, concluded a secret agreement with the Czechoslovak National Council, recognizing it as the *de facto* government of the future Czechoslovak state. When the Yugoslavs learned of this from Eduard Beneš, they hoped to induce Rome into a similar agreement with them. Sonnino, however, quickly dispelled their hopes. Counting on British and French concurrence in his plans, due to the Treaty of London, Sonnino turned his guns on Washington. True, he failed to stop Lansing from issuing the pro-Yugoslav statement on May 29. But he would not allow things to develop any further.

In Washington, on the other hand, the first step having been taken on May 29, Lansing was preparing to pursue his policy to its logical conclusion. At his initiative, the question of recognizing the national movements of the Habsburg empire was raised at an inter-Allied meeting at Versailles on June 3. Here it became evident that the Polish, Czechoslovak, and Yugoslav "questions" would be treated quite differently. None of the Allies opposed recognizing the Polish National Council. The same applied to the Czechoslovaks. In fact, in late March Premier Clemenceau had already promised Beneš French recognition for the Czechoslovak Council. A similar pledge was extended by the British on May 17. Rome, of course, had already granted recognition on April 21. The British and French, not to mention the Americans, were prepared to make the same gesture toward the Yugoslavs. Shortly before the June 3 meeting at Versailles, they sounded out Rome but met with a curt *no*.[68] At Versailles the Allies could therefore only agree that, in view of Italian opposition, it would be unwise to extend recognition to the Poles and Czechoslovaks without doing the same for the Yugoslavs. Actually, they compromised by recognizing the Polish Council and merely expressing sympathy for the Czechoslovak and Yugoslav national causes in an official communiqué. This compromise did not obscure the fact, however, that of the two, the Czechoslovaks could shortly expect more favorable Allied action.

Sonnino thus won a victory of sorts, though no one else was

68. E. J. Woodhouse and C. G. Woodhouse, *Italy and the Jugoslavs* (Boston, 1920), pp. 150–51; Paulova, pp. 456–58.

pleased. On learning the news, the Yugoslavs became embittered. Trumbić in Rome and Mihajlović in Washington protested to American and Italian officials and urged the Allies to reconsider their position.[69] They rightly argued the Allied war effort would suffer. Indeed, by the middle of June, Austrian propagandists were adroitly exploiting the Versailles communiqué to persuade the Czechoslovaks and Southern Slavs that they could not expect to achieve independence under Allied auspices. The Yugoslav Committee worked furiously to redress the psychological effects of Austrian propaganda through a barrage of messages sent behind Habsburg lines. On June 15 it also sent an urgent plea to all Allied governments to rectify the error of June 3.[70] Acting on his own initiative—for Pašić was keeping noticeably aloof—Ljuba Mihajlović appealed to Lansing to the same effect.[71] The plea fell on sympathetic ears.

Lansing had been far from idle since the Versailles decision of June 3. Displeased over Sonnino's intransigence, he was equally disturbed by British and French hesitancy in giving full force to a policy they all knew was required by the logic of the general situation. America's hands were clean and Washington was in no way bound by the Treaty of London. At the same time, however, neither Lansing nor Wilson was prepared to launch an argument over the secret treaty and risk impairing Allied solidarity. Instead, Lansing sought to find a way of exercising American initiative without causing an inter-Allied crisis. He discussed the whole issue with Wilson and recorded his own position in two memoranda prepared at the end of May and in late June. "In the first place," he wrote, "we should be perfectly frank with ourselves and admit that as long as there was a chance of entering into a separate peace with Austria-Hungary it was wise and expedient to attempt to do so, even though it was contrary to the just claims of the nationalities within the Empire." When these efforts failed, a "revision of policy became necessary. . . . It is my judgment that, primarily as a war measure, and also because it is wise and just for the future, we should encourage in every possible way the national

69. *FRUS*, 1918, Supp. *I*, 1, 811–13.
70. Paulova, p. 460.
71. Ibid., pp. 460–61.

desires of these people. If need be, I would favor going so far as to promise them their independence . . . if that would induce them to revolt against German-owned Austria-Hungary." [72] With no pretense at false morality, the argument was thus crystal clear. When the Yugoslav Committee's and Mihajlović's pleas were received, Lansing, with Wilson's approval, informed the Serbian minister on June 24, "in order that there may be no misunderstanding concerning the meaning [of the May 29 Declaration] I beg to state that the position of the United States government is that all branches of the Slav race should be completely freed from German and Austrian rule." [73] On June 28 Lansing repeated the same wording in an official circular, designed for public consumption within the Allied world and within the Dual Monarchy, to counteract Austrian distortions of the June 3 Versailles communiqué.[74]

Lansing's new statement also did not involve recognizing the Yugoslav Committee. But, in effect, it sanctioned the Committee's program as an integral part of Allied war aims and as such it marked a significant turning point. The United States was now committed to the Yugoslav project. Mihajlović and Trumbić were elated, though they knew the more difficult struggle to persuade Great Britain, France, and above all Italy to follow the American lead still lay ahead.

72. "Memorandum on our policy in relation to Austria-Hungary," May 30, 1918, and "Policy in Relation to the Nationalities Movement within the Austro-Hungarian Empire," June 25, 1918 (Lansing Papers ["Confidential Memoranda and Notes"], Manuscript Division, Library of Congress, Washington). See also Robert Lansing, *War Memoirs* (Indianapolis, 1935), pp. 269 ff.

73. FRUS, 1918, Supp. I, 1, pp. 815–16.

74. Ibid., p. 816. For a detailed account of the genesis of Lansing's declaration of June 28 see Mamatey, *United States and East Central Europe*, pp. 266–70.

2. The Genesis of Yugoslavia

FOLLOWING the Declaration of Corfu in July 1917, the Serbian government and the Yugoslav Committee coexisted in an uneasy association. On the surface they maintained a reasonably united front, but underneath, major differences persisted. The two sides clashed over the meaning of the joint document and, in every exchange, over the future internal relationship between Serbia and the other Yugoslav provinces. Within the Yugoslav Committee divergencies developed over the question of a republic as opposed to a constitutional monarchy. One Committee member, Hinko Hinković, launched an unauthorized campaign among Yugoslavs living in America to propagate the view that the declaration was not binding on either party. The Serbian government refused to regard the Committee as the proper agency for representing the Southern Slavs before the Allied world. Pašić refused to accept the word "Yugoslav," used though it was in the Declaration, because it suggested to him the demise of Serbia's individuality. And so forth.[1]

Until the summer of 1918, these differences were kept in control and, on the whole, out of public—Allied—view. But with the ever more evident approach of Allied victory, dissent ripened into open controversy. Part of the difficulty revolved around the Congress of Oppressed Nationalities and the Pact of Rome. Relegated into the background by the dramatic, albeit temporary, "success" of the Yugoslav Committee, Pašić became restive, disaffected, and, above all, diplomatically passive. He was also facing increased political resistance in Serbian circles. The parliamentary opposition, refusing to collaborate with his Radical cabinet, mounted a political offensive against him on Corfu and in the west. Pašić, in turn, governed without parliamentary sanction and, in

1. See Paulova, *Jugoslavenski Odbor*, pp. 325–79; Pavelić, *Trumbić*, pp. 92–105; P. Pekić, *Propast Austro-Ugarske Monarhije i Postanak Nasljednih Država* (Subotica, 1937), pp. 130–38.

response to his Serbian detractors, tightened his iron-fist rule.[2]

The Yugoslav Committee inevitably became drawn into the controversy of Serbian politics, a fact Pašić bitterly resented. He accused the opposition party leaders of conspiring with the Yugoslav Committee against him in an effort to take over the government. The opposition and the Committee, on the other hand, charged Pašić and the Radicals with betraying the "Yugoslav idea" and working only for a "Greater Serbia." The charges and countercharges reflected intense personal rancor, so much so that personal contact between the principals on both sides was broken off on several occasions.

The controversy broke into public view at the height of the diplomatic struggle for Allied recognition. R. W. Seton-Watson, long a friend of Trumbić and an outspoken critic of Pašić, decided to take matters into his own hands. Believing that he could shock Pašić into accepting the Committee's views by shaming him in Allied eyes, Seton-Watson published a sensational article, "Serbia's Choice," in the August 22, 1918, issue of his review, *New Europe*. A blistering attack, "Serbia's Choice" accused Pašić of ruling by illegal methods, of refusing to convene the Skupština, of suppressing all political opposition, and of undermining the cause of the "Union Sacrée." "Only a knave or a fool," Seton-Watson wrote, "would call his patriotism in question; but his outlook and standards are those of a vanishing era, and he is too old to shake off altogether the semi-Turkish traditions of his youth."[3] He then asked Pašić to form a coalition cabinet, to restore unity in Serbian ranks, and to dedicate his energies to supporting the *national* cause. But Pašić was hardly a man to be moved by violent words. "Serbia's Choice" inflamed feelings on both sides and, despite Seton-Watson's good intentions, the ill-tempered article deepened the gulf between Pašić, the opposition parties, and the Yugoslav Committee.[4] The conflict was not to abate until the final phase of the war, and then only due to the pressure of events.

2. See Djordjević, *Srbija i Jugosloveni*, passim; Paulova, passim.

3. *New Europe, 8* (1918), 127.

4. See Stojan Protić's defense of Pašić in "A Serbian Protests," *New Europe, 8* (1918), 258–59; "Serbia and the Entente," ibid., pp. 155–58; and M. Savčić, "A New Regime for Serbia," ibid., *9*, 105.

August 1918 witnessed yet another crisis in Yugoslav ranks. In a show of force, Pašić suddenly dismissed Ljuba Mihajlović as Serbian minister in Washington, ostensibly for repeated insubordination. Mindful of the background to Lansing's two declarations and the close liaison between Mihajlović and Trumbić, Pašić suspected his envoy of conspiring with the Yugoslav Committee. Mihajlović had, in fact, become quite independent in his actions. He failed to consult Pašić over several diplomatic moves, was known to favor a coalition government at Corfu, and was trusted by Trumbić and his associates. In actuality, Pašić had ample grounds for his decision, but its timing and manner of execution were designed more as a blow against his critics than a disciplinary action. The episode intensified ill feelings on all sides. More important, it caused understandable confusion among the Allies concerning Pašić's ultimate goals.

Coming at a critical juncture in the diplomatic struggle for recognition, the rift in Yugoslav ranks produced unpleasant echoes within the Allied camp. Sonnino tried to capitalize on these events by arguing that the Yugoslavs were so divided as not to merit Allied support. This tactic, however, had little immediate effect as the direction of American, British, and French policies was already set. Following Lansing's statements of May 29 and June 28, British and French statesmen felt keenly the anomaly of their situation. Both Foreign Secretary Arthur Balfour and Foreign Minister Stéphen Pichon were sympathetic to the Yugoslav cause, but determined not to offend Italy. They therefore set out to maintain a delicate balance between extending the Yugoslavs full moral support, in order to bolster Croat and Slovene resistance within Austria-Hungary, and at the same time withholding the formal recognition that would cause a crisis in their relations with Rome.

Since the Allies at Versailles had linked the Czechoslovak and Yugoslav cases—so as not to isolate the latter and demoralize the Southern Slavs in Austria—Beneš and Trumbić joined forces to bring the British and French governments around to their side. The first omens were encouraging. In a letter to Beneš on June 29, Pichon for the first time openly referred to a "Yugoslav State." Shortly thereafter he assured Trumbić of French support, though noting that "Sonnino represents an obstacle and that there are elements in Italy which would like to save Austria." [5] On July 1 Beneš and Trumbić obtained a statement from Balfour pledging British support for their national programs.[6] On July 25, in an address at Mansion House before the Serbian National War Aims Committee, Balfour went even further. In the presence of the Italian ambassador, he associated Great Britain with Serbia's war aims, including "the independence and unity of all Serbs, Croats and Slovenes in a single state." [7] Still, both statements fell short of granting recognition. "Honour bound" to the "regrettable" London treaty, as Balfour once wrote to Wilson,[8] the British and French governments simply would not force their views on the Italians. Yet how long could recognition be postponed?

Even in Italy that question began to be asked and openly discussed. Sonnino's abandonment of the Pact of Rome and his "victory" at Versailles came under steady attack from the liberal press, led by the *Corriere della Sera*. All through July, Leonida Bissolati, socialist reformer and minister without portfolio, waged a one-man campaign within the cabinet against Sonnino, but in vain.[9] Finally, when the British, French, and Americans broke the impasse by recognizing the Czechoslovak National Council "as a *de facto* belligerent government clothed with proper authority to direct the military and political affairs of the Czecho-Slovaks" [10]— Paris accorded the recognition on June 30, London on August 14, Washington on September 3—and the Yugoslavs became conspicuous in their isolation, public debate in Italy broke out in full force. The French, British and American actions were not actually meant to embarrass the Italian government; they were rather connected with the Clemenceau-Czernin *bagarre* over the issue of a separate peace with Austria-Hungary and the activities of the Czechoslovak legion in Siberia. Nonetheless, the Allied action caused a tumult in Italian circles.

5. Paulova, p. 467.
6. For the full text see ibid., pp. 464–65.
7. *New Europe, 8* (1918), 72.
8. On Feb. 27, 1918. See *Wilson Letters, 8,* 222–23.
9. S. Crespi, *Alla Difesa d'Italia in guerra e a Versailles (Diario 1917–1919)* (Milan, 1937), p. 121.
10. *FRUS,* 1918, Supp. I, *1,* 825.

Extreme nationalists, intoxicated by the prospect of victory, extolled Sonnino and his policy, while many prominent liberals called for a program of Italo-Yugoslav amity based on the Pact of Rome.[11] Their criticism of Sonnino abated briefly at the turn of September, when it was rumored that the cabinet had decided to recognize the Yugoslav Committee.[12] The rumor, however, proved false.

The Italian cabinet did indeed debate the Yugoslav issue at the beginning of September, with Sonnino and Bissolati as protagonists of two opposite policies. The debate came to a head on September 6–7 and was resolved temporarily by a compromise. Sonnino agreed to inform the Allies that the aim of Yugoslav independence and union was "consonant with the principles for which the Entente is fighting, as well as with the aims of a just and durable peace." [13] But no formal recognition would be granted. The statement only bound Sonnino not to oppose the dissolution of the Austro-Hungarian empire, though a month later he stated that the Italian government did not insist upon it.[14] He succeeded in skirting the issue of the future character of the Yugoslav state and, above all, in preventing any extension in the authority of the Yugoslav Committee or the Serbian government.

On September 26 the Italian government reiterated its sympathy for the Yugoslav cause, though noting that this declaration "in no way abrogates stipulations made for Italy by [the] pact of London." [15] On the same day, moreover, Sonnino told the American ambassador that Austria would again emerge as a great power and as such dominate, perhaps even absorb, the Southern Slavs.[16] In a number of pronouncements he also argued that the Croats and Slovenes opposed union with Serbia, were Austrophile by inclination, politically unreliable, and undeserving of Allied support. To lend weight to this argument, he persistently refused to free some 18,000 war prisoners of Croat and Slovene nationality

11. Woodhouse, *Italy and the Jugoslavss*, pp. 150–69.

12. Ibid., pp. 151–58. See also L. Hautecoeur, *L'Italie sous le ministère Orlando, 1917–1919* (Paris, 1919), p. 119.

13. For the full text see Paulova, p. 487.

14. Woodhouse, p. 162.

15. *FRUS*, 1918, Supp. I, *1*, 826.

16. Ibid., pp. 826–27.

and permit them to fight for the Allied cause on the Italian or the Salonika front.[17] On this issue he held fast to the end.

The military collapse of Bulgaria on September 29, 1918, brought the World War to its closing phase. Within six weeks military disaster overtook the Central Powers. The victorious Allies concluded armistices with Austria on November 3, with Germany on November 11, and with Hungary on November 13. The Habsburg commonwealth disintegrated. For the Yugoslavs, as for the Czechoslovaks and Poles, the moment of decision was at hand. Austria-Hungary's military collapse produced a chain of spontaneous nationalist revolutions that were neither controlled nor directed from the outside. In the Southern Slav provinces, Croat and Slovene leaders established a revolutionary government, the Narodno Vijeće of Zagreb, that immediately gained control of the entire land and proclaimed an independent state of Serbs, Croats, and Slovenes.

The Narodno Vijeće emerged as an entirely new factor in Yugoslav politics; it was a creation of neither the Yugoslav Committee nor the Serbian government. Yet neither Trumbić nor Pašić was taken by surprise. As early as September they began to explore ways of preparing for the expected revolt in Croatia and Slovenia. But their differences remained irreconcilable and all efforts at coordination failed. Since the Allies continued in their refusal to recognize the Yugoslav Committee as official representative of the Southern Slavs, Pašić journeyed to Paris in September to press Serbia's case. In several public statements he insisted on Serbia's "right to liberate" her brethren, but disclaimed any desire to dominate them in a future state.[18] At the same time, however, he did much to undermine the moral authority of the Yugoslav Committee. In a curious statement following Austria's last-minute attempt to save the empire by reconstituting it along federative lines, Pašić declared in an interview with Reuters that

> Serbia regards it as her duty to liberate the Serbs, Croats and Slovenes. Once freed, they will enjoy the right of free

17. *New Europe, 9* (1918), 41.
18. *La Serbie,* Oct. 7, 1918, and Oct. 28, 1918.

disposition, that is to say, the right to declare themselves either in favor of uniting with Serbia on the basis of the Declaration of Corfu or, if they so wish, of constituting themselves into small States as in the distant past. Not only do we not wish to pursue an imperialistic policy, but we do not desire to limit in any fashion the right of Croats and Slovenes to their self-determination; nor to insist upon the Declaration of Corfu, if it does not correspond to their own desires.[19]

Trumbić and his associates were furious. With victory in sight, Pašić was not only bypassing the Yugoslav Committee but creating doubts among the Allies about the wisdom of granting it official recognition. On October 10 Trumbić cabled Prince Alexander, asking the Heir Apparent to intervene with Pašić. Balfour and Pichon, Trumbić pointed out, had categorically assured him of their support for a Serb-Croat-Slovene state along the line propounded by the Yugoslav Committee. Pašić had done everything to undermine their confidence in such a solution, insisting only that the Allies recognize Serbia's right to liberate the Croats and Slovenes and create a united state under its aegis. Neither Balfour nor Pichon was swayed by Pašić's arguments, but under the circumstances both hesitated to interfere in the Yugoslavs' dispute, either by recognizing the Committee or by supporting the Pašić line.[20]

Several days later, Trumbić also wrote directly to Pašić, essentially to the same effect. But he added some additional thoughts. At this critical juncture, he wrote, the Serbian government and the Yugoslav Committee had to join forces to help create "the organs of authority in our future homeland," and to insure the "representation of our peoples as an entity" in the peace negotiations that would soon get under way. There was no time for delay; all existing differences between the parties involved had to be resolved. As a result, Trumbić now asked Pašić to convene a conference of representatives of the royal government, the Yugo-

19. Ibid., Oct. 28, 1918.
20. Trumbić to Heir Apparent Alexander, Paris, Oct. 10, 1918 (TP, F 10).

slav Committee, all Serbian political parties, and Andrija Radović, head of the Montenegrin Committee, all of whom subscribed to the Declaration of Corfu. He suggested that the conference take place in Paris, with Pašić as chairman, as soon as possible, preferably by October 25.[21] Pašić interpreted this proposal as a maneuver of the Committee and Serbian opposition leaders designed to thwart his policies, possibly even to remove him from the scene. He therefore refused. It is doubtful, in any event, whether such a conference would have significantly influenced the immediate course of events. For in a matter of days the center of gravity in Yugoslav affairs shifted decisively to the Southern Slav provinces of the crumbling Habsburg empire.

On October 29, six days before Austria signed the armistice, the Slovene (Father) Antun Korošec, the Croat Ante Pavelić,[22] and the Serb Svetozar Pribičević, principals of the Narodno Vijeće in Zagreb, solemnly proclaimed the independence of all Serbs, Croats, and Slovenes of Austria-Hungary and the creation of a "national" government, whose task it would be to effect a union with Serbia and Montenegro.[23] The proclamation was greeted with tempestuous popular acclaim and unrestrained demonstrations throughout the city of Zagreb and, within hours, in other parts of the now "ex-provinces." The Narodno Vijeće, comprised of all the Croat-Slovene political parties save the Frankist, was recognized by Emperor Charles of Austria-Hungary on October 31. On the same day the Emperor agreed to transfer the Austro-Hungarian fleet on the Adriatic to the Yugoslavs.

The October 29 "revolution" had been long in the making. All through the war the idea of an independent Serbo-Croat-Slovene state had been gaining strength in the Monarchy. After finding expression in May 1917 in the declaration of the parliamentary "Yugoslav Club" in Vienna, the idea was further propagated by the majority party of Croatia, the Serbo-Croat Coalition. From

21. Trumbić to Pašić, Paris, Oct. 15, 1918 (TP, F 39).
22. Not to be confused with the head of the Ustaša movement. Korošec was head of the Slovene Clerical Party, Pavelić of the Starčevic Party of Right, Pribičević of the Serbo-Croat Coalition.
23. See Šišić, *Dokumenti*, pp. 189–212.

mid-1917 on, the Coalition's popularity increased while that of Austrophile and Magyarophile circles steadily decreased.[24] Allied pronouncements of sympathy for the Yugoslav cause, such as Lansing's and Balfour's declarations of May 29, June 28, and July 1, 1918, prompted a number of anti-Habsburg demonstrations in Croatia and Slovenia.

In the late summer of 1918, as internal cohesion began to loosen and the prospect of military defeat began to loom as a real possibility, the Austrian government began a frantic search for ways of saving the empire. It discussed a number of projects, all involving some form of federative autonomy for the Southern Slavs. Thought was even given to the possibility of incorporating Serbia and Montenegro into the empire so as to fulfill the Southern Slavs' desire for unification. But no action was taken until it was too late. On October 16, with the military issue all but settled, Emperor Charles made the futile gesture of offering a federative reorganization of the Austrian half of the empire. Three days later, Woodrow Wilson decidedly rejected any idea of "autonomous development" for the subject nationalities within the Dual Monarchy—an idea, incidentally, that he had advanced in the Fourteen Points speech in January 1918. Wilson's note of October 19 not only threw cold water on all Austrian federative projects, it in effect gave the signal for internal revolt.

In Zagreb the next ten days were spent on organizing the revolt. Leaders of all political parties held frenzied meetings—in an atmosphere of open popular excitement—for the purpose of forming a multiparty national government and extending its control throughout the land. By October 28, preparations were completed and next day the page of history was turned. In a spontaneous chain reaction, the Narodno Vijeće proclamation of independence

24. See I. Gmajner, *Savremeni Pokret za Narodno Ujedinjenje* (Geneva, 1918); F. Cvijetiša, *Les Problèmes nationaux de l'Autriche-Hongrie—les Yougoslaves* (Paris, 1918); M. P. Tchoubinski, *L'Idée de l'unité serbo-croate* (Paris, 1918); V. Wilder (Vilder), *Dva Smjera u Hrvatskoj Politici* (Zagreb, 1918); *Le Mouvement yougoslave en Autriche-Hongrie pendant la guerre* (Paris, 1919); S. Budisavljević, *Stvaranje Države Srba Hrvata i Slovenaca* (Zagreb, 1958); F. Slipičević, *Prvi svjetski rat i stvaranje države Jugoslovenskih naroda* (Sarajevo, 1957). The author has also had access to the valuable study by Dr. Kruno M. Dinčić, "Le Fédéralisme chez les Slaves du Sud, *1804–1954*," MS (1955), in which this problem is treated in detail.

was followed by acts of accession of the provincial bodies of Vojvodina and Bosnia-Hercegovina, bringing into being a sizable Yugoslav state that extended from the borders of Serbia to the borders
of Italy. Remarkably, not a shot was fired to bring this "state"
into existence. On November 26, by resolution of the Podgorica
Skupština, Montenegro proclaimed its union with the other Yugoslav lands. Four days later the former Austro-Hungarian provinces
and Montenegro joined with Serbia to form the Kingdom of
Serbs, Croats, and Slovenes, by official proclamation of Regent
Alexander in Belgrade on December 1. Two independent states
—Serbia and Montenegro—voluntarily relinquished their sovereignty to bring about the Yugoslav union.

The Kingdom of Serbs, Croats, and Slovenes emerged with the
acquiescence of the Allies, but not at their instigation. Indeed,
after October 29, events moved with such rapidity that more
than once the Allies had only vague knowledge of what was really
happening. Thus Washington, London, and Paris learned about
the actions of the Narodno Vijeće from Trumbić and Pašić, not
directly from the scene. In Washington full details were not received until November 13, and even then conflicting rumors kept
circulating wildly.[25] The Italian government learned of the Vijeće's
formation via the radio on November 2, and was the first Allied
government to react. Greatly alarmed at the rumored transfer of
the Austro-Hungarian fleet to Yugoslav control—a rumor that
turned out to be correct—Sonnino immediately summoned the
American ambassador, Nelson Page. The Italian government protested against the announced intention of the Narodno Vijeće
to occupy the naval base at Pola and take possession of the former
Austro-Hungarian fleet. Page was told that the Italians planned
to do so themselves and that the United States should do everything to hold the Yugoslavs back.[26]

The time for implementing the Treaty of London was at hand
and Sonnino was not inclined to waste time. After asking Washington to restrain the Yugoslavs, he set about to prevent Allied

25. See *Papers Relating to the Foreign Relations of the United States. The Paris
Peace Conference, 1919, 2* (13 vols. Washington, 1942–47), 288 (hereafter cited as
FRUS-PPC).
26. *FRUS*, 1918, Supp. I, *1*, 862–63.

recognition of the Narodno Vijeće. On November 2 and again on the 6th, Trumbić cabled him, offering on behalf of the Narodno Vijeće full political and military cooperation with the Allied armies in the Balkans, and requesting formal recognition for the Zagreb government.[27] Pašić did the same.[28] Fearing that the United States, France, and particularly Great Britain were preparing to extend recognition—Imperiali had informed him that Balfour was ready to do so— [29] Sonnino pressed for a postponement. His intervention was successful, partly because the other Allies hesitated to antagonize Italy at the very moment of victory, partly because they regarded the Yugoslav situation as being too confused.

As one of its first tasks, the Narodno Vijeće sought to establish contact with the Serbian army and government and with the Yugoslav Committee. In quick succession two missions were sent forth from Zagreb: one, through the lines of retreating enemy units, to Belgrade; the other to Switzerland. In Serbia, however, the situation was still fluid. Belgrade was liberated only on November 1. The government, with Stojan Protić substituting for Pašić, who was still in Paris, was on the point of leaving Corfu for the liberated capital. The Vijeće mission thus arrived in Belgrade on the morning of November 8, twenty-four hours before the arrival of Regent Alexander and the Serbian General Staff, and several days ahead of Protić. On the ninth it was received by Alexander and from that point on close contact was maintained.

The other mission, composed of Antun Korošec, Melko Čingrija, and Gregor Žerjav, arrived in Geneva on November 1. Korošec immediately contacted Trumbić and Pašić to arrange a meeting. Both were in Paris, but not working together. Pašić, after bowing to the pressure of events, had finally begun to negotiate a coalition government with Serbian opposition leaders. The need for a coalition was evident, but the opposition leaders also wanted to include representatives of the Yugoslav Committee, to

27. Trumbić to Sonnino, Paris, Nov. 2, 1918 (Gab. 5368), and Nov. 6, 1918 (Tel. 7449, MFA, Rome).

28. Pašić to Sonnino, Paris, Nov. 8, 1918 (Note 72679, MFA, Rome).

29. Imperiali to Sonnino, London, Nov. 6, 1918, and Nov. 8, 1918, in *I Documenti diplomatici italiani*, R. Mosca, ed., *I* (6th Ser. Rome, 1956), 11, 24–25 (hereafter cited as *DDI*).

prepare the way for the imminent national union. Pašić temporized and would agree only to a Serbian coalition government. Further negotiations were interrupted by Korošec's message from Geneva. Trumbić, hopeful that the Narodno Vijeće mission might help to reconcile the differences between the Yugoslav Committee and Pašić, immediately informed Korošec of the substance of the dispute. Korošec, in turn, in his capacity as President of the Zagreb government, sent back a note empowering Trumbić to represent the Narodno Vijeće before the Allies, thereby not only establishing immediate contact with the Allied governments but lending Trumbić additional authority vis-à-vis Pašić.

The differences between Pašić and Trumbić, however, were not likely to be resolved at this point without the fullest review of all the issues involved. For this reason, and to prepare a plan of unification and joint action before the Allies, Pašić, Trumbić, and the Serbian opposition leaders left Paris to meet with Korošec and his colleagues. They arrived in Geneva on November 5. For the next three days talks were conducted almost without interruption. Pašić represented the Radical cabinet; Milorad Drašković, Marko Trifković, and Vojislav Marinković the parliamentary opposition (the Independent Radicals, Progressives, and Dissident Radicals, respectively); Korošec, Čingrija, and Žerjav the Narodno Vijeće; and Trumbić, Gustav Gregorin, and Dušan Vasiljević the Yugoslav Committee. At the outset, all agreed on an agenda of four principal points: 1) obtaining Allied recognition of the Narodno Vijeće as the legitimate government of the Serbs, Croats, and Slovenes of the former Dual Monarchy; 2) arranging for the creation of common organs for the united Yugoslav state; 3) protesting against Italian military occupation of Serbo-Croat-Slovene territory; 4) determining relations with Montenegro.[30] On points 1 and 3 agreement was quickly reached. Faced with the accomplished fact, Pašić agreed to recognize the Narodno Vijeće on behalf of the Serbian government. But on point 2, the creation of an all-Yugoslav government, the conference almost broke down.

Pašić began by insisting on a purely Serbian coalition government, in which the opposition parties would represent the Yugoslavs of the former empire. The Narodno Vijeće would designate

30. Šišić, *Dokumenti*, p. 238.

a committee of its own to serve as an *advisory* body to the cabinet in matters of foreign policy. This plan was turned down by everyone else. As an alternative, Drašković proposed a seventeen-member cabinet in which Serbia and the Narodno Vijeće each had an equal voice, a cabinet that would assume immediate jurisdiction over all Yugoslav lands and supplant existing governmental bodies. Both Pašić and Trumbić rejected this plan: the one because he would not share power with the Narodno Vijeće, the other still fearing that Pašić would retain too much control.[31]

Outnumbered and annoyed that the conference was laying concrete foundations for the new state (he had come to Geneva expecting rather to sign a declaration of solidarity designed for Allied consumption), Pašić now began to look for a way out. He suddenly proposed the formation of a joint political-military committee, with four Serbs and three representatives of the Narodno Vijeće, to conduct military affairs and prepare for the peace conference. Within the committee, Pašić would be foreign minister. In the meantime, the Serbian government and the Narodno Vijeće would continue to function, each conducting the internal affairs in its own sphere. The idea appeared suspect, because it ran counter to Pašić's long-held beliefs and because it suggested a convenient formula for Pašić to retain power in Serbia until he could return home and see what the immediate future held in store.[32] But in its general lines Pašić's proposal corresponded to Trumbić's own views. Thus Trumbić now counterproposed the establishment of a temporary Serbo-Croat-Slovene state, with its center in Zagreb, and the temporary continuation of the Serbian kingdom. The two *equal* sovereign entities would then negotiate and arrange their union. On hearing this, Pašić accused Trumbić of advancing a "purely Croat program of union" along the lines of a "Greater Croatia," designed, among other reasons, to keep the Serbs of the former Monarchy from joining Serbia.[33] He became irate at Korošec and the Serbian opposition leaders for supporting Trumbić's proposal, for the party leaders evidently hoped to use such a plan to eliminate Pašić as head of a Serbian coalition cabinet.

31. Dinčić, *"Fédéralisme,"* pp. 259–60.
32. This view is convincingly argued by Pavelić in *Trumbić,* p. 175.
33. Ibid.

In a heated debate Trumbić denied having any ulterior motives and argued rather that his proposal offered the only way out of the impasse. His view again received general support. Pašić now had to make up his mind. To reject a proposal supported by the other participants would make him appear as an opponent of the projected union; to accept it would violate his most cherished principles.[34] As he pondered the alternatives, an outside factor intervened.

The Allies were closely following what was happening at Geneva. The French, particularly interested in reconciling the various Yugoslav factions in order to stabilize the situation in Southeastern Europe, were alarmed by the possibility of a breakdown in the Geneva talks. On November 8, therefore, President Raymond Poincaré wired Pašić to urge that the "entire Yugoslav nation show itself to be of a single spirit, without even the smallest division, as is now more than ever required by our vital interests." [35] Poincaré's intervention left Pašić little choice. He quickly decided to give in—but also to make the agreement inoperative.

On November 9 the conferees drafted, signed, and released the so-called Geneva Declaration. The document announced the creation of a common Yugoslav ministry—of twelve portfolios, six from Serbia and six from the rest of the country—to conduct foreign policy and joint military affairs. The Serbian government and the Narodno Vijeće would continue to conduct the internal affairs of their respective territorial spheres until the adoption of a new national constitution, to be drawn up by a popularly elected constituent assembly of all Serbs, Croats, and Slovenes. Finally, Montenegro was invited to enter the national union.[36] The agreement also called for a vigorous protest to the Allies against Italy's occupation of Yugoslav territories.

This task done, Pašić immediately returned to Paris, followed shortly by all the signatories. The Geneva Declaration signified a major victory for Trumbić, but his triumph was short-lived. From Paris, Pašić sent separate reports on the conference to Regent

34. Ibid., p. 176.
35. Ibid., p. 177. See also Pekić, *Propast Austro-Ugarske Monarhije*, p. 313, and Paulova, *Jugoslavenski Odbor*, p. 562.
36. For the full text see Šišić, *Dokumenti*, pp. 236–37.

Alexander and Stojan Protić. Then he resigned as premier, and
Protić, with the rest of the Radical cabinet, followed suit. Trumbić and Korošec reached Paris on the 13th. Unaware of Pašić's
resignation, they proceeded to the Quai d'Orsay to discuss the
Geneva program with Pichon. To their consternation, the French
foreign minister informed them that the Serbian government had
resigned—Pašić and Milenko Vesnić had visited him the day before—and that the Geneva program was now a dead letter. Pichon
made no effort to conceal his deep irritation at the entire affair.

The following day, Korošec, as president of the Narodno Vijeće,
sent a note to the American, British, French, and Italian governments, requesting recognition of the Vijeće as a de facto government and of the Yugoslavs as an Allied nation. In the circumstances,
however, the Allies preferred to wait. On November 11, the day
of the German armistice, Colonel House relayed to Wilson Korošec's request for recognition. At the same time, the British and
French governments were again preparing to extend such recognition.[37] But news of the post-Geneva crisis and renewed Italian
pressure led the three governments to postpone formal action. As
to the Yugoslav crisis, significant new developments were under
way.

Having succeeded in nullifying the Geneva agreement, Pašić
proceeded to gain his way. First, he induced Ljubomir (Ljuba)
Davidović, Marko Trifković, and Vojislav Marinković to join
a Serbian coalition cabinet, with career diplomat Mihajlo Gavrilović as foreign minister. Then, on November 16 he announced
in Paris the formation of the new government. On the 18th he
received Trumbić, Korošec, and Čingrija, and explained that the
cabinet and the Regent had refused to accept the Geneva Declaration, thus forcing his resignation. He offered to accept several
members of the Narodno Vijeće into the Serbian cabinet, or alter-
natively, to allow a joint political-military committee to serve in
an advisory capacity.[38] That was his final offer. Trumbić and
Korošec insisted on the terms of the Geneva Declaration, whereupon Pašić broke off further talks and left Paris for London.

To complicate matters, Trumbić, Korošec, and the Serbian op-

37. *DDI*, p. 71.
38. Paulova, p. 571.

position leaders received reports indicating that Regent Alexander had not rejected the Geneva agreement.[39] In his report Pašić had apparently magnified the extent of his differences with the others, to justify his own resignation and force that of Protić and the cabinet. Korošec then informed Alexander of his side of the story. The whole episode led to an estrangement between Pašić and the Regent that, within a month, cost the old Radical the prime-ministership of the first all-Yugoslav cabinet.

With the deadlock in Paris, the center of gravity shifted again to Zagreb. There, the arrival of Colonel Dušan Simović,[40] as representative of the Serbian General Staff, opened a new channel of communications with Belgrade. Working closely with Svetozar Pribičević, Simović kept reporting to Belgrade the general desire for union with Serbia and the widespread popularity of the Karadjordjević dynasty.

At the same time, word arrived in Zagreb about the breakdown in Paris of talks between Pašić, Korošec, and Trumbić. There was already much nervousness over the postponement of actual unification because internal conditions were becoming strained. The landing of Italian troops in Dalmatia and their movements in Slovenia were causing considerable panic. The system of communication was largely disrupted; the economy was at a near standstill. In this atmosphere a general debate developed over the character of the proposed Yugoslav state, with partisans of federalism and centralism engaging in a bitter polemic.[41] Moreover, a number of politicians were distressed over the Geneva agreement because, they claimed, Korošec did not have the authority to negotiate any such compromise. With the passing of each day, the need for quick action increased. On November 25, therefore, the Narodno Vijeće decided to act without reference to the Geneva

39. In a lengthy report to the State Department on Dec. 24, Dodge wrote from Belgrade that Alexander had in fact not objected to a temporary dualistic arrangement. The Regent, rather, accused Pašić of keeping him ill-informed about the course of negotiations and of failing to convey messages from the opposition leaders. When Pašić returned to Belgrade, wrote Dodge, he was told he no longer enjoyed the Regent's confidence. (Dodge to Lansing, Belgrade, Dec. 24, 1918, 860H.01/39, Department of State, The National Archives, Washington, D.C.)

40. Who carried out the Belgrade *coup d'état* of March 27, 1941, and then briefly served as prime minister.

41. See Pekić, pp. 324–44.

Declaration. It sent a deputation to Belgrade with instructions to negotiate directly for the formation of an all-Yugoslav government. The final form of the new state would be determined by a national constituent assembly. But as a basis for negotiations, the Vijeće passed a new resolution proclaiming the union of all Serbs, Croats, and Slovenes of the former Monarchy with Serbia and Montenegro.[42]

On November 26 the Montenegrin Skupština in Podgorica passed a similar resolution, proclaiming the union of Montenegro with Serbia and all other Yugoslav lands.[43] The delegates of the Narodno Vijeće, led by Ante Pavelić and Svetozar Pribičević, arrived in Belgrade on the 28th and immediately began negotiations with Stojan Protić. The Zagreb Vijeće, however, had acted hastily, mainly at the instigation of Svetozar Pribičević.[44] It made no provision for the eventuality of a breakdown in the Belgrade talks, nor did it reserve the right of ratifying any agreement reached. Its delegates, in reality, had carte blanche. Protić and the Radicals were offered little resistance. They demanded acceptance of the House of Karadjordjević and the formation of a centralized administration for the entire country. The Zagreb delegates accepted, whereupon they were received in audience, one at a time, by Alexander. At eight on the evening of December 1, the Regent formally proclaimed the "union of Serbia and the lands of the independent state of Serbs, Croats and Slovenes into the united Kingdom of Serbs, Croats and Slovenes."[45]

The new state was thus born and its centralized character established. The task of forming a national government took two weeks. The Radicals, still the strongest single party in the land, could count on heading a national coalition. But Pašić, who had incurred the hostility of nearly every element outside his own party, would not be placed at its head. The final choice actually rested with Alexander. The Regent, however, for reasons of personal rivalry and practical politics, decided to remove Pašić from the scene—at least for the time being. By December 16 the main out-

---

42. Šišić, *Dokumenti*, 255–56.
43. Ibid., pp. 258–61.
44. See Pavelić, pp. 189 ff.
45. Šišić, *Dokumenti*, p. 282.

line of the coalition was worked out. By the end of the month the new cabinet was confirmed. Stojan Protić became the first Yugoslav Prime Minister; Korošec, Deputy Prime Minister; Trumbić, Minister of Foreign Affairs; Svetozar Pribičević, Minister of the Interior; Ljuba Davidović, Minister of Education; Marko Trifković, Minister of Justice. Nikola Pašić, veteran Prime Minister of Serbia, was appointed head of the Yugoslav peace delegation in Paris. For nearly a year and a half he would thus be away from Belgrade.

3. Italy Intervenes: The Occupation of Dalmatia and Fiume

AUSTRIA-HUNGARY AND GERMANY stood on the verge of laying down their arms. At three in the afternoon on October 31, the Allied Supreme War Council was convened at Versailles to approve the terms of the impending armistices. A representative of Serbia, Vesnić, was present. Earlier that day, however, representatives of the American, British, French, and Italian governments had already met and agreed on a joint draft. In respect to the Balkans, they called for the prompt evacuation of all Austro-Hungarian forces from the territories of the Dual Monarchy, along a demarcation line running from the Julian Alps in the northwest to Dalmatia and the Dalmatian archipelago in the southeast. The evacuated territories would be occupied by Allied, including American, forces. But the Italian army and navy would be the first to move, acting on behalf and as representative of all the Allies. The armistice demarcation line corresponded in almost every detail to the 1915 Treaty of London line.

At the afternoon meeting of the Supreme War Council the terms for the Austro-Hungarian armistice were adopted. Vesnić tried to persuade the Allies to occupy the whole Yugoslav territory and not just the areas coincident with the Treaty of London. Failing in this effort, in the end he approved the Allied plan on behalf of Serbia. During the next three days the Council also decided to divide the Austro-Hungarian fleet among the Allies. Vesnić fought to keep the fleet, which Austria had transferred to the Narodno Vijeće on October 31, in Yugoslav hands by having the Allies recognize the Vijeće as a cobelligerent government. This Orlando and Sonnino vigorously opposed. When the Narodno Vijeće cabled the Supreme Council, offering to transfer the Austro-Hungarian fleet to the American navy (to keep it from falling into Italian hands), Colonel House, Lloyd George, Clemenceau,

The Line of the Italian Occupation, 1918

and Orlando agreed to a new formula. They ordered the Yugoslavs to sail the fleet to Corfu and there place it at the disposal of the Supreme Commander of the Allied Forces. Thus within four days the Allies dealt two heavy blows to the Yugoslavs: they enabled Italy to occupy the Treaty of London line, and on political grounds they forced the Yugoslavs to relinquish control over the Austro-Hungarian fleet, including merchant vessels owned entirely by Southern Slav capital.

The Italians pressed their advantage with speed. The armistice with Austria was signed at the Villa Giusta in Padova on November 3, at the headquarters of General Armando Diaz, Commander-in-Chief of the Italian Army. No sooner was the armistice document signed than Italian land and naval forces began to move.[1] They entered Trieste and Pola in order to take over Austro-Hungarian vessels at the two naval bases, while in separate operations Italian warships proceeded to take over the islands of Korčula, Cres, Vis, and others. Within ten days key points in Istria and along Dalmatia were in Italian hands. On November 6 Šibenik was taken. The following day a naval squadron entered the bay of Zara and took possession of the city proper. Under Diaz' overall supervision, Italian troops even crossed the Villa Giusta demarcation line, moving into the hinterland of Dalmatia, in the direction of Fiume (excluded under the armistice terms, as well as under the Treaty of London), and toward Ljubljana.

Faced with such swift action, the Yugoslavs became panicky and tried to take countermeasures. The Narodno Vijeće ordered general mobilization, hoping to rush its own forces westward to take over as much of the littoral and of Slovenia as possible. At the same time, it appealed for military assistance to the Serbian Chief of Staff and to Marshal Ferdinand Foch, Allied Commander-in-Chief. Zagreb also requested the landing of French, British, and American forces along Dalmatia. Within a week, in fact, token French, British and American units did land—in conformity with the Versailles decision of October 31 and the armi-

1. The Villa Giusta armistice has been rightly characterized as a "document drawn with almost exclusive reference to the needs, demands and claims of Italy." See H. W. V. Temperley, ed., *A History of the Peace Conference of Paris*, *4* (6 vols. London, 1920–24), 122.

stice terms—but for the time being their combined size was not significant. Also, they were under Diaz' command!

At the same time, the Narodno Vijeće sent military delegates to Serbia and Corfu to obtain the help of Serbian and French forces under the command of General Louis Franchet d'Esperey, Allied Commander of the Armies of the Orient. Franchet d'Esperey was sympathetic and, apparently on his own authority, promised to lend his support.[2] The Austrian armistice, however, did not end the fighting with Hungary, and Serbia was still being cleared of the enemy. The Serbian army, therefore, was moving northward toward Syrmia and the Banat, and at the same time southward toward Albania and Montenegro. Until the end of November, its main efforts were expended on these two fronts, leaving only subordinate forces for the drive west—toward Dalmatia, Croatia, and Slovenia. Hungary capitulated only on November 13—the formal armistice was signed that day in Belgrade [3]— but the main body of the Serbian army still did not move west. In part, it was restrained by Franchet d'Esperey, who wanted to avoid conflict with Diaz and the Italian High Command. In part, the Serbian General Staff and the government were anxious to secure control over Bosnia-Hercegovina and the Banat, coincidentally lands promised to the Serbs by the Allies in 1915. In part, the Serbs reacted to Italian landings in Albania by hastily overrunning the northern part of the country, including Scutari, while the Italians proceeded to occupy Valona and central and southern Albania. In the chaotic days that followed the Austrian and Hungarian armistices, Belgrade could thus offer only limited help to the beleaguered government in Zagreb.

Yet the Serbian army helped in a number of critical areas, most notably in Slovenia. As Italians and irregular Slovene-Croat units raced toward Ljubljana, an armed clash seemed inevitable. At the same time, several units of the Serbian army, under the command of Colonel Simović, were fanning out together with Slovene and Croat irregulars across Styria and Carinthia. Simović, determined to prevent the Italians from taking over Ljubljana, dispatched a contingent to the Slovene capital that arrived there

2. Pekić, *Propast Austro-Ugarske Monarhije*, p. 296.
3. See F. Deák, *Hungary at the Paris Peace Conference* (New York, 1942), pp. 9–11.

before the Italians. Simović then informed the Italians that he intended to fight unless they withdrew behind the armistice demarcation line. Faced with a serious clash of arms, the local Italian commanders complied. This timely intervention was the main factor in preventing an Italian seizure of Ljubljana.

On another front, however, success eluded the Yugoslavs. By mid-November, Fiume was still unoccupied. The armistice demarcation line, running to the west of the city proper, specifically excluded Fiume from the Italian military zone, again in conformity with the Treaty of London line. While Italian units, camped to the west and the north, were waiting for word from Rome, a Serbian battalion under Major Maksimović entered and occupied the city on November 18. The Italian commander immediately contacted Maksimović and proposed that the Serbs withdraw fifteen kilometers southeast, along the coast, pledging that if the Serbs agreed the Italians would not enter the city. Maksimović naïvely complied, accepting the word of a fellow-Allied officer and hoping to avert a conflict with the Italians. The Serbs had barely left town when Italian units, headed by armored cars, moved in from nearby Abbazia (Opatija). Under the command of General Francesco Saverio Grazioli, they occupied the entire town, though soon "the arrival of two French, one American, and one British battalion gave an international character to the occupation." [4] The Americans, however, withdrew early, and despite the presence of other Allied forces, the occupation became almost purely Italian in nature.

Elsewhere, too, the Italians succeeded in carrying through with their plans. Disregarding the hostility of the local population, they quickly gained control of the principal islands and the mainland from Zara to Šibenik. With equal speed, their military occupation assumed a character of permanency, if not annexation. Admiral Enrico Millo assumed the title of "Governor of Dalmatia," and deliberately fostered the impression that Italy was there to stay and that the Treaty of London was finally enforced.[5]

---

4. Temperley, *4,* 122.

5. Almost everywhere they came, the Italians were received with open hostility. See H. Baerlein, *The Birth of Yugoslavia, 2* (2 vols. London, 1922), 29–46; *New Europe, 9* (1918), 151–56, 187–89.

In response to Italian actions, the Yugoslavs redoubled their efforts to gain control of the former Austro-Hungarian fleet. Raising the Croatian flag on all the warships and merchant vessels they took over from the Austrians, they wavered in complying with the Allied instructions to surrender the fleet at Corfu. The Italian navy, however, proceeded to sequester all former Austro-Hungarian ships, remove the Croatian flag, and escort them to Italian ports.[6] For obvious reasons, the Yugoslavs decided to avoid clashing with the Italians on the sea as well as on land. They therefore responded with a barrage of diplomatic protests but no armed challenge. They met with limited success, for an inter-Allied naval conference at Corfu finally adopted a compromise formula. At the initiative of Vice-Admiral Gauchet, commander of French naval forces in the Adriatic, the Yugoslavs were permitted to retain control of vessels captured after October 31 and sail them under the Croatian flag. The Italians, on the other hand, would retain control of the vessels they had seized, including those from which they had removed the Croatian flag. The Allied instructions to the Yugoslavs to surrender the fleet at Corfu were thus not implemented after all. But by the end of November the bulk of the former Austro-Hungarian fleet had passed into Italian control and Gauchet's compromise was, in any event, a temporary formula, leaving the whole problem to be settled by the peace conference.

The armistices of November 3 and November 13 were defective in several respects. They drew vague demarcation lines in Albania, the Banat, Carinthia, and Styria, thus giving rise to constant conflict between the contending occupation forces. They failed to provide for adequate coordination of policy between Generals Diaz and Franchet d'Esperey, thus allowing the Italians maximum leeway to pursue strictly national rather than joint inter-Allied goals. The Villa Giusta armistice, moreover, provided only for Adriatic territories and, as Seton-Watson rightly noted, "entirely (and perhaps inevitably) ignored the Balkan aspect of affairs."[7]

6. Pekić, pp. 298–99.

7. R. W. Seton-Watson, *Treaty Revision and the Hungarian Frontiers* (London, 1934), p. 19.

Predicated on the political premises of the Treaty of London, it pre-empted the task of the peace conference.

Considerable responsibility for this state of affairs must be laid at the door of President Wilson and Colonel House. Ever since the United States had entered the war in April 1917, American statesmanship had refused to come to grips with the Treaty of London issue. Though long opposed to the secret treaties on principle—and consciously never recognizing the Treaty of London as a valid basis for a future peace settlement—Wilson failed to make his position explicit or to deal with the issue before the end of the war. Despite State Department claims in early 1918 and Wilson's own testimony to the Senate Foreign Relations Committee in August 1919 to the effect that Washington had no precise knowledge about the Treaty of London (and the Treaty of Bucharest),[8] and therefore could do little about it, the evidence suggests that the President seriously considered taking up the issue with the Entente after America's entry into the war. He learned about the Treaty of London from Colonel House as early as May 1915.[9] In April 1917, however, Colonel House advised against making an issue of the secret treaties, fearing "the results of an American demand that the Allies renounce them. The time might come," the Colonel felt, "when the United States would be in a position to enforce such a demand as a necessary preliminary to a stable peace." [10]

While Wilson was formulating the Fourteen Points, another opportunity arose for American initiative in this respect. But as the Allies tried to find a basis for a separate peace with Austria-Hungary during the winter of 1917–18, Wilson was not inclined to take decisive measures regarding the future of the Habsburg empire or to jeopardize Allied solidarity by challenging Italy's right under the London convention. Yet he was deeply concerned about the secret treaties and asked Balfour to furnish him with the actual details and a statement of British views on the subject. This the Foreign Secretary did, together with the actual text. On

8. *House Papers, 4,* 61–63; *Wilson Letters, 1,* 493, and *8,* 20.
9. *House Papers, 3,* 40.
10. Ibid., p. 41.

January 31, 1918, Balfour candidly admitted that London was not happy about the secret arrangement, but he also served notice that "a treaty is a treaty: and we—I mean England and France (of Russia I say nothing)—are bound to uphold it in letter and in spirit. The objections of it indeed are obvious enough: it assigns to Italy territories on the Adriatic which are not Italian but Slav, and the arrangement is justified not on grounds of nationality but on grounds of strategy." [11] To Colonel House the President observed that without American support Italy could never secure "what she went into the war, on cold-blooded calculation, to get," [12] but he nonetheless refrained from raising the question with Rome.

The final occasion to press the issue arose during the inter-Allied discussions that preceded the Austrian and German armistices. At this point, however, Colonel House, representing the President in the Allied councils, specifically avoided discussion of this fundamental question. On October 31 and again on November 4, House steered discussion away from the subject for fear of getting bogged down over Italian issues. Anxious to reach quick Allied agreement and thus hasten the end of war, the Colonel acted in the belief that a political debate would only delay the armistice. In any event, he regarded the impending peace conference as the proper forum for such a debate. Yet in agreeing to an armistice demarcation line that corresponded to the Treaty of London line, he unwittingly compounded the dilemma for American, let alone Yugoslav, diplomacy at the peace conference. After the fighting had stopped, Wilson told the Italian ambassador in Washington that "inasmuch as the [London] pact was made to safeguard Italy from Austria-Hungary and now that Austria-Hungary no longer existed the pact itself might be supposed to have disappeared." As the first direct statement of his

11. Ibid., pp. 50–51. See also Baker, *Life and Letters, 7,* 74.

12. *Wilson Letters, 8,* 512. In December 1917 Wilson told former President Taft that he was opposed to any identification between American and British policies on this score. He "heartily disapproved" of British "self-interest" as expressed through the Treaty of London (ibid., p. 407). It may be noted that in March 1918 Balfour furnished Wilson and House with the details of the secret treaty (*House Papers, 3,* 49; *Wilson Letters, 8,* 5).

view, this was indeed strong language. But the Italian ambassador, who rightly "scented danger," failed to report the President's remark to Rome.[13] In any event, it was too late.

The Italian government proceeded after the armistice as though it were implementing the Treaty of London. Diaz was instructed to effect the occupation of Slav territory, but to avoid conflicts with the local populations and to pursue a policy of moderation.[14] At the same time, Sonnino demanded the evacuation of the Scutari region in Albania by the Serbian army, and after several interventions, Franchet d'Esperey was pressured by Paris into ordering the Serbs out and replacing them with French troops.[15]

The French government, however, was alarmed at the increasing prospect of clashes between Italians and Yugoslavs. In Dalmatia the Italian occupation began to encounter strong local resistance and cause daily incidents.[16] In Italy extreme nationalists launched a virulent campaign against the Yugoslavs, against the Pact of Rome and Italian proponents of rapprochement, against Italy's allies for their pro-Yugoslav attitude, and even against Wilson for abandoning Italy.[17] In these circumstances French Foreign Minister Stéphen Pichon considered asking for the stationing of American troops in all "critical" trouble spots in order to avoid major conflicts.[18] To underscore the gravity of the situation, even Colonel House urged Wilson, on November 11, to recognize the Narodno Vijeće and issue a "very guarded" assurance that Yugoslav territorial claims could be decided only by the peace conference, "in order to reassure them in the face of the Italian occupation of the Dalmatian coast along the line of the convention of London, against which I protested and consented only upon the explicit promise that this territory should have the same status as the territory to be occupied under the

13. Memorandum by Asst. Sec. of State Phillips, Nov. 26, 1918 (*FRUS-PPC*, 2, 315). Also see Mamatey, pp. 360–62, 369–70, and Bernardy and Falorsi, *Questione Adriatica d'oltre Atlantico*, pp. 130–31.

14. Diaz to Orlando, Nov. 5, 1918 (*DDI*, p. 3), acknowledging receipt of such a directive and promising to carry it out.

15. Ibid., pp. 5, 11, 62.

16. See Baerlein, 2, 29–46.

17. See Hautecoeur, *L'Italie*, pp. 132–50.

18. Bonin Longare to Sonnino, Nov. 6, 1918 (*DDI*, p. 12).

terms of the German armistice." [19] House's suggestion was echoed by Dodge, who at Corfu reported among else that

> The most disquieting element in the present situation is the attitude assumed by Italy which threatens to produce an open collision with the Yugo-Slavs in Dalmatia and Montenegro. Thus far the Italian forces are apparently the only ones of the Entente which have landed in these regions and the effect of this has been extremely irritating and alarming to the population. The attitude of the population is in no way hostile to a joint landing of the Entente forces but only to the Italians being allowed to act alone. This appears now to be realized and to be in a fair way to be corrected. The landing of American forces would be especially agreeable and quieting to the population. In this connection I may mention that the feeling between Italians and French at Corfu has become very bitter. Lately four large Italian battleships have arrived here whereas until their arrival there were only occasionally small Italian cruisers here. Since their unexpected arrival their Commander has acted on several occasions with singular tactlessness towards the French Commanding Vice Admiral. [20]

In Paris, Korošec—unable to return to Zagreb because Italian authorities would not issue him a transit visa—appealed directly to Colonel House for quick American intervention. On November 18 House, convinced that any other course would lead to major trouble, urged Wilson to send American troops to the scene. [21] While the proposal was being discussed in Washington, however, the Italian government did not remain inactive.

After much discussion, Orlando personally authorized on November 15 the plan to occupy Fiume. [22] This project was implemented four days later. At the same time, Sonnino moved on the diplomatic front. Determined to forestall Allied recognition of

---

19. *FRUS-PPC*, 2, 287.
20. Ibid., p. 290.
21. Ibid., pp. 298, 301.
22. *DDI*, p. 88. It appears that, unlike Orlando, Sonnino hesitated on whether to take Fiume at this stage. Since Fiume stood clearly outside the Treaty of London line, he did not wish to jeopardize the treaty (ibid., p. 78).

the Narodno Vijeće—for Italian military plans could hardly be carried out if the Yugoslavs obtained formal recognition and Allied support—he instructed his ambassadors to portray the Yugoslavs as lawless, politically unreliable, and incapable of forming a stable national union. In London, Imperiali thus openly referred to the Yugoslavs as "our worst enemies" and to the prospective Yugoslav union as no more than a "theoretical hypothesis." [23] On November 19, the day Italy seized Fiume, Orlando informed Camille Barrère, the French ambassador in Rome, that while the Allies had the right to send troops into every occupation zone, the Italian government would regard such action as distinctly "unfriendly." [24]

Before long, however, the French and British lost their patience with Rome. Not only Italian arbitrariness but also the anti-Allied press campaign, as well as a series of incidents, strained relations between Italy and her Allies. Admiral Paolo Thaon di Revel, head of the Italian Navy, objected to the sending of French and British warships into the Adriatic in such insulting terms as to cause Lloyd George and Clemenceau to explode into fits of anger. It took two weeks of painstaking effort on the part of Orlando to repair the damage caused by Thaon's remarks.[25] But Italian sensitivities never recovered from Lloyd George's bitter charge that the Italians contributed very little to the Allied campaign in Bavaria.[26] Nor would Rome forgive the fact that British and French officers in the Adriatic, acting from personal sympathies, encouraged local Yugoslav resistance to Italian occupation forces.[27]

On November 20 Vesnić urgently appealed to Washington to dispatch American warships into the Adriatic. The situation was clearly getting out of hand as the Italians met with increased hostility and resistance. In a secret report to Rome on November 21, Admiral Millo admitted that anti-Italian feeling was spreading and that local civil servants were taking an oath of allegiance to the Narodno Vijeće of Zagreb, despite the strictest order for-

23. *DDI*, pp. 82–83.
24. Ibid., p. 113.
25. Ibid., pp. 70, 95, 113.
26. Ibid., p. 104.
27. See Page to Lansing, Rome, Nov. 31, 1918 (*FRUS-PPC*, 2, 308).

bidding any manifestation in favor of the Vijeće.[28] Sonnino responded by recommending the reinforcement of Italian forces in Zara and Šibenik, particularly as he feared the Serbs might soon land their own troops in Dalmatia.[29]

But the Italians, too, became worried at the results of their own actions. On November 21, Count Lelio Bonin Longare wired Orlando—deliberately bypassing Sonnino—urging an agreement with the Yugoslavs. France and England, he noted, stood on the verge of granting recognition, while Wilson, he added, "will recognize without asking anyone else. I believe in this case it would not suit us to remain the only dissidents." [30] Orlando relayed Bonin's message to Sonnino with the observation that recognizing the Yugoslavs would in no way prejudice Italian territorial claims.[31] But Sonnino was in no mood to give way. Within hours after receiving Orlando's mesage, he simply replied: "In relation to Your Excellency's telegram No. 3697 of this day I wish to express the view that for the time being it is not convenient for us to proceed with recognition of the Yugoslavs without revising our future intentions." [32] Sonnino's intransigence led to renewed conflict within the Italian cabinet (Bissolati accused the Foreign Minister of betraying his own pledge of September 8 and, after weeks of vain efforts on his part, he resigned from the cabinet in disgust) [33] but no change in policy.

The British, French, and American governments, meanwhile, still could not bring themselves to recognize the Yugoslavs. They were sufficiently alarmed at the trend of events, and annoyed with Italy, to agree on the necessity of sending American troops into the Adriatic.[34] On November 22 Assistant Secretary of State William Phillips told the Italian ambassador in Washington that the United States government was "disturbed at the reports showing

28. *No. 207 di Protocollo,* Šibenik, Nov. 21, 1918 (Riservatissimo, MFA, Rome).
29. *DDI,* pp. 139, 142.
30. Orlando to Sonnino, Nov. 21, 1918 (Tel. Part. 3697, MFA, Rome). This document is not included in the *DDI* collection.
31. Ibid.
32. Sonnino to Orlando, Nov. 21, 1918 (Tel. 16635, MFA, Rome).
33. On Dec. 28, 1919. Bissolati hoped to provoke a public debate over Sonnino's policy and to carry on his fight against it from the outside. See Woodhouse, *Italy and the Jugoslavs,* pp. 164–69.
34. House to Lansing, Nov. 22, 1918 (*FRUS-PPC,* 2, 310–11).

Italian-Yugoslav friction in the Adriatic and that this government hoped that Italy would take no steps which would tend to increase such friction until all matters could be frankly discussed at the coming Peace Conference." [35] In response, Sonnino indicated his willingness to the landing of American and additional French and British forces—but only in areas "outside [the] territory occupied by Italy under the armistice." [36] The London treaty line would thus remain inviolate, despite Sonnino's own pledge to Colonel House on October 31 that the territory in question would have the same status as the territory occupied under the German armistice.

To complicate matters further, a new note of distress was sounded from Corfu. Dodge transmitted to Washington Yugoslav complaints that Italy was sending agents into Bulgaria in an effort to make trouble in Serbia and thus create the impression abroad that the Italian occupation of Fiume and Dalmatia was imperative for the maintenance of order throughout the Balkans. [37] All manner of Italian intrigues, machinations, and intelligence operations were indeed reported in eastern Serbia, Montenegro, and Albania. These accounts might easily enough be attributed to Yugoslav propagandists, were it not for Italian documentary evidence to the effect that the Rome government actually mapped out a program of subversive activities throughout Yugoslav lands and in adjoining areas, a program in effect designed to disrupt the Yugoslav union.

During the latter part of November, Italian policy came into sharp conflict with French military and political plans in the Balkans. The controversy ostensibly revolved around logistic considerations, but the political overtones were clear. French military authorities decided to establish the main logistic base of the Allied Armies of the Orient—commanded by General Franchet d'Esperey—in Fiume. To implement this plan, however, would involve preventing the consolidation of Italy's position in that

35. Ibid., pp. 309–10.
36. Ibid., p. 310.
37. Dodge to Lansing, Corfu, Nov. 22, 1918 (763.72/12364, Dept. of State, Washington).

city. Offering an ideal location for a military-naval base at the head of the Adriatic, Fiume also attracted the attention of the Serbian General Staff. Desirous of establishing a base of their own in Fiume—as headquarters for operations east of Trieste and south of Austria—the Serbs obtained Franchet d'Esperey's approval to participate with one battalion in the inter-Allied occupation of Fiume and Split. But this plan encountered vigorous Italian opposition.

On November 27 General Pietro Badoglio, then deputy to Diaz, took the initiative in asking Orlando to prevent the entire French plan from being put into force.[38] Orlando agreed, and in relaying Badoglio's request to Sonnino, added that the French should not be allowed to raise their flag at Pola, thereby suggesting possible doubts about the permanency of Italy's occupation of Istria.[39] A note to this effect was immediately handed to Philippe Berthelot, Secretary General of the French Ministry of Foreign Affairs, who disclaimed any intention to raise the French flag at Pola. On November 29, however, the French asked Thaon di Revel to withdraw Italian troops from Kotor, in the south, in the interests of maintaining local order. This the Italian admiral refused to do. On the same day the Italian commander at Pola accused French officers of openly spreading pro-Yugoslav and anti-Italian propaganda throughout Istria and of inciting the Slav population to open resistance.[40]

Unable to secure Serbia's participation in the occupation of Fiume and Split, Franchet d'Esperey next turned to Paris. On November 30 he demanded that Fiume be placed directly under his command.[41] The dispute now reached the highest governmental levels and was promptly placed on the agenda of the forthcoming inter-Allied conference, scheduled to meet in London on December 2–3.

At the London meeting, the issue resulted in an acrimonious debate on the whole state of affairs since the armistice. Sonnino accused the French of underwriting anti-Italian propaganda, of

38. *DDI*, p. 178.
39. Ibid., p. 177.
40. Ibid., p. 201.
41. Ibid., p. 212.

lending undue support to the Yugoslavs, of tacitly encouraging the Yugoslavs to seize the former Austrian fleet, of permitting their officers in Istria and Dalmatia to belittle Italy's contribution to the Allied war effort, and of supporting Franchet d'Esperey's scheme for a naval base in Fiume in order to frustrate Italian control there. Clemenceau repaid in kind by accusing the Italians of trying to prejudice the outcome of the peace conference and of frequently transgressing the spirit and the letter of the armistice, to which he added that the French nation was admittedly sympathetic to the Yugoslav union, anxious to recognize the new Serbo-Croat-Slovene kingdom, and opposed to Italian intrigues to break up that nation.[42] Unable to reconcile these divergent views, the Allies in the end decided to send a commission of admirals—British, French, American, and Italian—to investigate conditions in Fiume, Split, and other key trouble-spots. In addition, Generals Franchet d'Esperey and Diaz would be instructed to submit separate reports on the question of a naval base in Fiume to Marshal Foch, who would in turn recommend a specific course of action to the Allied governments.

Upon receiving these instructions, Franchet d'Esperey took matters into his own hands and ordered General Tranié to proceed with the establishment of an inter-Allied base at Fiume. But this General Grazioli, Italian commander in Fiume, would not allow. On December 6 Diaz demanded the immediate dispatch of the admirals' commission to Fiume, hoping to block Franchet d'Esperey's plans.[43] Diaz' demand caused furor in Paris. In a stormy session with Bonin Longare on December 8, Clemenceau accused Italy of heading "straight to war" with the Yugoslavs. On the same occasion, which Bonin characterized as "the most tempestuous that I recall in my none too short career," Clemenceau also accused Orlando of having "insulted" him in London and raised objections to the whole range of Italian policy.[44] Sonnino, in turn, held an equally intemperate meeting with Barrère in Rome, at which he repeated the familiar charges against France.[45]

42. On the London conference, see *FRUS-PPC, 1,* 333–43, and F. S. Marston, *The Peace Conference of 1919* (London, 1944), pp. 44–46.

43. *DDI*, pp. 249–50.

44. Ibid., pp. 266–67.

45. Ibid., pp. 278–80.

The Italian and French commanders, meantime, prepared their reports for Foch, as directed by the Allied governments. Diaz submitted his on December 10. In it he recommended the establishment of joint inter-Allied contingents over the entire former-enemy territory, provided that within the Italian zone they were under the exclusive jurisdiction of the Italian High Command and not of Franchet d'Esperey. At the same time, Diaz asked that the cities of Vienna, Graz, Linz, Salzburg, and Ljubljana, as well as the Adriatic islands of Veglia and Arba, be assigned to the Italian zone.[46] Franchet d'Esperey, on the other hand, in a report submitted on December 12, argued for a strict line of demarcation between his command and that of Diaz along the Fiume-Ljubljana-Maribor line, with those cities included within his zone. Fiume, he wrote Foch, "the only base of supplies possible for troops operating in the region of Belgrade and to the north, must be placed entirely under my authority, as well as the Fiume-Agram [Zagreb] railway." [47] He also urged the creation of international contingents, preferably under American command but his overall control, for all contested territories, to guarantee "a character of neutrality until the decisions of the Peace Conference." Serbian units, he felt, should participate in all inter-Allied contingents, especially in the region between Volosca in the north and the Italian Dalmatian zone in the south which should be under the control of an American; the English should control Split and Dubrovnik, and the French all of Montenegro.[48]

Foch deliberated for over a week. On December 22 he proposed to the Allied governments a compromise formula, based on the premise that the former Austro-Hungarian territory should *not* be partitioned into two great zones "in which the Italian command and that of the Allied Armies of the Orient could respectively act with entire liberty." As the major disputes revolved around Ljubljana and Fiume, he recommended the following solution:

> d) *The occupation of Laybach* [Ljubljana] can have no other object than the maintenance of order.

46. Diaz to Foch, Rome, Dec. 10, 1918 (*FRUS-PPC*, 2, 211–12).
47. Franchet d'Esperey to Foch, Salonika, Dec. 12, 1918 (ibid., pp. 213–14).
48. Ibid.

The present Serbian-Yougo-Slav garrison provides for this; the intervention of the Italians could only give rise to conflict. There is therefore every reason for maintaining the *status quo*.

e) *Occupation of Fiume*—To remove all cause of conflict, the surest solution would be to install at Fiume a regime of strict neutrality, by organizing there, for example, an interallied occupation, under the orders of an American general, who would be directly responsible to the Higher Council of War. Such a solution would be necessary as a last resort, if it seemed to be impossible to conciliate the conflicting interests. In the present situation it seems preferable to try to establish harmony by the adoption of a definite scheme of action based on the following points:

–The occupation of Fiume will be Italian and will be responsible to General Diaz.

–At the same time, there will be constituted, for the needs of the Allied Armies of the Orient, an autonomous base directly responsible to General d'Esperey, and the Commander of which will be a French general.

–The French general appointed shall be put into possession, by the Italian command, of the part of the port, installation and equipment necessary for the organization and functioning of the base, as well as of a zone of cantonment sufficient for the establishment nearby of a Franco-Serbian detachment assigned to this base.

Moreover, [General Franchet d'Esperey] will have exclusive control of the Fiume-Agram-Semlin railway and will regulate its operation.[49]

Finally, Foch stipulated that the occupation of Albania, except for Scutari, should remain Italian. His recommendations were implemented—all save the provision for the inter-Allied base at Fiume. The jurisdictional dispute along the Adriatic thus abated for the time being. In most respects, the Foch plan ratified the existing status quo. The Italians retained control of Fiume and their Dalmatian zone. But they failed to gain Ljubljana, once and for all.

49. Ibid., pp. 215–16.

The proclamation on December 1 of a Yugoslav kingdom of nearly twelve million inhabitants created a situation entirely unforeseen when the Treaty of London was negotiated in 1915. This development frustrated Sonnino's plans, yet he continued to fight a battle he was bound to lose. Unable to prevent the establishment of the Yugoslav union, he now concentrated on forestalling international recognition of the new state, on maintaining an economic blockade designed to crush the Yugoslav economy, and on continuing active support of the deposed King Nicholas of Montenegro in order to foster separatism within the Yugoslav state. Unless the central authority of Belgrade was undermined by constant tension and pressure and the Yugoslavs made to appear incapable of maintaining internal order, the Treaty of London would be placed in jeopardy. Yugoslavs and Italians would soon appear before the peace conference with conflicting territorial claims. His own allies, he knew, were sympathetic to the Yugoslav cause and bound to the principle of national self-determination. But Great Britain and France were also bound to the Treaty of London, and the only chance for implementing its terms—and thus gaining Dalmatia and Istria for Italy—lay in keeping them on his side.

The lengths to which Sonnino was willing to go in implementing his political program is revealed by a dramatic decision reached by the Italian government several days after the Yugoslav kingdom was formally proclaimed. During the latter part of November, General Badoglio, an inveterate opponent of Yugoslavism and a fervent advocate of the Treaty of London policy, drew up elaborate plans for disrupting the Yugoslav union. As deputy to Diaz, Badoglio had played a key role in formulating Italian occupation policies in Dalmatia, Istria, and Slovenia. An avid student of history and contemporary affairs, he had fairly sophisticated knowledge of Balkan and Southern Slav problems. With the approval, possibly even at the instigation, of Sonnino, he now prepared a detailed plan of action which he submitted for Sonnino's approval on December 3, while the Foreign Minister was at the inter-Allied conference in London.[50]

50. Badoglio to Sonnino, Dec. 3, 1918 (No. 90 Riservatissima Personale, Arch. Gab. 3687 [9/12/1918], MFA, Rome). Enclosed with Badoglio's letter to Sonnino was a copy of the "Progetto Per Lavoro Particolare Affidatomi da V.E.," addressed to "Commando Supremo, Ufficio del Capo di Stato Maggiore [Diaz]." Insofar as the

Badoglio's plan was centered on the premise that Italian action must not be limited to areas under Italian military control, but extended to cover the entire country. Convinced that "Yugoslavism" was supported only by intellectuals and parts of the educated bourgeoisie, he saw a fertile field for propaganda among the peasantry and workers. Imbued with "Bolshevik principles," the "proletariat" would not subscribe to a middle-class nationalist program. The potential for internal strife and conflict, therefore, abounded and needed only to be activated through "all possible means." To "augment the sense of disorientation that pervades all these classes, to intensify the inevitable differences of views," was the first stated objective of his plan.

Badoglio next surveyed the field of regional particularisms. In Serbia, he felt, the "dominant element has not yet taken stock of the positive fact that if Croatia today, pushed by the French, accepts Serbian leadership at the head of the unitary movement, she [Croatia] only views this as the first step in placing herself in turn at the head of the entire movement of the Southern Slavs." Thus Serbia, he predicted, would become the "unconscious instrument of Croatia which, convinced of her intellectual superiority over Serbia, will tend by all possible means to absorb her."

> To expose to the Serbian rulers the equivocation of Croatian conduct—possibly still the instrument of Austrian ruling circles which have not yet abandoned the hope of transforming the former empire into a great federation—to maintain among the Serbs the moral want they instinctively feel before the Croats, to remind them of the horrible tortures inflicted upon them over the decades by the Croats—unwitting instruments of the Austrians, but still their implacable enemies

---

heading "Progetto . . . Affidatomi da V.E." was addressed to Diaz, Badoglio's commission to prepare the project appears to have come from the Chief of Staff. But the brief covering letter of Dec. 3 to Sonnino leaves little doubt that the Foreign Minister knew what the project was about. Badoglio merely stated: "Excellency, I transmit a copy of the project for action to be undertaken among the Yugoslavs. If Your Excellency approves it and authorizes me to dispose of the required funds, on which I count, it suffices if Your Excellency will wire me indicated project approved. Devotedly, Badoglio." All following quotations are taken from Badoglio's document.

—can accentuate the alienation, even if this is not desired by the leaders.

The Croats, on the other hand, still dreaming of a "Greater Croatia" rather than a "Yugoslavia," should, he thought, be encouraged to suspect the Serbs as hegemonists. But since, as Badoglio put it, "the people [of Croatia] are primitive and often barbarian, and are fanatic and loyal to constituted authority: the only area to be exploited is the religious."

In Bosnia-Hercegovina he suggested that disunity be fomented through religious agitation among the Greek Orthodox, Catholics, and Moslems. "The Moslem element, primitive and fanatic, is easily convinced," he wrote.

By virtue of their separate language and different cultural exposure, the Slovenes he found even more susceptible to separatist propaganda than the others. In their case, because of popular religiosity, the clergy had to be won over to the cause of separatism.

Montenegro and Dalmatia represented no problem. In Montenegro, Badoglio felt existing conditions to be ripe for the dissemination of loyalist—pro-Nicholas—propaganda. In Dalmatia, Italian military forces would know what to do.

The actual program of action was divided into two spheres: 1) the Italian occupation zone, and 2) territories outside that zone. Within the occupation zone, military authorities would launch an intensive anti-Yugoslav campaign which, Badoglio noted, was already under way. Italian troops were to be encouraged to do their part, including fraternizing with Slav women, whose "susceptibilities," the practical General was certain, "will favor relations which can only lead to beneficial results." The clergy was to be approached directly, though the "most recalcitrant and intelligent [ones] will have to be deported because the population, religious as it is, is in their hands." Particular attention was to be given to former mayors and civil servants, now unemployed, for their grievances could be easily exploited.

As to the areas outside Italian military control:

1) A large squad of highly intelligent and well oriented agents is in the process of being organized. . . . [I] have already found reliable individuals to direct the activities in

Slovenia, Croatia, Dalmatia. I hope to have a suitable individual for Serbia as well within several days. The directives
which I shall give him, seeing to it that they are executed,
will be based on what I have put forth. . . .
2) I am seeking contact with two principal newspapers in
Ljubljana (*Slovenski Narod* and *Slovenec*), and three principal newspapers in Zagreb (*Obzor, Hrvatska Riječ, Novosti*)
in order to persuade them [to our side].
3) I will try to establish direct contact with the malcontent
elements of the former regime.

Upon the question of funds and special services, Badoglio
elaborated as follows:

NECESSARY MEANS

Special Squad—will reach some 200 agents divided into four
groups. We can anticipate on the average a minimum expenditure per agent of Lire 10,000 (two months of work).
Total minimum 2,000,000 Lire.
Press—We can anticipate an expenditure of Lire 150,000 per
newspaper. Given the fact that the most malleable are three
. . . an expenditure of 450,000 Lire.
Clergy . . . Lire 3–500,000.
Members of the Former Regime . . . 2 to 500,000 Lire.
Note—I am informed . . . that French unionist propaganda
is financed by the largest means. This explains the number
of agents I propose to engage. . . .

FACILITATIONS

a) Designation of the undersigned as member of international control commissions (fiction—only need the necessary
documents) . . . It would be useful to me to be theoretically
assigned to those [commissions] operating in Serbia and Hungary, so I could traverse the entire territory. . . .
b) Authorization to use all the resources of the Navy or to
request, in cases of urgency, a torpedo or motor boat. (Officers of the English information service operating along the
coast of Venezia Giulia, all have a torpedo boat at their disposal.)

These were the essentials of the plan Badoglio presented to Sonnino on December 3. Six days later, on the 9th, Sonnino replied:

PERSONAL

URGENT

Excellency,

In relation to Your Excellency's letter of December 3, No. 90, I have the honor to inform you that, following discussions between the President of the Council [Orlando], the Chief of the General Staff [Diaz] and myself, your project for *action to be undertaken among the Yugoslavs* has been accepted.

You may begin the action elaborated in the project immediately, turning for any elucidation that you may need directly to H. E. General Diaz.

I have, etc.

SONNINO [51]

Badoglio's activities—approved by Sonnino, Orlando, and Diaz —caused considerable difficulties for the Yugoslavs. But they did not disrupt the "union." While it is not possible to determine the details of how Badoglio's plan was carried out so long as the records of the Italian General Staff and its intelligence section remain closed, there is little reason to doubt that it was fully executed. Before long, American, British, French, as well as Yugoslav, intelligence officers began to report from various parts of the country that a concerted Italian propaganda and agitation campaign was under way, in a pattern bearing the distinct marks of Badoglio's plan. Throughout December 1918 and January–February 1919, field reports to this effect were gathered by the respective governments. Nevertheless, from the political point of view, the Italian action came too late. For once the peace conference got under way, the center of gravity shifted from the field to Paris, where the contest was fought along rather different lines.

In December 1918, actually, Italy's international standing was seriously affected by the continuing conflict with France. When Franchet d'Esperey ordered General Tranié to proceed with the establishment of an Allied base at Fiume, the Italians recipro-

51. Sonnino to Badoglio, Rome, Dec. 9, 1918 (Riservata alla Persona. Urgente, Arch. Gab. 3855 [Arch. Gab. Pos. 32], MFA, Rome).

cated by threatening to arrest all former Austrian vessels requisitioned by French naval authorities and now flying the French flag.[52] At the same time, they increased the pressure on the population of their occupation zone.

On December 15 Admiral W. H. G. Bullard, Commander of United States Naval Forces in the Eastern Mediterranean, reported that at Pola, Italian authorities had ordered sizable deportations and "are proceeding on the assumption that they are never to be moved. Their action certainly cannot be based on any terms of the armistice . . ."[53] Two days later he wrote: "The more I see and study conditions at Fiume, the more incomprehensible they seem. Italy has virtually taken possession of this city and to my mind without the slightest justification. . . . I took a long ride into the interior . . . and I was greatly surprised to see the extent to which the Italian domination extends in and near the city, but in the country hardly any but Jugo-Slav or Serbian flags were seen."[54] And on December 25 General Tranié "explained that he found the city [Fiume] in Italian control and that every obstacle was put in the way of establishing a base. . . . The base question causes very strained relations between the French and the Italians."[55]

By mid-December this tension began to affect relations with the British as well, and London now warned Rome that Italy's claim to Fiume stood clearly outside the limits of the London treaty. If the Italians were to persist with it, it would create great difficulties for them as well as for continued Allied unity.[56] The Foreign Office did not challenge the validity of the Treaty of London, though it was aware of increasing American objections to it.

By this time, indeed, American policy came to rest on the view that the Treaty of London would in no way bind the United States. Realizing as much, Count Vincenzo Macchi di Cellere, Italian ambassador in Washington, appealed on December 25 to David Hunter Miller for American support of Italy's claims. He argued not on the basis of any American obligation to validate the

52. See Bullard to Benson, Fiume, Dec. 15, 1918 (*FRUS-PPC*, 2, 328–30).
53. Ibid., pp. 330–31.
54. Ibid., p. 332.
55. Ibid., p. 340.
56. *DDI*, pp. 321–22.

London treaty but on the basis that the treaty's terms were just toward Italy.[57] American officialdom was not easily persuaded, particularly as disturbing field reports kept flowing in. For example, on December 23 General Tasker H. Bliss, member of the American Commission to Negotiate the Peace, wrote to President Wilson that "it is the unanimous opinion of the American Peace Commission that Captain Gherardi's statement of facts as observed by him indicates that the American troops are being used to further a policy of occupation and penetration which, if not contrary to the terms of the armistice with Austria-Hungary, is at least unnecessary under that armistice. In one case, an attempt was made to use a small American force to effect, without any apparent justifiable reason, a penetration into Montenegro." [58] Bliss also charged the Italians with making various attempts to use American units "not for legitimate military purposes but to further political aims." [59] He demanded that the American contingent in the Adriatic be reassigned to the United States Supreme Command and this Wilson agreed to do. Three days later, Admiral Bullard, the American member of the Inter-Allied Naval Commission of Investigation set up in London on December 3, complained that the Italian member, Admiral Mola, was doing everything in his power to obstruct the investigation.[60] This pattern continued for some time.

As a result, Italy was moving toward a crisis with her allies, and particularly with France. The Fiume base was still the central problem. Since the city, technically, lay outside the Italian zone, the French suddenly decided to disembark at Fiume, whereupon General Grazioli simply reinforced the Italian contingent in the city and the suburbs in order to tighten his grip over the entire district.[61] Orlando, at the same time, sent a strong protest to Clemenceau over French movements in Fiume,[62] while Grazioli tried to limit the French force to 2,000 men. Franchet d'Esperey

57. David Hunter Miller, *My Diary at the Conference of Paris, 1* (20 vols. privately printed, 1928), 55–56 (hereafter cited as Miller *Diary*).
58. *FRUS-PPC, 2,* 337–38.
59. Ibid., p. 338.
60. Ibid., pp. 342–43.
61. See *DDI,* pp. 341–42.
62. Ibid., pp. 346–47.

complained that the Italians were interfering with the Command of the Armies of the Orient, and Clemenceau replied to Orlando's protest with a counterprotest of his own.[63] Though both Paris and Rome were anxious to find a solution to the Fiume base question, by December 26 tension between the two capitals had reached a high point. From Paris, Bonin Longare urged Orlando and Sonnino to moderate their stand and quickly work out a compromise with the French. On December 27, however, Sonnino insisted on registering yet another protest against the "petty politics" of French authorities in the Adriatic and their open support of the Yugoslavs.[64] Next day, moreover, Admiral Mola unilaterally suspended the work of the Inter-Allied Naval Commission of Investigation because the commission "began to transform itself into a veritable commission of inquiry, investigating everything and everyone, particularly in regard to the activities of our Government." [65]

The dispute was actually not resolved, though through the tacit concurrence of the French and Italian governments, the tension suddenly decreased. The peace conference was about to open and both governments were anxious to restore a semblance of unity. King Victor Emmanuel paid a state visit to Paris, where he was greeted with popular enthusiasm as well as official cordiality. The visit was in fact timed to break the tension and provide a basis for reconciliation. More important, world attention was already focused on the coming peace conference. President Wilson's arrival in Europe and his triumphant tour of Allied capitals caused a swelling wave of popular excitement and expectation of a new era of peace. Under the circumstances, the Fiume problem temporarily receded into the background. Nothing more could be done until the peacemakers embarked on their formidable task.

63. Ibid., pp. 355–56. With Bonin Longare's help, negotiations were now launched for a possible coexistence between the Italian and French commands in Fiume.

64. Ibid., p. 363.

65. Ibid., p. 369. On the same day Diaz informed Sonnino that the situation in Fiume was untenable and that Franchet d'Esperey must be replaced by someone more "moderate" (ibid., p. 369).

PART II

At the Peace Conference

4. On the Eve of the Conference

UNION and independence are not political panaceas. Of this the founding fathers of the Yugoslav state were fully aware. They were, if anything, more sensitive to the dangers than to the opportunities inherent in the nationalist revolution that had come to pass. For there was, to be sure, cause for apprehension. In 1918 Yugoslav nationalism was not sustained by an underlying philosophy of government that commanded widespread agreement, despite great popular support for the principles of democratic processes. "Serbia" and "Croatia" were uneven quantities and largely unknown to each other. Popular enthusiasm could become the catalyst of national unity, but it could not undo the political differences and the material problems which required immediate resolution.

Between the chaos of victory and the approach of the peace conference, there was little time to devote to fundamental issues. Within a month a government had to be formed; a national administration established; the case for the peace conference prepared; economic integration begun; relief to war-ravaged areas dispatched; a dissolving army reformed; communications re-established—all in the face of Italy's military occupation and economic blockade along the Adriatic, as well as constant armed clashes in the Banat, Carinthia, and elsewhere. Under the merciless pressure of events, the leadership of the new state in effect faced an unending series of crises.

At the same time, to the world at large the union of Southern Slavs appeared as the culmination of a nationalist struggle which had historical logic as well as political practicality to it. And indeed, from the points of view of ethnic kinship and Balkan geopolitics, it did. Yet in December 1918 the Kingdom of Serbs, Croats, and Slovenes was in some ways an anomaly. The voluntary union of territories and peoples whose traditions and attainments were considerably varied had been carried out through internal efforts, not external pressure. Without the Allied victory and the defeat of the German-Magyar empires, the Yugoslav union would not then have been possible. Without Allied sympathy and ultimate support, it might not have endured and flourished. Yet the Yugoslav state came into being without formal Allied sanction and, significantly, it became a political reality long before the peace conference convened. By January 1919 it had already weathered grave internal trials, diplomatic isolation, and active Italian opposition as well.

But the kingdom was a state without frontiers. This bitter fact of life affected every major aspect of national existence—its military security, economic viability, political stability, and psychological well-being. It inflicted, in short, a strain on the creative energy of the entire nation. The problem of frontiers could be resolved only by the peace conference, and there Allied support was obviously essential. Yet the Yugoslavs, unlike the Czechs and Poles, were coming before the peace conference without international recognition and the overt encouragement which Allied recognition implied. Facing serious territorial disputes with each neighboring state save Greece, they felt vulnerable to diplomatic blackmail.

Yugoslav territorial claims would inevitably be opposed by all vanquished enemies, by Bulgarians, Magyars, and Austrians alike. A greater danger, however, lay in the territorial disputes involving members of the Entente, for both Italy and Rumania could conceivably resist Yugoslav claims in Austria, Dalmatia, and the Banat by forming a *mariage de convenance* with the vanquished states.

The Italians, moreover, possessed every strategic advantage. They were privy to the inner councils of the great powers; they were in military control of the territories in dispute; and they could use the Treaty of London to tie the hands of the British and the French. Trumbić even expected Sonnino to trade Italian support for the League of Nations and harsh peace terms for Germany in return for a *Pax Italiana* in the Adriatic. He was hardly reassured by Wilson's public and private pronouncements urging the principal Allies to maintain solidarity on all major issues of the day.

Pašić, on the other hand, was apprehensive on a different score as well. He who had once described Serbia as a 'dinghy attached to the Russian ship of state' had always looked to Russia for support within the Allied camp. Now that the Bolshevik Revolution had removed the Slavic colossus from the diplomatic stage, Pašić and most Serbian Radicals felt uncomfortably alone.

The Yugoslavs thus came to Paris imbued with a mixture of hope and anxiety. They looked to "Wilsonianism" as the revolutionary doctrine that gave meaning and impetus to their very national existence and which, if it prevailed at the peace congress, would assure them justice. But they were less than confident that Wilsonian ideas and the principles of nationality and self-determination would triumph over traditional Realpolitik, from which they feared they could expect little satisfaction.

If, however, there were grounds for concern over the political climate in Paris, there were in fact more serious problems on the internal front. The Yugoslavs had no difficulty in conceiving a favorable territorial settlement. The Slovenes had precise ideas about their rightful frontiers with Italy, Austria, and Hungary, and so did the Croats about theirs. The Serbs had worked out a general program for frontiers with Rumania, Bulgaria, and Albania, and so did the Montenegrins for their southern parts. But for lack of time and domestic expediency as well, the Yugoslavs had no coordinated national territorial program when they came to Paris. In view of repeated Allied warnings to small and large powers alike about the need for moderation and sacrifice, and in view of the predictable opposition of Italy, Rumania, and the defeated neighboring states, there was little likelihood of fulfilling maximum territorial programs. In coming to the peace conference without some prior agreement about essential versus expendable elements of their own program, the Yugoslavs exposed themselves to considerable danger. For, once in Paris, they faced not one but two major tasks—the working out of basic compromises among themselves while concurrently dealing with the peace conference. The danger of agreeing upon maximal territorial demands so as to maintain surface solidarity within the delegation and to placate conflicting opinions at home was very real indeed. But inflexibility can be a costly luxury for a small and vulnerable nation, especially one so dependent upon the good will and support of friends who were themselves concerned with myriad problems of their own.

Yet the Yugoslav peace delegation was not initially at fault. Before the peace conference, there was little time to coordinate the national case. Much of the delegation assembled on an ad hoc basis. Communications with Belgrade were incredibly poor, making normal contact with the government a practical impossibility. While Belgrade was not abreast of latest developments around the world, the delegation in Paris was not abreast of all developments at home. There was little preparatory work, such as is normally undertaken before a major international congress, to depend on for guidance. Under these circumstances, to steer a steady course between the exigencies of international politics, on the one hand, and domestic politics, on the other, called for talent, wisdom, experience, and tact, which few peace delegations have ever been known to possess.

Pašić and Trumbić! Seldom have circumstances bound two more antithetical characters to a common cause. Seldom, indeed, have two antagonists been forced to become partners so quickly.

The selection of Pašić as head of the peace delegation was natural—and logical. Alexander's decision to keep him from the premiership implied also that he wanted Pašić out of Belgrade. But the presidency of the peace delegation was not merely (though mostly) a substitute reward. Even as head of government, he might logically have been sent to Paris. For not only was he "boss" of the largest Serbian political party but a genuine popular hero as well. Pašić personified Serbia, and Serbia was, after all, the oldest partner of the wartime Entente. A venerable figure at home as well as abroad, Pašić knew all the Allies and they all knew him.

Trumbić's selection as foreign minister and second-in-command at Paris was perhaps just as logical. During the December parleys in Belgrade, called to establish a national government, it was Josip Smodlaka who first proposed Trumbić for the portfolio of foreign affairs.[1] As president of the Yugoslav Committee in London, representative of the National Council in Western Europe, and, finally, as a Croat who would balance a national cabinet with

---

1. See B. Krizman, "Kako je Dr. Ante Trumbić Postao Prvi Jugoslavenski Ministar Vanjskih Poslova," *Slobodna Dalmacija,* April 17, 1956.

a Serbian premier and a Slovene vice-premier, Trumbić was the obvious choice.

But he was anathema to the Radicals, and Protić clearly said so. Pašić let it be known he would refuse to serve with Trumbić. Still Smodlaka persisted. Supported by Korošec and Pribičević, he argued that Trumbić was indispensable to the Croats. He was also the leading expert on Dalmatia (and therefore needed for the impending battle in Paris), as well as a man with important connections abroad. Trumbić indeed knew the leading statesmen of the West and counted influential opinionmakers—Steed, Denis, et al.—among his closest foreign friends. In reality, though this was not openly flaunted in Protić's face, Trumbić would be a greater asset abroad than Pašić.

When Protić and the Radicals continued to object—the wartime wounds were very slow to heal—Korošec proposed Smodlaka for the job. The latter refused on grounds of ill health and only continued to press for his friend and fellow-Dalmatian. After days of wrangling, Pašić and Protić gave in on December 16.

In Paris, meantime, Trumbić knew next to nothing about the Belgrade talks. On the 17th he first read a press report indicating his selection and later the same day received a cable from Belgrade inquiring about his willingness to collaborate with Korošec and Pašić. Believing that Pašić had been appointed premier, he replied in the affirmative on the 18th. In a lengthy reply, however, he laid down certain conditions. Pašić, Korošec, and he were to be given equal accreditation to the peace conference as representatives of the Kingdom of Serbs, Croats, and Slovenes, thinking evidently that the premier, vice-premier, and foreign minister would all be present at Paris. If instead of becoming foreign minister he (Trumbić) were given a post without portfolio,[2] the foreign ministry, he urged, should still go to one of the former Austro-Hungarian regions. If "Foreign Affairs" were to go to a Serb, the new national government, he warned, might not obtain proper international recognition.

"On my part," he added, "I declare that I will remain in the

2. Ibid. A separate cable was in fact sent to him jointly by Trifković, Davidović, Pribičević, and Smodlaka, asking *inter alia*, whether he would prefer to enter the cabinet as foreign minister or minister without portfolio.

cabinet only to the end of the peace conference," [3] a promise he was indeed to keep. Meanwhile, he "assumed" that the head-quarters of the foreign minister, and by implication the ministry, would be in Paris for the duration of the peace conference and that all major policies would be formulated there. Lastly, Trumbić asked for specific information regarding the cabinet's domestic program and for the immediate appointment of a peace delegation fully staffed with various commissions of technical experts, particularly naval and military, the latter to be headed by the Vojvoda Živojin Mišić.

It was after, but not as a result of, this exchange of cables that Pašić was vetoed as premier by Alexander and assigned to head the peace delegation in Paris. At the same time, it was decided to keep Protić, the substitute premier, in Belgrade.

Trumbić, of course, knew none of these details. Since the inquiry of December 16 and his reply of the 18th, he had received no official communication. Therefore, on the 29th he cabled Alexander (through the Serbian military attaché in Paris) to ask for news. He (Trumbić) had heard that Alexander was preparing to visit Paris and then that the trip had been postponed; that Pašić had rejected the premiership (!); that the cabinet had in part been changed and had already taken the oath of office; that a peace delegation had been named, but already changed; that Protić was signing all cables as premier and proxy foreign minister; that he (Protić) had dismissed Jovan M. Jovanović as minister to London, an act which had created a very bad impression in Allied as well as Yugoslav circles abroad, etc., etc. "I have no official news. Am asked on all sides for information which I cannot give . . ." [4]

Next day Trumbić received the first official cable from Protić. It simply announced that for "unavoidable official reasons" Jovanović had to be dismissed. As his replacement the cabinet was considering Smodlaka or Vojislav Antonijević (the minister to

3. Ibid.
4. For the full text of this cable see B. Krizman, "Pred Početak Konferencije Mira 1919 godine," *Slobodna Dalmacija,* April 19, 1956. Alexander, incidentally, never replied.

Rome) and would Trumbić please name candidates of his own. "For political reasons," Protić added, "the matter is urgent." [5] To this Trumbić immediately shot back the following reply:

> I am very surprised. You demand answer about important foreign service questions before I am officially informed of being foreign minister and before I formally assume office . . . With regret I am unable to give you any answer. Before I decide anything it is vital to clarify all matters personally with cabinet. Therefore I have decided to go to Belgrade (by way of Switzerland) and will notify you by cable about my departure. Meanwhile, no action should be taken in regard to foreign minister.[6]

In the end, Trumbić did not go to Belgrade, but his sudden decision of the 30th reflected extreme annoyance at the turn of events at home and, in general, an increasingly anguished state of mind. After dispatching the above telegram to Protić, he was further alarmed at receiving a brusque message from the Premier ordering him, in effect, to take the oath of office as foreign minister.[7] This message was actually sent on December 21 through Salonika, where it was delayed, and was finally transmitted by Vesnić in Paris. It was followed next day by a letter from Vesnić, informing him that Pašić, Trumbić, Vesnić, Ivan Žolger, Smodlaka, Bošković, and Otokar Ribarž had now been appointed peace delegates.[8]

Before replying to Protić's telegram about the oath of office, Trumbić received still another, and this time a lengthy, cable from Belgrade. Sent on January 3, it arrived in Paris on the 5th. After explaining that "you still do not know about composition of cabinet and your nomination as foreign minister only because of bad telegraphic connections," Protić went on to report that the cabinet had been appointed on December 21; that the government's juris-

---

5. Protić to Trumbić, Belgrade, Dec. 27, 1918 (No. 5659, TP, F66).
6. Trumbić to Protić, Paris, Dec. 30, 1918 (TP, F66).
7. Protić to Trumbić, Belgrade, Dec. 21, 1918 (Conf. No. 5892, TP, F66).
8. "Mission du Royaume des Serbes, Croates et Slovènes au Congrès de la Paix," TP, F63/3.

diction extended over the entire country; and that a provisional parliament was being planned for March 1, 1919. But then Protić added these significant points: first, that the new government had asked for the recognition of all Allied and neutral states, and while none had yet been granted (due to Italian opposition), "some Powers will continue to regard the Serbian Kingdom as an international factor"; and second, that the foreign ministry must be "governed by the customs of Serbia. Accordingly, a minister cannot run the ministry abroad, but must have a substitute who will conduct its regular affairs." The King had appointed him (Protić) as proxy foreign minister, while Mihajlo Gavrilović would serve as deputy minister of foreign affairs. As for the peace delegation, no specific instructions had yet been drawn up. The cabinet was to "decide whether this is necessary." [9]

Trumbić exploded. Was he to be foreign minister in name only? And mere window dressing for Pašić in Paris? Belgrade had not asked his opinion on any matter of national policy and had dismissed Jovanović in London without any prior consultation with him. To make matters worse, the Narodno Vijeće had now ceased to exist,[10] and on January 2 Protić had decreed that the Yugoslav Committee no longer had "any authority" to conduct conversations abroad "because all national policy is now being carried out by the government." Adding insult to injury, Protić also ordered financial support to Yugoslav Committee members discontinued as of January 1 and the peace delegation in Paris was ordered so to inform all Allied governments as well as the individuals concerned. The government was not averse to employing some of them in various legation press-bureaus and as technical attachés to the peace delegation, but would tolerate no independent political action on their part.[11]

Trumbić was stung by this cavalier treatment of the Committee,

9. Protić to Trumbić, Belgrade, Jan. 3, 1919 (No. 20, TP, F66).

10. Vesnić to Trumbić, Paris, Jan. 11, 1919 (No. 109, TP, F66), transmitting a telegram from the Narodno Vijéce to Trumbić, dated Dec. 21, 1918 (which, wrote Vesnić, "I received today"), declaring that all its functions ended with the formation of the national government. The same applied to the functions of the Vijéce's representatives abroad, i.e. the Yugoslav Committee.

11. Protić to Delegation, Belgrade, Jan. 2, 1919 (No. 6345, TP, F66).

and a crisis was developing in his relations with Belgrade. He considered resigning, but realized this would cause a serious split within the country. It would also jeopardize the fruits of all his labors abroad, not to mention his work on the "Adriatic Question." He no doubt consulted with other members of the Yugoslav Committee and quite possibly with some of his French and British friends. In the end he decided to wait and see.

It is not known exactly when he abandoned the trip to Belgrade. January 4, the day originally scheduled for his departure, simply came and went. After that, no further mention of the trip was made.

In Belgrade, meanwhile, some preparations for the peace conference were launched. But no one knew exactly when the conference would formally open; it could happen momentarily. Wilson's triumphal reception in Western Europe of course echoed throughout Yugoslav lands and only added to the general confusion and the frenetic tempo of activity in Belgrade.

The foreign ministry, still mostly staffed by Serbian diplomatic personnel, was understandably ill-prepared for its new tasks. The Paris delegation, and indeed the ministry, would have to include scores of experts from former Austro-Hungarian regions, but these were largely unknown to the Serbs. Moreover, once Pašić and Trumbić were assigned to their respective posts, the other delegates remained to be selected.

The government expected the Yugoslavs to receive four conference seats at Paris. It decided to name four plenipotentiaries and three additional delegates with full authority within the delegation, but without the right of signing any of the peace treaties. In the end, Pašić, Trumbić, Žolger, and Vesnić were designated as plenipotentiaries; Smodlaka, Ribarž, and Bošković as "governmental delegates"—in all, three Radical Serbs, two Dalmatian Croats, and two Slovenes.

Korošec was the natural candidate to represent Slovene interests in Paris. He preferred, however, to remain in Belgrade with Protić and suggested Žolger instead. Since the latter was a controversial figure, Korošec's motivations are not entirely clear, though all evidence suggests that he thought Žolger more amenable than any other Slovene [12] and he thus expected to remain in control.

Žolger—lawyer, writer, and university professor—had all his life been politically obscure. He briefly rose to prominence in the Habsburg service and held a ministerial post in Vienna. In 1918 he thus symbolized the past and not the future. His appointment to Paris would doubtless be exploited by Sonnino. It was. The Italians used his presence repeatedly to revive their old "pro-Habsburg" charge against the Southern Slavs, and their propaganda was not without effect. Moreover, Žolger's needless appointment discouraged many of the Yugoslavs' friends.

The appointment of Vesnić, by contrast, made a good deal of sense even though it was bound to displease Trumbić and all ex-members of the Yugoslav Committee. But aside from being a confidant of Pašić, Milenko Vesnić was without doubt Serbia's ablest diplomat. Experienced, urbane, and of superior intellect, Vesnić was solidly steeped in both Balkan and Western cultures. Politically and socially at ease, he had close connections with French and other Western statesmen. He was, it will be recalled, the only non-American consulted by Wilson and House about the Fourteen Points in advance of the President's address. Last but not least, marriage to an American heiress—who counted Mrs. Wilson among a wide circle of acquaintances—brought him not only fortune but also useful political connections. The Vesnić salon in Paris was frequented by notables of many nations and could provide a valuable link between Pašić and the Allied diplomatic world outside the ordinary restraints of protocol.[13]

Ribarž and Smodlaka also added strength to the Yugoslav delegation, but of a different kind. As prominent, experienced, and popular political figures, both men commanded respect in all

12. Vošnjak (Interview, Nov. 9, 1955, Washington, D.C.) suggested that Korošec was determined to keep him (Vošnjak) from the rank of delegates. In the end, to soothe his feelings and those of his advocates—for example, Županić—Vošnjak was appointed head of the delegation secretariat.

13. Social connections were important and Vesnić made good use of them. Even Crespi complained about this, lamenting the fact that Orlando and Sonnino were too isolated during their stay in Paris. Characteristically, however, Crespi pays gallant tribute to the "great beauty, intelligence and attractiveness" of Mme. Vesnić. (Crespi, *Alla Difesa d'Italia*, p. 428).

quarters. As, respectively, Slovene and Croat deputies in the Vienna Parliament, both men had unassailable records and a reputation as vigorous champions of the "national cause."

Bošković, by contrast, was a mediocrity at best. A cynic, he also was a man of the past. Vain to the extreme, this former ambassador to London suffered in near-equal measure from a political submissiveness to Pašić, an obsessive resentment of Trumbić, and a consuming passion for the sartorial creations of Savile Row. To no one's surprise, Bošković came to play a strategic role in all the major conflicts that developed within the delegation in Paris.

To the Allied world Nikola Pašić was the main enigma. Now that circumstances had sent him abroad to be spokesman of a country for which he could scarcely harbor unmixed feelings, how enthusiastically and effectively would he champion its cause? In Paris, Pašić at first attracted great attention. Though never as popular in Western circles as Venizelos, Beneš, or Paderewski, he still enjoyed great prestige. Parisians acclaimed him on the streets to show appreciation of Serbia's valiant war effort.

But Pašić did not enjoy the limelight. He preferred to work in the *coulisses,* partly because he was taciturn by nature and partly because he was unfamiliar with Western ways. In important respects he epitomized the nineteenth-century Serbian nationalist. Intimately acquainted with Balkan history and geography, he knew relatively little beyond the Slavic and Balkan worlds, despite his student days in Zurich and his wartime travels throughout Allied Europe. Now in his seventy-fourth year, he could look back on a brilliant political career and a lifetime of service to his beloved Serbia. As leader of its first progressive modern political party, Pašić—partly inspired in his formative political years by Bakunin—had been instrumental in causing the downfall of Obrenović despotism and the triumph of constitutionalism after 1903.

Pašić had also been instrumental in orienting Serbian nationalism toward Russia. He looked East for the fulfillment of Serbia's "destiny," and over the years developed certain geopolitical principles to which he adhered until the end of his life. Aside from viewing Russia as the motive force in East European politics, he believed that the security and stability of the Balkans—and the fulfillment of Serbian national goals—depended on the establishment of a solid Greek-Serbian axis as opposed to a Bulgaro-Albanian one.[14] Having explored the possibility of a Serbo-Bulgarian rapprochement in the 1880s and again in 1905–06, he gave up that idea as historically futile, especially after the second Balkan War and the Bulgarian attack of 1915. He came to the peace conference four years later profoundly convinced of the necessity of a close Yugoslav-Greek liaison. This meant, in practical terms, establishing as wide a Serbian-Greek frontier as possible and keeping Bulgaria completely isolated in the Balkans.

In this frame of mind, Pašić indeed appeared as an enigma. He knew next to nothing about Croatia and Slovenia. He was not well-read or proficient in languages. Even his use of Serbian was far from polished or accomplished.[15] He also had great distrust for all Catholic Slavs.[16] Pašić was somewhat more familiar with Trieste and the northern littoral, partly because of his wife's Istrian origins, but his command of geography west of Bosnia left much to be desired. In the east, by contrast, Pašić was second to none in regard to the history and geography of Serbia, Montenegro, Mace-

14. Slobodan Jovanović, Interviews, Jan.–April 1955, London. While Pašić is not known to have spoken in terms of actual geopolitical axes, his policies bear out Jovanović's terminology. Pašić wrote very little, and little has been written about him by way of biographical material. The existing literature is neither adequate nor objective. A sketch of his life, however, may be gleaned from the following: *Nikola Pašić* (Belgrade, 1937); Sforza, *Nikola Pašić;* B. Purić (Pašić's son-in-law), "Nacionalna Politika Nikole Pašića," *Sloboda* (Chicago, 1952–54); J. M. Prodanović, "Nikola Pašić," *Srpski Književni Glasnik,* 20 (1927); M. Trifunović, "Nikola Pašić," *Srpski Književni Glasnik,* 20 (1927); M. Trifunović, "Nikola Pašić," *Srpski Književni Glasnik,* 20, (1927); *Nikola Pašić u Novoj Evropi* (Zagreb, 1926); Randi, *Nicola P. Pašić;* and Slobodan Jovanović, *Pašić.*

15. Languages were not his forte. Pašić was conversant with Bulgarian and Russian, but his knowledge of French and German was rudimentary. He was even occasionally sloppy in Serbian, as can readily be seen from his correspondence and dispatches. As for his interest in general literature, during the years of his Bulgarian exile in the 1880s, Pašić developed a taste for history alone. After returning to Serbia, however, most of his historical reading was limited to Russia and the Balkans. See Randi, pp. 10 ff.

16. In the 1890s Pašić began writing a treatise on the bases of Serbo-Croat cooperation in which this view is developed. While the treatise was never completed or published, its views were reflected in Pašić's subsequent actions. (N. Pašić, "Sloga Srbo-Hrvata," MS, Arhiv Srpske Akademije Nauka, Belgrade, No. 11857.)

donia, and Bulgaria—so much so in fact that he personally drafted some of the territorial memoranda pertaining to eastern frontiers.

The forces that led to the creation of a Yugoslav state rather than a widely expanded Serbia were not really comprehensible to him. And therefore the inherent conflict between Pan-Serbianism and Yugoslavism, and perhaps between the nineteenth and twentieth centuries, haunted him until the very end. In vital ways, Pašić was captive to the realities of a bygone age.

By the end of the first week of January the leading figures and many technical experts of the Yugoslav peace delegation had gathered in Paris. Headquarters was the Hôtel de Beau-Site on the Rue de Presbourg, which partly encircles the Étoile. The delegation, which before long numbered ninety-three members,[17] was a microcosm of the new nation itself. It included members of all ethnic groups and religions and political (save the Communist and Stjepan Radić's Croatian-peasant) parties. Pašić's Radicals were more numerous than any other group. The universities, especially that of Belgrade, were well represented at all levels. As for the rest, the delegation included many figures from both public and academic life.

Jovan Cvijić, for example, the former rector of Belgrade University, became head of the geographic and ethnographic section of the delegation. His function was indeed strategic. A Balkan geographer of European renown,[18] Cvijić in effect became arbiter over many of the technical disputes that developed within the delegation. Yugoslav demands in the north, northeast, and east bore the unmistakable traces of his hand.[19] Slobodan Jovanović—historian,

17. See below, Appendix. Over the months Trumbić felt that the technical sections were understaffed. Budgetary limitations, after June 1919, also proved to be an impediment.

18. Cvijić's most famous work, *La Péninsule balkanique. Géographie humaine* (Paris, 1918), earned him wide attention and acclaim in the west. But his earlier works on Macedonia and Serbia were also known and admired. See *Cvijičeva Knjiga* (Belgrade, 1927); Cvijić, *Iz Uspomena i Života* (Novi Sad, 1923); P. Slepčević, *Jovan Cvijić* (Sarajevo, 1927).

19. Though he worked closely with other ethnographers at the peace conference—J. Radonić, A. Belić, S. Mihaldjić, N. Županić, and the historians L. Vojnović and F. Šišić—the collective effort resulted for the most part in conclusions reached by Cvijić between 1895 and 1914.

academician, legal theorist—similarly influenced Yugoslav policy, especially in regard to such questions as war guilt, the League, and international law.

But of greater political significance was the absence in the delegation of members of the former Yugoslav Committee. Only two held positions of responsibility and influence: Ante Trumbić and Bogumil Vošnjak, the Slovene who served as Secretary-General of the delegation. Several other members were occasionally used on a consultative basis, but none were given responsible posts. Thus the Yugoslav Committee had indeed dissolved and its voice was no longer heard in 1919.

The national territory of the Kingdom of Serbs, Croats, and Slovenes, as envisioned by the Yugoslavs for presentation to the peace conference, encompassed: Serbia, Montenegro, Bosnia, Hercegovina, Croatia and Slavonia (including Fiume [Rijeka] in the south and Medjumurje in the north), the Banat, Bačka and Baranja, Prekomurje, Southern Styria, Southern Carinthia, Carniola, Istria and the Istrian Isles, Trieste, Gorizia, Dalmatia, and the Dalmatian archipelago.[20] This program did not basically differ from that proposed by Supilo to Izvolski in December 1914, or from the Yugoslav Committee's declaration of May 1915.[21] It called for a nation of 14 million people, including over one million non-Slavs, and a territory of some 250,000 square kilometers, or somewhat less than half of France.[22]

But to implement this program was not going to be easy. For it did not call merely for the union of Serbs, Croats, and Slovenes on the basis of national self-determination; it also rested upon a combination of strategic, geographic, economic, and historic considerations, which in some instances conflicted with the purely

20. See *Memorandum Presented to the Peace Conference, in Paris, concerning the Claims of the Kingdom of the Serbians, Croatians and Slovenes* (Paris, 1919); *The National Claims of the Serbians, Croatians and Slovenes* (Paris, 1919); J. Smodlaka, *Jugoslav Territorial Claims* (Paris, 1919).

21. See *The Southern Slav Programme*, pp. 11–13; "Mémoire présenté par le Comité Yougoslave aux Ministères des Affaires Étrangères de France, de Grande-Bretagne et de Russie," May 15, 1915, in *Question Adriatique*, pp. 113–22. For Supilo's memorandum to Izvolski see ibid., pp. 30–36.

22. Actually, in 1919 the total population turned out to be twelve million, including some two million non-Slavs.

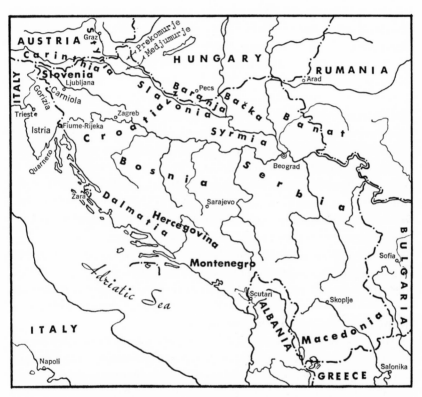

Regional Map of Yugoslav Territories

ethnic. It foreshadowed territorial disputes with six of the seven neighboring states, with Greece as the exception. The Yugoslavs not only faced disputes on every side but had to cope with formidable Allied opposition as well. Indeed, Italy and Rumania, and the secret inter-Allied treaties which supported their territorial claims, soon came to represent serious obstacles to the fulfillment of Yugoslav demands. When the *New Europe* sympathetically declared that of "all the new states which the war has brought into being, none is confronted with so many delicate problems as Yugoslavia," [23] it recorded a fact that all peacemakers soon came to lament.

In view of the complexities involved, it is essential to survey the specific frontiers the Yugoslavs proposed:

1. *Albania.* The Yugoslavs first of all demanded that Albania be maintained as an independent state with the frontiers established by the London Conference of 1913. The independence of Albania was sought principally as a block to Italian expansion, for under the Treaty of London, Italy was scheduled to obtain sovereignty over the strategic port of Valona and a protectorate over central Albania.

When in June 1917 the Italian government suddenly proclaimed an Italian protectorate over all of "independent Albania," despite vigorous French and Serbian protests, the Serbs responded by occupying Scutari and part of northern Albania, which they refused to evacuate at the end of the war.

In 1918 the Montenegrin Committee for National Union insisted on the inclusion of the Scutari region into the Yugoslav state and in effect made this part of the official territorial program.[24] Scutari was claimed on economic, historic, and ethnic grounds, which were for the most part unconvincing. But there was a sufficient element of logic to the claim to make it politically useful. If need be, Scutari and northern Albania could be claimed in an effort to keep Italy away from Montenegrin and Serbian frontiers.

2. *Bulgaria.* Here the Yugoslavs asked for a strip of territory

23. *New Europe, 10* (1919), 97.

24. See *Albania* (Paris, 1919); *The Question of Scutari* (Paris, 1919); *La Paix de Versailles, 10* (Paris, Éditions Internationales, 1932), 70.

along the entire Bulgarian frontier from Greece to Rumania, mainly on strategic and partly on ethnic grounds.[25] Since the old Serbo-Bulgarian frontier had proven militarily vulnerable and indefensible, the Yugoslavs were determined to prevent a recurrence of the military disaster which followed Bulgaria's unprovoked aggression in 1915. The Belgrade-Niš-Skoplje and the Niš-Kneževac-Zaječar-Negotin railway lines, central to the entire Serbian communications system, were particularly exposed by proximity to the Bulgarian frontier. The proposed line extended the Yugoslav frontier some twenty kilometers eastward in the Strumica salient and in the area adjacent to Vranje. It ran from the river Struma in the south, to and including the strategically important Dragoman Pass on the Niš-Sofia line, to the fortress of Vidin in the north. Insofar as it followed the summit of the mountains from the village of Izvor northward, the proposed line envisaged a natural topographical barrier which reinforced the strategic security of the Vardar and Morava valleys and the eastern branch of the Niš-Skoplje railway system.

3. *Rumania.* The dispute with Rumania centered on the Banat, a region inhabited by Magyars, Germans, Serbs, and Rumanians, which up to November 1918 had belonged to Hungary.[26] The Yugoslavs claimed the western and part of the central Banat on ethnic, strategic, economic, and historic grounds.[27] The Rumanians, on the other hand, claimed the entire Banat in fulfillment of the secret 1916 Treaty of Bucharest and on ethnic grounds as well.[28] The Allies thus had to choose between honoring a pledge made under conditions of wartime expediency or keeping faith with the principles of nationality and self-determination.

25. *The Serbo-Bulgarian Relations and the Question of the Rectification of the Frontier* (Paris, 1919).

26. For the history and ethnic composition of the Banat see B. Auerbach, *Les Races et les nationalités en Autriche-Hongrie* (Paris, 1917), pp. 315–53, 432–37.

27. See *Delimitation between the Serbians and the Roumanians in the Banat* (Paris, 1919), the official Yugoslav memorandum. Also, J. Cvijić, J. Radonić, et al., *La Question du Banat, de la Batchka et de la Baranya. Le Banat* (Paris, 1919).

28. See the Rumanian memoranda *Roumania before the Peace Conference. The Banat of Temeshvar* (Paris, 1919); and *La Roumanie devant le Congrès de la Paix. Ses Revendications territoriales* (Paris, 1919). For the Rumanian case see also Sherman David Spector, *Rumania at the Paris Peace Conference: A Study of the Diplomacy of Ioan I. C. Brătianu* (New York, 1962).

In 1919 the Banat was, as Seton-Watson put it, "so inextricably mingled" that "however the future frontiers may be drawn, minorities belonging to each of the four principal races will inevitably be left in each of the newly constituted states." [29]

Of the region's three component *comitats*, the mountainous Krasso in the east, the central Temes plain, and the Torontal plain in the west, the Serbs held an undisputed plurality over Rumanians only in Torontal. According to the Hungarian census of 1910, the ethnic composition of Torontal and Temes was as follows:

	Magyars	Germans	Rumanians	Serbs	Croats	Slovaks	Others
TORONTAL:	128,405	165,779	86,937	199,750	4,203	16,143	13,923
TEMES:	89,960	165,883	169,030	69,905	350	3,080	12,627

In the area claimed by Yugoslavia—all of Torontal and part of Temes—there were 327,444 Slavs (the figure includes Czechs, Slovaks, Ruthenes, and Slovenes) and 212,997 Rumanians.[30] The important railway centers of Temesvar and the Danube port of Bazias, neither a predominantly Serbian town, were claimed on economic grounds. The proposed Yugoslav line was bounded in the north by the river Maros, in the west by the Tisza, in the south by the Danube, and in the east by an irregular line from Arad due south to the Danube.

The Yugoslavs, unlike the Rumanians, argued with reasonable validity that the Banat had in fact no geographic, economic, ethnic, or historic unity. The western Banat had had close historic and cultural links with Serbia ever since the great Serb migrations of the fifteenth century.[31] Economic ties had also been historically strong and Temesvar had long served as a great commercial center for the Balkans. The water routes of the western Banat converge southward toward Belgrade, thus connecting the Banat

29. "The Question of the Banat," *New Europe, 10* (1919), 98.

30. Cvijić, et al., *Le Banat,* p. 13. The category "others" included various Slav elements, but was set apart in order to reduce the "Serb" figure. A precise breakdown of this category is impossible. Auerbach gives figures only for Serbs and Rumanians: 191,000 vs. 86,000 respectively in Torontal and 57,000 vs. 160,000 respectively in Temes (Auerbach, *Races et nationalités,* p. 434).

31. For the history of the Serbs in the Banat through the mid-19th century see E. Picot, *Les Serbes de Hongrie* (Prague, 1873).

with the Morava and Vardar valleys. Even though the *Ausgleich* of 1867 separated the Banat and Serbia economically (as a result of deliberate Magyar policy), the Banat's economy had been historically more related to Serbia than to Rumania. Strategically, the western Banat had always controlled the northern approaches to Belgrade and the Morava valley, and has been a traditional invasion route into the Balkans. The strategic exposure of Belgrade, so effectively exploited by the Austrians in 1914, was therefore presented as a further compelling reason for claiming this land to the north.

The Rumanians, by contrast, claimed the entire Banat and demanded the fulfillment of promises made to them in August 1916 by Great Britain, France, Italy, and Russia, in the secret Treaty of Bucharest, in return for which they joined the Entente. Yet even in 1916 Allied statesmen were fully aware of the ethnic complexities involved. As early as May and August 1915, Sir Edward Grey and Sazonov admitted that to assign the western Banat to Rumania would violate Serbia's indisputable right to the region.[32] American opinion on the subject was similarly expressed by the United States minister in Bucharest who, at the end of 1918, stated that "two thirds of the population of the western Banat are Servians and only one third Roumanians, so that if the principle of nationality is adopted the Servians should get the western portion of the Banat." [33]

As for the Yugoslavs, since the terms of the Bucharest agreement had never been divulged to Belgrade, and since the Serbs had never been consulted, they simply refused to recognize the treaty at all.[34] They also argued that Rumania's separate peace treaty with the Central Powers, concluded in 1917, invalidated the treaty even though the Rumanians rejoined the Entente in 1918. Toward the end of the war Pašić made one serious attempt to reach agreement with Rumania about the Banat. In October 1918

---

32. *House Papers, 1,* 462–63; *Int. Bez.,* III, 8, ii, pp. 770–71.

33. Vopicka to Polk, Bucharest, Dec. 5, 1918 (*FRUS-PPC,* 2, 400). Vopicka also added: "Not only should Servia receive this part of the Banat on the nationalities question but also for the protection of Belgrade . . ." (p. 401).

34. This was repeatedly stressed by Alexander to Dodge. See Dodge to Lansing, Belgrade, Jan. 28, 1919 (86oh.01/46), and Jan. 17, 1919 (763.72119/3427; Dept. of State, Washington).

he met with Take Ionescu (and Eleutherios Venizelos, who enter-
tained hopes of mediating this dispute) on several occasions in
Paris. After prolonged discussions, they reached an amicable understanding by which Rumania was to get the largest part of the
Banat, including the southern bank of the Maros to its confluence with the Tisza and the Temesvar-Bazias trunkline, and
Serbia the rest.[35] But this "sensible" partition, as Nicolson has
called it,[36] was not destined to be carried out. Designed as a preliminary step in the formation of the Little Entente, the agreement was repudiated by Bratianu and bitterly attacked by the
Rumanian chauvinist press as a betrayal of the national cause.
Bratianu's action, of course, embittered the Yugoslavs immensely
and in large part explains the acrimony which developed on both
sides during the peace conference.

4. *Hungary.* Here the Yugoslavs claimed Bačka, the region between the Tisza and the Danube; Baranja, between the Danube
and the Drava; Prekomurje, to the north of the Mur; and
Medjumurje, between the Drava and the Mur.[37] As with the Banat,
a purely ethnic line could not be achieved. Not only was the
ethnic mosaic as complex, but the absence of adequate physical
barriers made a natural delimitation equally impossible.

In Bačka and Baranja, in addition to Magyars, Germans, and
Orthodox Serbs, there were substantial pockets of Catholic Serbs
(or Croats, according to some)—the so-called Bunjevci and Šokci.
Little is known about them to this day, though they are presumed
to have come from Dalmatia. In Bačka alone, they numbered over
150,000, according to the Serbian census of 1919.[38] Many were set-

35. R. W. Seton-Watson, *A History of the Roumanians* (Cambridge, Eng., 1934),
pp. 537–38. See also G. I. Bratianu, *Origines et formation de l'unité roumaine*
(Bucharest, 1943), passim.

36. H. Nicolson, *Peacemaking, 1919* (New York, 1939), p. 136.

37. See *Delimitations between Serbians and Magyars in the Batchka* (Paris, 1919),
the official memorandum; *Delimitations between the Serbians, Croatians and Slovenes
and the Hungarians in the Baranya and Somogy* (Paris, 1919), also an official memorandum; J. Cvijić, *Frontière septentrionale des Yougoslaves* (Paris, 1919); J. Cvijić,
J. Radonić, et al., *La Question du Banat, de la Batchka et de la Baranya* (with
separate studies on Bačka and Baranja); and E. Haumant, *La Frontière septentrionale
de l'État yougoslave* (Paris, 1919).

38. Cvijić, et al., *La Batchka,* appendix. For the historical background, see I. Ivanović, *O Bunjevcima. Povjesničko-narodnopisna rasprava* (Subotica, 1894), and V. Bogdanov, *Živa Prošlost* (Zagreb, 1957), pp. 233–54.

tled in purely Magyar territory. To complicate matters further, there were also sizable groupings of Russians (Ruthenes), Slovaks, and Jews. According to Yugoslav figures, the overall population distribution was as follows:

| | Serbo-Croat | | | | | | | |
	Ortho-dox Serbs	Bun-jevci-Šokci	Slo-vaks	Rus-sians	Mag-yars	Ger-mans	Jews	Others	Total
BAČKA	165,372	156,691	67,564	14,241	208,758	179,902	19,659	7,152	819,339
BARANJA	51,352	24,127	140	—	48,256	58,459	—	1,573	183,907 [39]

Discounting the German element—for it could not be joined to either Austria or Germany and was hence automatically destined to remain a minority in Hungary or Yugoslavia—the Yugoslavs had an ethnic plurality in both Baranja and Bačka.

Historic and economic arguments were added to the ethnic. Historically, the cultural and commercial roles of both regions were similar to that of the Banat. Moreover, in 1919, as a region endowed with extremely fertile soil (partly because it lay below the level of the Danube), Bačka was particularly important. The Yugoslavs were also anxious to obtain the Subotica-Novi Sad, Subotica-Sombor, and Subotica-Baja railway lines—for otherwise they would have lacked a northern communications system—as well as the navigable waterways of the Danube and the Tisza.

With regard to Medjumurje and Prekomurje the issue was mainly ethnic. In each case there was a clearcut Yugoslav major-ity,[40] even though both regions lay north of the Drava, the his-toric frontier between Hungary and Croatia. Neither was sig-nificant in size or economic importance; both were too densely populated and relatively poor.

5. *Austria.* West of Prekomurje, the proposed frontier ran to the Italian border at Pontafel. The Yugoslavs claimed Lower Styria and most of Carinthia along a course which corresponded roughly to a line of linguistic partition. They claimed four major towns, however, which had a German majority in 1919: Radkersburg

39. Ibid. See also A. Belić and S. Mihaldjić, *La Question du Banat, de la Batchka et de la Baranya. La Baranya* (Paris, 1919), p. 21.

40. Haumant, p. 4; M. Slavić, *La Question du Prekmurje, de la Styrie et de la Carinthie. De la Statistique du Prekmurje* (Paris, 1919), p. 21.

(Radgona), Maribor (Marburg), Klagenfurt (Celovec), and Villach (Beljak).

The problem of separating mixed populations in this region was not simplified by Austrian statistics which, for political reasons, were grossly distorted.[41] Claiming an actual Slovene majority in the region as a whole, the Yugoslavs resolved to ask the peace conference to lay aside the Austrian census figures. Their own calculations showed a majority of 426,000 Slavs to 78,000 Germans in Styria, and 124,000 Slavs to 38,000 Germans in Carinthia.[42] As for the four German towns, each was surrounded by a purely Slav hinterland and had, moreover, been forcibly Germanized after 1850, a contention which was supported with considerable historical evidence.[43]

To the ethnic argument were joined historic and economic considerations. Lower Styria and Carinthia had had close cultural and economic ties with Slovenia. Southern Slav nationalism

41. Austrian and Magyar manipulations with census figures have stirred up a considerable scholarly controversy. For critiques of the figures and analyses of Austrian and Magyar nationality policies see the following: R. A. Kann, *The Multinational Empire* 2 (2 vols. New York, 1950), 299–307, analyzing the "nonexistence of uniform Austro-Hungarian nationality statistics"; O. Jászi, "The Distribution of Nations and the German-Magyar Hegemony," in his *Dissolution of the Habsburg Monarchy* (Chicago, 1929), pp. 271–82; L. Dominian, *The Frontiers of Language and Nationality in Europe* (New York, 1917), who observes that "as a rule an increase of 10% in the number of Slavs, Rumanians and Italians can be safely added to figures set forth in government statistics" (p. 76); A. J. May, *The Hapsburg Monarchy, 1867–1914* (Cambridge, Mass., 1951), pp. 305–87, on Magyarization and Germanization among the Southern Slavs; L. Léger, *La Liquidation de l'Autriche-Hongrie* (Paris, 1915), pp. 15–19; J. Roglić, *Le Recensement de 1910. Ses Méthodes et son application dans la Marche Julienne* (Sušak, 1946); A. J. P. Taylor, "Political and Ethnographic Structure of the Hapsburg Monarchy," in his *Hapsburg Monarchy, 1809–1918* (new ed. London, 1951), pp. 262–69; L. Niederle, *La Race slave. Statistique-démographie-anthropologie* (Paris, 1916), pp. 141–44, 163–67; R. W. Seton-Watson, *The Southern Slav Question* (London, 1911), pp. 1–12; A. E. Moodie, *The Italo-Yugoslav Boundary* (London, 1945), pp. 133–34, 146–47.

42. F. Kovačić, *La Question du Premurje, de la Styrie et de la Carinthie. La Styrie* (Paris, 1919), pp. 13, 16. See also I. Žolger, et al., *La Question du Prekmurje, de la Styrie et de la Carinthie. La Carinthie* (Paris, 1919), p. 31.

43. See R. J. Kerner, *The Yugoslav Movement* (Cambridge, Mass., 1918); H. Wendel, *Der Kampf der Südslawen um Freiheit und Einheit* (Frankfurt, 1925); F. Šišić, *Jugoslavenska Misao* (Belgrade, 1937); B. Vošnjak, *Yugoslav Nationalism* (London, 1916), and *A Bulwark against Germany: the Fight of the Slovenes for National Existence* (London, 1917).

flourished in both provinces in the nineteenth century. Both, but especially Carinthia, also possessed important railway lines connecting Istria with the Danubian plain.

6. *Italy.* From Pontafel to the Adriatic, the Yugoslavs drew an ethnographic line between Italy and Yugoslavia, running for the most part some 15 kilometers west of the Isonzo (Soča) down to but excluding Monfalcone.[44] They claimed the whole Istrian peninsula, including Trieste and Pola; the counties of Gorizia and Gradisca; Fiume (Rijeka) and the Quarnero islands; and Dalmatia with its archipelago.[45]

With the exception of Trieste and Pola and the town of Gorizia, the Slavic element had a clearcut majority throughout Istria and the county of Gorizia.[46] The Italian minority was not compact. Italian communities in Istria were concentrated along the coast west of Pola; none were to the east. The Yugoslavs conceded that Trieste, Pola, and the town of Gorizia were predominantly Italian, but argued that their "Italianity" had been artificially stimulated, and that they represented "buttons on the Slav mantle." A generation earlier, in 1881 to be precise, even Sonnino publicly admitted that to "claim Trieste as a matter of right would be an exaggeration of the principle of nationality and would not present any real interest for our defense." [47]

Be that as it may, the Yugoslavs' claim to Trieste weakened their case considerably, not to say unnecessarily. It met with little sympathy abroad, because the Italians claimed it on incontestable ethnic evidence. The Yugoslavs were warned repeatedly not to

44. *Frontiers between the Kingdom of the Serbians, Croatians and Slovenes and the Kingdom of Italy* (Paris, 1919), the official memorandum; the ethnographic map of A. Lazić, *Frontière éthnographique italo-yougoslavo-allemande* (Paris [1918]). Cvijić regards the Isonzo as the westernmost natural limit of the Balkans (*La Péninsule balkanique*, p. 6), a premise accepted by Moodie (p. 157).

45. *The Territories of Goritza and Gradiska and the Town of Trieste* (Paris, 1919), the official memorandum; *The Town of Trieste* (Paris, 1919); *La Ville de Ryeka (Fiume)* (Paris, 1919); and, L. Vojnović, F. Šišić, et al., *The Question of the Adriatic. Fiume (Rieka)* (Paris, 1919).

46. *The Territories of Goritza*, pp. 4–5; *L'Istrie* (Paris, 1919), p. 4. In Istria as a whole, the population was 58% Slav and 38% Italian according to the census of 1910, as well as independent Yugoslav calculations. In the city of Trieste proper, however, the population was 57% Italian and 43% Slav. For historical background see M. Rojnić, *Istrie. Aperçu historique* (Sušak, 1945).

47. In the *Rassegna Settimanale*, No. 29, p. 338.

ask for Trieste, and even their most ardent supporters—Seton-Watson, Steed, and others—thought this demand excessive and harmful to their cause. Nicolson was less patient but more succinct: "The idiots claim Trieste," [48] he wrote in his diary on February 18, expressing a view that was indeed widely shared.

Yet the reasons for Trieste being claimed have never been fully brought to light. The Yugoslavs disagreed among themselves and many shared the view of Vesnić, which he stated on December 25, 1918, to the Associated Press: "Italy's claims to Trieste have been so persistent and continuous for a long period that we are willing to leave that question apart." [49] The final decision to claim Trieste, as will soon be seen, was indeed not taken lightly.

Istria was also claimed for historic and economic reasons. The historic argument that the Slavs had been settling in the region in the seventh century was transparently weak. But the argument that in the nineteenth century, when the Slavs were in absolute majority, Habsburg policy deliberately stimulated the growth of the Italian element, was supported by sound evidence and was more to the point. After 1867 in fact, Southern Slav nationalist activity in Istria grew in direct ratio to the anti-Slavism of the Imperial bureaucracy.

Economically, Istria was presented, with considerable justice, as being of much greater importance to the Yugoslav than to the Italian state, both for its economic resources and the maritime-commercial facilities of Trieste. Trieste had long served as one of the principal commercial outlets for the Slav hinterland as well as for all of East Central Europe. It was the principal Adriatic port of the Austrian Empire; 40 per cent of total Triestine traffic on the eve of World War I was directed to and from Southern Slav lands, with the rest mostly to and from Austria and Bohemia.[50]

7. *Fiume-Rijeka.* The case of Fiume presented a special problem. Long the natural port of Croatia, it had not been an object of Italian irredentism before 1918. Nor had it ever been of economic interest to Italy. The Treaty of London had specifically assigned it to Croatia and, as Albrecht-Carrié put it, why the Italians claimed

48. Nicolson, p. 264.
49. *New York Times,* Dec. 25, 1918.
50. *Trieste et la Yougoslavie* (Ljubljana, 1919), p. 5.

Fiume "is hard to tell." [51] But in 1918, with the support even of such moderates as Bissolati and Salvemini, Fiume was placed on the sacred altar of the irredentist program under Sonnino's guidance.

The Yugoslavs responded to this challenge apprehensively but vigorously. For them "Rijeka" was a magic word symbolic of the Serbo-Croat Coalition and of Croatian Yugoslavism in the years before World War I. More important, however, in Fiume-Rijeka they saw the key to their maritime and economic future.

No one disputed the fact that in 1919 Fiume proper had an Italian majority, though with the twin city of Sušak the majority was distinctly Yugoslav. In 1910, according to Hungarian census figures, Fiume consisted of 24,212 Italians, 15,687 Yugoslavs, and 6,492 Magyars. But thirty years earlier there had been 10,227 Yugoslavs and 9,237 Italians. In 1851 there were 11,581 Yugoslavs to 691 Italians.[52] Before 1900, significantly, there were almost no Magyars.

The rapid growth of Italian and Magyar elements in the decades before World War I was deliberately fostered by Budapest, for after 1867, Fiume became the subject of a bitter political contest between Budapest and Zagreb. Historically, Fiume had little connection with Italy except for a brief period in the Middle Ages and again when it fell under Venetian sway. In the sixteenth century it fell to the Habsburgs. In 1776 Maria Theresa joined it to the Hungarian Crown of St. Stephen. In 1868, as a result of the Croatian-Hungarian *Nagodba* which followed the Austro-Hungarian Ausgleich of 1867, Fiume proper was assigned as a *corpus separatum* to the Kingdom of Hungary, while Sušak was assigned to the Kingdom of Croatia-Slavonia. But the corpus separatum provision resulted from a falsification of Article 66 of the Nagodba and has been disputed ever since by the Croats.[53] After 1868,

---

51. Albrecht-Carrié, *Italy*, p. 102.

52. *La Question de Fiume* (Paris, 1919), pp. 2, 4. For further detail and historical background see F. Hauptmann, *Rijeka: od Rimske Tarsatike do Hrvatsko-Ugarske Nagodbe* (Zagreb, 1951); R. Maixner, *Rieka* (Sušak, 1945); F. Šišić, *Abrégé de l'histoire politique de Riéka-Fiume* (Paris, 1919).

53. The Magyars falsely claimed that the Croats indeed renounced Fiume through the Nagodba. See G. Horn, *Le Compromis de 1868 entre la Hongrie et la Croatie* (Paris, 1907); L. Eisenman, *Le Compromis austro-hongrois* (Paris, 1904), pp. 541–44.

Italian growth in Fiume began in earnest, encouraged mostly by Magyar economic and political concessions.

The economic issue was more consequential. As the second largest port (after Trieste) in the northern Adriatic, Fiume possessed excellent railway facilities. The main Fiume port (Sušak's Porto Baroš serviced mostly Croatian commerce in lumber) and the railway system were vital for the Yugoslav economy, which had neither similar port facilities elsewhere nor an adequate maritime fleet. Fiume was developed by the Magyars for the purpose of rivaling Austrian Trieste. Should Fiume now go to Italy, the Yugoslavs argued, it would languish, because it would be used only for Italo-Yugoslav maritime trade, which was insignificant. Trieste would flourish while the Yugoslavs would be denied a port which they would develop further and use for the world's markets. Italy had great ports elsewhere, Mediterranean as well as Adriatic, while they had none at all.

8. *Dalmatia*. By contrast, the Dalmatian question seemed deceptively simple. In essence it amounted to this: would the Allies honor the Treaty of London or the principles of nationality and self-determination?

On their side the Yugoslavs had a foolproof ethnic case. The Austrian census of 1910 divided the population of Dalmatia into 610,669 Yugoslavs and 18,928 Italians, or a ratio of 96 per cent to less than 3 per cent.[54]

Zara (Zadar) was an exception, as the only Dalmatian city with an Italian majority. The islands of Veglia (Krk) and Lussin (Lošinj) had sizable Italian minorities, but nowhere a clearcut majority. The Yugoslavs suggested varying measures of local autonomy as well as special cultural guarantees in these cases, but strictly within a Yugoslav national framework.

As for the Italian argument that the Dalmatian mainland and islands promised to Italy by the Treaty of London were essential to her security in the Adriatic, the Yugoslav answer was simple. A threat to Italian security arose only from Austro-Hungarian policies, and this situation no longer obtained. The Yugoslavs wanted friendly relations with Italy and had no designs against her. On the other hand, if Italy got part of Dalmatia and impor-

54. *Mémoire sur la Question Dalmate* (Paris, 1919), p. 7; Dominian, pp. 76, 92.

tant offshore islands, Yugoslav security would be endangered and its sovereignty impaired. Moreover, the Yugoslavs would be denied a natural frontier in the south.

In Italian eyes Dalmatia was part of a broader design. The Italian memorandum of claims to the peace conference demanded fulfillment of the London treaty terms, plus Fiume. Thus possession of Istria, Fiume, part of Dalmatia, several strategic islands, the Albanian port of Valona, and control over the rest of Albania would make Italy master of the Adriatic—not on the basis of "nationality" but on the basis of compensation for Italy's war effort. Save for Fiume, this program was opposed by most Italian liberals—Bissolati, Borgese, Salvemini, Ghisleri, Della Torre, and the *Corriere della Sera* group—but without effect on official policy. Thus even though various Italian ethnographic studies disputed Sonnino's demands to the east of Pola,[55] the old axioms of Dante and Mazzini that "Italy" ends at the Quarnero were quickly laid aside.

9. *Yugoslav-Czechoslovak Corridor.* During January and February 1919 there was some talk of a possible Yugoslav-Czech corridor through northern Slovenia and western Hungary, along a narrow strip of territory inhabited by clusters of Croats, Slovenes, Czechs and Slovaks. The idea for a direct link between the two successor states appears to have originated with Beneš as a step toward creating the Little Entente. Though mentioned in the general Yugoslav memorandum, it never received much support in Belgrade. Cvijić went so far as to prepare a special map demonstrating the feasibility of the project.[56] As soon as the matter was brought up in the peace conference Subcommittee on Czechoslovak Affairs on March 8, however, it was shelved due to American opposition and was not heard of again.

Before this overall territorial program could be worked out— and elaborated in specific memoranda for presentation to the peace conference—other more immediate problems required action.

On Friday morning, January 10, 1919, the Yugoslav delegation

---

55. See, for example, Carlo Errera, *Italiani e Slavi nella Venezia Giulia* (Rome, 1919); A. Ghisleri, *Italia e Jugoslavia* (Rome, 1945), p. 36.
56. Cvijić, *La Frontière septentrionale,* map.

held its first executive meeting.[57] It began on a bad note. Pašić reported on having seen Pichon, who told him that the Yugoslavs could count on three conference seats at best. The discussion that followed was animated, and when Trumbić after a while proposed preparing a definitive memorandum of territorial claims for early submission to the Allies, it became evident that rough sailing lay ahead. The delegation, moreover, did not know that new decisions affecting its immediate interests were coming to a head in inter-Allied councils.

In the maze of confusion that reigned throughout Paris in the week before the peace conference finally opened (January 18), the issue of Yugoslav representation at the conference table was perhaps a minor matter when judged against the multitude of problems that awaited solution by the Allies. But the very fact that problems of this kind—vital to each state concerned—were left unresolved until the very last, or even completely ignored, reflects poorly on the political wisdom of the peacemakers of 1919.

Post-armistice discussions among the Allies had led to a formula of allocating three (rather than the four expected by Belgrade) conference seats to Serbia, Belgium, Greece, and Rumania. Poland and Czechoslovakia, as newly formed states whose belligerency had been recognized shortly before the end of the war, were each

57. The session was attended by Pašić, Trumbić, Vesnić, Ribarž, General Petar Pešić (head of the military mission), and Dr. Ante Tresić-Pavičić (former deputy for Dalmatia and now a delegation expert on regional affairs of the kingdom). "Zapisnik Delegacije S.H.S. na Mirovnoj Konferenciji u Parizu, 1919–1920" (hereafter cited as Zap.), Session 1, Vol. 1, Jan. 10, 1919. These minutes of the Yugoslav peace delegation are now on deposit at the Yale University Library, Division of Historical Manuscripts, in certified typescript copy generously made for the author by the Manuscript Division of the University of Zagreb Library. My study is based on this copy of the minutes. In late 1960 the Institut Društvenih Nauka (Odeljenje za Istorijske Nauke) in Belgrade published the minutes: Bogdan Krizman and Bogumil Hrabak, eds., *Zapisnici sa Sednica Delegacije Kraljevine SHS na Mirovnoj Konferenciji u Parizu, 1919–1920* (Belgrade, 1960) (hereafter referred to as K&H). The main difference between the unpublished and published versions is that the latter is extensively annotated, includes the record of 11 sessions for March–June 1920 not included in the manuscript, and gives the texts of various dispatches in the notes and several official memoranda in the appendixes. For the reader's reference and convenience I have added to all citations from the manuscript equivalent page references in K&H.

to be given only two. But on January 12, when Wilson met with the premiers of France, Great Britain, and Italy at the Quai d'Orsay to settle on rules of procedure and the conference agenda, Lloyd George, fearing an "unwieldy assembly" [58] if too many small states were given three seats each, argued to limit each to two. His formula carried the day, with the proviso, however, that each case be separately studied. When, next day, Wilson succeeded in raising the quota of Brazil to three, a storm of indignation broke loose among the Belgians, Greeks, and Yugoslavs.

For the Yugoslavs the Allied decision spelled political disaster.[59] Having only two seats would mean being represented by Pašić and Trumbić and no Slovene at all. Domestic repercussions among the Slovenes were inevitable, especially since their solid support for the government and the peace delegation was vital in every way. To exclude them from the front ranks in Paris meant courting the charge that Belgrade was more interested in Dalmatia and the east than in Istria, Carinthia, and the northwestern frontier.

That was not all. During the week preceding the opening of the peace conference, the Allies reached agreement on two other issues, each of momentous consequence to the Yugoslavs. In a series of interlocking decisions affecting the relationship between the lesser states and the Supreme Council of the peace conference in general and the nature of Yugoslav representation in particular, the Allies, under heavy Italian pressure, decided to postpone granting formal recognition to the Kingdom of Serbs, Croats, and Slovenes as such.[60] Ominously, they also decided to reserve one conference seat for the state of "Montenegro." [61]

On the very eve of the conference, the Yugoslavs thus suffered serious political setbacks. The peace delegation heard of these decisions from Pašić, shortly before noon on Tuesday, January 14.[62] After a two-hour discussion it decided to lodge a strong

58. Marston, *Peace Conference,* p. 60.
59. The delegation heard about the Allied action from Pašić, on the morning of Jan. 14. Zap., *1,* 4 (K&H, p. 21).
60. Moodie, *Italo-Yugoslav Boundary,* p. 155. Alexander was told that he would be received in Paris only as Regent of Serbia. His trip was immediately postponed.
61. Marston, p. 61.
62. Zap., *1,* 4–5 (K&H, pp. 21–22).

protest against any reduction in the Yugoslav quota and any change in accreditation which would substitute "the Kingdom of Serbia" for "the Kingdom of Serbs, Croats and Slovenes." At the same time, however, the delegates placed little hope in this protest. If the Allies insisted on allotting them only two seats and on accepting only Serbia, there was little choice, they felt, but to send Pašić and Trumbić to the conference table anyway.

Drafting the note of protest took almost two days. But more important than the protest was the dissension this task generated within the delegation. At this, the very beginning of their labors, the delegates resorted to a tone of overt political rivalry that did not augur well and indeed came to plague their relations on countless future occasions. Since the minutes of delegation proceedings and the archives of Trumbić and others have until recently been sealed, students of Yugoslav diplomacy and historians of the Paris Peace Conference have ignored this aspect almost completely.[63] Yet intradelegation conflicts weighed heavily on Yugoslav policies at Paris and therefore inevitably lend a new dimension to a study of the Yugoslav settlement as a whole.

Given their mutual wartime antipathy, it is no accident that Pašić and Trumbić emerged as the leading antagonists at Paris. But their personal bitterness and hostility sprang from profound differences in political conceptions. And, insofar as their personal quarrel often led to a split of delegation ranks into Serb and non-Serb elements, it foreshadowed the tragic conflict that overtook internal Yugoslav politics in the years to come.

In January 1919 Trumbić, already perturbed by evidence of Serb centralist tendencies, sought to achieve delegation unity on two vital scores: 1) obtaining immediate recognition for the Kingdom of Serbs, Croats, and Slovenes; and 2) securing for the peace delegation as much autonomy from Belgrade as possible. Pašić resisted both and resisted with success. Secure in the knowledge that he could count on Protić and the dominant Radical element

63. This is true of Yugoslav and western historians alike. The only exception is found in the articles of Dr. Bogdan Krizman (for entries, see below, Bibliography), who, as research associate at the Državni Arhiv and at the Jadranski Institut in Zagreb, has made use of the delegation minutes, the Trumbić Papers, the archives of the Narodno Vijeće S.H.S. at the Državni Arhiv, and other collections as well.

in Belgrade to support his view, Pašić indeed stimulated the delegation's dependence upon the government at home. And this began at the very start.

Thus on January 15 Trumbić presented his draft of the protest that was to be handed to Pichon.[64] It began by summarizing the events that had led to the union of "the former Kingdom of Serbia" with other Southern Slav lands, and the establishment of the Kingdom of Serbs, Croats, and Slovenes and its first national government. It next argued that the "former" Serbian kingdom no longer existed and therefore could not be represented at the peace conference. Then it concluded that in view of the Serbian (and Southern Slav) contribution to the war effort, the reduction in Yugoslav representation should not be carried out. When the delegates had read his draft, Trumbić added that Belgrade should be consulted about the text of the note. If the government reply, however, were not received by the 17th, the day before the conference was to open, the note should be submitted anyway.

Pašić at first agreed with the argument that the delegates should represent the Kingdom of Serbs, Croats, and Slovenes, and not that of Serbia. But he strongly objected to having this matter linked with the question of the conference seats quota. He demanded instead that each issue be dealt with in separate notes. Then Vesnić took the floor and argued that, since the Allied decision was transmitted orally and the formal peace conference note concerning the exact accreditation had not yet been received, it would be premature to formulate an answer. When a formal note was received, he (Vesnić) would prepare an appropriate reply.

At this point General Petar Pešić entered the debate. He objected to Trumbić's use of the term "former Kingdom of Serbia" as though "Serbia no longer existed" and added that one can speak about "former Austria-Hungary," but not about "former Serbia." [65]

The delegates thereupon agreed to postpone consideration of the whole issue. Trumbić, obviously vexed by the opposition of all the Serbs present, proposed asking the government in Belgrade

64. Zap., *1*, 6–9 (K&H, pp. 22–23). Those present were Pašić, Trumbić, Ribarž, Pešić, and Tresić-Pavičić.

65. Ibid., p. 11 (K&H, pp. 23–24).

to grant the delegation *pleins pouvoirs* for resolving all questions pertaining to the peace conference. This suggestion, as the recording secretary (Dr. Ninko Perić) noted in the minutes not without some sarcasm, "could not be adopted, because the mandate received by the first delegate, Mr. Pašić, which will also be received by the other Messrs. delegates, states that the delegates will work under government instructions." [66]

Next day, January 16, Vesnić simply announced that he, *"as minister of Serbia"* (sic), received an invitation for two delegates of the *"Kingdom of Serbia"* (sic) to participate at the conference opening. And he then proceeded to read a draft of the reply he had prepared. Next he reported on a meeting with the minister of Belgium at which they discussed the possibility of joint action before the Allies. And at the end Vesnić announced that he had "already sent" a letter to Lloyd George, "protesting the fact that the notification of the Kingdom of Serbs, Croats and Slovenes has not been taken into account, and that Serbia has been allotted only two delegates for the Peace Conference." [67] The protest was not a strong one; it did not demand recognition. "Taken into account" were euphemistic words. Trumbić, the Foreign Minister, was kept from taking formal action of his own.

In one regard, however, Vesnić's action did bear fruit. The joint Serbian and Belgian protests—Belgium even threatened to boycott the conference unless placed on an equal footing with Brazil —induced the Allies to alter their earlier stand. On Friday the 17th, at the strong insistence of Clemenceau, Lansing, and Pichon, both quotas were raised from two to three. [68] The news was relayed to Vesnić shortly after 3:00 P.M., just as the delegation had convened for that afternoon's session, whereupon Vesnić triumphantly announced that he had "this moment received a telephone call from M. Dutasta," the Secretary-General of the French peace delegation, informing him of the Allied decision. [69]

The Allied decision was of course strictly procedural. The

66. Ibid. (K&H, p. 24).
67. Ibid., pp. 12–13 (K&H, pp. 24–25).
68. Marston, p. 61.
69. Zap., *1*, 14 (K&H, p. 25).

broader issue of diplomatic recognition was left for the peace conference to decide and, meanwhile, the Yugoslav delegates were to be admitted in the name of Serbia alone.[70] Distasteful as it was, Trumbić went along with this formula. His first project within the delegation, however, had in fact come to naught.

Nor was satisfaction forthcoming with regard to Montenegro, a political problem closely linked to that of Yugoslav recognition and to the policies of the Italian government. When Protić cabled on January 3 that "were it not for Italy, we would already have general recognition," [71] he also warned that Italian policy would continue to strive to make a major issue of Montenegrin independence. And indeed, from the vantage point of Rome, the existence of a Montenegrin separatist movement served as an important political lever to be used, not unlike the Badoglio Plan, in behalf of the policy of challenging the Yugoslav union itself.

Italian efforts in this direction were materially aided by the actions of the ex-King Nicholas and his entourage. In November 1918, when the Podgorica Assembly resolved to join the Yugoslav union, Nicholas and his principal adviser, Jovan Plamenac, launched a campaign to maintain the fiction of Montenegrin independence. With the aid of his son-in-law, Victor Emmanuel III, and the Italian government, Nicholas established Plamenac as head of a government-in-exile which asked for separate admission to the peace conference at Paris and even submitted a series of Montenegrin territorial demands, including a part of Hercegovina.[72]

At the same time, Sonnino repeatedly refused to recognize the Podgorica Assembly resolution as a reflection of Montenegrin popular will, on the ground that this action was taken in the ab-

70. The text of Vesnić's letter to Lloyd George is not given in the minutes. The discussion, however, suggests that Vesnić implied to Lloyd George a willingness to accept the label of "Serbia." He made more of an issue over the number of conference seats.

71. Protić to Trumbić, Belgrade, Jan. 3, 1919 (No. 20, TP, F66).

72. Jovan Plamenac, *Montenegro before the Peace Conference* (Paris, 1919), three memoranda dated March 5, 1919.

sence of the king and his government.[73] He argued, moreover, that the Podgorica Assembly had acted under Serbian pressure and force, a line he was to maintain in all his dealings with the Allied statesmen. Meanwhile, he continued to support Nicholas and Plamenac, as did his successor at the Quirinale.

There is of course no question that Serbian agents did indeed enter Montenegro in October and November 1918 to spread unionist propaganda and that Serbian influence was exerted in the Podgorica Assembly. But the bulk of pro-unionist propaganda came from various Montenegrin groups whose activities by far overshadowed those of the Serbs. Most of the Montenegrin activities were directed by the Committee for National Union, established in Geneva in 1917 under the leadership of Andrija Radović, Janko Spasojević, and others, many of whom had been ministers in various of Nicholas' cabinets. By the end of the war, moreover, Nicholas had little popular support, partly because of earlier royal pro-Austrian intrigues and partly because of the tragic military debacle suffered at Mount Lovčen.[74]

As a result of Italian support of Nicholas, the Yugoslavs thus also faced a "Montenegrin Question" at the peace conference.

While considering the question of Yugoslav representation in Paris during the week before the peace conference opened, the Supreme Council had to act on Nicholas' demand for admission. The matter was a delicate one for the Allies. Nicholas and Plamenac could and, indeed, did cite letters from Wilson, Clemenceau, and other Entente statesmen promising Allied aid for the restoration of Montenegrin independence in accordance with the principles expounded in the Fourteen Points.[75] In 1918, however, the Allies appear to have been more interested in seeing Montenegro freed from Austrian and German military control than in the less pressing issue of Montenegrin independence versus union with Serbia. This is particularly significant in view of the fact that as early as the autumn of 1916 the British Foreign Office had decided that an independent Montenegro would "serve no

73. *DDI*, passim.
74. For the wartime background of the Montenegrin question see, Woodhouse, *Italy and the Yugoslavs*, pp. 88–111; J. Spasojević, *Ujedinjenje Crne Gore sa Srbijom* (Geneva, 1917).
75. Plamenac, Memo. I, pp. 2–5.

useful purpose" if a larger Southern Slav union were to come into being or even if Montenegro were to be absorbed into Serbia.[76] There is no evidence that French and American views differed from the British in this regard, even though Wilson did not really have concrete ideas on the subject.

The "Montenegrin question" was actually launched and placed on the inter-Allied agenda by Italy, following the armistice.[77] By January 1919 it had assumed considerable proportions. Mostly at Sonnino's prompting—and well-publicized refusal to accept the Podgorica resolution—the British began to express concern with Serbian actions in Montenegro and made official inquiries in Belgrade. Protić refused to discuss the subject with London, precipitating a strong reaction at Whitehall.[78]

On January 7, 1919, Wilson received a plea from Nicholas asking for a general review of events in Montenegro and admittance to the peace conference.[79] In view of his earlier correspondence with Nicholas and the fact that the Yugoslav union was as yet unrecognized, the President was now placed in a quandary. He had received conflicting reports about the Podgorica action, and rather than to disavow Belgrade openly, he instructed Lansing to have a "frank talk" with Vesnić and tell him that "serious questions are arising in our minds because of the dealings of Serbia with Montenegro. Undoubtedly," Wilson concluded, "the sympathies of the people of the United States are as much with Monte-

---

76. Lloyd George, *Truth about the Peace Treaties, 1,* 37–38. Also, Nicolson, *Peacemaking,* p. 150.

77. Bonin Longare in fact appealed for American help to "preserve" Montenegrin independence a week before the Podgorica resolution was passed (Bonin Longare to Sonnino, Paris, Nov. 20, 1918, *DDI,* p. 123).

78. On Jan 4, 1919, the Foreign Office expressed annoyance with Protić for refusing to discuss Montenegrin affairs and for allegedly trying to present the Entente with a fait accompli, "thus attempting to prejudice the decisions of the Peace Conference." The Foreign Office next urged Washington to join in a protest against Belgrade (*FRUS-PPC, 2,* 362). On Jan. 6 James Rennel Rodd, the British ambassador in Rome, informed Sonnino that the British would make an issue of Montenegro at the peace conference (Sonnino to Bonin Longare, Imperiali, et al., Rome, Jan 6, 1919, *DDI,* p. 422). Sonnino approved wholeheartedly. On Jan. 10, however, the British minister in Belgrade informed the Italian chargé d'affaires that Montenegro was a closed issue and nothing would be done about it (Galanti to Sonnino, Belgrade, Jan. 10, 1919, *DDI,* p. 448).

79. Nicholas to Wilson, Paris, Jan. 7, 1919 (*FRUS-PPC, 2,* 362–65).

negro as with Serbia." [80] When two days later, however, Nicholas asked for a personal meeting, Wilson, on advice from Lansing, politely declined.[81]

With Wilson's action the threat of peace conference interference with the Podgorica resolution waned.[82] During the week of January 12 the Supreme Council adopted a compromise plan to the effect that "in principle" Montenegro should be represented at the peace conference by one delegate whose official designation would "not be established until such a time when the political situation of that country will be clarified." [83] Thus, as Nicolson put it, the conference resolved the quandary by characteristic hedging.[84] Prior moral obligations toward Nicholas were fulfilled at least in form, while from the Allies' point of view, Yugoslav susceptibilities were supposedly allayed by indefinitely deferring Montenegrin representation. In the end, Nicholas failed to gain separate admittance to the conference. The issue dragged on through December 1919, at which time the Supreme Council officially closed its books on this entire affair.[85] But none of this could be foreseen on the day the peace conference opened.

80. Wilson to Lansing, Paris, Jan. 9, 1919 (ibid., p. 367).

81. Ibid., p. 370.

82. Though the British investigating mission of Count de Salis in Montenegro reported that the Podgorica Assembly had been rigged, no action was taken to follow this up (Nicolson, pp. 150–51).

83. *Actes du Conseil Suprême. Recueil des résolutions* (Paris, Imprimerie Nationale, 1934–35), No. 4, Jan. 12, 1919; No. 12, Jan. 12, 1919 (hereafter cited as *Résolutions*).

84. Nicolson, p. 150.

85. On March 3 (*Résolutions* 141) the Council agreed to receive a Note on behalf of Nicholas. This was subsequently delivered by General Gvozdenović. On May 7 Wilson received a new plea for the admission of Montenegro and he urged the Council to decide the matter once and for all (*Résolutions* 416). Ten days later the entire issue was again unresolved and officially postponed. But the Council had, meantime, used a new formula—"Yugoslavia (including Montenegro)"—indicating that the matter was considered settled (*Résolutions* 482, May 15). On Sept. 26 Plamenac sent a note to the Council threatening the conclusion of a separate peace with Germany, Austria, and Bulgaria. On Dec. 1 the Council resolved unanimously to disregard the Plamenac communication (*Résolutions* 1521). With this, the "Montenegrin question" was resolved.

5. The Politics of Frontiermaking: Phase I

ON JANUARY 18, 1919, the peace conference finally opened. The dignified atmosphere of the Quai d'Orsay, where the opening session was held, belied of course the general pandemonium which had prevailed in Paris and Allied capitals for weeks. Clemenceau's ruthless, even cavalier, treatment of the lesser Allies that afternoon did not augur well for the newly established states.

Victory has seldom been conducive to self-abnegation on the part of victors. It was therefore not unnatural for the twenty-seven victors that convened at Paris to approach the problems of continental and global peace in terms of their special, all too often conflicting, interests. Yugoslavia and Italy proved no exception to the rule.

Even Wilson could not temper the stark reality of Allied cross-purposes, or indeed keep power politics from becoming the leit-motiv of the peace conference. The idea, so fashionable in the 1920s, of a conference seized by a "fatal two-mindedness," [1] with the idealism of the "new" diplomacy battling the cynicism of the "old," deserves continued attention today. In an age of limitless potential for human development or destruction, the key to stable peace may well lie in the spirit of approach. And if indeed 1919 marked "the high watermark of democracy in world history," [2] it would be well to remember that the recession of the tide began in part at Paris in that very year.

As one of the most complex and explosive issues at the peace conference, the Italo-Yugoslav controversy contributed its due share to the prevalence of power politics. The rivalry was naturally aggravated by the time lag between armistice and peace conference, for the intervening two months led to an intensification of

1. R. S. Baker, *Woodrow Wilson and World Settlement, 2* (3 vols. Garden City, N.Y., 1922), 128.
2. Hajo Holborn, *The Political Collapse of Europe* (New York, 1951), p. 96.

nationalist fervor on both sides of the Adriatic. In Italy the possibility for compromise waned with each passing week, while in Yugoslav lands popular passions were increasingly inflamed by the Italian military occupation. Had the conference, as originally expected, convened right after the armistice,[3] the bitter contest over Fiume might not even have arisen.[4]

As did most of the Allies, the Italians used each successive delay to propagandize their national program at home as well as abroad. And even after the conference had opened, time remained a vital political factor in Rome. The government insisted that Italian claims against Austria receive the same urgent consideration as French claims against Germany. But the conference brushed aside Italian issues until April. Thus, by concentrating first on the problems of Germany and the League of Nations, Clemenceau, Lloyd George, and Wilson compounded Italian disappointments and, unwittingly, encouraged nationalist agitation throughout Italy. As impatience gave way to frustration, Orlando and Sonnino became, in Charles Seymour's words, "more insistent as they observed the concessions which Wilson was obliged to make to the French and the British." [5] They began to look upon Germany and the League as diplomatic levers for obtaining concessions of their own in the Adriatic. And in Wilson—who had unfortunately failed to discuss the Treaty of London during his visit to Rome,[6]

3. For the reasons behind the delays, see Temperley, *Peace Conference, 1,* 238–45; Marston, *Peace Conference,* pp. 28–54.

4. Before, that is, the Italians made a formal claim to that city. Once Fiume had become an issue, as André Tardieu observed, "Italy's interest in the conference was far too much confined to the question of Fiume" (A. Tardieu, *The Truth about the Treaty,* Indianapolis, 1921, p. 101).

5. *House Papers, 4,* 433–34.

6. Wilson's visit was brief and chaotic. The occasion provided a golden opportunity for a thorough exploration of the Adriatic issues, including that of the London treaty, and both the President and the Italian government must clearly have known it. Yet both sides hesitated, partly because the schedule was overfilled with ceremonial functions, partly because neither side (particularly the President) wished to embarrass the other, and partly because Italian attitudes had not yet become fully crystallized. Thus, for example, in a speech in Rome before an enthusiastic audience Wilson pleaded for friendship between Italians and Yugoslavs, but deliberately failed to refer to the London treaty once. (See *New York Times,* Jan. 3, 1919.) One interesting sidelight of Wilson's trip pertains to a brief meeting between him and Bissolati, who had just resigned from the cabinet. The meeting was held at Bissolati's request and was arranged by the American embassy. Wilson

though he subsequently kept disapproving the secret treaties in general—they began to see an adversary rather than a friend.[7]

For the Yugoslavs the time lag was, paradoxically, a godsend. For while it is true that nationalist fervor had increased, the delay enabled them to come to Paris in the name of a new national state, whose establishment was their own internal work and not the product of inter-Allied politics.

Ever since 1919 both Yugoslavia and Czechoslovakia have been popularly portrayed as creations of "Versailles," a view that even most scholars have failed to dispel. Yet as Victor Mamatey recently pointed out, by the time the peace conference finally convened, "the Habsburg Empire had been dead for over two months, and its heirs were already well entrenched. . . . The Allies made their independence possible by crushing the main obstacle to it: the military might of the Central Powers." [8] But the initiative and main effort in each case came from within and not from the Entente. By January 1919 the reality of the Yugoslav union was not questioned by the Allies, despite their temporary refusal to extend it diplomatic recognition.[9]

Had the peace conference opened before the end of November, the union of Serbia, Montenegro, and the Serbo–Croat–Slovene state proclaimed by the Narodno Vijeće in Zagreb would not yet have been effected.[10] In such circumstances Italy might well have raised the very issue of the union for sanction by the Allies. Had the conference opened before December 21,[11] the Yugoslavs would have been caught without a national government, with all the attendant implications. In this regard, the delay worked to their advantage.

---

attributed relatively little significance to it, but the interview doubtless irritated both Orlando and Sonnino. (For details see Albrecht-Carrié, pp. 81–85.)

7. As a result, they even tried to circumvent Wilson on occasion by negotiating directly with House, believing the latter to be more pliable than the President. See Nicolson, *Peacemaking*, pp. 167–68.

8. Victor S. Mamatey, *The United States and East Central Europe, 1914–1918* (Princeton, 1957), p. 380.

9. Ibid., p. 384.

10. Given the complete breakdown of communications within the country and the multiplicity of negotiations in Geneva, Zagreb, Belgrade, and Cetinje, the union could hardly have been proclaimed before Dec. 1.

11. The day on which the first national government was installed.

In other respects, however, the situation was the reverse. Conditions throughout the Italian military occupation zone deteriorated rapidly in the two months after the armistice. The continued blockade caused hardships for the economy as a whole. Ultimately, while neither peace nor war prevailed, the government and the country at large could hardly begin performing the routine tasks required for a normal, stable national existence. Moreover, with the problem of national frontiers unresolved, the country was bound to remain politically and psychologically vulnerable to basic instability.

Preparation of the territorial case and the official memoranda was assigned from the outset to the Yugoslav delegation in Paris.[12] In this vital task, as in the matter of recognition and representation at the conference table, the delegation soon split into factions which fed on personal as well as regional differences. It also began to rely on Belgrade to resolve almost any impasse, thus relinquishing much of the initiative that it could normally have used. While it is natural for a peace delegation, not led by the head of government, to refer significant conflicts of opinion to the home government, unfortunate consequences can arise if the government often fails to take decisive action. In the case of Belgrade, because of internal political predicaments, it became increasingly the pattern (especially after June 1919) to refer the problems back to Paris. Thus an unfortunate cycle was gradually set in motion, and when both government and delegation tried to avoid making unpleasant decisions, as was to happen within several months, a national policy simply did not exist. But the consequences of the delegation's actions were at first not evident, largely because immediate pressures in Paris did not permit a prior discussion of strategy and tactics.

Even before the delegation had formally convened, General

12. The precise date of the government directive to the delegation is not certain. It does not appear on the "Directive to the Royal Peace Delegation" (TP, F38), though it was received in Paris before Jan. 10. In addition to preparing the official memoranda, the delegation was also instructed to sponsor pro-Yugoslav propaganda in Paris, to prepare estimates of war damages for every region of the country, to prepare materials regarding Yugoslav maritime needs and the former Austro-Hungarian fleet which was to be claimed "without reference to territorial decisions made by the peace conference," etc. It is interesting to note from this document that the government expected the peace conference to last no more than 3 months.

Pešić was invited by the headquarters of Marshal Foch to indicate the extent of Yugoslav territorial demands. In consultation with Pašić, Trumbić, and Ribarž, General Pešić submitted to the French army command a map showing Yugoslav frontier claims on all sides. In reporting the French reaction at the first delegation meeting on January 10, Pešić told his colleagues that the French Chief of Staff "doubts that we can get Trieste and Pola, and that it would be well if our Kingdom did not ask for these parts." [13]

Pešić's report at this session actually followed a preliminary exchange between Trumbić and Pašić, with the former raising the subject of territorial claims and the latter replying that he had already prepared two memoranda on his own which he now wanted to submit to those present. As a result of the French warning about Trieste and Pola, however, discussion turned to the western frontier with Italy, and the delegates agreed to ask for a line which would run along the "old Austrian-Italian frontier, and to ask arbitration for Gorizia, Trieste and western Istria." [14]

This important decision, reached on the spur of the moment in response to the French warning, was taken without calculating its broader implications. The principle of adopting arbitration as a means for resolving territorial disputes had not been previously agreed upon, nor indeed explored. When the arbitration formula was hurriedly adopted for Trieste, Gorizia, and western Istria, no one suspected that a basic question had been raised.

During the days that followed the first delegation meeting, the Yugoslavs' attention was repeatedly distracted from the problem of frontiers. Conference representation, disquieting reports about local conflicts in the Banat and the Italian occupation zone, and news that the Regent would leave Belgrade on January 16 and arrive at Toulon on the 20th or the 21st all required immediate consideration.[15] Still Pašić and Trumbić managed to prepare drafts for the territorial memorandum which they submitted for study to the delegates on the 15th.[16] These were discussed over the next two days, but without any concrete result.

On the morning of Saturday the 18th, the day the peace confer-

13. Zap., *1*, 3 (K&H, p. 20).
14. Ibid.
15. Ibid., p. 12 (K&H, p. 24).
16. Ibid., p. 11 (K&H, p. 24).

ence opened, the delegation met again to discuss the problem of frontiers. After a lengthy but inconclusive debate, Trumbić suggested that the delegation, in prior consultation with Belgrade, petition the Allied governments to end all military occupation in the Adriatic region as provided for in the Armistice of November 3. The request, Trumbić explained, should be based on two arguments: 1) that the occupation had originally been directed against Austria-Hungary, which now no longer existed and could not, therefore, pose a threat to the Allies; and 2) that the occupation had lost its raison d'être with the establishment of the Yugoslav state, a state now fully capable of maintaining order in the region.[17]

Vesnić objected to Trumbić's proposal because a) it was doomed to failure, and b) it might irritate the Allies. The delegation, he said, should take steps against Italian military policies in Dalmatia and lodge a protest against Italy's disregard of armistice provisions. But before taking any action, the delegation should first collect all available data regarding Italian infringements on civilian rights in Dalmatia. Meanwhile, he would remain "decisively opposed to Mr. Trumbić's proposal" for demanding Italian evacuation.[18]

Bošković heartily seconded Vesnić, while Pašić simply ruled that the proposal be referred to Belgrade. Before discussion on this item ended, Smodlaka rose in defense of Trumbić, arguing that an end to Italy's occupation in Dalmatia ought certainly to be asked.

The same afternoon Pašić, Trumbić, and Vesnić went to the Quai d'Orsay to attend the opening conference session, and following dinner, the delegation reconvened at 9 P.M.[19] On this occasion some underlying principles of Yugoslav policy were for the first time brought up at length.

Turning to the question of frontiers after a brief report on the ceremonies at the Quai d'Orsay, Pašić opened the discussion by referring specifically to the map General Pešić had turned over to Foch's staff. This prompted Smodlaka to declare, quite solemnly,

17. In this masterful document (TP, F3) Trumbić managed to abstain from mentioning Italy even once.

18. Zap., *1*, 15–16 (K&H, p. 26).

19. Present were Pašić, Trumbić, Vesnić, Bošković, Smodlaka, Ribarž and General Pešić.

that Yugoslav demands had to "adhere strictly to the ethnographic boundaries of our nation." The General's map, he said, set a dangerous precedent because it included areas not inhabited by Yugoslavs "in a measure sufficient to claim [them] under the principle of nationality." If Yugoslav demands were to exceed ethnic boundaries, "we will facilitate and lend justification to Italian claims in Dalmatia and will, moreover, incur retribution in the future."[20]

To this Pašić retorted that

> it is important to adhere to the principle of nationality, but even from this point of view our claims are justified and to the ultimate limit of possibility this principle will be maintained. Italian claims against us, as an Allied country, cannot be equated with our demands against enemies. Our demands for a rectification of the frontier with Bulgaria do not violate that principle, as is also the case with our claims in the Banat, where we are in conflict with the Rumanians who have no right to the Banat, if one holds strictly to the principle of nationality. A political frontier cannot be drawn strictly along an ethnographic line, because the nationalities are mixed, and as much as we might receive of a foreign element so much of ours will have to go to others.[21]

Thereupon General Pešić asked that the future strategic needs of the country be fully kept in mind, adding, not without a cynical note, that strategic criteria "will govern the delegates of all countries at the peace conference." It would be an error, concluded the General, to begin with minimum demands, a proposition immediately seconded by Bošković and Ribarž.

Thus on the day the peace conference opened the Yugoslavs stood on the threshold of basic disagreements. With Trumbić generally agreeing with Smodlaka on the principle of ethnic frontiers, two clear groupings emerged from the discussion. When four days later the same subject was again raised, the lines of division became somewhat more blurred. Žolger, who had previously kept aloof, suddenly demanded that Ivnica in Styria be claimed because the whole area, though Germanized in recent times, was actually

20. Zap., *1*, 17 (K&H, p. 27).
21. Ibid., p. 18 (K&H, p. 27).

Slovene—besides being quite rich in mines. Surprisingly, Ribarž, who only four days earlier opposed presenting "minimum" demands, rebuked his fellow Slovene on the grounds that Ivnica "is German" and that it should not be claimed for its mines lest a similar pretext be used by other states, especially Italy, for claiming strictly Yugoslav regions.[22] Before general debate could develop, Pašić again intervened, this time ruling that the specific case be given to the experts for further study.

Then Pašić turned to a bigger theme. He had just been to see Marshal Foch, from whom he gathered, exactly as had General Pešić, "that we cannot ask for Trieste and Pola." [23] That was not all. In the course of their conversation, reported Pašić, Foch suddenly asked, "How would it be if Fiume became a free city?", to which Pašić replied, "This absolutely cannot be," because Fiume is "the only port for our state." [24] As though to allay the fears of his Croat colleagues, Pašić added that he had succeeded in convincing the Marshal, and there would be no more talk about Fiume as a free city.

Next, General Pešić reported on a conversation with General Franchet d'Esperey, quoting the French commander in the Balkans as declaring that Italy would insist only on Zara and readily give up the rest of Dalmatia.

Trumbić did not directly react to either report. Having decided to reopen discussion about governing principles, he turned to a separate topic. The Regent, Trumbić pointed out, had just issued a proclamation, countersigned by every member of the cabinet, stating that Yugoslav territorial policy would adhere strictly to the principle of nationality. This proclamation obviously bound the peace delegation. Though he did not say so, Trumbić now addressed his colleagues not only as a fellow delegate but as Foreign Minister and member of the cabinet as well. He ended by categorically insisting on adherence to Alexander's proclamation in letter and spirit combined.

Pašić, as though personally challenged, countered that the delegation had scrupulously observed the principle of nationality in

22. Ibid., p. 20 (K&H, p. 28).
23. Ibid.
24. Ibid.

its work thus far, adding that if General Pešić's controversial map violated that principle "somewhere," necessary corrections would be made. But he warned again that the principle of nationality was not susceptible to implementation everywhere; and if the Yugoslavs had to give up Slav villages here and there, they would also have to take foreign villages in exchange. The Regent's proclamation, he concluded, was a statement of intentions which would be followed wherever possible. It would guide the delegation and no nation would adhere to it more faithfully than "we." For the moment, Trumbić let it go at that.

Next day the same conflict broke out again.[25] Pašić began by warning that an Allied request for the Yugoslav memorandum could come any moment and that, therefore, agreement must be reached quickly. General Pešić's map, said Pašić, "is not the official definitive proposal of the Delegation . . . but, in general, it can serve as a basis . . ." [26] This said, Pašić proceeded to a detailed presentation of his proposed boundary lines in Bulgaria, the Banat, Bačka, and Baranja. With regard to Slovenia, he said, "we should adopt the frontier projected by Dr. Ribarž, while in regard to Italy, where we must come to agreement, I wish to hear your views." [27]

Was this a maneuver to gain Slovene support and, if possible, to isolate Trumbić? Pašić's main interest lay after all in Bulgaria and, in the second place, in the Banat. He had even personally prepared the Bulgarian memorandum—"About Relations with Bulgaria and Rectification of the Frontier" [28]—which he now read to the delegates for their approval. More revealing, however, was the following remark, made during his general exposé about eastern frontiers: "We are not thinking of punishing the Bulgarians territorially; we hope that they too will become wise for once *and join our union.*" [29]

There can be little doubt that Pašić tried to establish himself

25. Present at the session of Jan. 23 were Pašić, Trumbić, Vesnić, Žolger, Bošković, Smodlaka, Ribarž, and General Pešić.

26. Zap., *1*, 23 (K&H, p. 29).

27. Ibid., p. 24 (K&H, p. 30).

28. This document was officially submitted to the peace conference under the same title.

29. Zap., *1*, 23 (K&H, p. 29). Italics mine.

as the final arbiter of territorial policy in the east and the northeast. In this he wanted no interference from Trumbić or anyone else. The Slovenes, from his point of view, could have whatever they wanted in return for supporting, or at least not opposing, him in the east. Subtly, he began to curry their favor by adopting the Ribarž line in toto. In the west, however, he was not going to solicit *only* Trumbić's views about Italo-Yugoslav frontiers and thus jeopardize whatever control he had over the unpredictable and generally hostile foreign minister.

Trumbić sensed his antagonist's trend of thought, for he countered with a maneuver clearly designed to forestall a special Serbo-Slovene arrangement within the delegation and to maintain his own control over frontier decisions on all sides. He returned, first of all, to the theme of the Regent's proclamation—concerning strict adherence to the principle of nationality—ending, in effect, by declaring that the Yugoslavs must "ask only for the ethnographic frontiers of our people." [30] Then, as a direct challenge to Pašić (and indirectly to Bošković and General Pešić), he demanded that the delegates consult the ethnographic experts. "We are not sufficiently informed about this matter," said Trumbić, "and could not make a definitive judgment without such expert opinion about our ethnographic frontiers." [31] Specifically, he suggested hearing the views of Cvijić, Aleksandar Belić, and Jovan Radonić (experts for the Banat, Bačka, Baranja, and Bulgaria), hoping, quite possibly, to embarrass Pašić through the testimony of the leading Serbian scholars in the field.

What followed was a contest of wills and a test of political strengths. Pašić stated that the matter was urgent and that referring it to the experts would involve a loss of precious time. In his opinion, moreover, the delegates were political personages who should have been well acquainted with the views of such experts as Cvijić, whose findings on Balkan ethnography had already been published in his various writings. To depend on the experts at this point would have been tantamount to avoiding political responsibility. While he (Pašić) had no objection to the principle of consulting experts, he felt it should be done quickly and without any intention of taking refuge in their views.

30. Ibid., p. 26 (K&H, p. 30).
31. Ibid. The quotations that follow are taken from the same minute.

Vesnić echoed the same line. "We are here to attend a political Congress," and to submit a map proposing specific frontiers whose basis should be ethnographic. "But it goes without saying that these frontiers must be [drawn] . . . so as to assure a peaceful existence to the new state." The map, he thought, should be accompanied by "the briefest possible written elaboration of our claims, without engaging in lengthy academic explanations." Next, General Pešić. We must hurry, he said. The delegates are expert enough to resolve these questions. The experts are only their assistants.

Then Ribarž! The delegates, said the Slovene also, are expert enough to settle the matter themselves. Where Bulgarian frontiers were concerned, little help could be expected from the technical experts, for they could not even agree on the basic ethnographic data to be used. This was true of Bulgarian and other foreign ethnographers as well. The whole frontier issue was urgent and required immediate resolution.

But Trumbić did not budge. The experts had to be consulted, "especially in view of the mentioned proclamation." Smodlaka, as before, rose to his support. The map General Pešić gave the French could not be adopted under any circumstances, for it violated the principle of nationality. Since the delegates could not agree, all the more reason to consult the experts.

Vesnić objected once again. The delegates could not follow the experts' views since they alone carried political responsibility. Concluded Vesnić, "I do not wish . . . ever to protect myself with someone else's opinion. The proclamation enunciates a principle which we have already proclaimed long ago and by which we still adhere. If we do not agree on details, neither will the experts. Men charged with such a lofty and delicate mission must be prepared to bear responsibility for their work." [32]

And so on. But as Trumbić would not be swayed, Pašić and Vesnić in the end gave in. They insisted, however, on a curious formula by which Bošković, Žolger, General Pešić, Ribarž, and Smodlaka would meet next morning with the six senior experts of the ethnographic section [33] to draw up a precise ethnographic map of the Yugoslav people. Pašić, Vesnić, and Trumbić were not to attend.

32. Ibid., pp. 28–29 (K&H, p. 31).
33. Cvijić, Belić, Stanojević, Radonić, Mackovšek, and Tihomir Djordjević.

Consideration of frontiers was resumed on January 26. The day before, a telegram had arrived from Belgrade relaying Slovene complaints, mainly Kramer's, about alleged sacrifices imposed on Slovene territory. Pašić read this telegram in which the cabinet also instructed the delegation to draw a precise boundary with Italy, "adhering as far as possible to the principle of nationality." [34] This was followed by a message from Cvijić, asking the delegates to consult the ethnographic section before editing the final memoranda. Cvijić and his colleagues evidently feared that their opinions would be mostly disregarded. For at the meeting of delegates and experts on the 25th, while an ethnographic map was indeed drawn up, the experts were told nothing about the final claims that would be officially presented to the Allies.

Pašić in fact now declared that, since the views of the experts had been obtained (!), the delegates should immediately turn to working out the various claims. But with regard to Bulgaria he asked the adoption of General Pešić's original line, save for a correction around Pernik. Bošković, who had also prepared a memorandum on Bulgarian frontiers, went a step further. He argued that all Yugoslav claims against Bulgaria involved ethnically Serbian areas and demanded a pledge by the delegation that claims against Bulgaria be declared sine qua non. To this Trumbić took strong exception, fearing that categorical insistence on rectification of the Serbian-Bulgarian frontier would tend to open the explosive issue of Macedonia. He agreed on the need for greater strategic security vis-à-vis the Bulgarians, especially for the safety of Serbian railroads, but he was opposed to basing these claims on the grounds of ethnic justice. Nor would he agree to treating the Bulgarian case as a sine qua non or in any way differently from other frontiers. In view of the differences that had emerged, he now proposed to refer this matter to Belgrade.

Ribarž and Smodlaka, as well as Pašić, agreed that the main argument should be military and strategic rather than ethnic. Vesnić thereupon asked for the immediate adoption of the proposed line along Bulgaria, adding that as far as Macedonia was concerned, "this is a question which will never arise." [35]

34. Zap., *1*, 31 (K&H, p. 32).
35. Ibid., p. 33 (K&H, p. 33).

Vesnić had barely finished when Smodlaka offered a bold plan of his own. Fearing that any Yugoslav demand against Bulgaria that might be interpreted as excessive, i.e. not based on nationality, would only encourage the Italians to press their own excessive demands, Smodlaka proposed the following: let the Yugoslavs take only what is *absolutely* necessary for strategic security, but as a political gambit, let them merely describe their strategic needs and leave it to the peace conference to determine the details of the actual frontier with Bulgaria. Pešić and Pašić, he said, wanted to include some areas not indispensable to Yugoslav security, including pockets of population where Serbian national consciousness had not developed. "As we behave towards the Bulgarians," he concluded, "so the Italians will behave towards us . . ."[36]

To this General Pešić retorted that no one could tell whether the claimed population would or would not vote for Serbia. But everyone knew that they were Serbs, and that included the experts. The proposed line resulted from extensive work done since 1917 by the Serbian ministers of foreign affairs and war, as well as by the General Staff. Smodlaka would not accept this, arguing that the delegation could not be bound by earlier Serbian studies. Circumstances had changed and so had the government and ministers. The ideas of the "Serbian" foreign minister—Pašić—were not shared by the current incumbent and the latter indeed agreed with Smodlaka's proposal to let the conference decide the Bulgarian frontier.

For the moment, this brought discussion to an end.[37] As no substantive agreement could be reached, the delegates decided to refer the entire matter to Belgrade. If the government failed to act before the Allies asked for an official Yugoslav memorandum on Bulgaria, they agreed to put forth the Pašić-Pešić line.

The last days of January gradually moved toward a showdown within the delegation. On the 28th a meeting was convened to continue mapping out frontier claims, and at the outset Bošković

36. Ibid., p. 34 (K&H, p. 33).

37. At this session Trumbić was appointed, at his own request, Yugoslav delegate to the Commission on Harbors, Railroads, and Waterways, and Vesnić to the Commission for the League of Nations. Trumbić requested the appointment in order to participate in the negotiations about the former Austro-Hungarian fleet.

demanded an assurance that, during the past two days, no one had
told the French that the Yugoslavs would be willing to reduce
claims against Bulgaria or accept whatever the peace conference
decided. Pašić, who the day before had again seen Foch, assured
him that no such thing had been intimated. The discussion then
proceeded to the Banat, Bačka, Baranja, Slovenia, and Italy, with
the aid of maps prepared by the ethnographic section.

In regard to the Banat, Pašić again took the position that a political frontier could not coincide with a strictly ethnic line, because,
as he rightly observed, self-determination could not be practically
implemented. The German element, for example, could not be
joined to Austria or Germany, while Rumanians, Magyars, and
Serbs were frequently so intermixed that complete separation was
practically out of the question. If the delegation, he argued, would
adopt General Pešić's line in the Banat, a number of Rumanians
would enter the Yugoslav state, but in turn many Yugoslavs would
go to Rumania. Bošković promptly endorsed Pašić's proposal. So
did Ribarž.

Smodlaka, however, again raised objections of principle, urging
the delegation to "ask only what is clearly ours and then not budge
an inch." [38] As with Bulgarian frontiers, he was opposed to proposing a specific line, preferring to leave that to the peace conference.
The inclusion of substantial foreign elements would weaken the
new state and, as he greatly feared, sow the seeds of future conflict.
Since, however, the government directive required specific lines
and the General Staff had already submitted a map to the French
"with the approval of the majority of delegates at that," he now
thought it would be silly to change their minds in a matter of a few
days. The delegates were therefore forced to keep the Pešić line
(in the Banat), but he would insist that the memorandum specify
that the Yugoslavs wanted only "our national territory."

Vesnić thought the Pešić line reasonable and, so far as he knew,
the French did too. Thereupon the delegates voted to adopt it for
the official memorandum, though no decision was taken on Smodlaka's proviso. [39] Discussion regarding the rest of the Hungarian

38. Zap., *1*, 42 (K&H, p. 36).

39. Ibid., pp. 42–43 (K&H, pp. 36–37). The Pešić line of division with Rumania
ran from the Serbo-Bulgarian-Rumanian frontier between the village of Akcar and

frontier followed the same course and agreement was speedily reached.[40]

When the Slovene-Austrian frontier came up for review, Smodlaka asked that Klagenfurt (Celovec) and Villach (Beljak) be excluded from Yugoslav claims, because a demand for these "German" towns would mean "certain war." Trumbić disagreed. Both towns were important railroad centers and should be claimed openly, as he saw it, on economic and strategic rather than ethnic grounds. Ribarž and Žolger asked that these towns be claimed on historic grounds as well, to which Bošković (!) responded that Slovene wishes in this matter must be respected by everyone present.

After two and a half hours, the meeting recessed for lunch. Reconvening at 5:30 P.M., the delegates now turned to Italy. Within minutes they agreed to abide by the earlier decision to claim the line of the old Austro-Hungarian frontier to Monfalcone, with arbitration for Trieste and western Istria. When Smodlaka took the floor, he proposed making Trieste a free city and granting western Istria to Italy outright, on the basis of nationality—a dramatic and far-reaching suggestion in itself. But it remained for Trumbić to drop the real bombshell of the day.

---

the river Skomlija, along the Danube toward Brufak (on the right bank), thence northward along the mountain-ridge across the river Nira through the village of Iladija (which was assigned to Rumania), thence to Gornja (assigned to the Serbian side), across the river Berzava to a point east of Nim Bagzan; thence northwest to Izgar (assigned to Yugoslavia), to Bazias, Temes, Bekes, and Romon Benesek (assigned to Rumania), to Segenthem (to Yugoslavia), and thence north to the river Maros, between the town of Arad and the village of Zadarlac. For the text of General Pešić's memoranda, prepared for the French General Staff, see K&H, pp. 312–25.

40. The proposed frontier with Hungary ran from the Yugoslav-Rumanian frontier on the Maros, along that river to its confluence with the Tisza (Theiss); thence along the Tisza to a point north of Hargos, thence westward toward Malukit (assigned to Hungary), across the Danube; from the Danube, southwest to a point near the village of Szederkeny (assigned to Hungary), thence west toward Babocka, northwest toward Bereny (assigned to Yugoslavia), and again west toward the river Mur; along the Mur to the mouth of the river Lendav and thence due north to the river Raab, east of St. Gotthard; along the Raab to the old Austro-Hungarian frontier to Illoch (assigned to Yugoslavia), thence southwest to the river Mur, to its confluence with the river Sulem, south of the town of Leibnitz; thence west to Radellberg and a line running south of Wolfnitz and St. Donat, and north of Villach, from which point the line ran south along the mountain-ridge to the town of Pontafel.

Long apprehensive that the Allies, especially the French, might give in to Italian demands for strategic security in the Adriatic [41] in return for Italian support elsewhere, Trumbić had been brooding over possible ways of countering Sonnino's claims. Since everyone at Paris expected the Italians to claim most of northern Dalmatia and a majority of the islands—on both historic and strategic grounds—Trumbić had prepared a countermove of his own. He first announced it to the delegation on the 28th, and on the 29th it was discussed in full detail.

The plan was as simple as it was bold. Let the government, Trumbić asked, authorize the delegation to propose in its memorandum to the peace conference the complete neutralization of the whole Adriatic, in war and in peace, under the protection of the League of Nations. By neutralization he meant excluding the war fleets of all nations from the Adriatic and expressly prohibiting fortifications and military installations along the entire coast.

As arguments in favor of neutralization, Trumbić cited these:

1. The Italians claim that their Adriatic coastline is devoid of protective islands, unsuitable for adequate fortification, in short, vulnerable to attack. Since the eastern coast is endowed with an excellent physical configuration, a multitude of islands and maritime channels, the Italians have tried to gain control of part of the eastern coast through the Treaty of London. Their strategic reasoning has met with considerable sympathy abroad and there is the danger that they may be given territories on the eastern coast, and especially the islands.

2. Neutralization of the whole Adriatic would place the Yugoslav nation on the same *niveau* with Italy. It would correspond to the Yugoslavs' best interests, and even if they received the entire ex-Austro-Hungarian littoral, without neutralization, they would still be inferior in position to Italy, a great power with a strong fleet that greatly outnumbers their own.

3. Neutralization would appear as the best, indeed the only,

41. On Jan. 26 he wrote to Pichon protesting the occupation of Dalmatia by Italians alone and asking that Serbs be admitted to the region as they had been to the Banat. On Jan. 29 Pichon replied, saying that this whole matter rested with General Diaz and that the French government could do nothing about it. See B. Krizman, "Iza Kulisa Vijećanja Naše Delegacije," *Slobodna Dalmacija,* April 26, 1956.

means for protecting the coast and the islands, in time of peace, against possible chicanery and pressure from the Italian fleet, and in time of war, against outright attack. It would also be the best manner for implementing the idea of a free Adriatic Sea, already called for in the Corfu Declaration.

4. Neutralization would free the state from the heavy financial burdens normally required for safeguarding the coast.[42]

Considering the far-reaching implications of this proposal, not to mention the problem of obtaining Italian agreement, Trumbić could hardly expect complete and quick acceptance by the delegation. Still the degree of opposition he encountered was surprising, for Smodlaka turned out to be his lone supporter.

Vesnić rejected the plan out of hand, because it would, in his view, (1) involve a limitation of national sovereignty; (2) imply Yugoslav recognition that Italian claims, as put forth in the Treaty of London, were valid; and (3) mean giving up too early a tactical weapon for obtaining Italian agreement to complete and reciprocal neutralization. But the last point was not uppermost in Vesnić's mind, for he immediately added that even if the Italians agreed, this formula would involve a "great and serious sacrifice of our moral and political position in the future international community."[43]

Pašić and Ribarž also objected and proposed submitting the plan to Belgrade. Significantly, neither man was willing to enclose a delegation recommendation to the government.

Trumbić appears to have been shocked by the reception his plan evoked. He said little in the debate. Smodlaka, however, argued fiercely, asking his colleagues pointedly, "is our position so difficult that this formula must be adopted? It is!"[44]

The majority, however, had its way. The Trumbić neutralization plan would be sent to Belgrade with a note putting forth the conflicting points of view but without a specific recommendation, thus killing it in channels. And so the first proposal for a Yugoslav grand gesture to break the Adriatic deadlock came to naught.

42. Zap., *1*, 46–47 (K&H, p. 38).
43. Ibid., p. 48 (K&H, p. 39).
44. Ibid.

While the Yugoslavs were thus hammering out their territorial case, the peace conference gradually began to tackle the myriad of problems that beset the world. But no one knew when each problem would come up. With their anterooms invaded by a relentless procession of advisers, advocates, and special pleaders, even the leading statesmen began to work at cross-purposes, not to mention the attending armies of diplomats, delegates, generals, technical experts, journalists, and various political adventurers, who had all descended upon Paris. In this atmosphere,[45] at once so promising and so forbidding, the lesser states were at a disadvantage. Actual decision-making power rested with the Council of Ten, of which they were not a part. The Council in turn, so unwieldy that on March 24 its functions were taken over by the Big Four, faced not only the task of producing treaties of peace but also that of administering the affairs of war-torn Europe from one day to the next.

When would Balkan frontiers be discussed? No one knew for sure. The Yugoslavs assumed that it could happen at any moment and set out immediately to explore the attitudes of the Allies. Pašić's talks with Foch, as well as those of Trumbić with Pichon, Nicolson,[46] and others, were designed to sound out and to influence both the British and the French. Both the British and the French were favorable to the Yugoslavs up to a point—to the point of not having to denounce the Treaty of London and their commitments to Italy.

The unknown quantity was the United States. How far would Wilson be willing (and able) to press Sonnino, Lloyd George, and Clemenceau? Wilson, no doubt, felt genuine sympathy for the Yugoslav cause and equally genuine distaste for the secret treaties. But would he champion their cause as a test case for self-determination, if his closest Allies did not go along? And could he break down Italian insistence on implementing the Treaty of London?

45. See Nicolson's memorable "Scenario of the Peace Conference," in *Peacemaking*, pp. 152–56.

46. Trumbić lunched with Nicolson on Jan. 30. On the 24th Nicolson had also seen Vošnjak. He apparently liked neither one, calling the Croat a "gloomy man" and the Slovene "very imperialistic" (pp. 248, 253).

Wilson's attitude thus became the main problem in Yugoslav eyes. Yet no understanding of Wilson's involvement in the Yugoslav-Italian conflict can be complete without a glance at the attitudes of his advisers and the evolution of American thinking on this entire problem.

As has already been noted, prior to 1917, American officialdom knew little about Southern Slav nationalism and the Yugoslav movement. The United States' entry into the war changed this picture considerably.[47] A fairly systematic effort was undertaken to gain information about various parts of the world, including the Balkans, in response to the challenge of American wartime responsibilities. A concerted effort to gather information and materials about the Balkans for the purpose of formulating specific policies was made by a group of scholars and political and territorial experts, established under the overall supervision of Colonel House in the summer of 1917. The Inquiry,[48] as this body came to be known, had been called together specifically in order to prepare advance positions that the United States should adopt at the peace conference following the end of the war.

During their first year of activity the Inquiry experts (many of whom came to Paris in 1919 as members of the American Commission to Negotiate the Peace) tended to echo rather than initiate official Washington policy. Thus in 1917, at the time when there was no official American inclination to even contemplate the creation of an independent Southern Slav state, the first Inquiry report, dated December 22, 1917, simply stated that "no dismemberment of the [Austro-Hungarian] Empire is intended." [49] This report paid greater attention to Italian aspirations, recommending that Trieste be given to Italy. But this did not imply approval of the Treaty of London program as such, for the Trieste proposal was followed up with a specific warning that the United States should not yield to "those larger ambitions [of Italy] along

47. For further details, see Mamatey, *The United States and East Central Europe,* pp. 77 ff., 258, 314–15, and passim.
48. For the organization and work of the Inquiry, see *FRUS-PPC, 1,* 9–118; Lawrence E. Gelfand, *The Inquiry: American Preparations for Peace, 1917–1919* (New Haven, 1963).
49. *FRUS-PPC, 1,* 48.

the eastern shore of the Adriatic for which we can find no substantial justification." [50]

The Inquiry held to this general line through the months that
followed Wilson's Fourteen Points and endorsed neither the
creation of a Yugoslav state nor the dissolution of the Habsburg
empire until the latter program became part of official Allied war
aims in the summer of 1918. During the last few months of the
war the Inquiry began to think seriously and favorably about a
Yugoslav state. By the time of the Austro-Hungarian collapse, most
of the American specialists in charge of Central European, Danubian, and Adriatic affairs—including Dean Charles Haskins and
Professors Dana Munro, W. E. Lunt, Charles Seymour, and Robert
Kerner—had become ardent advocates of a "Yugoslav solution."
From December 1918 on, these men, with a number of other colleagues, tenaciously clung to this solution as being consonant with
Wilsonian ideas as well as indispensable to a stable peace in Central Europe and the Balkans.

Their impact on Wilson and American policy cannot be under-
estimated, for the Inquiry served as the foundation of American
territorial policies throughout the peace conference.[51] The report
of January 21, 1919, for example, spelled out a policy for the
Adriatic which, in effect, called for recognition of the Yugoslav
state, while at the same time opposing Italian expansion in the
eastern Adriatic.

A significant aspect of this report was its approach to the Treaty
of London. It generally reflected the position formulated by David
Hunter Miller [52] and by Colonel House, who, on January 9, informed Orlando that he was opposed to giving any territory to
Italy which might "sow the seeds of future discord and war . . .
[for] if the Italians insisted upon the line drawn by the Pact of

50. Ibid., p. 50.

51. On Dec. 30, 1918, for example, the American peace delegation completed a
skeleton draft of the peace treaty in which Adriatic and Balkan problems were
defined in terms which the delegation largely upheld throughout the peace conference (ibid., p. 301).

52. Miller to House, Jan. 11, 1919: "any provision of the Pact of London . . .
which may be inconsistent with [inter-Allied agreements and Wilson's note of
November 5, 1918] were by that agreement abrogated and are no longer in force"
(Miller *Diary, 3,* 437).

London, which included Dalmatia, it would certainly mean war." [53] This attitude was obviously shared by the Inquiry experts [54] and represented the major premise upon which the January 21 report was based.[55]

The report included the following specific recommendations:

1. That an independent "federated" Yugoslavia be established, to consist of Serbia, Montenegro, and the Serbo–Croat–Slovene territory of the former Austro-Hungarian Empire: "It is from every standpoint desirable that the proposed state not be broken up . . . It is our conclusion that the Adriatic interests of these peoples and the size and strength of their immediate neighbors make it desirable that strong efforts be made to amalgamate the political and economic interests of the group."

2. That Yugoslav boundaries with Austria and Hungary be drawn up "so as to coincide roughly with the language boundary," with the exception of two areas, the Banat of Temesvar, where a compromise with Rumanian interests should be reached, and the Istria-Isonzo region: "The proposed line in Istria should be along the Carnic and Julian Alps' watershed and along the remaining high ridges down the peninsula. This deviation from the ethnic principle is justified primarily by economic considerations, giving to Italy those portions of the Slavic hinterland in Istria and the Isonzo valley deemed vital to the economic viability of Italian urban centers. The Yugoslavs are to be assigned the eastern coast of Istria, all of the Dalmatian coast and archipelago claimed by Italy as well as Fiume." This line of partition would place 370,000 Yugoslavs in Italy and leave 75,000 Italians in Yugoslavia. "Fiume should be assigned to Yugoslavia because it is vital to the interests of the latter, and likewise assures to the more remote hinterland, including Austria and Hungary, the advantages of two competing ports [Trieste and Fiume] under the control of different nations."

3. That Yugoslav frontiers with Rumania, Bulgaria, Greece, and Albania be based upon the old Serbian frontiers of 1913, with the exception of Albania, where Yugoslavia's claim in the north should

53. *House Papers, 4,* 437.
54. See D. W. Johnson, in E. M. House and C. Seymour, *What Really Happened at Paris* (New York, 1921), pp. 112–39.
55. See Miller *Diary, 4,* 235–39.

be approved. With regard to the rest of the country, Italy should obtain control over Valona, but only as a mandatory power rather than in sovereign possession, given the "doubtful" nature of the Italian claim.

In its entirety the report [56] represented, as Albrecht-Carrié observed, a "sane and fair-minded analysis of local situations" which struck a "moderate compromise" between ethnographic, economic, and strategic considerations.[57] It left room for specific negotiations despite insistence on the primacy of Wilsonian principles. But in setting the major lines of long-range American policy, it gave Wilson the strategic tools with which to approach the conference and in so doing it augured American support for the Yugoslavs, without which their case could not succeed.

While the reports of the American experts were being considered within the Commission to Negotiate the Peace, Yugoslav-Italian relations deteriorated rapidly as a result of events in Dalmatia and Slovenia, the recognition impasse, the naval blockade, and Italian activities in and around Montenegro.

The military occupation of Slav territories and the naval blockade against Austro-Hungarian lands continued after the peace conference opened. By mid-January, Belgrade began to complain that the blockade was inflicting serious damage on the Yugoslav economy.[58] Not only had exports of Dalmatian and Bosnian products and imports of needed foreign goods and equipment, which would normally have moved through Trieste, Fiume, and other Italian-controlled ports, almost completely stopped, but substantial quantities of perishable fruits and foods had begun to stockpile in Bosnia, Hercegovina, and Serbia, waiting to be moved via the Adriatic.

Belgrade protested against the blockade in Rome and in other Allied capitals as well. Sonnino, however, refused to budge, since the blockade was specifically sanctioned by the armistice. The

56. According to Nicolson, *Peacemaking*, pp. 106–07, these recommendations were backed by the British, and indeed an informal joint Anglo-American "position" may have been worked out at a meeting on Jan. 6 in, as Nicolson put it, "what had once been the *cabinets particuliers* of Maxim's."

57. Albrecht-Carrié, *Italy at the Paris Peace Conference*, p. 94.

58. Protić to Delegation, Belgrade, Jan. 17, 1919 (TP, F66).

blockade was yet another step in the campaign against Yugoslavia, which included withholding recognition, maintaining the occupation, encouraging separatist movements throughout Yugoslavia (especially in Montenegro), and was designed specifically to force Yugoslav concessions in the matter of the Austro-Hungarian fleet.

Protić's protestations against the blockade were simply ignored by Sonnino on the technical grounds that the Yugoslav government had not been recognized. Thus, when on January 11 the Yugoslav legation in Rome lodged a strong protest against the blockade at the Consulta,[59] the Foreign Ministry referred it to Orlando's office with the terse notation that the "Serbian" protest was made in the name of the "Legation of the Kingdom of Serbs, Croats, and Slovenes." [60] On January 22 the Vice-President of the Italian Council of Ministers, Giovanni Villa, informed the Foreign Minister that "the name assumed by the Serbian Legation is not authorized" and therefore nothing further could be added to the question of the blockade.[61] The Yugoslavs were given no reply.

In other quarters, however, new efforts were being launched in behalf of Italo-Yugoslav conciliation—by the Italian minority, which the year before had sponsored the Pact of Rome, and the Yugoslav minority around Seton-Watson and Steed.[62]

Significantly, one of the leading architects of this campaign was Bissolati. In one of the first public speeches since his resignation from the Italian government, Bissolati appealed to the government and to Italian public opinion to reconsider the whole problem of the Treaty of London. There are districts in the Treaty area, he said,

> whose vindication would lead Italy to draw a frontier contrary, as I believe, to her fundamental interests. . . . The question is wrongly posed when it is said that to oppose the annexation of Dalmatia—even of the part assigned to Italy by the Treaty of London—implies an abandonment of the sureties and guarantees to which our kinsmen are entitled

59. Note Verbale, Arch. Gab. 1168, Jan. 11, 1919 (MFA, Rome).
60. Foreign Ministry (Biancheri?) to Orlando, Jan. 19, 1919 (Arch. Gab. Tel. Part. 1044, MFA, Rome).
61. Villa to Foreign Ministry, Jan. 22, 1919 (Tel. Arr. 5388, MFA, Rome).
62. See Dinaricus, "Italy and Serbia," *New Europe, 10* (1919), 9–12.

where they are in tiny minorities. No, the question is whether, in the interest of Europe's safety against a fresh German menace and of a lasting peace, such guarantees should be secured by *means of annexation*. . . . But if Italy renounced the annexation of Dalmatia, she might obtain from Jugoslavia or from the Conference the joy of pressing to her heart the most Italian city of Fiume, which the Treaty of London renounced.[63]

While the Yugoslavs were not likely to consider Dalmatia as a *quid pro quo* for Fiume,[64] since they looked upon both as theirs, Bissolati's Milano speech offered a basis for possible agreement by suggesting the protection of minorities as a formula for breaking the deadlock. Though an unofficial gesture, it appeared as a step forward.

Bissolati's speech was similar in tone to the arguments of Seton-Watson, who did not, however, propose to give either Zara or Fiume to Italy. Seton-Watson and Wickham Steed, in some ways more influential than Bissolati or the *Corriere della Sera* group, were both close to the Foreign Office as members of Lord Northcliffe's wartime Crewe House staff. Steed, furthermore, could use the power of the *Times* and thus naturally enjoyed enormous prestige. Seton-Watson, on the other hand, both as a result of wartime services and his general reputation as an authority on Central and Eastern Europe,[65] came to play a fairly significant role at the conference. Nicolson records instances when Seton-Watson, for example, argued the Yugoslav case before the British delegation, insisting that the Yugoslavs be given Fiume and the hinterland. In

63."Italy and the League of Nations" (speech in Milano, Jan. 11, 1919), *New Europe, 10* (1919), v–vii, suppl.

64. According to the London *Daily Mail*, Jan. 15, 1919, Orlando was prepared to trade Dalmatia for Fiume, but was opposed in this by Sonnino. The story, emanating in Paris from an "unofficial Italian source," predicted an open break between the two, but was immediately and vigorously denied by the Italians. Imperiali to Sonnino, London, Jan. 15, 1919; and Sonnino to Imperial, Rome, Jan. 16, 1919 (*DDI*, pp. 468–69).

65. During the war Seton-Watson did much to establish contact between the Foreign Office and Masaryk, Beneš, Trumbić, and others. At the peace conference he did the same with regard to the British delegation. For his wartime role see H. Hanak, *Great Britain and Austria-Hungary during the First World War* (London, 1962), passim.

his own words, Nicolson and Allen Leeper "never moved a yard without previous consultation with experts of the authority of Dr. Seton-Watson who was in Paris at the time." [66] His advice, according to Wickham Steed, was sought upon Yugoslav-Italian, Yugoslav-Austrian, and Italo-Austrian frontiers,[67] and he was never long out of touch with the experts of the British as well as American delegations.

More than anything else Seton-Watson, Steed, and other partisans of the New Europe wished to bring about a new atmosphere in which Yugoslavs and Italians could return to the spirit of the Pact of Rome. In their view an Italo-Yugoslav reconciliation could take place only if Italy agreed to end the blockade and give up Dalmatia, and if the Yugoslavs renounced Trieste and western Istria. But which side should be the first to break the deadlock was of course the cardinal question. Since the Yugoslavs saw themselves as victims of Italian aggression, they were on the defensive and not prone to magnanimous gestures. The Italians, led by Sonnino, on the other hand, saw Italy victimized by Allies who refused to implement the Treaty of London, and they too were not likely to seek a rapprochement.

For the time being, therefore, the efforts of Bissolati, Steed, and Seton-Watson failed. But the groundwork they laid at the time the conference opened was not devoid of promise, and before long their efforts were to be renewed.

The wheels of the peace conference, meanwhile, were set in motion at the end of January. On the 31st the Yugoslavs were suddenly summoned before the Council of Ten to present their claims in the Banat.[68] On the same day they also received indication of favorable developments in the American camp.[69] Yet optimism

66. Nicolson, pp. 126, 231.

67. "R. W. Seton-Watson," typescript article prepared for the *Dictionary of National Biography*, written by Steed shortly before his death in 1956 (Steed Papers, Wootton-by-Woodstock, Eng.). Speaking of his own role, Seton-Watson observed: "I myself spent about four months in the *coulisses* of the Conference and made it my business to find out what the 'experts' were thinking and doing . . ." (*Treaty Revision and the Hungarian Frontiers*, p. 22).

68. At noon that day, Pašić told the delegation that the Yugoslavs had just been invited to appear before the Council at 3 P.M. (Zap., *1*, 50 [K&H, p. 39]).

69. That morning Pašić and Trumbić had received an encouraging cable from

with regard to the peace conference quickly resolving the deadlock between Italy and Yugoslavia was clearly premature.

Wilson, who had accepted the recommendations of the American experts' report of January 21, apparently decided to broach
the problem of the Treaty of London directly with Orlando and
Sonnino, in the hope of persuading them to give it up. Neither,
of course, had any intention of doing so. Quite the contrary, Steed,
who lobbied actively in the *coulisses*, "gathered" from a Rumanian
diplomat on the 26th that the Italians and Rumanians "had made
a compact to stand or fall together over the maintenance of the
Secret Treaties." [70] Small wonder then that Wilson's meetings with
the Italians went "very badly." On the 27th Wilson had a "stormy
interview" with Sonnino who, as Steed put it, "seems to have lost
his temper and to have gone to the length of telling Wilson not
to meddle in European affairs but to stick to his American last.
When referring to Sonnino, Wilson clenched his fist and used un-
parliamentary language." [71] Next morning, Sonnino, in turn, told
George Herron that he "not only rejected all idea of a compromise
upon the Secret Treaty of London, but talked of preparing for
another war a few years hence and declared that Italy must guard
herself against the Franco-Serbian Alliance that was certain to be
formed against her." [72]

---

the Yugoslav minister in Bern, who had been told by Stovall, the American
ambassador, that Wilson was anxious to end the conference quickly because of the
Bolshevik danger. Stovall, who had seen Wilson in Paris, "gave no hope to the
Italians and their claims because Wilson feels that these must be resolved by the
Peace Conference without regard to previously concluded agreements. . . . The
American ambassador also noticed a greater willingness on the part of the British
and the French to give in and this is a good sign. He asked me," the Yugoslav minister reported, "about our frontier demands and further asked whether we are
willing to make concessions in western Istria where the Slovenes are in a minority.
I answered that we ask only for the application of the principle of nationality and
Wilson's principle of the self-determination of peoples. He asked whether we would
permit transit across our territory to the Magyars and Austrians and give them
access to our harbors. I answered that so far as I knew we would make no difficulties for exports through Rijeka or any other port." (Jovanović to Pašić and
Trumbić, Bern, Jan. 30, 1919, TP, F66).

70. Steed,*Thirty Years, 2,* 273.
71. Ibid.
72. Ibid., p. 275.

The Yugoslavs knew none of this. When Pašić, Trumbić, and Vesnić went before the Council of Ten on January 31, they did not even know whether the discussion on the Banat would lead to a general review of Yugoslav territorial claims. It did not. But from the very first discussion on the Banat, it was clear that all Yugoslav claims, not just those affecting Italy, were in for a difficult time.

The January 31 session before the Big Ten produced a head-on clash between Yugoslavs and Rumanians, with the Council unable to untie the Gordian knot.[73] The main controversy revolved around the validity of the secret Treaty of Bucharest, which the Yugoslavs of course refused to accept since Serbia had neither been a party to the agreement nor indeed been informed of its text. But Sonnino adopted the tactic of lending wholehearted support to Rumania's claim, as much for the purpose of defending all of the secret treaties as for the purpose of merely harassing the Yugoslavs.

In the official Rumanian presentation, Bratianu claimed the whole Banat on three grounds: the validity of the secret treaty, the economic-geographic unity of the whole region, and the ethnic preponderance of 600,000 Rumanians over 400,000 Germans and 300,000 Serbs.

Vesnić, who preceded Pašić and Trumbić in presenting the Yugoslav case, countered with these arguments: the treaty "as far as we are concerned does not exist since we do not even know about it"; [74] the Yugoslavs want to see the Banat partitioned on the basis of national self-determination; the strategic security of Belgrade (exposed to attack from the west and the north, as well as from the east) makes possession of part of the Banat indispensable; and finally, the Serb-inhabited portions of the Banat have been historic centers of Serbian culture and intellectual activity, or, as Trumbić put it a few moments later, the Banat has "for centuries been the foyer of Serbian culture." [75] Trumbić also observed that the part claimed by Yugoslavia included 278,000 Serbs, 328,000 Germans, 251,000 Magyars and 266,000 Rumanians, thus challenging the ac-

73. For the minutes of the Council session, see *FRUS-PPC, 3,* 822–29. For a discussion of the Rumanian position see Spector, *Rumania,* pp. 79 ff.

74. Zap., *1,* 51 (K&H, p. 41). At this point Clemenceau intervened to say that the treaty could not have been kept a secret, but Pichon admitted that it had.

75. Ibid., p. 53 (K&H, p. 41).

curacy of Rumanian figures. Of the three component *comitats* of the Banat (Torontal, Temes, and Krasso), the Yugoslavs claimed the first two, convinced that this corresponded with the actual wishes of the populations concerned.[76]

Bratianu accused the Yugoslavs of proposing an "unnatural" partition of the Banat, demanding at the same time an immediate withdrawal of Serbian troops from the whole region and their replacement by an inter-Allied occupation force. Thereupon Clemenceau inquired whether the Rumanians would abide by a popular plebiscite, as suggested by Trumbić. The Rumanian answered firmly "no," adding that the entire question had already been settled by the secret treaty. After further prodding, Bratianu agreed at least to consider a plebiscite, though he remained adamant on the withdrawal of Serbian troops.

The Council session was thus inconclusive and the Allied statesmen decided the same day to refer the Banat problem to the territorial Commission on Rumanian Affairs. But at this first appearance the Yugoslavs, thanks partly to Bratianu's obstinate approach, made a favorable impression, presenting their position in moderate tones and with reasoned arguments. Their willingness to abide by a plebiscite scored a major point.

Yet, from their point of view, the "interview" had a most disagreeable side. They, as well as the Rumanians, had appeared not as partners of the alliance but rather as suppliants. They found the working method of the conference unpleasant for small states, since the promised equality between small and great states, whenever small-power interests were at stake, had not and indeed would not materialize.

Even the guarded optimism Pašić, Vesnić, and Trumbić felt because of the impression they had made before the Council on the 31st was soon to be dispelled. Within six days an angry telegram arrived from Belgrade informing them that the French command in the Balkans had ordered all Serb units to evacuate the Banat and make room for French troops. Protić's telegram threatened that the Yugoslavs would "not leave." [77] In fact, however, the government immediately ordered the Serb army to withdraw some

76. Later that evening the delegation reaffirmed the proposed Banat line.
77. Protić to Vesnić, Belgrade, Feb. 4, 1919 (No. 1091, TP, F66).

15 kilometers to a line beyond which it was not to "move another inch." But when, a few days later, Franchet d'Esperey ordered Mišić to effect complete withdrawal, the cabinet was thrown into panic. With its prestige, as well as that of the army, at stake and fearing open humiliation vis-à-vis the Rumanians, the government met in emergency session to draft a reply to the Allied commander. Unwilling to agree to evacuation, it finally asked d'Esperey to postpone executing the order until the peace conference had decided the fate of the Banat, implying that it would abide by a decision made in Paris. Nonetheless, warned Protić, "we fear conflict and bloodshed." [78]

On the diplomatic front back in Paris, things were not going well. On February 2 the Yugoslavs were suddenly invited to visit Pichon, the French Foreign Minister, at the Quai d'Orsay. Pašić, Trumbić, and Vesnić went, hoping possibly to learn something about the Banat. Instead, Pichon wanted to discuss the Adriatic and asked whether the Yugoslavs thought an agreement with Italy possible. But before they had a chance to reply, Pichon said: "We are bound by the agreement to Italy; neither Britain nor France can be disloyal and denounce the pact; it is up to Italy to disengage us from it. As your friends we wish to see agreement reached and that is why we are now interceding." [79]

The reference to the Treaty of London was disquieting at best. Was it meant as a warning that the Yugoslavs should not count on Britain and France? Or was it an effort to help them? It was hard to tell. The Yugoslavs replied cautiously. The London treaty could not be a basis for agreement, because it was made without them.[80] They were not asking for "concessions" from Italy but only what was right and just. When Pichon inquired as to their "minimum" demands, they outlined the entire western frontier: the whole of Friuli up to the Cormons–Gradisca–Monfalcone line to Italy; Trieste and the western Istrian coast to be submitted to arbitration; central and eastern Istria with Gorizia up to the Cormons–

---

78. Protić to Pašić (?), Belgrade, Feb. 17, 1919 (No. 1702, TP, F66).
79. Zap., *1*, 56 (K&H, p. 42).
80. Pašić told Pichon that Sonnino had recently asked him (Pašić) whether he would accept the treaty in principle, to which Pašić said flatly "no."

Gradisca–Monfalcone line to Yugoslavia. (Several days later Trumbić learned that Pichon thought this excessive.[81]) Pichon listened attentively to Pašić, Trumbić, and Vesnić, and took notes on everything they said. He repeated again that Britain and France were bound by the treaty and ended on the ominous note that, though both powers were anxious to facilitate an amicable agreement, "a settlement will be difficult to reach." [82]

The meeting lasted about 45 minutes. Less than an hour later, Pašić, Trumbić, and Vesnić met their anxious colleagues—Žolger, Bošković, Smodlaka, Ribarž, and General Pešić—and told them what had happened.

Then Trumbić asked for the floor. Without the slightest hint that a dramatic proposal was about to unfold, he began to speak in measured tones. Several conversations he had had lately with "Frazier, the first secretary of the American peace delegation, as well as this afternoon's talk with Pichon" [83] had given him the distinct "impression" that the Yugoslavs would soon receive an invitation from the Allies to submit the whole Yugoslav-Italian conflict to arbitration by President Wilson. The delegates should think seriously about this possibility. Such an invitation could mark a turning point in Yugoslav destinies at Paris.

Sensing that something important was afoot, even though Trumbić was being somewhat cryptic, everyone agreed that Wilson would be a "most favorable" arbiter. The pros and cons of the principle of arbitration and the question of submitting all the western territories or only a specific part were not discussed. The delegates for once made a quick decision: to cable the government for immediate instructions on a matter they unanimously deemed to be most urgent.

Trumbić had in effect asked the delegation to consider submitting the *entire* dispute with Italy to Wilson. His colleagues, without yet committing themselves to concrete action, seemed generally receptive to the idea. They had become conscious lately that Yugoslav problems were coming up for discussion and this put them under pressure to close ranks, so much so that between Jan-

81. Trumbić to Cabinet, Paris, Feb. 7, 1919 (TP, F66).
82. Zap., *1*, 58 (K&H, p. 42).
83. Ibid. (K&H, p. 43).

uary 31 and February 6, they hastily approved the final memorandum of claims.[84] The Banat hearings before the Council of Ten did not lead to an improvement in their position, while the interview with Pichon gave cause for further alarm. Foch and others had warned them not to ask for Trieste, western Istria, and Pola, and sacrifices seemed to be inevitable.

Still, Wilson was being sympathetic, and so long as he continued to enjoy the confidence of Yugoslavs everywhere, neither the delegation nor the government would be criticized for placing their trust in him. If Wilson then *made* the Yugoslavs accept a compromise, *he* would bear the blame and not the regime. The Serbs could not be charged with abandoning Croat and Slovene interests. The Croats and Slovenes could not be charged with giving in to the Serbs. In any event, no one could be expected to protect Yugoslav interests more than Wilson. From many points of view, therefore, Trumbić's proposal had appeal.

Trumbić had obviously talked with Arthur Hugh Frazier and Douglas W. Johnson in more detail than he indicated to the delegation. From his point of view, however, he had to be quite careful, for the idea of Wilson's arbitration was not his own. It came from the American side. Thus he wrote to the cabinet on February 7: "A serious American source [Frazier] suggested to me the idea of Wilson's arbitration. I was told that Wilson will soon be off to the United States. Whether he returns will depend on various circumstances. It is better for you [Yugoslavs] if your problems are settled while he is here." [85] Trumbić could not, of course, reply before sounding out the delegation. In addition to Frazier and Johnson, however, he had also held important discussions with Lansing, Wickham Steed, and Wilson himself.

Trumbić had no doubt used his meetings with Frazier and Johnson to discuss the question of recognition. The timing was propitious on several counts. The President, who was shortly to return to the United States, was anxious to bring the Yugoslav-Italian dispute to an early end. His mind at this time was mainly preoccupied with the League of Nations, and nothing would have pleased him more than to take the finished Covenant back home. But at the

84. Ibid., pp. 50–62 (K&H, pp. 39–44).
85. Trumbić to Cabinet, Paris, Feb. 7, 1919 (TP, F66).

beginning of February, Wilson also had to cope with Orlando and Sonnino, both of whom were getting increasingly insistent on having Italian problems taken up. Hence the American effort to sound out the Yugoslavs. At the same time, the Americans were now also ready to break the recognition deadlock.

On February 1, one day before the meeting with Pichon, Trumbić made an official call on Lansing, who invited him to review the whole history of Yugoslav unification, the current state of affairs within the country, the composition of the government, and the nature of Yugoslav parliamentary plans.[86] Trumbić used this opportunity to press the need for Allied recognition. Lansing asked many questions but did not promise immediate recognition, though by this time, with the support of Allen Dulles, Clive Day, and Charles Seymour, he had apparently already decided to grant it.[87] Five days later, within hours after seeing Wilson, Trumbić received a personal message from Lansing informing him that on the following day, February 7, the United States would extend recognition to the Kingdom of Serbs, Croats, and Slovenes.[88] As promised by the letter, Lansing next day made public a declaration recognizing the new state, whose "final frontiers will be determined by the Peace Conference in accordance with the wishes of the peoples concerned." [89] Thus the impasse was finally broken. The American action raised Yugoslav morale immensely. It also settled the fate of Montenegro, and it was now only a question of time before the other powers would follow the American lead.

In the evening of February 2 Trumbić also talked with Steed. Steed had been contacted earlier in the day by Colonel Stephen Bonsal, a member of the American delegation and a close associate of Colonel House,[90] with a request to "extract from the Yugoslavs

86. For the full text of Trumbić's report to the cabinet on his meeting with Lansing, see B. Krizman, "Pitanje Medjunarodnog Priznanja Nove Države," *Slobodna Dalmacija*, May 16, 1956.

87. See *FRUS-PPC, 11*, 6 ff.

88. Krizman, "Pitanje Medjunarodnog Priznanja," *Slobodna Dalmacija*, May 16, 1956.

89. Ibid.

90. Bonsal, incorrectly identified as Major by Steed, was attached to the American delegation and performed several missions in Germany and Central Europe during the peace conference. His memoirs, *Suitors and Suppliants, the Little Nations at Versailles* (New York, 1946), unfortunately contain little information about these talks.

their final terms so that, if those terms were just, the President might insist upon Italian acceptance of them." [91]

Steed informed Trumbić that the Yugoslavs would jeopardize their standing with Wilson by insisting on the "maximum" line in the west and argued that they must adopt a fresh approach. The pressure on Trumbić was mounting on all sides. This meeting lasted late into the night, and as Steed records, Trumbić proved a hard "nut to crack," fighting the "old battle" and refusing to "commit himself to definite terms for a settlement with Italy." [92] At first glance, Steed's version would not seem wholly credible, since Trumbić by this time had already decided upon Frazier's formula for arbitration. But Trumbić probably hoped to use Steed to obtain better terms from the Americans. When Steed promised to get Trumbić a personal interview with Wilson in return for a "proposal that Wilson could adopt," the foreign minister still wavered. But next morning, Steed records,

> his friend and fellow delegate, Smodlaka, came to see me, after conferring with Trumbitch, and brought a map showing six different lines of possible settlement, including an extreme Southern Slav line on the west and an extreme Italian line on the east. In his view, something between the two central and most moderate lines would be acceptable. Roughly, these lines left the centre of the Istrian Peninsula as debatable ground, while the eastern portion would go to Yugoslavia, and the coast from Pola to Trieste would go to Italy.[93]

At Steed's request, Seton-Watson took these proposals to Colonel House and Major Johnson, both of whom were delighted with the results. They wanted at once to submit this map to Wilson, who was soon to see Orlando. Steed then proposed that Wilson see Trumbić first, and on the 6th a meeting was arranged by Frazier an hour or so before Orlando was to arrive.

The meeting between Wilson and Trumbić was of decisive importance. The President, Trumbić found, was cordial and "very kind." [94] They discussed the Trumbić-Smodlaka map, and when

91. Steed, *Thirty Years*, 2, 278.
92. Ibid., p. 279.
93. Ibid.
94. Krizman, "Priznanje," May 16, 1956.

Wilson asked which specific line the Yugoslavs would accept in Istria, Trumbić replied, according to Steed's information, that he would be willing to leave that to the President's judgment. Wilson pointed out that he could arbitrate only if asked to do so by both sides and suggested that Trumbić make a formal proposal for arbitration through the president of the peace conference, Clemenceau.[95] Trumbić agreed, but did not immediately so inform either the cabinet or the delegation. For on the Yugoslav side two episodes took place that threatened the recently evidenced solidarity in the delegation.

In Paris, Bošković suddenly started a petty argument on February 6 by accusing Smodlaka of deliberately slipping the term "Yugoslavia" into the territorial memorandum in place of the official label, "Kingdom of Serbs, Croats and Slovenes." [96] In Belgrade, however, a more serious development was taking place at the same time. Korošec, who strongly opposed arbitration for Istria, because both the Trieste hinterland and Gorizia were predominantly inhabited by Slovenes, decided to take matters into his own hands. Fearing that the cabinet would agree to arbitration for Trieste and western Istria, or to place the fate of the entire peninsula into Wilson's hands, he sought out Dodge, the American minister, and told him that the Yugoslavs would refuse to sign any peace treaty which left Trieste and Gorizia to Italy.[97] Next, he cabled Žolger and Ribarž in Paris telling them, as Slovenes, not to accept arbitration for western Istria and Trieste. Agreeing, Žolger and Ribarž immediately so informed Pašić. On February 8 Pašić in turn informed the whole delegation. When the majority of delegates refused to change the memorandum and claim Trieste and Gorizia outright, thus reneging on the pledge made to Pichon, Žolger and Ribarž threatened to resign.[98]

With a new crisis at hand, all other problems were laid aside. Pašić cabled Protić, protesting against Korošec's action. "Today" (February 8), he pointed out,

95. Steed, *Thirty Years*, 2, 280.
96. Zap., *1*, 61 (K&H, p. 44).
97. Dodge to Lansing, Belgrade, Feb. 6, 1919 (86oh.01/45, Dept. of State, Washington).
98. Zap., *1*, 63 (K&H, p. 45).

we voted on our frontiers with Italy. A question was raised as to whether we should suggest arbitration for Trieste and the western coast of Istria or just claim them without mentioning arbitration. As you know from my earlier reports we had already agreed once about Trieste and western Istria and communicated our decision orally to Pichon . . . Now suddenly Ribarž and Žolger inform the delegation about the letter [sic] from Korošec saying that Slovenes cannot agree and that they demand Trieste and western Istria on the principle of nationality, because Trieste cannot live without the hinterland which is completely Slovene . . . This happened after we spoke with Pichon . . . The delegation is unable to agree. Ribarž and Žolger threaten to resign . . . Trumbić and the others say they cannot agree to renounce arbitration since this was told to Pichon . . . A change in delegation composition would have bad consequences at this stage . . . We cannot take an intransigent line with the Allies who are anxious to settle the German treaty and will side with Italy if we try to blackmail them. . . . Actually we would gain if the Allies agreed to limit arbitration to Trieste and west Istria. They tell us they are bound to Italy and agreement will be impossible if we insist [on everything] . . . Britain and France are in a dilemma because they want good relations with both Italians and Yugoslavs. Consequently, they say both will have to give way. . . . Government should make decision quickly . . . before we have to submit the memorandum. Otherwise, we either submit memorandum or have to say that we must wait for instructions. It would be bad to renege on earlier offer. But a change in delegation must be avoided.[99]

Trumbić, who the day before urged the cabinet to submit *all* of Istria to Wilson's arbitration, despite probable Italian opposition,[100] tried hard to induce Žolger and Ribarž to change their minds. Both refused to budge. But a compromise, designed to avert an open break within the delegation, was adopted on the

99. Pašić to Protić, Personal and Strictly Confidential No. 148, Paris [Feb. 8, 1919] (TP, F64).

100. Trumbić to Cabinet, Paris, Feb. 7, 1919 (TP, F66). Trumbić felt the Yugoslavs could get eastern Istria without arbitration and perhaps more with arbitration.

morning of February 9. The memorandum would be changed in the following manner: Trieste and western Istria would be claimed outright for Yugoslavia, without mention of arbitration, with the proviso that if "the other side" offered arbitration, it would be accepted in accordance with the earlier declaration to Pichon.[101] The Allies would thus still know that the Yugoslavs were willing to accept arbitration, though, of course, this change represented a serious departure from the delegation's earlier stand.

The surrender of the delegates to Žolger's and Ribarž's ultimatum would probably have become public knowledge had the cabinet not acted at this very juncture. By coincidence, the cabinet voted on February 7 to accept Wilson's arbitration of the whole Italo-Yugoslav dispute, thus in effect overruling Korošec. At the same time, however, it rejected Trumbić's proposal for neutralization of the Adriatic on the grounds that, though neutralization was acceptable in principle, its implementation could not be assured so long as Italy maintained a strong Mediterranean fleet which could be sent into the Adriatic whenever the Italians pleased. Protić cabled Trumbić to this effect on the 7th.[102] The telegram (dispatched via Salonika) arrived in Paris late on the 9th and was read to the delegation on the 10th.[103] As a result of this intervention, Trumbić was instructed to inform Frazier immediately that the Yugoslavs would accept Wilson's arbitration for the whole dispute with Italy.

Trumbić promptly went to Frazier on the 10th, told him the news and asked him to inform Wilson. The President was obviously pleased, for he in turn instructed Frazier to tell the Yugoslavs that he was "deeply moved" by the confidence they showed in him. As before, he suggested that they write a formal letter to both him and Clemenceau. Then, as Trumbić told his fellow-delegates next day, "Frazier himself furnished the drafts for both letters." [104] These were approved by the delegation on the 11th and dispatched to their destinations on the 12th.[105] "We are con-

101. Zap., *1*, 64 (K&H, p. 46).
102. Protić to Trumbić, Belgrade, Feb. 7, 1919 (No. 1245, TP, F66).
103. Zap., *1*, 65 (K&H, p. 46).
104. Ibid., p. 66 (K&H, p. 47).
105. For the text of the letters, see F. Šišić, *Jadransko Pitanje na Konferenciji Mira u Parizu. Zbirka Akata i Dokumenata* (Zagreb, 1920), pp. 22–23.

vinced this is the right step . . . the French and British are also
favorably impressed. . . ." wrote Trumbić to the government next
day.[106]

In the meantime, however, new clouds began to gather on the
horizon. Immediately after seeing Trumbić on February 6, Wilson
received Orlando and informed him of the "Yugoslav proposal."
Orlando appeared agreeable to the principle of American arbitration—pending approval by the Italian cabinet. More than that,
according to Steed he gave Wilson "distinctly to understand that
the official Italian decision was likely to be favourable." [107] If Wilson was cheered upon hearing this, his optimism was to be short-
lived. For next day the Italian delegation submitted to the peace
conference a formal statement of claims which went substantially
beyond the terms of the Treaty of London, especially with regard
to the Tyrol, Albania, and Fiume. The claim to Fiume, in fact,
received as much space in the memorandum as any other region.[108]
The Italian claims, drawn up by the Triestine Giacomo Barzilai,
were in every respect maximal and scarcely conducive to a reasonable settlement. Indeed, in urging House and Frazier to discount
Orlando's apparent willingness to accept American arbitration,
Wickham Steed had hit the mark.

By contrast, the Yugoslav proposal for arbitration appeared, as
Albrecht-Carrié put it, as "undoubtedly a skillful move" [109]—even
as a stroke of diplomatic genius. And in many ways it was. Only
the idea did not originate with them, as has been believed ever
since 1919. Trumbić, and ultimately the cabinet, deserve the
credit for quickly adopting the American suggestion and using it

106. Trumbić to Cabinet, Paris, Feb. 13, 1919, TP, F66. He also added: "The
general situation is not satisfactory. During the whole month nothing has been
settled. The conference moves too slowly. . . . The general feeling is that too much
time is given to frontier questions instead of making preliminary peace with Germany. Hence the Powers have decided to concentrate on that and postpone frontier matters for the time being. This is justified from the general point of view
but is dangerous for us. The Italian army would remain where it is. Hence the arbitration proposal is all the more important. . . . I hear the Italians are opposed
to the proposal but will be forced to accept it."
107. Steed, *Thirty Years*, 2, 280.
108. See *The Italian Claims on the Alps and in the Adriatic* (Paris, 1919).
109. Albrecht-Carrié, *Italy*, p. 107.

to full advantage. It placed the Italians, already "terribly upset" [110] over American recognition of the Yugoslav state, in an unpleasant quandary. The proposal flattered Wilson and made him appear as the Southern Slavs' champion. If the Italians accepted the challenge, it would mean giving up the Treaty of London, Dalmatia, and probably Fiume; if they refused, it would imply that they lacked confidence in Wilson and that their own claims were admittedly excessive. In either case the Yugoslavs would profit.

The Italian delegation learned of the proposal on February 11. While it debated what course of action it should take, Orlando went to see Wilson on the 12th, "moaned and wept, said that the Southern Slavs had taken him by the throat," [111] but promised to reply immediately after consulting the King and the cabinet in Rome on the 14th, the very day Wilson was scheduled to leave for home.

The Council of Ten entered the picture on the 17th. In the absence of both Wilson and Orlando, Clemenceau announced receipt of the Yugoslav letter, but made no further comment. Thereupon Sonnino announced that the Italian government found the proposal for arbitration unacceptable and therefore had decided to reject it.[112] Wilson learned the news in mid-Atlantic, but the Yugoslavs, who learned of it through other channels, were not officially told until March 3.[113]

110. Steed, *Thirty Years*, 2, 280. Albrecht-Carrié observes euphemistically that the news was "naturally not welcomed in Italy, but was received with apprehension and disappointment rather than violent objection" (*Italy*, p. 106).

111. Steed, *Thirty Years*, 2, 281.

112. *FRUS-PPC, 4*, 27–28. Steed reports that Sonnino threatened to resign if the Yugoslav proposal were accepted (*Thirty Years*, p. 281). Crespi, who helped Sonnino frame the Italian reply, makes no mention of such a threat (*Alla Difesa d'Italia*, p. 292). Neither does Albrecht-Carrié.

113. Already on the 17th, while Sonnino was in fact addressing the Council, Trumbić was preparing the following dispatch to the government: "The question of Wilson's arbitration broke into print in Paris this morning. Rumor has it that Orlando would be willing to accept the proposal, but that Sonnino is opposed to it. Unofficial Italian sources, worthy of attention, maintain that arbitration would invalidate the Treaty of London which they cannot accept. Also, Italy demands complete fulfillment of the treaty, or Rijeka in exchange for Dalmatia. . . . Altogether, Italian propaganda is making headway on all fronts. It is estimated that they are employing 2000 individuals. Now the Italians have placed the question of Rijeka in the first category of importance and echoes of their agitation are heard on all sides. . . . I do not believe that this will influence Wilson, but it is

On the 17th, however, Clemenceau also announced that, barring any objection, the Yugoslavs would present their claims to the Council next day. But Sonnino refused to engage in open debate with the Yugoslavs before the Council. Instead, he proposed that either the Italians absent themselves while the Yugoslavs put forth their claims, or if the Italians were to be present, there be no discussion at all. The latter formula was adopted and the Italian, at Clemenceau's behest, was assured that no discussion would take place. Sonnino thus succeeded in keeping the Yugoslavs from gaining equal status with Italians in matters pertaining jointly to both. As for the Yugoslavs, the long-awaited moment of presenting their claims to the peace conference now finally arrived.

---

influencing public opinion . . . In general our position in the conflict with Italy is difficult. From what we hear, our press at home is given to exaggerated optimism and this could mislead our public." (Trumbić to Cabinet, Paris, Feb. 17, 1919, TP, F66).

6. The Politics of Frontiermaking: Phase 2

AT 11:00 A.M. on February 18 the Yugoslav delegation learned from Pašić that it was to appear before the Council of Ten at 3:00 P.M. that same day. The conference secretariat had called Pašić the night before and a letter was sent to him earlier that morning, but neither the telephone call nor the written notification had specified the purpose of the Council meeting.

Pašić thought the Council would either take up the whole range of Yugoslav claims or only those pertaining to Italy; the delegation had to prepare for either contingency. Vesnić, with everyone's concurrence, expressed bitterness at being kept in the dark by the Allies and proposed a formal protest.[1] Then came the practical question: if *all* Yugoslav claims were to be discussed, who should make the presentations? Evidently, there was no time to prepare. Under the circumstances it was agreed that each delegate who appeared before the Council that afternoon would take part in the discussion; each man would refer to *all* the territorial claims so as to show collective interest and purpose, and then develop in detail the area of his immediate competence.[2]

Trumbić then raised a legal point. If Italy, a party to the dispute, also sat as a judge in the Council (with Britain and France bound to her by treaty), the situation would be hopeless and the Yugoslavs should protest such an arrangement at the start of the afternoon meeting. They should ask the President of the peace conference whether they were invited only to give a report and whether the Council was convened as a court of judgment over Yugoslav claims. If the answer were *yes,* Trumbić wanted to declare that the Yugoslav delegates were sent to Paris to participate as full and equal members of the conference. They should then either ask for a suspension of proceedings until new instructions

1. Zap., *1*, 73 (K&H, p. 50).
2. Ibid., pp .73–74 (K&H, p. 50).

were received from Belgrade, or object to the composition of the present "court" and declare themselves not bound by any of its decisions.[3]

Pašić disagreed. First, he doubted Italy could be removed from the "court," even where Adriatic questions were concerned. Second, Trumbić's proposal would "altogether risk falling out with the whole peace conference," for if the Allies refused to budge, the Yugoslavs would then have to withdraw from the conference.[4] Vesnić and Bošković sided with Pašić; Ribarž and Smodlaka with Trumbić. By way of compromise, however, they agreed that during the afternoon session, but not at the very beginning, Vesnić would state "in an appropriate form" that the Yugoslavs expected to receive the same treatment as Italy in regard to their dispute and that Italy be considered a litigant rather than a judge. Not a very forceful plea, but the best the delegates could agree upon.

The Yugoslavs adjourned at 1:45 P.M. An hour and a quarter later, Pašić, Trumbić, Vesnić, and Žolger were ushered into Monsieur Pichon's room at the Quai d'Orsay, where the Council of Ten had convened.

Clemenceau immediately invited the Yugoslavs to present their entire case. Vesnić spoke first, beginning with "an apology. It had not, up to the present, been possible to supply the Conference with a full memorandum. There were [the American minutes record] certain difficulties due to distance, bad communications, etc. . . . A memorandum giving general considerations had been supplied. Separate memoranda of a more technical order would be prepared subsequently." [5] Then he went on to review the overall Yugoslav claims, concentrating on southern, eastern, and northeastern frontiers.[6] He closed by asking the Council to grant the Yugoslavs equality with Italy in all matters of interest to both. Žolger spoke next, mostly about the northern line and the dangers of Pan-Germanism, followed by Trumbić, who dwelt on the western frontier and the Adriatic. (Pašić made no statement of his own.)

3. Ibid., pp. 74–75 (K&H, p. 50).
4. Ibid., pp. 75–76 (K&H, pp. 51–52).
5. *FRUS-PPC, 4,* 45.
6. When he explained Yugoslav claims against Bulgaria, Clemenceau whispered to Vesnić: "With this, I think, you will have no difficulty." Zap. *1,* 80 (K&H, p. 53).

In its entirety, the Yugoslav exposé [7] followed closely the arguments developed in the separate memoranda that were about to go to press.

As soon as they had finished, the Yugoslavs retired and the Council began to consider their case. Wilson was of course not present. Balfour suggested the matter be turned over to a territorial commission on the precedent of Greek, Czechoslovak, Rumanian, and other cases, noting at the same time that some of the powers had incurred special obligations in regard to the Yugoslav case. Sonnino responded by stating that the whole subject was most difficult. Italy would not permit any commission to deal with the Italo-Yugoslav dispute; that would have to be done exclusively by the Supreme Council. When Clemenceau asked whether Sonnino would object to the formation of an experts' commission for Yugoslav northern and eastern frontiers, Sonnino said no, so long as questions affecting Italy (Dalmatia, Albania, Istria) were left within the jurisdiction of the Council. This formula was then adopted and the problem of Yugoslav frontiers with Bulgaria, Rumania, Hungary, and Austria was assigned to the Committee on the Banat (actually, on Rumanian Affairs). A communiqué to this effect, from which the Yugoslav delegates learned of this decision, was released the same afternoon.

Thus, where Yugoslavia was concerned, the Council adopted a double standard which had no parallel at the peace conference. The Yugoslav case was to be decided on two separate levels and treated as two separate issues. Claims affecting Italy (in Istria, Dalmatia, and Albania) were assigned to the Council, where Italy could exercise a veto; all others to a regular commission of experts. The prospects were hardly reassuring.

In Belgrade, Protić nearly exploded upon learning this news. Already bitter over the Allied order to withdraw in the Banat, he cabled Trumbić on February 23, complaining that Allied actions had made

> a heavy impression here. The Cabinet cannot understand the
> inconsistency of the powers. We made a good impression with

7. A "long and dull presentation," according to Baker, *Woodrow Wilson and World Settlement,* 2, 141. An "exceedingly able statement," according to Lloyd George, *Truth about the Peace Treaties,* 2, 958.

our declaration regarding Banat yet now Velika Kikinda and Subotica are endangered for us,[8] while the Rumanians who made a bad impression get what is not even properly theirs. . . . Regarding the conflict with Italy the Cabinet also cannot understand the position of our friends among the great powers. The Cabinet feels there can be only one course between these two: either France, England and Italy should give up the London Treaty and then the conference can freely resolve the dispute . . . or, accept our proposal for American arbitration. If neither is accepted, the Cabinet will seriously have to consider whether there is any sense in our participating in the peace conference. Apparently the attitude in Paris is this: let us guard the Serbs, Croats and Slovenes, but land, people and money we will give to the Italians, Rumanians and Czechs, if not even to the Magyars. In such a case it would be better to have this done without our participation. Please inform the whole delegation of this as the disposition of the entire Cabinet.[9]

A similar cable was received by Pašić three days later, instructing the delegation to declare officially that "we cannot agree that the Conference resolve our dispute while the Treaty of London remains in force, for that would mean that the litigants would act as judges." [10]

Faced with these instructions, the delegation took fright and quickly decided to cable Protić that "things have not yet come to the point of our leaving the peace conference." [11] At the same time, however, Trumbić also informed Belgrade that according to all reports the Italians had turned down the arbitration proposal and that Sonnino would not give up the Treaty of London because it had been de facto fulfilled. Wilson had of course refused to recognize the treaty, Trumbić added, and this "is our only hope." [12]

8. This reference was made in response to Trumbić's telegram of Feb. 13, reporting rumors that the two towns, and Temesvar as well, would be assigned to Rumania (Trumbić to Ministry of Foreign Affairs, Paris, Feb. 13, TP, F66).

9. Protić to Trumbić, Belgrade, Feb. 23, 1919 (Personal No. 2009, TP, F66).

10. Protić to Pašić, Belgrade, Feb. 26, 1919 (Personal No. 2107, TP, F66).

11. Trumbić to Protić, Paris, Feb. 27, 1919 (TP, F66); Zap., *1*, 102 (K&H, p. 62).

12. Trumbić to Ministry of Foreign Affairs, Paris, Feb. 27, 1919 (No. 198, TP, F66).

Then, on March 3, Clemenceau suddenly informed the Yugoslavs that at the February 17 session of the Supreme Council "the Italian delegation declared that it cannot accept [the Yugoslav] propositions." [13] And thus ended the plan for Wilson's arbitration.

The maneuver to break the impasse had not worked. In fact, the Yugoslavs were worse off than before, because the Italians would now press for agreement on the Adriatic before President Wilson's return. The peace conference, having for the most part cleared the issues of colonies and the League, now turned to the German treaty. Sonnino seized the opportunity to demand consideration of the Austrian settlement, craftily using the specter of revolution in Italy as a lever for forcing immediate action.[14]

The Yugoslavs tried to play for time and to forestall any action prior to the President's return in mid-March. They learned from various quarters that the Allies considered their demands excessive,[15] which only increased their misgivings. Conditions at home were becoming increasingly strained and so indeed were personal relations within the delegation.

In the last days of February a rash of bitter arguments broke out again, causing general mistrust and deep personal rancors beneath the outward façade of delegation solidarity. The old conflict between Pan-Serbianism and Yugoslavism received new impetus when Trumbić (on February 22) complained that the memoranda nowhere listed each claimed territory by name so as to "clarify matters for the Allies." [16] Pašić pointed to a previous decision to submit only a map rather than a special list, but Bošković would not let it go at that. Infuriated, he declared that in any circumstances a separate list should include no reference to the Kingdoms of Serbia and Montenegro, both former *sovereign* states and thus not subject to Allied discussion. Trumbić angrily rejoined that each region had to be individually listed in order "to deter-

13. Šišić, *Jadransko Pitanje,* p. 28.

14. Miller *Diary, 19,* 530.

15. Trumbić to Ministry of Foreign Affairs, Paris, March 5, 1919 (TP, F66). "We have no hope of getting Beljak or Celovec. . . . I am also afraid for Maribor. . . . our situation is getting more difficult every day. . . . Our greatest hope lies in Wilson, if he comes back before our questions are resolved and if he is willing to help us."

16. Zap., *1,* 86–88 (K&H, pp. 55–56).

mine its legal position." Serbia and Montenegro, he said almost mockingly, could appear separately as "independent sovereign states." But Pašić ruled the entire matter out of order on the basis of prior resolutions. If Trumbić wanted to assert the principle of parity between Serbia and the former Austro-Hungarian provinces, he scored no victory at all; if he merely wanted to remind Pašić and Bošković that Croatia and Slovenia had not been *annexed* to Serbia, he scored a point or two.

Two days later a new argument developed. Trumbić proposed a new formal demand for diplomatic recognition from all Allied and neutral states, declaring that he did not view Lansing's letter of February 6 as granting unqualified American recognition. Pašić and Vesnić disagreed, arguing that Lansing's letter involved complete recognition and a firm precedent which the other powers were now bound to follow. This exchange was leading nowhere when Bošković suddenly changed the subject, noting that Vesnić had employed the term "Yugoslavia" in the speech before the Council on the 18th. This he (Bošković) greatly "resented." [17] And as though this issue were of capital importance, it cropped up time and again, developing into a one-hour debate on the afternoon of March 2.[18]

The problem—to use or not to use the term "Yugoslavia"—was finally referred to Belgrade. Protić replied, sensibly but to no avail, by urging that they leave such matters aside until "we are all at home . . . Unfortunately there are many who know about our disharmony and that makes our difficult position even more difficult." [19]

Following Italian rejection of the arbitration proposal, the Yugoslavs began to explore new strategies. In view of the Banat crisis, Sonnino's "victory" in the Council, and the alleged Allied

17. Ibid., p. 95 (K&H, p. 59).
18. Ibid., pp. 110–12 (K&H, pp. 65–66). This polemic included a bitter debate about the Corfu Declaration, with Smodlaka and Trumbić arguing against Pašić, Vesnić, and Bošković that the term "Yugoslavia," used even by Alexander himself, was perfectly valid. Smodlaka then asked for a vote on the subject. Pašić refused, but agreed to refer the matter to the cabinet. It was brought up all through March and April.
19. Protić to Trumbić, Belgrade, March 17, 1919 (No. 3092, TP, F66).

disenchantment with the Yugoslav exposé of February 18, on March 4 Smodlaka urged adoption of a formula that would at once reassure the Allies, seize the initiative from Sonnino, and help break the impasse. "We could put forth," Smodlaka proposed, "an open offer for a plebiscite in all territorial disputes with our allies." [20] Surprisingly, the delegation readily agreed—in principle. After a day of discussion, the proposal was referred to Belgrade by Trumbić, with these comments:

> Our situation is difficult . . . Italian propaganda, aided by French censorship, makes us appear imperialistic. . . . This proposal is limited to disputes with Rumania and Italy, because they are friendly and allied states . . . and excludes enemy states. We are all convinced that this step would be tactically appropriate and could not hurt us at all. It corresponds to Wilson's principles and we can expect that he will receive it well. It will give proof of our moderation and objectivity.[21]

While the government deliberated over Smodlaka's proposal, the situation in Paris grew worse. On March 11 the Council of Ten turned to the question of equal treatment for Italians and Yugoslavs. In the course of the debate that followed, Orlando and Sonnino succeeded in making an issue of whether the Yugoslavs should be considered as allies at all. They would welcome Serbia as an equal party, but not the Croats and Slovenes who fought against the Entente and should therefore be considered enemies. That was why Italy would not recognize the new state. Sonnino even pointed to the new status of Žolger, a former Austro-Hungarian minister, as testifying to the bad faith of the Yugoslavs. Lansing objected, but Sonnino succeeded in having the entire issue shelved. The latter also succeeded in persuading the Council to remove the Yugoslav-Albanian problem from the territorial commission to which it had earlier been assigned and having it placed within the jurisdiction of the Council.[22]

20. Zap., *1*, 118 (K&H, p. 68).
21. Trumbić to Ministry of Foreign Affairs, Paris, March 6, 1919 (TP, F66).
22. See *FRUS-PPC, 4*, 320–26.

By coincidence, the delegation learned this the next day simultaneously with the arrival of a telegram from Belgrade, warning that the Italians had launched a campaign to portray the Yugoslavs as "enemies." Under the circumstances, the cabinet instructed the delegation to press for immediate Allied recognition because "this situation cannot be tolerated any longer." [23] Also, it was again considering withdrawing from the peace conference.

The Yugoslavs of course were hardly in a position to defy the Allies at that moment. They had neither the requisite diplomatic support nor the internal means to implement their territorial program for any length of time. Nonetheless, Protić and his colleagues in Belgrade had neared the point of desperation as both domestic and external pressures mounted.

What tried their tempers even more was the arrival in Belgrade of Prince Luca Livio Borghese, the new Italian minister, with a letter of accreditation to the Kingdom of Serbia. Protić had the document returned to him with a note stating that it should be addressed to the Kingdom of Serbs, Croats, and Slovenes. Borghese replied that Italy did not recognize such a state and warned that he would leave Belgrade if the original letter were rejected. And for the time being no further action was taken.

The episode, however, intruded unpleasantly into the work of the delegation in Paris. On March 12 Trumbić explored the plebiscite idea with the Americans (with Steed's help) and found them most favorably impressed. Two days later the proposal was approved in Belgrade, and Protić instructed the delegation to draw up an appropriate note. But a new conflict developed over the drafting of the note which imperiled the fate of the whole plebiscite proposal.

Following agreement on the first rough draft, Bošković brought up the Borghese incident in Belgrade. In his view the government had acted rashly, and the delegation, he thought, should urge the cabinet to prevent a rupture of relations with Italy at all cost. Pašić, who had probably inspired Bošković's maneuver, agreed. He added, moreover, that the government should have accepted Borghese's letter, giving him to understand that he was in effect

23. Zap., *1*, 140 (K&H, p. 76).

accredited to the new state. Trumbić objected strongly to this line and praised the cabinet for its forthright stand.[24] No one, it should be noted, questioned the right of the delegation to advise the government on matters such as this.

As for the plebiscite proposal, two full days of discussion followed on drafting the right kind of note. Then, on the 18th, Vesnić questioned the idea that it be sent immediately. He had had second thoughts and had now concluded that the note should not be sent at all. The Allies, he argued, would not act without consulting the Yugoslavs, and an unsolicited proposal of this nature would only give the impression that the Yugoslavs were trying to circumvent the conference. Besides, a plebiscite could be suggested later on as well.

Smodlaka then revealed that Steed, who had doubtless consulted the Americans, had told him that now was the best moment for the formal note. Trumbić, who had discussed the matter with Frazier, supported this view, but Pašić and Bošković sided with Vesnić. All eyes turned to Ribarž (Žolger happened to be absent) and the Slovene agreed with the Serbs, explaining that "we must take into account the sensitivities of the great powers, and especially of France which does not much care to have the principle of plebiscite discussed." [25] The gulf between the two sides deepened when Pašić demanded that the views of *all* friends (Italians included?) be further explored. This provoked a stormy exchange of accusations and counteraccusations that in the end led Smodlaka to say angrily: "This is a struggle between ourselves and Italy. No one will advise us, nor should we expect it. This step does not come through American initiative. . . . We are duty bound to use this means in our own interest, to regain the sympathy of public opinion which we lost in submitting our memorandum." [26] (The reference to American initiative was evidently meant as a barb at the Serbs' sensitivity to the close liaison between the Croat delegates and the United States mission and to draw obliquely a parallel to the Wilson arbitration affair.)

In the end, Smodlaka and Trumbić were outvoted. The note to

24. Trumbić to Ministry of Foreign Affairs, Paris, March 12,(1919 (TP, F66).
25. Zap., *1*, 152–53 (K&H, p. 82).
26. Ibid., p. 154 (K&H, p. 82).

Clemenceau was postponed pending further exploration of Allied views, and thus the plebiscite proposal—probably the most statesmanly idea advanced within the Yugoslav delegation—was shelved.

The uneasy peace, which had prevailed in the Yugoslav borderlands since the armistice, broke down in February and March 1919. A wave of incidents erupted in the Banat, northern Albania, throughout Dalmatia, and in the Klagenfurt basin. As prospects for a quick peace settlement waned in Paris, tension between Italian occupation forces and local populations increased. In Belgrade there was much talk about mobilization, while in Italian-held districts mass meetings and demonstrations occurred almost daily. The Italians refused to repatriate Croat and Slovene prisoners of war and applied severe sanctions against all recalcitrants.

In the military occupation zone they acted as though the Treaty of London had been in fact implemented. They launched a campaign of political and cultural Italianization on the mainland and islands as well. Italian archives reveal that these measures were coordinated in Rome as part of overall Italian policy vis-à-vis the Southern Slavs. On the island of Krk, for example, the Glagolitic liturgy was banned and forcibly replaced by Latin. Clergymen who resisted were exiled with the full concurrence of the government in Rome.[27] Public expressions favoring the Yugoslav union were forbidden, censorship was strictly enforced, and in one instance a newly elected member of parliament was prevented from attending the opening session of the Skupština in Belgrade.[28]

The Yugoslav government and peace delegation protested regularly but without effect. Oddly enough, even the issue of these "protests" caused disagreements within the delegation, as on

27. The Bishop of Krk, Dr. Antun Mahnić, for example, was confined near Rome for nearly a year for refusing to cooperate with Italian authorities. Prior to his exile his diocese was subjected to countless molestations. While in exile, his contact with the diocese was completely cut off. In a general report on the Mahnić case, Baron Monti, then in charge of the office of religious affairs in the Ministry of Finance, admitted to Count Sforza that injustices had been committed against Mahnić and that many of the charges brought against him were in fact fabrications. (Monti to Sforza, Rome, Nov. 21, 1919, MFA, Rome [no ref. no. given]). See also *New Europe, 141* (1919), 255; *Bulletin yougoslave, 18* (Geneva, Feb. 21, 1919).

28. *Stenografske Beleške Privremenog Narodnog Pretstavništva Srba, Hrvata i Slovenaca, 1919–1920* (5 fascs. Belgrade, 1920), p. 6 (hereafter cited as *Sten. Bel.*).

March 2 when word came that the Italians were preparing to occupy Split. Trumbić proposed that the four plenipotentiaries go immediately to Clemenceau and lodge an oral protest. Vesnić and Pašić objected on general grounds, while Bošković declared that if a protest were made about Split, one should also be made about Allied policies in the Banat and Bulgaria, which, he said, were as important as the frontiers with Italy. Žolger quickly added that if mention were made of the Banat, and he thought it should be, then the frontier with Austria should certainly not be neglected.[29] In keeping with precedent, no action was taken on the original motion for Split, until twelve days later, when Italian troops fired on civilians in that beleaguered town. At that point Pašić and the others agreed to demand prompt Allied intervention in Split.[30]

As other incidents developed, Yugoslav headquarters in Paris were bombarded with reports, pleas, and suggestions from Belgrade, Yugoslav legations abroad, and municipalities throughout the country. Two reports concerning Montenegro were particularly alarming: one, on March 4, that separatist Montenegrin cadres were being trained and equipped in Italy for an impending insurrection; the other, on March 12, that two Italian divisions had disembarked at San Giovanni di Medua and that one battalion was on its way to the Yugoslav frontier through Albania.[31]

Of the several trouble-zones, however, none had become more critical at this time than Carinthia, where Yugoslav and Austrian forces had been fighting since the beginning of January. Due to an unclear demarcation line, the conflict had increased to a point that led to the dispatch of an American investigating team to determine the merits of the dispute.

The so-called Miles-King mission—both Colonel Sherman Miles and Lieutenant Leroy King were members of Professor Archibald Coolidge's mission in Vienna which, in turn, served as the Central European field quarters of the American peace commission—actually extended its investigations beyond Carinthia. Its reports throw an interesting light on several of the trouble-zones around

29. Zap., *1*, 112–15 (K&H, p. 66).
30. Ibid., p. 142 (K&H, pp. 77–78).
31. Ibid., pp. 120, 139 (K&H, pp. 68, 76).

the country.[32] Though Miles and King (of the two, only Miles had had some prior experience in the Balkans) came to Carinthia in mid-January charged only to gather information, they soon found themselves mediating between Yugoslavs and Austrians. With the aid of Major Lawrence Martin and Professor Robert Kerner, who joined them in the field, they proposed some modifications for the demarcation line in Carinthia. In mid-February, Miles set off to report to the American commissioners in Paris, while King went on to Belgrade and Zagreb. In March, Miles returned, and following a brief stay in Fiume, proceeded to Dalmatia and Montenegro.

In Carinthia fighting did not end with the departure of the American team. For a while it even increased, to the diplomatic embarrassment of the Yugoslavs in Paris, since Yugoslav units were on the offensive. But the peace delegation had only the scantest information about the Carinthian operations. Trumbić repeatedly asked the cabinet and the war ministry for full and accurate information regarding troop dispositions and operations not only in Carinthia but everywhere.[33] The Paris representatives were in fact at great disadvantage in having to respond to various charges and rumors on the basis of meager and often impressionistic information.

Fiume too was a center of continuous unrest. A stream of incidents involving Italian, Serb, and French forces, not to mention the local population, was largely provoked by Italian actions.[34] By March 11 the situation had become so grave that the Council of Ten ordered an investigation there, as well as all along Dalmatia.

In Slovenia, meantime, a crisis long in the making broke into the open at the end of February. When the Yugoslav command in Ljubljana learned that the United States had recognized the Yugoslav state, it expelled the Italian mission from Slovenia and re-

32. See *FRUS-PPC*, 12, passim; also, Jerome Jareb, ed., *Leroy King's Reports from Croatia, March to May 1919* (New York, 1960).

33. Trumbić to Ministry of Foreign Affairs, Paris, March 21, 1919 (TP, F66).

34. On April 9, for example, Franchet d'Esperey informed the French government that the incidence of bloodshed had increased and that the Italian authorities in Fiume were interrupting the flow of munitions intended for French and Serbian forces (Franchet d'Esperey to Ministry of War [Paris], Belgrade, April 9, 1919, Dossiers Klotz, A-12, BDIC, Paris).

fused to issue travel and residence papers to its officers. The Italian government retaliated by closing the frontier (armistice line), thus interrupting the flow of food and supplies into Slovenia, which led to considerable privation in both town and country. This action also led to a series of armed clashes between opposing border patrols.[35]

The Council in Paris responded by creating an inter-Allied commission (four generals, one each from the United States, Great Britain, France, and Italy) to recommend measures for the restoration of peace. In its final report, the commission charged Italy with responsibility for most of the incidents in Slovenia and along the coast,[36] though actual Allied intervention never materialized. Colonel Miles, meanwhile, wrote separately to Coolidge in Vienna: "The Italian determination to antagonize the Yugoslavs is a most amazing piece of stupidity, when one thinks of the opportunity Italy might have seized in the Balkans." [37]

Throughout the rest of the country conditions did not differ greatly. Constant frontier tension and the uncertainty of success in Paris weighed heavily on the government in Belgrade and did little to help economic rehabilitation and general domestic integration. Political integration was further complicated by yet another factor—Italian-sponsored separatist propaganda.

The extent to which Badoglio's "project" of December 1918 resulted directly in the Italian propaganda onslaught of February–April 1919 cannot be precisely ascertained until Italian military and intelligence records of the period are opened. But there is not enough reason to doubt that they were closely linked, particularly in view of subsequent events.[38] Allied field reports—from Dodge,

35. Dodge to Lansing, Belgrade, March 16, 1919 (763–72119/4461, Dept. of State, Washington). Crespi records having received specific orders to cut off all supplies and having obeyed instructions to the letter (*Alla Difesa d'Italia*, pp. 305, 319–20). See also *New York Times*, Feb. 28, 1919.

36. See *FRUS-PPC, 4*, 255–61; "Report of the Military Commission of Inquiry, Split, Fiume, etc.," April 12, 1919 (Dossiers Klotz, A-9). The Italian commission member prepared a minority report charging the Yugoslavs with acts of provocation against Italian authorities.

37. Miles to Coolidge, Split, March 20 (?), 1919 (*FRUS-PPC, 12*, 492).

38. For Badoglio's later role and Italian uses of Croat separatist elements, see

Miles, King, and Major Temperley, as well as other British and French officers—from various Yugoslav regions spell out an Italian intelligence and propaganda pattern resembling Badoglio's plan too closely to be considered mere coincidence.

On February 3, for example, Dodge reported to Lansing on conditions in Montenegro and drew special attention to Italian propaganda supporting the ex-King Nicholas. Active agitation, the report continued, was supplemented by distribution of arms to disaffected Montenegrins and roving bands of Albanians for the purpose of encouraging resistance to Serbian troops and Montenegrin unionist forces.

Commenting on another front, King wrote Coolidge in Vienna: "The Italians are choking Croatia by their occupation of Fiume, and are doing everything to cause discontent and trouble, both there and in Slovenia. They are determined to break up Jugo-Slavia if they can." [39] As for the Serbo-Bulgarian sector, King noted (on the basis of British and Yugoslav sources) that the Italians "have a general and troops at Sofia and . . . are everywhere trying to hamper the Jugo-Slav state. The Italians allow Bulgarian soldiers to be transported in Italian motor trucks back along their lines of communication into Albania. The Italians are doing all they can to inflame the Albanians against the Serbs, and trouble is expected in that quarter." [40] Other reports to Coolidge warned that the "Italians are doing their utmost to separate the Croats and the Serbs," by means that included distribution of pro-Hungarian literature whenever it seemed useful.[41] On February 27 Coolidge, now in possession of numerous similar reports, cabled the American Commission in Paris: "Reason for thinking Italy is encouraging Croatian Separatist Movement." [42]

In actuality, Croatian separatism made little headway in 1919 and was largely overshadowed by the popular enthusiasm that so

Giovanni Giurati, *Con d'Annunzio e Millo in difesa dell'Adriatico* (Florence, 1954), passim. See also Paolo Alatri, *Nitti, d'Annunzio e la Questione Adriatica* (Milan, 1959).

39. King to Coolidge, Belgrade, Feb. 24, 1919 *(FRUS-PPC, 12, 478)*.
40. Ibid.
41. Storey to Coolidge, Vienna, Feb. 25, 1919 (ibid., pp. 394–95).
42. *FRUS-PPC, 12, 475*.

recently attended the end of the war, victory, and national unification. There were of course various disgruntled groups in Croatia, including former officials of the old regime, unemployed war veterans, and Radić's republican peasant movement. Radić did not have a strong following at this time, though within two or three years he became a central figure in Croatian and national politics. Nor was republicanism a popular ideology in 1919.[43]

At the beginning of that year the Italians established contacts with various groups as well as with Radić. In April they produced in Paris an alleged appeal from Radić to Sonnino, dated April 6, asking for Italian help against "the Serbian occupation of Croatia," [44] but the authenticity of that document is subject to serious doubts. According to Vladko Maček, Radić's collaborator and successor, Radić had indeed drafted a memorandum at this time, but one calling for a Peasant Republic of Croatia which he planned to submit to the peace conference in Paris. Prevented from doing so by sudden arrest, he entrusted the document to associates who turned it over to the Italian military mission in Ljubljana for transmission to Paris.[45] While en route, the memorandum appears to have undergone considerable textual revision, and though originally addressed to the peace conference, it re-emerged addressed to Sonnino.

By contrast to the much smaller oppositional groups, the principal political parties of Croatia supported the national union and stood firmly behind its foreign policy. Their unity on this score was fully expressed in the first Yugoslav national assembly, convened in Belgrade on March 1, 1919.

The Privremena Skupština, or Provisional Parliament, was called mainly to organize a constituent assembly and to pass interim legislation.[46] All through March, April, and May, however,

43. Marxist historians, particularly Ferdo Čulinović and Vaso Bogdanov of the University of Zagreb, have in recent years sought to prove the contrary. The extent of peasant republicanism in 1919 has also been overstated by Vladko Maček, first Radić's assistant and then his successor. See V. Maček, *In the Struggle for Freedom* (New York, 1957), pp. 78 ff.

44. A copy of Radić's "appeal" to Sonnino is located in the Dossiers Klotz, A-8, 9.

45. Maček, pp. 81–82.

46. It was so organized as to include delegates from all Yugoslav lands, including those under dispute. Out of a total membership of 296, Serbia had 84 delegates, Croatia (including Fiume and Medjumurje) 62, Slovenia 32, Vojvodina 24, Dalmatia

it met in the shadow of the peace conference. All news from Paris as well as from the disputed regions greatly affected its proceedings. A constant flow of messages and appeals for help against Italian occupation authorities, particularly from Dalmatia, helped to create an atmosphere of crisis, subjecting the members of the Skupština to considerable psychological strain.[47] The pressure of events kindled feelings of national solidarity in the realm of foreign policy and led to repeated expressions of support for the government and its peace delegation in Paris. The Skupština as a whole reacted with emotional abandon when on March 16 Protić announced—in order to generate pressure on the Allies and foster unity at home—that, according to all indications from Paris, some half million Yugoslavs would be assigned to neighboring states. This prognosis followed closely upon a bitter statement by Regent Alexander, accusing the Allies of favoring Italians over Yugoslavs, a statement he repeated bluntly to the American minister.[48]

The first formal debate on foreign policy opened on March 27. For several days individual delegates rose in support of the government and the peace delegation. The Wilson arbitration proposal, though by now officially buried, was praised by one and all. Hope was even expressed that it might yet be revived.

But the debate also produced a tone of frustration, impatience, and anger, matching that of Protić, Alexander, and the press. Feelings ran so deep that, as Dodge had already warned some days earlier, if the peace conference failed to conclude a favorable settlement, the prevailing mood of the country was to fight.[49]

12, Bosnia-Hercegovina 42, Montenegro 12, Macedonia 24, Istria 4. (Čedomil Mitrinović and Miloš N. Brašić, *Jugoslavenske Narodne Skupštine i Sabori,* Belgrade, 1937, pp. 341–49.) All the major political parties were represented. Radić's Croatian Peasant Party refused to seat its two members. The great majority favored the Yugoslav union and the monarchy. A bloc of some 30 members, known as the National Club and composed of the Starčević group and several splinter groups, approved of the monarchy but insisted on much greater regional autonomy than the majority. (Dodge to Lansing, Belgrade, March 8, 17, 1919, 86oh.01/64–65, Dept. of State, Washington.)

47. See *Sten. Bel.,* sessions 1–21.

48. Dodge to Lansing, Sarajevo, March 12, 1919 (86oh.01/56, Dept. of State, Washington).

49. Dodge to Lansing, Belgrade, March 21, 1919 (763.72119/4325, Dept. of State, Washington).

In Paris, meantime, the forging of Yugoslav frontiers began in earnest. As instructed by the Council of Ten on February 18, the Committee on Rumanian and Yugoslav Affairs had taken under consideration all Yugoslav frontiers save those with Italy and Albania. All the territorial committees—there were six in all [50]— were instructed to produce final reports by March 8, a deadline clearly impossible to keep. After various postponements, therefore, the deadline was extended to April 6, a deadline which, with much difficulty, the Rumanian-Yugoslav committee was able to observe.

The territorial committees were created on the theory that territorial disputes not directly involving immediate great-power interests should be submitted to the judgment of technical experts in the interests of objectivity. Though initially proposed by Lloyd George, the committees were largely the handiwork of Wilson, who, in answer to some opposition, threatened that unless the idea were adopted, his position would be based on the recommendations of the Inquiry rather than on "common expert advice." [51] When finally approved, however, the committees were haphazardly appointed (and subsequently treated) and their work suffered from imprecise instructions as to their tasks and methods. The experts were naïvely enjoined to disregard political considerations in all their proceedings, a lofty objective which, as the Italians realistically warned, was quite impossible to fulfill.

As did everyone else (Czechs, Poles, Belgians, et al.), the Yugoslavs expected the privileged position of "full and equal" membership in their own territorial committee. But the committee quickly turned into a microcosm of the Committee of Ten, staffed and governed by the great-power experts alone. With Italian and Albanian frontier questions set aside for the Council of Ten, the committee procedure soon enabled Italy to wield great influence over all other Yugoslav frontiers as well.

In view of Italian policy objectives, the Italian members of the committee could hardly agree to any solution inconsistent with their national aims. But their membership was used as a political

50. For the makeup and history of the territorial committees see Marston, *Peace Conference*, chap. 9.

51. Ibid., p. 115.

weapon designed to advance Sonnino's broader strategy. As Harold Nicolson confided to his diary: *"February 21, Friday.* Greek Committee. . . . I can't understand the Italian attitude. They are behaving like children, and sulky children at that. They obstruct and delay everything—and evidently think that by making themselves disagreeable on every single point they will force the Conference to give them fat plums to keep them quiet." And again, on February 25, to his father, Lord Carnock:

> On the whole I find that the Americans are a great help, since they are well-informed, broad-minded and extremely honest. The French are behaving far better than I imagined . . . The great difficulty comes from the side of the Italians, and Sonnino is the evil genius of the piece. He appears to have given a mot d'ordre to his Delegation that they are to adopt the tactics of delay and obstruction, with the result that unanimity of action is frustrated at every point by perfectly wilful obstruction on the part of the Italians. It is all working up to a real row, and I am extremely anxious lest the Italians will saboter the whole thing rather than give way. The obstinacy and malevolence of Sonnino are quite unrealisable.[52]

From the very start, the Italian members of the committee—Giacomo de Martino and Count Luigi Vannutelli Rey—supported Rumanian claims as a means of blocking the Yugoslavs.[53] They stubbornly defended the Treaty of Bucharest in line with their defense of the Treaty of London. They also supported Bratianu's position on the "indivisibility" of the Banat, though they eventually had to give way on this point in the face of vigorous American, British, and French opposition.

By February 19 the Rumanian claim to the whole of the Banat was, in principle, rejected. The experts, however, could not agree on a joint line of partition. They adopted a partial line along the Danube, to a point from which British and French proposals began to diverge markedly. The French, supported by Charles Seymour of the United States, favored the Yugoslav line which was

---

52. *Peacemaking*, pp. 266, 270–71.

53. "Committee on Rumanian and Yugoslav Affairs," *Procès Verbal* 1, Feb. 8, 1919 (181.2160/1, Dept. of State, Washington.) (Hereafter cited as CRYA-PV.)

mainly intended to give strategic protection to Belgrade and the Morava valley. The British, on the other hand, favored a compromise, and in order not to disrupt the existing communications system in the Banat, proposed assigning most of the course of the Maros to the Rumanians. When the Allies failed to reach agreement on either line, they decided to hear Rumanian and Yugoslav views directly.

Bratianu and Alexandru Vaida Voevod were called before the committee on February 22. They asked for the whole of the Banat on the basis of the Treaty of Bucharest. Three days later the Yugoslavs—Pašić, Trumbić, Žolger, Cvijić, and General Pešić—were called. They claimed the same line in the Banat, Bačka, and Baranja as put forth in the formal memoranda. Nothing had changed and the two positions remained at such variance that an "amicable settlement" was obviously out of the question.

For six weeks the committee worked on alternate lines in the Banat. For lack of better alternatives it used 1910 census figures as a basis for dealing with particularly controversial localities. This had the unfortunate consequence of basing decisions about the ethnic composition of several areas on inaccurate statistics, a fact freely admitted by the British, French, and American experts.[54]

As for the Council's injunction against admitting political criteria into committee deliberations, it soon became apparent that this directive could not be carried out. Within ten days after Yugoslav affairs were entrusted to the territorial committee, the political differences between Britain, France, and the United States, on the one hand, and Italy, on the other, came out into the open. On February 28 the American, British, and French delegates agreed on a northern line in the Banat by which the entire Szeged area was to be left to Hungary. In Bačka, they drew a line corresponding roughly to the Yugoslav proposal, which would have placed 110,000 Yugoslavs and 50,000 Magyars within Yugoslavia.[55] The Italians, however, refused to accept either line. De Martino would

---

54. CRYA-PV 3, Feb. 13, 1919 (181.2160/3). Yugoslav figures were also based on the 1910 census, but broke down the category "others" which included numerous Slavs. Yugoslav statistical revisions were most often accepted by the French and British members.

55. Miller *Diary, 18,* 95.

agree only to placing Szeged in Hungary. As for the rest, he reserved any decision, though during the same session, in spite of earlier declarations, he reverted to the position that Italy, "faithful to the Treaty of 1916," was still disposed to give Rumania the entire Banat. De Martino conceded that the Bucharest Treaty might have been invalidated by Rumania's withdrawal from the war, thus creating a basis for giving Serbia at least part of the disputed region. But, he argued, Yugoslavia should receive no more than the "natural frontier" of the Tisza and the Danube, thus in effect rejecting the American-British-French line in the north, a line based on the principle that "it is proper to take other factors [other than geography and ethnography] into consideration, means of communications for instance." [56]

Similarly, when discussion turned to Baranja in early March, agreement was reached only on a partial line, along the Drava to its confluence with the Mur. Beyond that point, numerous alternatives were proposed. During the ensuing debate the Italians suddenly brought up the irrelevant issue of Montenegro. And when Sir Eyre Crowe of Great Britain, in an effort to dispose of the subject quickly, stated that Montenegro was strictly an internal Yugoslav affair and hence fell beyond the committee's competence, De Martino blandly replied that in the Italian view "Montenegro is an independent state" and had to be treated as such.[57] This obstructionist tactic worked, for it led to a prolonged polemic extending over several committee sessions. Finally, on March 3 the American, British, and French experts managed to have the "problem of Montenegro" referred to the Council of Ten, where it technically belonged from the very start and where, for reasons of their own, the Italians now wanted to raise it all over again.

All during March the committee worked intermittently on the Banat and all the other frontiers. Where the Banat was concerned, it was bombarded continuously by Yugoslav and Rumanian communications, appeals, statistical material, and the like. The controversy became so acute that the committee chairman, André Tardieu, repeatedly complained about its violence. The Yugo-

56. CRYA-PV 8, Feb. 28, 1919 (181.2160/8).
57. CRYA-PV 9 (181.21601/9).

slavs insisted that peace could not be maintained unless their full demands were met, while the Rumanians insisted that if the Banat, "in its natural frontiers, is refused to them, the revolt of national sentiment in their country will overthrow the cabinet and bring about the triumph of Bolshevism." [58]

After repeated argument, the committee on March 10 again refused to agree to the "indivisibility of the Banat." Vannutelli Rey submitted to the majority view, but complained that it was "inadvisable." Italy, he said, would give in only to uphold Allied solidarity.[59]

When both Yugoslavs and Rumanians realized that neither side would yield, they suddenly switched tactics and indicated willingness to resolve the dispute by plebiscite. For the Yugoslavs this line was consistent with their January 31 statement before the Council of Ten and with the government's approval of the Smodlaka proposal. For the Rumanians, however, it appeared as a basic shift of position.

In reality, the Yugoslav and Rumanian proposals were again at such variance as to make the whole gesture meaningless. The Yugoslavs demanded a plebiscite district by district; the Rumanians for the Banat as a whole. The former plan was thus bound to result in the desired partition (western Banat to Yugoslavia, the rest to Rumania), while the latter was likely to assign the whole region to its sponsors. The committee rejected both.

This episode led Vannutelli Rey to revive the issue of secret treaties once again. He demanded the application of the Treaty of Bucharest, accusing Britain and France of failing to honor their commitments. Crowe and Jules Laroche denied that their governments regarded the treaty as invalid. When Rumania concluded a separate peace with Germany, the Allies had tacitly agreed to regard the Bucharest convention as null and void. But that agreement had never been formalized and therefore could not be construed as binding. In their zeal to defend their governments' actions, Crowe and Laroche fell into the trap of admitting that Vannutelli's position had a sound basis in fact. They managed to resolve the problem only by persuading the Italian to have the

58. CRYA-PV 6, March 13, 1919 (181.21601/16).
59. Ibid.

Signers of the Corfu Declaration, July 1917

Standing, left to right: B. Vošnjak, D. Trinajstić, F. Potočnjak, M. Ninčić, V. Marinković, M. Djuričić, M. Drašković. *Seated, left to right:* D. Vasiljević, H. Hinković, A. Trumbić, N. Pašić, N. Nikolić, S. Protić, Lj. Davidović.

Nikola Pašić

Ante Trumbić

Regent Alexander hears the Address of the Narodno Vijeće of Zagreb
Belgrade, December 1, 1918

Trumbić signing the Treaty of Rapallo, November 12, 1920

Standing: Extreme right, Italian Foreign Minister Sforza; 2nd from right, Italian
Premier Giolitti; 4th from right, Yugoslav Premier Vesnić.

whole question of the 1916 treaty referred to the Council of Ten, a move that served Sonnino well.

The case of the Yugoslav-Hungarian frontier in Bačka and Baranja led to quicker agreement than the Banat. The course of the rivers Danube, Drava, and Mur was adopted without much dispute. But west of Baranja the conflict was resumed.

The first problem concerning the Yugoslav-Austrian frontier lay in determining how far west the committee's jurisdiction extended. A second and more difficult problem was that of the Klagenfurt basin. The first issue was resolved with relative ease on March 13, when the committee voted to limit its competence to the Klagenfurt-Ljubljana road, with everything further west to be referred to the Council of Ten. But agreement on the Klagenfurt basin was not so easily (and inexpensively) obtained.

The Italians sought to have the whole basin assigned to Austria; the Americans suggested a compromise, with Klagenfurt to Austria and Maribor to Yugoslavia, and the French and British at first favored Yugoslav demands. To Seymour's formula of "Maribor for Klagenfurt," De Martino responded by refusing to consider *any* specific line in the basin until the fate of Maribor was settled. In Italian eyes Maribor became a key issue due to its strategic position as a railway center lying directly on the Italy-Austria-Hungary route. Hence it had to be in "friendly" Austrian hands. When the British and French delegates accused Italy of favoring a line of communications through "enemy" Austria rather than "allied" Yugoslavia, De Martino launched a disquisition about Yugoslav "treachery." The promise of international guarantees to safeguard Italian economic interests did nothing to modify his views. Tardieu and Crowe, in turn, refused to yield and proposed to adopt the Yugoslav line up to and including Maribor, which, they argued, was vital to the Yugoslav communications system and also involved the fate of all Prekomurje.

Partly in order to break the impasse and partly to complement the line taken by Sonnino and Orlando in the Council of Ten, the Italians now began to circulate reports about an alleged "deal" between the Yugoslavs and Hungary. In return for Hungarian support of the Yugoslavs' claim to Fiume, the latter were supposed to have agreed to grant concessions in Bačka and Baranja. Though meant to embarrass the Yugoslavs and to persuade the Allies of their political unreliability, the reports carried little weight. For it was obvious to anyone that Fiume was subject to the Council of Ten, where Yugoslav and Hungarian views counted very little, while in Bačka-Baranja the Yugoslavs admitted no compromise in their statements to the territorial committee. Under the circumstances, Belgrade had little reason to contemplate any bargains with Budapest, let alone enter into concrete negotiations.[60]

Another major problem facing the territorial committee was the Yugoslav-Bulgarian frontier. Here, in contrast to other regions, the great-power experts felt from the start that Yugoslav claims were excessive and ethnically unsound. If the Yugoslav line were adopted on the basis of strategic needs, Sofia, they maintained, would become militarily exposed. The Italians argued, not without foundation, that the military balance between Bulgaria and Serbia had been severely altered in the latter's favor through the creation of the large Yugoslav state. The rest of the committee agreed. But characteristically, the Italians proceeded from a sound general argument to extreme and unwarranted conclusions. They simply insisted on leaving the old frontier unchanged and on dismissing reasonable Yugoslav demands for the strategic protection of eastern Serbia. In sum, they proposed to ignore the reality of the historic Serbo-Bulgarian antagonism and the Bulgarian onslaughts of 1913 and 1915. In their view of Balkan geopolitics Bulgaria was clearly to serve as a counterweight to the new Yugoslav union.

The American, British, and French experts refused to go along with this. Though not favoring the entire Yugoslav claim, they urged some frontier rectification, particularly that most of the Strumica salient be assigned to the Serbs. The Vranje sector, on the other hand, was to be studied further by a military subcom-

60. See Crespi, *Alla Difesa d'Italia,* p. 348. In Belgrade, Dodge heard such a rumor in the middle of March and broached the matter to the Foreign Ministry. The Asst. Foreign Minister, Gavrilović, told him that he (Gavrilović) had been approached indirectly by the Hungarians with an offer of Hungarian support for the Yugoslav claim to Fiume in return for Yugoslav evacuation from Hungary. The feeler was turned down and never reached a negotiating stage, as alleged by Crespi, who attributes the initiative to the Yugoslav side. (Dodge to Lansing, Belgrade, March 22, 1919, 763.72.13031, Dept. of State, Washington.)

mittee. This subcommittee agreed upon a common line for the Strumica and for Vranje, but could not agree on the strategic Dragoman Pass and Caribrod. Of the four powers, only France (Laroche, Haumant, and General Le Rond) argued for a sweeping revision in favor of Yugoslavia, because the old line afforded the Bulgarians a "real offensive bridgehead against Serbia." [61] The French were willing to adopt a compromise line "following the watershed without giving special advantages either to the Bulgarians or to the Serbs." The Bulgarians, they felt, should retain the Dragoman Pass to protect their positions at Slivnica, "but not to keep the foot of the pass, which allows them to menace the Valley of Nish and the Morava." [62] This the Italians would not accept.

The Council of Ten, meanwhile, again demanded final reports from the territorial committees. Thus in the middle of March, though many of its positional conflicts were still unresolved, the Rumanian-Yugoslav committee began to prepare its final report. Countless drafts were drawn up for the separate frontiers and then debated in the greatest detail. Up to the last minute—the full report was submitted on April 6—agreement concerning the frontiers with Bulgaria and Rumania could not be reached, largely due to Italian insistence on reducing Yugoslav gains to a minimum.

During its existence, the committee split into two factions, with the French, British, and Americans constituting one and Italians the other. The Americans, however, did not really act as part of a given bloc. They pursued an independent line (particularly vis-à-vis Bulgaria and Klagenfurt) which most often coincided with the Anglo-French position rather than the Italian. In the case of the Banat, for example, the American experts refused to uphold the Treaty of Bucharest, to which the United States was not a party. The British and French experts agreed to regard the treaty as an entirely separate matter, though their governments were signatories to it. In the case of Bulgaria, the Americans sought a compromise line that would assure a "reasonable equality of strategic advantages" for both sides.[63] As for the Austrian frontier, they held to

61. CRYA-PV 11, March 5, 1919 (181.21601/11).
62. Ibid.
63. CRYA-PV 16–17, March 13, 18, 1919 (181.21601/16–17). During this session an

the formula "Klagenfurt for the Austrians, Maribor for the Yugo-slavs."

On the whole, American policy in the committee rested mainly on the principle of ethnic justice or self-determination, modified only in cases of urgent economic or strategic needs. This differed from the others in one important respect. French policy took into account future French influence in the Balkans, and therefore sought to strengthen the Yugoslav state even where this may have been inconsistent with purely ethnic principles. The Italians hoped to extend Italy's influence in the Balkans at the expense of Yugo-slavia, and therefore sought to buttress Bulgaria, Hungary, and Austria. The British, whose continental interests in 1919 did not extend beyond Western Europe, generally sided with the French and Americans, mainly because they were committed to support the new Yugoslav state and because supporting Italy served none of their broader political or economic interests.

On April 6 the committee's formal report was submitted to the Supreme Council (the Council of Four). Its boundary recom-mendations ranged from Bulgaria to Austria to the Klagenfurt-Ljubljana line. Everything to the west, being regarded as of "di-rect interest" to Italy, was left to the jurisdiction of the Council.[64] The Yugoslav-Albanian frontier was also left untouched.

The lengthy document on Yugoslav frontiers began on the Bul-garian side. It assigned to Yugoslavia the upper valley of the Strumica and most of the Vranje sector. As no agreement was reached on the Pirot region, two separate reports were submitted. The first was an Anglo-French proposal recommending that Serbia be given Caribrod and several positions to the east, with the Drago-man and Ginci passes, which control the approaches to Sofia, to Bulgaria. This plan was designed to give both sides maximum strategic security. The second, a joint Italo-American report, pro-

---

interesting dispute developed over the wording of the draft report. The Italians insisted on omitting any reference to Bulgaria's past aggressions. The Americans, however, though convinced that Serbian territorial claims were excessive, joined the British and French in insisting that the report underscore Serbia's unfortunate past experiences with the Bulgarians.

64. "Report [Nos. 1 and 2] Presented to the Supreme Council of the Allies by the Committee for the Study of Territorial Questions Relating to Rumania and Yugo-slavia," April 6, 1919 (181.21602/6–7, Dept. of State, Washington).

posed leaving this sector unchanged so as not to expose Sofia. Further north, the four-power experts agreed to leave the old frontier unchanged and reject the Yugoslav bid for Vidin. In its entirety the new proposed frontier fell materially short of Yugoslav demands, though in the south the strategic security of eastern Serbia was greatly improved. The underlying principles of the new frontier were mainly strategic (and historic in the sense of condemning Bulgaria's past aggression). The maximum Yugoslav line was rejected mainly because its total acceptance would place Bulgaria in a position of political and economic subordination vis-à-vis the new Yugoslav state and, the experts feared, prejudice the chances for a stable peace.

Turning to the Banat, the committee recommended assigning the Szeged area to Hungary and the remainder to Yugoslavia and Rumania. Yugoslavia was allotted part of the western Banat, excluding Temesvar which was to go to Rumania. The principles governing the partition were, in the first place, the maintenance of an equitable equilibrium between the nationalities—75,000 Rumanians were left in Yugoslavia, 65,000 Slavs in Rumania [65] —and in the second, a practicable distribution of rail and river communications (the latter under proposed international control) between the two Balkan states. The section on the Banat concluded with the statement: "Considering the complexity of the problem and the diverging passions manifested, the commission insists on the necessity of reciprocal engagements for the protection of minorities in conformity with the provisions of the League of Nations." [66] By these recommendations the Yugoslavs suffered a great blow, mainly in Temesvar. But they scored a tangible victory by securing, in effect, the rejection of the Treaty of Bucharest and the Rumanian claim to the indivisibility of the Banat.

Along southern Hungary the technical experts tried the impossible by combining the principles of natural frontiers, ethnic justice, and economic viability. As a result, they drew a line that reduced Yugoslav claims to a minimum. They rejected the Yugoslav demand for Prekomurje on the tenuous argument that the Slavic majority in the region, if joined to the Yugoslav state, would con-

65. Ibid., Report No. 2.
66. Ibid.

stitute too pronounced and exposed a salient. Medjumurje, however, was assigned to Yugoslavia, together with part of Bačka and
Baranja. The recommended line ran from the Tisza (south of
Szeged) to the Danube in such a way as to leave Subotica and
Sombor in Yugoslavia, but so as to exclude a sizable portion of the
claimed territory. From its junction with the Danube the line
ran to that river's confluence with the Drava, to its confluence with
the Mur. The rivers, corresponding to no ethnographic lines, were
adopted on the grounds of natural frontiers. They could hardly
satisfy the Yugoslavs from the ethnic point of view and were, therefore, immediately attacked as inadequate.

The Austrian frontier recommendations reflected sharply the
political divisions of the Allies. Two reports were submitted, with
the Italians strenuously objecting to the majority position. With
regard to Maribor, the French, British, and American experts advised assigning it to Yugoslavia due to the Slovene predominance
in the region, while the Italians would have it go to Austria. As
for the Klagenfurt basin, no concrete proposals were put forth.
The report merely pointed out that this region contained many
prevalently Slovene strongholds, but that it constituted a geographic entity, delimited in the south by the natural barrier of
the Karawanken chain. Due to this natural barrier, the experts
regarded the region as having greater economic unity with the
north than with the south. But they admitted lacking adequate
information about the desires of the local populations and urged
the establishment of a commission of inquiry.

Thus despite strenuous Italian opposition,[67] the Yugoslav-Austrian problem was left wide open. The report as a whole concluded by emphasizing the necessity of reciprocal guarantees between Yugoslavia and her neighbors to protect the rights of all
minorities.

The boundaries drawn by the experts effected for the most part
a reasonable compromise between factors of nationality, econom-
ics, strategic security, and historical precedent. They were not very
favorable to Yugoslavia. Where Yugoslav demands were so maximal as to be questionable—in Trieste, Scutari, and Klagenfurt—
the committee either had no jurisdiction or left the problem open.

67. The Italian delegate submitted a minority report. (ibid.).

Elsewhere, with the exception of the city of Temesvar and possibly Vidin in northern Bulgaria, Yugoslav demands were neither excessive nor contrary to the principle of nationality. The entire northern frontier involved areas of mixed populations where it was impossible to draw a strictly ethnographic line, a fact compounded by the absence of real natural barriers. Inevitably, therefore, *none* of the contestants could expect complete satisfaction.

In these circumstances, political considerations could not but affect the outcome. The Italians recognized this reality from the start. Consequently, they used their position in the technical committee to further Italian political objectives, attaining considerable success, even though they were more often in the minority than not. Their intervention favored the Austrians, Hungarians, Rumanians, and Bulgarians, all of whom (with the exception of the Rumanians) had been wartime enemies. The Serbs, recent Allies in the war, found their claims substantially reduced along Bulgaria and in the Banat, not to mention Croat and Slovene claims in the north.

Nonetheless, the Yugoslavs had some cause for satisfaction. They gained significant concessions in southern Bulgaria and the Banat, as well as important territories in the north. Moreover, the committee recommendations of April 6, which were eventually revised to their benefit, recognized the validity of the very principles upon which Yugoslav demands were based. In many ways, the most unfavorable aspect of the April 6 report lay in its failure to make progress on the explosive issues relating to Italy, Dalmatia, and Albania. For these problems the center of gravity remained at the highest political level of the conference, the Council of Four, where toward the end of March the conflict began to assume decisive proportions.

7. Enter Woodrow Wilson

UPON HIS RETURN to Paris on March 14, Woodrow Wilson found on his desk the Italian memorandum of claims. It formally demanded the application of the Treaty of London and Fiume as well, while a second memorandum depicted in bleak terms Italy's inferiority on the Adriatic.[1] With the presentation of these notes, the Italo-Yugoslav dispute moved into high gear. The Yugoslavs of course had no say in determining when the issue would come up for review. Pašić could not gain admittance before the Supreme Council.[2] The initiative lay strictly with the Americans and Italians.

Even prior to Wilson's return, the American delegation undertook a general review of the Adriatic problem under the guidance of Colonel House. On March 10 the latter met with Lloyd George and Clemenceau, and obtained their agreement to support the American experts' line rather than the Treaty of London. They also agreed to assign Fiume to Yugoslavia or propose its internationalization as a compromise.[3]

The Italian memoranda, however, served notice that such an agreement would not be accepted, prompting the American experts to re-examine the whole range of issues once again. Their report concluded that Italian strategic requirements were amply protected in the north and that neither the Tarvis region (Slovene and German in population) nor the Ljubljana-Fiume railway should be assigned to Italy. Moreover, Fiume was vital to the Yugoslav economy, especially if Trieste went to Italy, while Dalmatia (except for Zara) was to go to Yugoslavia on clearcut ethnic grounds.[4] A second report pertaining to Fiume alone listed

1. Miller *Diary, 6,* 454–56; Steed, *Through Thirty Years,* 2, 327–28.
2. Miller *Diary, 19,* 1529–30; *Résolutions* 172, March 11, 1919.
3. *House Papers, 4,* 359–60.
4. Miller *Diary, 6,* 411–13.

annexation to Italy, municipal autonomy, or an Italian mandate as further alternatives, but none of these was endorsed.[5]

Meanwhile, a rift developed in American ranks over Fiume and the Treaty of London. On March 16 Sidney B. Mezes wrote to House (probably with the approval of Miller), taking issue with the other experts. He recommended adopting the London treaty line in the north, various changes in Italy's favor along the western line, granting Fiume (with provision for a free port) and all the Dalmatian islands sought by Rome to Italy. In return, the Italians were to give up the Dodecanese and all Albanian and Asia Minor claims.[6] This letter caused consternation among Mezes' colleagues. Within two days Seymour, Day, Lunt, and Johnson wrote to House urging that Fiume and all of Dalmatia be given to the Yugoslavs. Johnson in particular, "whose judgment Wilson regarded as authoritative," [7] opposed any compromise with Italy.[8]

News of this rift apparently leaked out, and in order to put pressure on the Americans, the Italian delegation announced on March 21 that it would withdraw from the conference unless the Italian claims were taken up in the Council immediately and Fiume were assigned to Italy.[9] Three days later the "Ten Autocrats of Paris," as *New Europe* had baptized the Council,[10] reconstituted themselves as the Council of Four in order to expedite work on Italian problems as well as the growing Bolshevik menace in Hungary and Russia.[11] The Italian claims were placed on the agenda for the beginning of April.

The Yugoslavs were not consulted. But feeling that Wilson's return to the peace conference would lead to action very soon, they tried to exert some pressure of their own. In Paris, Pašić

5. Ibid., pp. 414–15.
6. Ibid., pp. 451–53.
7. *House Papers, 4,* 439.
8. Miller *Diary, 6,* 457–59.
9. C. T. Thompson, *The Peace Conference Day by Day* (New York, 1920), p. 256.
10. *New Europe, 10* (1919), 241.

11. In this connection it may be noted that on March 30 Smodlaka reported to the delegation that information which reached him from several Yugoslav regions, especially Primorje, claimed that Bolshevism was taking strong root in the country. He attributed this to economic dislocation and the lack of international support and recognition of the new state. (Zap., *1,* 177–78 [K&H, p. 91].)

asked for the abrogation of the Treaty of London on March 16,[12] while in Belgrade, Alexander and Protić successfully rallied Skupština support for the government.[13] They also informed the American minister that they would turn down any solution that denied the Yugoslavs either Fiume or Dalmatia.[14] On March 22 Protić accused the peace conference in the Skupština of using a double standard in dealing with Italy and Yugoslavia, while a week later Pašić wrote to Clemenceau in the same sense, adding a complaint against the Allied tendency to treat the former Austro-Hungarian Slav provinces as enemy territory.[15] These interventions, however, had little impact on events.

Wilson had planned to have House explain the American position to Orlando on April 4, when Lloyd George unexpectedly raised the Adriatic issue in the Council the day before. Great Britain, France, and the United States had, of course, already agreed that Fiume should not be assigned to Italy. Therefore, when Lloyd George brought up the subject on the 3d, they proposed hearing the Yugoslav side before proceeding any further. They decided to invite one Yugoslav delegate to appear that afternoon, but Orlando, refusing to be present, decided to spend the afternoon with House.

The invitation to appear before the Council at 4 P.M. arrived at Yugoslav headquarters precisely at 1 P.M., [16] in the midst of a delegation session devoted mainly to Albanian-Montenegrin affairs. After selecting Trumbić to go before the Big Four, the session was adjourned. Wilson, Clemenceau, and Lloyd George were friendly and discussed Fiume with Trumbić for over two hours. Though the Yugoslav offered to testify about the entire Adriatic problem, the questions were limited to Fiume. Wilson at one point asked whether Split could not serve as a port for the hinterland, and

12. *Pravda* (Belgrade), March 16, 1919.

13. *Sten. Bel.*, pp. 18–19.

14. Dodge to Lansing, Belgrade, March 18, 1919 (763.72119/4462, Dept. of State, Washington).

15. Dodge to Lansing, Belgrade, March 25, 1919 (763.72119/4319, Dept. of State, Washington); *Sten. Bel.*, p. 47; Pašić to Clemenceau, Paris, March 31, 1919 (Dossiers Klotz, A-7).

16. Zap., *1*, 191 (K&H, p. 96).

when Trumbić replied in the negative, Lloyd George agreed, pointing to the parallel of the rocky English coastline. In Trumbić's view the session went very well and in his reports to the delegation and the government next day, he expressed optimism about the Allied position on Fiume.[17]

Orlando and House, meantime, had also been exploring the problem of Fiume, but failed to come any closer to agreeing. As the Colonel ruefully recorded in his diary: "We would have little difficulty if it were not for Fiume. If the peace settlement had been made just after the Armistice, all these questions could have been settled without difficulty, for Fiume would never have been injected into the terms by the Italians."[18] Still, the issue was clearly moving into an advanced stage. By common tacit consent, the questions of Trieste and the Dalmatian *mainland* (except Zara) receded into the background. It had also become clear that Orlando was not unwilling to trade Dalmatia for Fiume, while on their side the Yugoslavs were no longer pressing for Trieste. As the conflict thus began to narrow, the main focus fell on Fiume.

Meanwhile, the American experts added a new dimension to the problem. Appealing directly to Wilson on April 4, they proposed for the first time the idea of an "independent" city or state for Fiume,[19] an idea that was to play a central role in the critical days that followed. On April 7 Orlando offered House a plan for a free city "to the west of Fiume," asking him to propose it to Wilson, who flatly turned it down.[20] Next day several American experts asked Wickham Steed (because of his intimacy with the Yugoslavs) to prepare a memorandum for Wilson to back up their position.[21] Steed advised the President not to dictate to either side.

17. Ibid., pp. 193–94; Trumbić to Ministry of Foreign Affairs, Paris, April 4, 1919 (TP, F66). See also the minutes of the Council meeting, in P. Mantoux, *Les Délibérations du Conseil des Quatre, (24 Mars–28 Juin, 1919)*, *1* (2 vols. Paris 1955), 132–39 (hereafter cited as *Délibérations*).

18. *House Papers, 4,* 441.

19. See Albrecht-Carrié, *Italy at the Peace Conference*, pp. 440–42, Doc. 34.

20. *House Papers, 4,* 441.

21. Steed, *Thirty Years, 2,* 327. At one point during this critical period the Italians tried to discredit Steed by circulating reports that before 1914, Steed had offered his services to Rumania for an annual fee of 100,000 lire. (Biancheri to Sonnino and Imperiali, Rome, April 12, 1919, Tel. 1262, MFA, Rome.)

Several days later (April 12) Steed was asked to serve as intermediary between the two sides, a task he both relished and carried on during the next four weeks.

The idea had gradually developed (in meetings of Western experts between April 7 and 11) of bringing the Italians and Yugoslavs face to face in hopes of facilitating direct negotiations. Neither side, however, fancied such a prospect so long as responsibility for an unpopular compromise could not be attributed to Wilson. Orlando—for Sonnino now receded into the background, as he disapproved of giving up Dalmatia and was hardly the man to negotiate a compromise—preferred not to meet directly with the Yugoslavs for the time being. Or at least it seemed so on the surface, for actually at this very juncture the Italians approached the Yugoslavs—though most quietly and privately. But they hardly expected that their initiative would lead to unfortunate results.

On March 31 the Yugoslavs held a plenary session attended also by four of the delegation experts on maritime and merchant shipping affairs. After a discussion of routine matters, the delegates were startled by a special report from the shipping magnate, now a technical expert, Božo Banac. After a recent meeting of the inter-Allied subcommission for merchant shipping, he was approached confidentially by one of the Italian members (Ceita) with the suggestion that Italy and the Yugoslav Kingdom come to an agreement concerning the division of the former Austro-Hungarian fleet. He suggested a private meeting of the two, to which Banac agreed in an "unofficial" capacity. During their friendly exchange the Italian argued that Great Britain and France were likely to participate in dividing the former Austro-Hungarian fleet —and take away the major part. Since this would not be in the best interests of either Italians or Yugoslavs, Ceita proposed an agreement between the two, based on the principle "the Adriatic for the Adriatics!" The Yugoslavs, he thought, should receive some 250,000 tons of shipping, and the Italians the rest (ca. 600,-000).[22] Furthermore, the Italian emphasized, there was need for a general political agreement and he urged that a meeting be ar-

22. Zap., *1*, 181 (K&H, p. 92).

ranged between the two sides involving several persons from each.

Banac's report was major news. After a short debate (in which Vesnić warned that any Yugoslav-supported move to cut out the British and the French might lead to unhappy results), Božo Banac and Melko Čingrija, also a maritime expert, were empowered to explore further the Italian offer and intentions, but strictly unofficially.

Several days later, on April 5, Čingrija reported that he, Banac, and Filip Wolf-Vuković had met with three Italian experts who had expounded the principle that all Adriatic shipping should belong only to the Adriatic states and again proposed 250,000 tons for the Yugoslavs with the rest for Italy. Banac, acting clearly beyond his instructions, then told the Italians that in his view such private discussions should be broadened to include political personalities as well, suggesting concretely the presence of the Italian plenipotentiary Silvio Crespi and of Trumbić. The Italians immediately responded that "Crespi gladly agrees to come." [23]

Now the delegation had to decide whether to agree and whether Trumbić should become involved. The Italians, reported Čingrija and Banac, were a) in a hurry to reach agreement on the merchant fleet, and b) determined to use this occasion to broach a whole range of other issues affecting the two sides.

The question of the fleet alone was a major one for the Yugoslavs, and the prospect of breaking the six-month deadlock was pleasing in itself. With the blockade of Dalmatia (and the remaining littoral) still in force and nearly the entire Austro-Hungarian fleet in Italian hands since the armistice—indeed, Italian interests were at this very time actively (and in violation of armistice stipulations) buying stock in former Austro-Hungarian shipping lines to gain control and even outright ownership [24]—the issue was urgent. Since the beginning of the peace conference, Trumbić and the Yugoslav maritime experts had devoted much energy to it. According to their estimates, about 250,000 tons of shipping was owned by Slav interests, [25] a figure the Italians re-

23. Ibid., p. 198 (K&H, p. 98).

24. Dr. Branko Kojić, "Postanak Jugoslavenske Trgovačke Mornarice," MS (Zagreb, 1956), p. 20. I am grateful to Dr. Kojić for permission to use and cite this valuable study.

25. Ibid., p. 19.

fused to accept until the unexpected offer at the turn of April.

But what lay behind this sudden Italian move? Having learned of the substantial Italian purchases of stock in the shipping companies, the Yugoslavs had protested to the Supreme Economic Council on several occasions. The Economic Council planned to review the matter on April 9, which it indeed did. On that day it also created an investigating subcommittee, under the chairmanship of John Foster Dulles, to examine the Yugoslav charges and also consider the Adriatic blockade. In anticipation, the Italians suddenly announced cancellation of the blockade and the subject was dropped from the subcommittee agenda. But as a side result of the investigation, the Allies decided to add the Austro-Hungarian fleet to the general merchant shipping pool already established for the German fleet. This was to be divided among the Allies in ratio to their wartime losses. Since total Allied losses amounted to some 9 million tons and available former enemy shipping amounted to roughly 4 million tons, each ally could count on regaining only 45 per cent.[26] Such a formula would have hurt the Italians, yielding about 370,000 tons in return for the 800,000 they claimed to have lost. As for the Yugoslavs, the formula would have been catastrophic, for *Serbia* had not been a maritime state and had had no merchant fleet, hence no maritime losses.

From every point of view, therefore, a direct arrangement—if it could be carried out—would favor both Italians and Yugoslavs. This the Italians quickly recognized, even before the Adriatic shipping was added to the Allied "pool," and hence the approach to the Yugoslavs. But since agreement to grant 250,000 tons to the Yugoslavs represented in their view a major concession, they planned to reap political dividends as well. The Yugoslav delegation felt understandably uneasy when Čingrija and Banac gave their report on April 5.

The experts, including Wolf-Vuković, strongly favored the division offered by the Italians as the only way to obtain a proper Yugoslav share. Trumbić wholeheartedly agreed. But Vesnić cautioned again against compromising Allied interests and acting behind British and French backs. "The matter," he said, "involves both political and legal aspects. From the political point of view, should we take the bait and make something separate of the

26. Ibid., p. 23.

Adriatic; is it our political interest to indulge in solidarity with the Italians in an egoistic affair and to the detriment of better and more certain friends?" From the legal point of view, Vesnić added, the entire venture would not succeed because the Allies would never agree to it. The proper legal procedure, he concluded, would be to argue not "the Adriatic for the Adriatics," but to ask for the removal of Adriatic shipping from the inter-Allied pool.[27] Bošković and Ribarž agreed with Vesnić, while Smodlaka supported Trumbić. The latter went on to argue that

> one must look at things realistically. This Italian proposal combines their interests and ours. We do not relinquish our territorial demands. . . . And who are the Allies [whose sensitivities worry Vesnić]? Neither France nor England ever recognized Serbia as an Ally; now they concluded a treaty with Poland, but never with Serbia; and they still regard our former Austro-Hungarian parts as enemy territories. What is involved here is our economic interest and we have to follow it because there is no other way. Perhaps the Allies will even welcome such an agreement on our part with Italy, because our dispute is one of the most difficult problems before them, and so they will sacrifice getting part of the shipping in the interest of this agreement.[28]

Vesnić disagreed, adding that their "strength always lay in that we have had no secret agreements, especially none that clearly violate all Allied interests . . ."[29] Pašić concurred.

In the end the delegation outvoted Trumbić and Smodlaka. It resolved to reject the Italian proposition and the principle that all Adriatic shipping be removed from the pool for exclusive division between the two Adriatic states, with the reservation that an agreement could be reached to remove from the pool only ships clearly owned by either Yugoslavs or Italians. The maritime experts were authorized to convey this to the Italians.

On April 8 Čingrija reported that he, Banac, and Wolf-Vuković had again met with the Italians, who agreed with the Yugoslav formula and dropped their own. A joint agreement to this effect

27. Zap., *1*, 200–01 (K&H, p. 99).
28. Ibid., pp. 202–03 (K&H, p. 100).
29. Ibid., p. 203 (K&H, p. 100).

was drafted and was approved by the delegation. Only the Italians insisted on using the term "Yugoslavia" rather than "Kingdom of Serbs, Croats and Slovenes." (When asked to change it two days later, they refused, saying that such a "political" gesture could only be effected by Crespi and not by mere technical experts.) Next day (on April 9) Vesnić was visited by an aide of Colonel House, who informed him that Wilson favored direct Italo-Yugoslav talks, while Banac reported that Crespi was anxious to meet Trumbić to explore other problems as well. In view of these developments, the Yugoslavs were bound to follow through. The government in Belgrade was not consulted. The Italian and Yugoslav experts now arranged a meeting for Crespi and Trumbić for April 11. On the 10th an agitated exchange developed in the delegation as to whether Trumbić should discuss general political questions or limit himself to the issue of the fleet and only listen to Crespi's exposé. This was the formula adopted, though Trumbić warned that his position as foreign minister would lead the Italian to expect more.

The encounter took place as scheduled, but far from yielding its intended result, it deepened the Adriatic rift. Trumbić, as he reported to the delegation the following day (April 12), opened the discussion with a review of the events leading to this meeting. Then, pointing out that he had come at the express wish of Crespi, he noted the Italian refusal to use the term "Kingdom of Serbs, Croats and Slovenes."

Crespi first stated that he had come with the knowledge of Orlando but not that of Sonnino, and then replied that the phraseology was only part of the general problem between the two states that had to be resolved. Then, going straight to the heart of the matter, he told Trumbić: "We must solve the question of Fiume; we Italians cannot give it up and you cannot get it. If Fiume were ours, we would grant you every concession for your trade. What Wilson wants is some sort of neutralization which would be good for neither you nor us. Only great hatred would prevail between us. So: Fiume to us, and to you the agreement, recognition, concessions, ships and the rest [*drugo*]." [30]

30. Ibid., 2, 17 (K&H, p. 108); and "Zapisnik Razgovora Trumbić-Crespi" (Trumbić's notes of the meeting), April 11, 1919 (TP, F66); Trumbić to Ministry

To this Trumbić replied: "I speak here only privately, but I am convinced that my view is shared by my whole nation: Fiume must be ours and about this there can be absolutely no discussion." [31] He elaborated all the reasons behind this stand, but the real end of the exchange had already come with the categorical declarations of both men. Concerning the fleet, Crespi simply announced that the agreement now remained *in suspenso* and on that note the two parted company. The meeting could have served a very useful purpose; instead, it only accelerated the crisis.

On April 14 Woodrow Wilson took things into his own hands. He saw Orlando twice that day—*à deux*. After one session in the morning, according to the Italian version, Orlando returned in the afternoon, bringing with him Andrea Ossoinack, the former Fiuman delegate to the Hungarian parliament, who argued for the annexation of Fiume to Italy.[32] Ossoinack told the President that the Italian majority in Fiume desired union with Italy, and had so indicated in a declaration on October 18, 1918.

Wilson used the occasion to present the American position to Orlando.[33] Essentially restating the views of his own staff, he offered Orlando a line coinciding with the Treaty of London only in the north, plus a partition of Istria. To this he added the island of Lošinj, demilitarization of the other islands, and control of Valona, all of which should afford, he argued, ample strategic security to Italy. Fiume, however, could not go to Italy because it was essential to the Yugoslavs. As a palliative, Wilson proposed a free city of Fiume within a Yugoslav customs framework.

By agreeing to the Treaty of London in the north but rejecting it in the east and south, Wilson weakened his position. The offer was inconsistent with his prior stand on the treaty as a whole. Orlando quickly detected the flaw, though the Italians were even less consistent than Wilson. For on the one hand, they insisted on

---

of Foreign Affairs, Paris, April 14, 1919 (TP, F66). In this report to the government Trumbić remarked that the conversation had been "loathsome." Interestingly, Crespi makes no reference to the meeting in his diary.

31. Zap., 2, 17–18 (K&H, p. 108).

32. Crespi, *Alla Difesa d'Italia*, pp. 424–28.

33. The following day Wilson complained to House that he had had a very "unhappy time . . . with Orlando yesterday" (*House Papers, 4,* 443).

the Treaty of London in order to get Dalmatia, while on the other hand, they brushed it aside in order to get Fiume. The meeting of April 14 produced no result, except that the "Wilson line" of partition in Istria quickly became the new Yugoslav symbol.

Next day Trumbić was apparently informed about the Wilson-Orlando talk by Johnson, for within twenty-four hours the Yugoslav delegation suddenly resolved to advance their plebiscite proposal to Clemenceau and submit the entire Italo-Yugoslav dispute to a popular vote.[34] As Trumbić reported to Belgrade, "the moment is right" and "Wilson's man" assured him that the President "knows our problem well and will remain faithful to his principles." [35]

And so on the 16th the plebiscite proposal was formally presented to Clemenceau, with copies sent to Wilson, Lloyd George, and Orlando. Wilson was sufficiently pleased and impressed to receive Pašić on the following day. The meeting was cordial. Pašić reviewed the Yugoslav position at great length (not only in regard to Fiume and Istria but everywhere), ending with an appeal to the President to help the Yugoslav cause which, he repeatedly stressed, was based on the principle of national self-determination. Wilson listened attentively and sympathetically, referring occasionally to the maps Pašić had brought along. He made no promises, but said at the end, as Pašić later reported to his delegation, that "he will help us with our just claims." This interview no doubt influenced Wilson's whole attitude in the mounting crisis.[36]

Orlando, meanwhile, went to Clemenceau, Balfour (Lloyd George had briefly gone to London), and Colonel House to complain about Wilson. House tried to bolster his spirits and offered to make Fiume a free city under League of Nations administration. This formula was opposed by Johnson, Day, and other experts, but Wilson apparently approved of it, telling Johnson: "I am ready to fight for the line you gentlemen have given me, with one possible exception: It may seem best to make Fiume an independent port." [37] But Orlando, fearing the fall of his cabinet if

34. Zap., 2, 22 (K&H, p. 110).
35. Trumbić to Ministry of Foreign Affairs, Paris, April 16, 1919 (TP, F66).
36. Zap., 2, 28–31 (K&H, pp. 113–14).
37. *House Papers, 4,* 442.

he failed to obtain Fiume, rejected the plan outright. The Italian attitude so discouraged House that on the 18th he told Wilson: "I have about come to the conclusion that since we cannot please the Italians by compromise, we might as well do what seems best in the judgment of our experts, and that is to give it [Fiume] directly to the Jugo-Slavs, safeguarding the rights of all those contributory to the port." [38]

He also urged Wilson to so press Lloyd George and Clemenceau and "commit them in order to present a united front." Lloyd George and Clemenceau refused, however, fearing that if they promised Fiume to the Yugoslavs, the Italians would demand the whole Treaty of London to which they were formally bound. House finally tried another approach: eastern Istria (the area which Wilson's line assigned to Yugoslavia) to Italy, and Fiume with northern Dalmatia under League trusteeship for an unspecified number of years. It was Lloyd George who put this plan before the Italians on April 20, because Wilson felt it "yielded too much," but Orlando refused it too.

And so the Italians, having failed to win over Trumbić or Wilson, now decided to press the issue in the Council of Four. But by April 19, when the Council met for this purpose, their position had been weakened. For by now Wilson had openly and firmly come out against Italian annexation of Fiume. In pressing such a solution further, so evidently misjudging their man, they drove Wilson into a position that could only hurt them—into the position, in effect, of becoming the chief spokesman for Yugoslav interests at the peace conference.

Orlando opened the Council discussion of the 19th with a detailed exposition of the Italian position, which, he argued, was affected by serious unrest at home. The problem, in his view, revolved around the Treaty of London. Though ordinarily he would not have based his arguments on the treaty, since the United States was not a party to it, he ended by demanding its total implementation *plus* Fiume, the latter on the grounds of self-determination.[39]

Wilson, however, reiterated his previous stand. The London

38. Ibid., p. 444.
39. *FRUS-PPC, 5,* 82.

agreement could not serve as a basis for settlement, at least not for the United States. He granted the validity of the strategic argument in the north, but south of Trieste and Pola it could not apply. As far as Fiume was concerned, the city was an Italian island in a Slavic sea, economically dependent on Yugoslav lands and Central Europe. Dalmatia was clearly Slavic and in a strategic sense would only place a burden on Italy in the event of hostilities. He (Wilson) doubted that the Yugoslavs posed a real menace to Italy, but in any event League of Nations supervision should provide adequate guarantees. Moreover, the United States was anxious to prevent the Balkans from again becoming involved in power politics.

Clemenceau and Lloyd George, whose governments were bound by the Treaty of London (though neither statesman had personally signed it), shared the President's views. They were particularly apprehensive about Italy's insistence on Fiume, because of its specific exclusion from the 1915 agreement. Lloyd George even expressed the view, which Clemenceau immediately echoed, that if the Italians insisted on the principle of self-determination for Fiume, that principle would have to be applied everywhere from Trieste to Split.

After three long hours of discussion, no solution could be found. Afterward, the Italian delegation held a "stormy meeting," [40] at which it decided to continue to stand by the Treaty of London.

The following morning, Easter Sunday, the Council debate was resumed. Orlando appeared with a declaration stating: "I must maintain all the declarations which I have made so far as the question of Fiume is concerned . . . if Fiume is not granted to Italy there will be among the Italian people a reaction of protest and of hatred so violent that it will give rise to the explosion of violent contrasts within a period that is more or less close." [41] He concluded, however, that since the Allies refused to recognize the right of Italy to break the alliance in the event that her claims were not satisfied, he, Orlando, pledged that he would not break the alliance.

Wilson immediately responded by asserting that he still could

40. Albrecht-Carrié, *Italy*, p. 133.
41. *FRUS-PPC*, 5, 95.

not be bound by the Treaty of London and that he regretted Orlando's intransigence with regard to Fiume. But then Wilson committed the blunder of conceding to Orlando that Italy was not bound by the Fourteen Points,[42] a tactical error that damaged the force of his main argument. The meeting yielded no result, save that Lloyd George's suggestion that the three signatories of the Treaty of London hold a separate meeting was accepted. Wilson now began to consider whether to wait for the outcome of these talks or to take independent action of his own. For the time being he decided to wait.

The meeting of Italian, British, and French leaders took place on the morning of April 21, producing little change. Lloyd George and Clemenceau indicated a willingness to stand by the Treaty of London, but not if they had to grant Fiume as well. Sonnino— who had re-entered the negotiating arena after the Wilson-Orlando talk of April 14—insisted on both. But since Wilson was resolutely opposed to the cession of either Fiume or Dalmatia, Lloyd George and Clemenceau were now at a loss for further suggestions. Both were unwilling to trade Wilson's good will for that of Italy, and they could only think of bartering a few additional islands off Dalmatia in return for an agreement on Fiume. When Sonnino returned to the theme of a revolution within Italy, Balfour impatiently noted that Italy could neither dispense with Fiume nor with American economic aid and thus might have to put up with revolution in the end.[43]

Wilson, at the same time, consulted with his advisers in regard to a public statement he had prepared and now proposed to issue. House urged him to wait and first consult with Lloyd George and Clemenceau.

The Yugoslavs, meanwhile, were active on the sidelines. The positive impression made by their formal offer on the 16th to submit the dispute to a popular vote, followed by Wilson's friendly reception of Pašić next day, raised their hopes somewhat. They now heavily counted on the American President. But alarming reports kept arriving from home, where the government was evidently

42. "J'ai toujours pensé et j'ai toujours reconnu que l'Italie n'était nullement liée par les Quatorze Points" (*Délibérations, 1,* 295).

43. Albrecht-Carrié, p. 135.

restive.[44] Furthermore, the peace conference secretariat refused to show them the final (April 6) territorial committee report, which they correctly took to augur ill. Dutasta's refusal to show the report and Tardieu's to reveal its details caused much bitterness in the Yugoslav delegation, leading Trumbić to write acidly to Belgrade: "They will probably inform us when they will need our signature." [45]

As for the Big Four talks, the Yugoslavs were kept informed, but not about specific details. Thus in the evening of April 18 they were reassured about the trend of events by Johnson, who dined with Professor Michael Pupin.[46] On the 21st, Trumbić learned that Wilson had again refused to recognize the Treaty of London and received "assurances" that the President was still "determined." [47]

Wilson, meanwhile, followed House's advice and discussed his proposed public statement with Lloyd George and Clemenceau. Both urged him to wait. The Italians at the same time drafted a letter announcing their readiness to sign the German treaty once their frontier problems were settled and cautioning their Allies to observe the joint agreement against signing a separate peace.[48]

44. On April 20 Protić cabled Trumbić to point out that political debate at home concerning Serbo-Croat relations was causing great anxiety. The Croat press, particularly the *Obzor,* made frequent allusions to the Pan-Serbianism of Pašić and the Radicals and to Serbian hegemony throughout the country. Many of the Croat critics were making use of Trumbić's name to support their position, or as Protić put it: "They also use your name without your knowledge as though you subscribed to their views. Please believe me I find it unpleasant to speak to you about this . . . Please prevent if you can the misuse of your name in this political agitation." And then: "Pašić has, like all of us, made many mistakes. But to accuse him of having worked against the union is criminal." (Protić to Trumbić, Belgrade, April 20, 1919, Personal. Tel. 4881, received in Paris on April 23, TP, F66.) At the same time Dodge reported "much unrest" everywhere. Korošec, incidentally, had told him that if the peace conference assigned Fiume, Trieste, and Istria to Italy, he (Korošec) would resign and withdraw his party from the coalition "so as, with greater freedom, to begin a formidable Irredentist movement." (Dodge to Lansing, Belgrade, April 16, 1919, 763.72119/4642, Dept. of State, Washington.)
45. Trumbić to Ministry of Foreign Affairs, Paris, April 21, 1919 (TP, F66); Zap., 2, 23–26, 32–33 (K&H, pp. 110–12, 114).
46. Pupin to Trumbić, Paris, April 19, 1919 (TP, F65)
47. Trumbić to Ministry of Foreign Affairs, Paris, April 21, 1919 (TP, F66).
48. Albrecht-Carrié, p. 136.

The next forty-eight hours saw some of the most frantic and confusing activity of the entire peace conference. Orlando in effect threatened to leave Paris—without signing the German treaty—if Italian demands were not met.[49] (Through Steed,[50] the Italians informed the Yugoslavs that a political agreement, apparently based on Crespi's offer, had to be reached within twenty-four hours.) Lloyd George scurried back and forth trying to effect a compromise. He succeeded in getting Wilson, now incensed over the Italian threat, to propose: Fiume a free city, the strategic islands to Italy, and Zara and Šibenik free cities under League of Nations protection.[51] Orlando turned this down, still demanding the annexation of Fiume. The Yugoslavs apparently did not know about Wilson's concession regarding the islands and Šibenik (the delegation held no meeting from April 21 to 24, hence the point is not recorded in the minutes), for on April 23 Trumbić cabled Protić that the situation had improved, that the British and French had refused to implement the London treaty, and that Wilson had made no new suggestions, hence the Italians had effectively failed.[52]

With Orlando's rejection of Wilson's last offer, the die was finally cast. On the morning of April 23 House advised Wilson to call the Italian bluff and put an end to this "game of poker."[53] At the same time, Lloyd George and Clemenceau made a last-minute appeal to Orlando to reconsider his stand on Fiume, the Treaty of London, and the decision to return to Rome.[54] Later in the day, knowing well the effect it was bound to have on Italian public opinion, Wilson took the irrevocable step and released his statement "Regarding the Disposition of Fiume" to the press.[55] The "manifesto" reviewed the whole problem of the Treaty of London, the dissolution of the Austro-Hungarian empire, the principles of the Fourteen Points, and the peace settlement.

49. Ibid.
50. Steed, *Thirty Years*, 2, 328–29.
51. Albrecht-Carrié, p. 136.
52. Trumbić to Ministry of Foreign Affairs, Paris, April 23, 1919 (TP, F66).
53. *House Papers, 4,* 446.
54. Miller *Diary, 19,* 536.
55. For the full text, see Baker, *World Settlement, 3,* 287–90.

Fiume, it said, must serve not only Italy but also Yugoslavia and all of Central and Eastern Europe. The President repeated the arguments of his April 14 memorandum, defending the Wilson line as the fulfillment not only of Italy's natural frontier but of her strategic security as well.

The manifesto's tone was one of explanation, not recrimination. As a restatement of Wilsonian principles, it was nothing short of brilliant. However this aspect was overshadowed by the sensation it produced. The breach in Allied ranks was now complete, endangering the chances of an early settlement. And as Seymour put it, "When the storm of Italian fury broke . . . upon the President's head," [56] Wilson found himself in isolation. He was now in effect appealing to the Italian people over the head of their government, without apparently calculating that his action would bring the government and the people closer. For he had obviously misjudged the temper of Italian nationalism where Fiume and the Adriatic were concerned. Italian popular feelings had been skillfully aroused by Sonnino who, together with Orlando, could now present their case on the unanswerable argument of *national honor.*

The Yugoslavs greeted the manifesto with a mixed reaction. "We are naturally elated over [Wilson's] stand, his restatement of Wilsonian principles, denunciation of the London treaty and refusal to give Fiume to Italy," Trumbić cabled to Belgrade. "But at the same time we regret that our issue is not yet resolved." [57] These sentiments were shared by the entire Yugoslav delegation: elation over Wilson's support of the Yugoslav cause and his firm stand on Fiume, tempered by disappointment over the "sacrifice" of great numbers of Istrian Slavs to Italy.[58] Žolger even wanted to write "privately" to Wilson in this sense, but the others wisely dissuaded him from doing so.[59]

---

56. *House Papers, 4,* 447.

57. Trumbić to Ministry of Foreign Affairs, Paris, April 24, 1919 (TP, F66). Trumbić added that Wilson's declaration had been approved by the American experts, "who according to American democratic ideas are not mere functionaries, but personalities with independent opinions." [!] At this point he also predicted rather accurately that if Orlando fell, his successor would be Nitti.

58. Zap., 2, 36 (K&H, pp. 115–16.)

59. Ibid. (K&H, p. 116).

The Italians of course reacted sharply. They were stunned and immediately prepared to leave for Rome. On the 24th, Orlando released a formal reply and departed for Rome, to be followed by Sonnino next day. Under the circumstances, Orlando's letter was a model of tact—and biting irony:

> The practice of addressing nations directly constitutes surely an innovation in international relations. I do not wish to complain, but I wish to record it as a precedent, so that at my own time I may follow it, inasmuch as this new custom doubtless constitutes the granting to nations of larger participation in international questions, and personally, I have always been of the opinion that such participation was a harbinger of a new order of things.[60]

And then it proceeded to reject Wilson's proposals and renew the demand for Fiume. In Italy, incidentally, publication of Wilson's manifesto was held up until the release of Orlando's reply so that the two statements could appear side by side, a tactic that paid good political dividends.

Hours before his departure from Paris, Orlando was handed a memorandum drawn up by Balfour, setting forth the British position on the crisis. In it Balfour noted that while Great Britain was a signatory to the Treaty of London, none of the premises of 1915 prevailed in 1919. Austria-Hungary no longer existed. Russia was no longer a factor. The United States was not a signatory, hence could not be held bound. Finally, the entire peace settlement would be undermined if based on anything but the manifest will of the populations concerned. Balfour essentially argued that conditions had so far changed that the signatories, while technically bound to the letter, could not feel morally bound to the spirit of the treaty, though it contained no *rebus sic stantibus* clause.

The British memorandum had little effect. It is interesting, however, to observe that neither the British nor the French made any use of the argument that Italy, contrary to obligations contracted in the Treaty of London, refrained from declaring war upon Germany until August 27, 1916, an omission which Nicol-

60. Woodhouse, *Italy and Jugoslavs*, p. 243. See also Baker, *World Settlement, 3,* 281–86.

son records as having been regarded in some British circles as "sufficiently serious to invalidate the whole Treaty of London." [61] This argument would, of course, have exasperated the Italians even more. Yet within two months even this argument came to be used.

The Yugoslavs regarded Orlando's reply to Wilson as "clever," but Trumbić for a moment mistakenly thought the new situation might force Orlando to accept compromise.[62] They became worried when Steed, on April 25, relayed a rumor that the Italians were planning to seize Fiume and proclaim its annexation.[63] Apprehension grew when later that day a senior journalist of the Paris *Temps* visited Trumbić and said that the French government feared the Italians might move on Ljubljana and even Zagreb. Was this a subtle communication from the French government, or an inquiry as to whether the Yugoslavs were militarily prepared? In any event, Trumbić replied that the Allies would be expected to intervene and then cabled Belgrade urging a military alert.[64] In a second telegram the same day, Trumbić sent a revised political estimate, predicting that Orlando and Sonnino would obtain a free hand at home. Great danger existed in regard to Fiume, and Lloyd George and Clemenceau might press for "autonomy," a solution Wilson's manifesto did not exclude. In view of all this, Trumbić suggested—in a move not so dissimilar to Wilson's—that the Skupština send a resolution to Congress in Washington asking it to protect the Yugoslav people from Italian infringements on their rights.[65]

All in all, the events of April 23–24 marked a climax in the diplomatic war. The Yugoslavs were willing to accept the Wilson line, despite the sacrifices it entailed, and place the blame on the American President without, however, injuring his prestige in the eyes of Yugoslav public opinion. They would thus emerge as paragons of moderation and champions of Allied unity. This line

61. "That," Balfour said at one point, "is a lawyer's argument." Shortly, however, Balfour came to use it himself. (Nicolson, *Peacemaking*, p. 161.)

62. Trumbić to Ministry of Foreign Affairs, Paris, April 25, 1919 (TP, F66).

63. Ibid.

64. Trumbić to Ministry of Foreign Affairs, Paris, April 26, 1919 (TP, F66).

65. Trumbić to Ministry of Foreign Affairs, Paris, April 26, 1919 (separate dispatch, TP, F66).

in fact was taken by the Yugoslav press at home. But a stalemate had now developed, causing great anxiety for the immediate future. From Belgrade, Dodge reported general awareness that a decisive stage had now been reached. The air was again filled with talk of possible war, into which, wrote Dodge, the people and the army, "although tired to the utmost of war, would rush with enthusiasm . . . to liberate [their] territories." [66]

The Adriatic crisis did not interrupt the administrative work of the peace conference. On the contrary, in late April the conference secretariat, believing the end to be in sight, began to prepare for the formal conclusion of the peace settlement. A note was sent to each delegation inquiring as to who would sign the documents of peace. Among the Yugoslavs, this routine request precipitated a disagreeable episode, exposing the very essence of their political dilemma.

Pašić relayed the secretariat's request at the delegation meeting of April 25. Vesnić, quite logically and in keeping with the tacit assumption prevailing for three months, proposed Pašić, Trumbić, and Žolger as signatories: one Serb, one Croat, and one Slovene. Whereupon Ribarž pointed out that Žolger might well refuse to sign. To avoid the embarrassment of making a last-minute change (after the official document forms were printed), he suggested that Vesnić sign instead. Žolger indeed confirmed the warning. Foreseeing the "territorial sacrifices" that would be imposed on the Slovenes in particular, he thought it "politically wiser" not to sign the peace treaty, for his signature would be used to stifle future Slovene irredentism. The others [67] all tried to make Žolger change his mind, but to no avail. The only recourse left was to refer the issue to Belgrade.

Pašić and Trumbić immediately cabled Protić, both agreeing that the peace treaty must be signed by a Serb and a Croat, as well as a Slovene. Žolger's argument, said Trumbić, is "wrong," since he does not represent the Slovenes as such but the entire nation.

---

66. Dodge to Lansing, Belgrade, April 30, 1919 (763.72119/5099, Dept. of State, Washington).

67. Pašić, Trumbić, Vesnić, Bošković, Smodlaka, and General Pešić, Zap., 2, 39–40 (K&H, p. 117).

The same argument, moreover, could be applied by the Croats. If Žolger did not sign, the Slovenes would blame everything on the Serbs and Croats.[68] Protić and the cabinet were evidently of the same view, for within ten days a cable arrived from Belgrade instructing Žolger to act as the third signatory.[69] For the moment at least, this question seemed to be solved.

But the conference secretariat note provoked another issue as well, for it was addressed (as all its previous communications) to the delegation of "Serbia" rather than to the "Kingdom of Serbs, Croats and Slovenes." To this Trumbić objected, categorically declaring that he would never agree to signing a peace treaty using such a form. Agreeing quickly, the delegation resolved to ask the peace conference secretariat for the appropriate "editorial correction" and also to so advise Belgrade. In this matter, too, the cabinet concurred, instructing the three delegates to sign "only as plenipotentiaries of the Kingdom S.C.S." [70]

Since it obviously involved serious political considerations, the editorial correction, it turned out, was not so easy to effect. All during May, Trumbić and Vesnić had to spend exasperating hours with conference secretariat officials and with members of the Allied delegations to obtain some satisfaction. The draft treaty presented to the Germans on May 7, for example, listed the country as "Serbie-Croatie-Slavonie [sic]," while the League of Nations statute listed simply "Serbie." But since the draft treaty (May 7 version) included "Serbie-Croatie-Slavonie" in the category of Allied and Associated Powers, Trumbić was prompted to observe: "I regard the question of our recognition resolved. We must only correct the terminology." [71]

Trumbić's optimism, without his own knowledge of the details, was actually well founded, for one unforeseen dividend of the Italian "walk out" from Paris was that it facilitated British and French recognition of the Yugoslav state. On the day following Orlando's departure, Clemenceau noted in a meeting with Wilson and Lloyd George that Britain and France had withheld recogni-

68. Trumbić to Protić, Paris, April 25, 1919 (TP, F66).
69. Zap., 2, (May 5, 1919), 52 (K&H, p. 122).
70. *Ibid.*
71. Trumbić to Ministry of Foreign Affairs, Paris, May 8, 1919 (TP, F66).

tion only "in order to please the Italians," [72] but that the time had come for a decision. With encouragement from Wilson, the French and British leaders then decided that if the Italians were still absent when negotiations with the Germans began, they would simply recognize the Yugoslav state. Formal action was postponed so as not to further antagonize the absent Italians and also to seek their approval when they returned. But since Rome's approval was not given, Great Britain and France bowed to the inevitable on their own and granted formal recognition on June 1 and 5 respectively.[73]

The conference secretariat of course effected the "editorial correction" only after the British and French governments had acted, managing quite effectively to ignore vociferous Italian objections. And so in the end procrastination came to a halt. The Yugoslavs' long battle was won and the term "Royaume des Serbes, Croates et Slovènes" was formally adopted. But by that time other crucial decisions had come to pass as well.

In abruptly leaving Paris, the Italians not only broke the façade of Allied unity and upset the conference schedule; they also rendered a quick Adriatic settlement impossible. No one doubted that they would come back and sign the German treaty, for Italy could ill afford isolation from her allies, with all its political and economic ramifications.

The Allies tried hard to persuade the Italians to return, at one point even threatening that Italian claims against Germany, mainly reparations, would be ignored unless Orlando came back. As for the Adriatic issue, Wilson declared on April 30: "As far as I am concerned, I declare that Italy can have all she can obtain by plebiscite," [74] thereby rejecting the idea of a compromise. This tough line was reinforced next day when the Council received word that the Germans would not exploit Orlando's withdrawal

72. *Délibérations, 1,* 385.

73. Their action was followed by Belgium on June 13, Rumania on July 3, and Spain on Aug. 4. Most other countries officially recognized the Kingdom of Serbs, Croats, and Slovenes prior to the signing of the Austrian peace treaty in September. Italian recognition may be said to date in effect from the signing of the Treaty of Versailles on June 28, 1919. See Temperley, *Peace Conference, 5,* 158–59.

74. *Délibérations, 1,* 422.

in order to delay negotiations; for now no olive branch had to be offered to Rome. In fact, to increase the pressure, the Big Three decided in the first week of May to begin work on the Austrian peace treaty, which directly involved Italian interests and could hardly be ignored by Rome.

Orlando and Sonnino, meanwhile, were anything but idle. Under their direction a massive nationalist campaign was launched in the Italian press, attacking Wilson and demanding Fiume. On April 26 the Italian National Council of Fiume "proclaimed" the annexation of the city to Italy,[75] a theatrical gesture designed to further inflame public feelings, but in reality signifying little. On May 1 Orlando again publicly demanded Fiume. In Paris, Lloyd George and Clemenceau responded two days later by deciding to invalidate the Treaty of London if Orlando did not return to work on the German treaty. But because Wilson objected that this implied American recognition of the London treaty, the Italians were not immediately informed of this decision.

Even so, Orlando and Sonnino began to realize that their absence from Paris was only hurting the Italian cause. Their allies showed no inclination to give in. On May 4 Orlando admitted this reality and decided to return to Paris, and two days later the Italians resumed their seats at the peace conference.[76] Their ten-day absence had accomplished nothing.

One of its by-products, however, was the publication in the Italian press of a story that caused some dismay within the Yugoslav peace delegation. According to the newspaper *Tribuna,* in a detailed account of the Wilson-Orlando talks in Paris, the President informed the Premier that Trumbić had told him that the Yugoslavs were prepared to give up Trieste, Gorizia, and Istria in the interests of reaching agreement with Italy. The story came to the ear of Žolger who (on May 2) demanded to hear from Trumbić whether it was true. If it was not, he expected the latter to issue a prompt public *démenti.*

Trumbić denied having told Wilson anything of the sort, adding that the *Tribuna* did not quote him but Wilson. Any démenti should come from Wilson; for him (Trumbić) to do it would be to

75. See G. Benedetti, *La Pace di Fiume* (Bologna, 1924), p. 32.
76. For further details see Albrecht-Carrié, *Italy,* pp. 153 ff.

disclaim the President. In any event, he would first have to find out from the American side whether Wilson had actually made such a statement and whether he would be willing to issue the démenti. Žolger, now seconded by Ribarž, was far from satisfied, but the delegation authorized Trumbić to explore the matter with the Americans. Under the circumstances, it also resolved to thank Wilson in writing for his defense of Yugoslav interests in his declaration of April 23, but to point out the "sacrifices" of Yugoslav lands that it entailed.[77]

During the next few days Trumbić met with Frazier (who had been present at the Wilson-Trumbić meeting) three times, and Frazier discussed the matter with Wilson once. Neither Wilson nor Frazier recalled, Trumbić reported to the delegation, his alleged offer to the President, nor indeed that Wilson had made such a statement to Orlando. Wilson never issued démentis, nor would he do so now. As to a démenti by Trumbić, Frazier advised against it, because it would appear as censuring the President. But if the delegation insisted, said Trumbić, he was ready to issue a statement disclaiming the *Tribuna* story, regardless of consequences.

Žolger, either disbelieving Trumbić's account of what Frazier had said or out of anger at the inevitable Slovene losses, demanded the démenti from Trumbić. Pašić and Vesnić, however, intervened, arguing that Wilson must be given no cause for offense. They suggested instead that Trumbić issue a statement in the near future, and, without referring to Wilson or the *Tribuna* story, restate all the Yugoslav territorial claims. Thus, by reiterating the claim to Trieste, Gorizia, and Istria, the *Tribuna* claim would automatically be rejected. So much discussion followed this proposal that Trumbić became exasperated and gave an ultimatum: "I submit to the Delegation only one question. Am I to issue a *démenti* stating: 'It is not true that I declared to Wilson that the Kingdom SCS is ready to give up Gorizia, Trieste and Pola, as announced in the *Tribuna* of April 25.' And nothing else." [78] This was of course not accepted, but Trumbić would hear of no alternative. Either this or nothing. A decision was postponed and on

77. Zap., 2, 46–47 (K&H, pp. 119–20).
78. Ibid., p. 55 (K&H, p. 123).

May 9, when Trumbić again refused to budge, the delegation voted that "Dr. Trumbić should not issue a *démenti* in the form he proposed." [79] This brought the incident to an end, but not without leaving bad feelings between Trumbić and the others.

In the international arena, meanwhile, Colonel House initiated a new line of action to break the Adriatic deadlock. His idea was to bring the Italians and Yugoslavs face to face and in effect force them to compromise. It stemmed, perhaps logically, from a series of moves and countermoves that threatened to make the crisis even worse.

On May 4 Trumbić went to Steed asking him to transmit a new Yugoslav proposal to the Americans, calling for the demilitarization of the Dalmatian coast and islands, with Italy free to fortify those outer islands ultimately assigned to her.[80] Why Trumbić used Steed when he saw Johnson several times between May 5 and May 10 [81] is not entirely clear, unless he acted entirely on his own, without authority from the Yugoslav delegation.[82] Steed took the plan to Johnson. Meanwhile, the Italians too asked Steed to transmit a new proposal to the Americans, by which the "municipal territory" of Fiume would be assigned to Italy and then be leased to Yugoslavia for ninety-nine years.[83] The American experts, however, refused to approve this, preferring to place Fiume under the League of Nations for an unspecified number of years and then settle its fate by plebiscite.

On May 8 Johnson composed a memorandum embodying the League plus plebiscite idea and concluding that a "plebiscite in Fiume would, in the opinion of competent observers, show a majority in favor of Jugoslav sovereignty for economic reasons under present economic conditions." [84] In the event of an Italian majority, the annexation of Fiume to Italy, he added, should be postponed until the Italians built a new port for Yugoslavia at

79. Ibid., p. 59 (K&H, p. 125).
80. Steed, *Thirty Years, 2,* 331.
81. Trumbić to Ministry of Foreign Affairs, Paris, May 13, 1919 (TP, F66).
82. The delegation minutes of May 5–10 contain no record that Trumbić reported on his conversations with either Steed or Johnson.
83. Steed, *Thirty Years, 2,* 331.
84. Baker, *World Settlement, 3,* 297.

Bakar (a plan the Italians had advanced in return for getting Fiume) in every way equivalent to that of Fiume. If the Italians failed to meet these conditions, Fiume should be given to Yugoslavia.

Johnson's memorandum contained additional provisions by which Italy would get the Treaty of London line in the north, the Tarvis district (which American experts recommended for Italy "on condition that Fiume go to Jugoslavia"), and the islands of Lussin (Lošinj), Pelagosa (Palagruža) and Lissa (Vis). This plan was unanimously endorsed by the American experts, with the recommendation that the Wilson line be adopted in Istria. It stipulated that Italian troops east of the line be withdrawn pending a future plebiscite in the whole area; that a plebiscite be held in Italian-claimed Dalmatia (as a unit, however, to avoid giving Italy widely separated enclaves); that Zara become a free city; that there be Italian sovereignty over Valona, with a "sufficient" hinterland; that there be possible mandates in Asia Minor and Africa; and finally, that a favorable American loan be made as evidence of American "friendship for Italy." [85] A common condition to all these provisions was the immediate withdrawal of Italian troops from Slav territory.

When Johnson consulted Trumbić about this plan, the latter accepted it at once. In fact, to strengthen it further, he now formally offered the demilitarization of the entire Yugoslav coast, which Johnson quickly included in his plan, together with a guarantee of free Yugoslav passage through the Straits of Otranto, "even in time of war." [86]

The plan in effect guaranteed that Fiume would eventually go to the Yugoslavs, which horrified the Italians.[87] They rejected it, and on May 10, in half-desperation, suggested to Steed that he promote direct Italo-Yugoslav negotiations.[88]

Colonel House, meanwhile, with the aid of David Hunter Miller, had already explored the possibility of sponsoring an Italo-Yugoslav meeting with Vincenzo Macchi di Cellere, the Italian

85. Ibid., pp. 299–302.
86. Ibid., p. 302.
87. See Albrecht-Carrié, p. 164.
88. According to Steed (*Thirty Years*, 2, 332), they even informed House that barring a favorable solution "Sonnino would commit suicide."

ambassador to Washington. On May 12, House met with Sonnino and Di Cellere, with whom it was decided to let Miller and
Di Cellere work out a new proposal. Later that day House suggested to Wilson the idea of placing Fiume under the League
until "good sense and calm judgment" prevailed.[89] Wilson, who
had become so annoyed with the whole imbroglio that he refused
to see personally either the Italians or the Yugoslavs, apparently
approved, for House proposed the same plan to Orlando the following day. Orlando accepted it, in principle at least, agreeing to
work out the technical and legal details with Miller. But the two
failed to reach a satisfactory understanding, though, according to
House, they "made some progress."

Learning about the talks, Wilson feared that Orlando might
interpret the overtures as a binding offer, but agreed to their continuation when House assured him that Orlando understood them
to be no more than a *pourparler*. The failure to reach an agreement thus far was due mainly to Orlando's determination to make
certain that Fiume would not go to the Yugoslavs—under any circumstances.

On May 14 Orlando informed House that the Italian delegation
was willing to reach a direct agreement with the Yugoslavs "on the
whole Adriatic question, including Fiume," and asked whether
the President would object to such an arrangement. Wilson sent
word that he had no objection so long as the agreement were
"freely reached." [90] Wilson also agreed that such a meeting could
take place under American auspices, a point requested by Orlando,
probably as a face-saving device in the event of failure.

Next morning (May 15) House called Trumbić over and proposed a direct Italo-Yugoslav meeting, but in such a way that one
party would occupy one room and the other party a second room,
with the Americans acting as go-betweens.

In his lengthy report to the cabinet,[91] Trumbić noted that
House had warned that in the event of failure Orlando and Son-

---

89. *House Papers, 4,* 463; Miller *Diary, 1,* 300–02.
90. Specifically, without pressuring the Yugoslavs. See *House Papers, 4,* 464.
91. "Izvještaj od 15–20 Maja Delegata Trumbića za Kraljevsku Vladu," Paris, May
21, 1919 (TP, F66).

nino might force the British and French to implement the whole Treaty of London. Trumbić merely replied that he would immediately place the proposal before the Yugoslav delegation.

The delegation agreed to the meeting with the Italians and selected Trumbić for the task. Trumbić, however, asked ("before I undertake this unpleasant mandate") for precise instructions concerning the Yugoslav position. After an "exhaustive debate," Trumbić's report continued, "the Delegation resolved unanimously that the final limit of our concessions" in Istria would coincide with Johnson's memorandum, while with regard to the Adriatic, from the Raša south, Italian sovereignty on any islands or the mainland must be "absolutely and unconditionally" prevented: "This was to be the underlying basis. With regard to questions of detail, however, such as Fiume, Zara, Šibenik, Vis and Lošinj, which come into question as a result of Italian claims, our delegation took the position that once Italian sovereignty in any of these centers is excluded, it is prepared to negotiate, if necessary, special arrangements in regard to individual cases." [92]

Having in the meantime found out that the territorial committee had left Prekomurje to Hungary, the Yugoslavs feared the Allies might make further concessions at their expense, particularly in Carinthia. They therefore decided to link the Adriatic issue with the north and northwestern frontiers and to explore the matter with House. On the morning of the 16th, Trumbić discussed all this with him. House, determined to proceed with the planned Italo-Yugoslav meeting, called in Johnson and the two together tried to reassure Trumbić, promising to urge Wilson to champion the Yugoslav claims in the north. Johnson also suggested that the Yugoslavs obtain British support in this regard, which Smodlaka attempted later in the day. [93] House tried to soften Trumbić's position, but the Yugoslav, while agreeing to the

---

92. Ibid.

93. Nicolson, *Peacemaking*, p. 340. At the same time Trumbić and Pašić also cabled Protić asking approval of the delegation's position. Protić's reply came too late, but gave complete approval: "I approve direct talks . . . We do not approve any concessions from principal claims . . . nor to recognize to Italy Fiume or Zara. On our part we have done everything possible by offering arbitration, plebiscite, national self-determination." (Protić to Pašić, Belgrade, May 21, 1919, TP, F66).

meeting with Orlando, refused to make any concrete commitments.[94] Undaunted, House arranged the meeting with the Italians for that afternoon.

What followed was a bizarre session in the Colonel's suite at the Crillon, in which Trumbić was closeted in one room with Johnson and Frazier, while Orlando and Di Cellere were in another with Miller and George Louis Beer (the American expert on colonial questions), with House using the middle room as a control center. The meeting—Trumbić and Orlando never came face to face—lasted four hours and resulted in a complete deadlock. House exaggeratedly noted that "we got them so nearly to an agreement that it was a matter of deep regret that we could not bring them all the way." [95] For in fact, while the Americans frantically scurried from room to room trying to find some commonly acceptable formula, neither Trumbić nor Orlando would yield on the central points. The Italian actually came hoping to use the Americans to apply pressure on the Yugoslavs.

The final formula offered to Trumbić by House involved making Fiume with Sušak an independent city under League guarantee, with a free port (and improvements financed by the great powers); giving Dalmatia (neutralized) to Yugoslavia, and the islands of Lošinj, Vis, and Palagruža to Italy—with the open questions being eastern Istria, Zara, and Šibenik, and the other islands mentioned in the Treaty of London. Trumbić accepted Fiume as an independent city, provided Italian sovereignty was forever excluded, and demanded that everything else (including Sušak with Porto Baroš) go to Yugoslavia.[96] This Orlando rejected, and after further negotiations the meeting finally broke up. Trumbić's hands were tied by the instructions he received. But it is worth noting that these were issued by the delegation at his own insistence, a fact probably reflecting his determination to commit the Serbian members in particular to a firm stand on the northern Adriatic.

Despite the deadlock, the Crillon meeting had one important result. Both the Italians and Yugoslavs came to accept the princi-

---

94. *House Papers, 4,* 464–65.
95. Ibid., p. 465.
96. "Izvještaj od 15–20 Maja Delegata Trumbića . . ." (TP, F66).

ple of an independent Fiume under some form of League control
—provided of course that ultimate sovereignty would not be assigned to the opposing party. The acceptance of this principle
immediately focused attention on eastern Istria, for the main issue now would concern the land connection between (independent) Fiume and Italy. For obvious reasons Orlando insisted on
extending Italian sovereignty all the way to Fiume, while for
equally obvious reasons Trumbić would not yield an inch east of
the Wilson line. This became the crux of the problem following
the Crillon talks.

Wilson, who received detailed accounts of the talks from
House,[97] was no more in a mood to coddle the Italians after May
16 than he had been before. During the next few days, in talks
with Lloyd George and Clemenceau, as well as with his own advisers, the President remained ill-disposed toward the Italians,
even on learning (from Lloyd George) that Orlando would gladly
trade all Italian concessions in Asia Minor for Fiume. Unmoved,
Wilson merely observed (on May 19) that Orlando would do best
to make the Italian people understand that it was not in Italy's
interest to ruin its relations with the United States.[98] The same
day Miller made an effort to bring Sonnino around to a more
conciliatory view. When he failed, further talks between the
American and Italian sides were, for the time being, allowed to
lapse.

With the Americans temporarily out of the picture, Orlando decided to enlist the French. Troubled by the precarious situation
at home—an increasingly restive public opinion and political opposition based on lack of results—Orlando had to move lest the
cabinet fall. When the Adriatic issue came up at the Council
meeting of May 26, the Italian Premier again found himself in a
minority of one. Wilson spoke in terms of a plebiscite, to which
Orlando responded by demanding the Treaty of London all over
again. This so infuriated Clemenceau that at the end he growled:
"You propose the Treaty of London: that's not a solution; that is

97. Trumbić, meantime, reported to Belgrade that House told him Orlando was
to blame for the failure of the talks (TP, F66).
98. *Délibérations*, 2, 113.

anarchy . . ." [99] Nonetheless, he asked Orlando to come forth with a new proposal.

But instead of presenting a new proposal, Orlando approached Tardieu suggesting that *he* advance a *French* plan. Tardieu consulted Clemenceau and House, and with their concurrence, agreed to do so. This *French* scheme, known ever since as the Tardieu Plan, was hammered out after a long night-session with the Italians on May 27–28. It embodied most (but not all) of the ideas advanced by Orlando at the Crillon talks of May 16. The plan called for the establishment of a temporarily independent, demilitarized buffer state of Fiume—excluding Sušak—with a hinterland extending to the Assling triangle, the latter to go to Austria. The western boundary of this state would run roughly along the Wilson line—thus denying eastern Istria to the Yugoslavs—and include the island of Krk (Veglia). The buffer state would be administered by a five-member commission: one named by Yugoslavia, one by Fiume, one by the League of Nations, and two by Italy. The port would become a free zone, and a League-supervised plebiscite would decide the ultimate fate of the entire state after fifteen years. Furthermore, Italy would annex Zara and Šibenik, the islands of Cres (Cherso), Vis (Lissa), Lošinj (Lussin), and Palagruža (Pelagosa), and receive a mandate over Albania, with the Yugoslavs to participate in the construction of the North Albanian railroad. Finally, all of Yugoslav Dalmatia would be neutralized.[100]

Wilson demurred. He opposed *forcing* this plan on the Yugoslavs—though House would have done so [101]—and feared the consequences of granting Italy the Fiume-Sušak islands and a mandate over Albania. Due to his intervention, the American experts made certain modifications in the Tardieu Plan, mainly to make Zara and Šibenik free cities under League protection. Then, on May 30, the United States delegation invited the Yugoslavs to a joint meeting, which Wilson did not attend, and presented them with this latest package-proposal.

99. Ibid., p. 227.

100. Šišić, *Jadransko Pitanje*, pp. 32–33.

101. House argued that "we have the Adriatic question whittled down to the vanishing point" and urged the President not to complicate matters (*House Papers, 4,* 471).

The Yugoslavs now faced a trying test. The fact itself that the new plan was being presented by the Americans, with Wilson's knowledge and approval, amounted to considerable pressure. Great sacrifice was being asked, but to reject the plan outright would alienate Wilson, their principal protector and only genuine "friend." Moreover, at the meeting of the American and Yugoslav delegations Secretary Lansing argued that Wilson's position had become difficult due to the impatience for peace of American public opinion and that "for the American people Fiume cannot and must not be the sole obstacle to peace . . . Therefore, sacrifices are called for on our side as well." [102] The Yugoslavs were asked to reply by 10 A.M. next day.

The reply was given at the appointed hour.[103] It sought to meet the Americans half way, recognizing that political realities had been asserted over abstract principles: "In the interests of world peace and taking into account the difficult position of the Great Powers, which have given us so much proof of their friendly attitudes, we are forced by circumstances to agree on the whole also to these new sacrifices." While in effect rejecting certain provisions of the Tardieu Plan, the Yugoslav delegation agreed to abandon the claim to Gorizia, Trieste, most of Istria, southwest Carinthia, and parts of Carniola—on the "assumption" of being assigned the southern part of the Klagenfurt basin, without the city of Klagenfurt. It further agreed to a free state of Fiume (with about 160,000 Yugoslavs and 30,000 Italians), provided it included all of eastern Istria and the island of Cres (Cherso), and assigned Sušak, Porto Baroš, and the Croatian hinterland to Yugoslavia; with Italy and Yugoslavia to have equal representation on the governing council of the Fiume state; with a plebiscite in the "free state" after three years to determine whether it wanted to join Italy or Yugoslavia (and if the latter, the Fiume *municipality* would be obliged to hold a further plebiscite to choose between joining the Serbo–Croat–Slovene state or gaining free city status

102. Zap., 2, 87 (K&H, p. 138).

103. Ibid., pp. 88–90 (K&H, pp. 138–39); "Neslužbeni Odgovor Delegacije SHS na Projekt Što joj ga je Predložila Američka Delegacija kao Posrednik u Pokušaju Direktnog Sporazuma Italo-Jugoslavenskog o Jadranskom Pitanju," Paris, May 31, 1919 (TP, F66). The document was drafted by Smodlaka, Ribarž, and Cvijić, and approved by the entire delegation.

like Danzig); with the Lošinj, Vis, Lastovo, Palagruža island groups placed under League control for three years pending final plebiscite (but under no circumstances to fall under Italian sovereignty); and with Zara and Šibenik under Yugoslav sovereignty, but enjoying wide autonomy.[104] In sum, the Yugoslav position excluded Italian sovereignty anywhere on the Dalmatian mainland or islands, arguing on the basis of popular self-determination. However, it accepted the permanent loss of western, and the temporary loss of eastern, Istria. As to Fiume proper, the possibility of its permanent loss (provided it did not go to Italy) was conceded for the first time. This position entailed considerable sacrifice and a major accommodation to the great powers.[105]

The Big Four discussed the Yugoslav reply on June 6.[106] They decided to have Wilson draft a definitive memorandum on the proposed Fiuman state to forestall Yugoslav rejection. Wilson did not relish this role, but with the approach of the final German treaty, the pressure of domestic and other international affairs, as well as the seemingly endless Adriatic crisis, he was becoming more susceptible to his partners' entreatments. On June 7, nonetheless, he warned Orlando that the American government would yield no more than it already had. But Wilson did make a further concession: he agreed to let Italy have Lošinj and the Zara islands outright, as well as Lastovo and Palagruža. (Fortunately for the Yugoslavs, Orlando was still not satisfied.)

Ten crucial days went by and none of this was communicated to the Yugoslavs. But Smodlaka somehow discovered the truth—how is not clear—and promptly went to Johnson, who confirmed it.[107] Dismayed, Smodlaka informed his fellow delegates on June 19 about Wilson's concession on the islands, and the delegation immediately resolved to write to the President directly, asking that no final decisions be made before hearing the Yugoslav side.

But by this time a bigger drama had unfolded. Unable to sway Wilson on Zara and Šibenik and Cherso, Orlando had returned to

104. "Neslužbeni Odgovor."

105. The government was kept fully informed, though due to the pressure of time, the delegation acted on its own authority. Belgrade gave its subsequent approval.

106. *Délibérations*, 2, 322 ff.

107. Zap., 2, 121 (K&H, p. 151.)

Rome to mend political fences. Faced with a rebellious parliament, and in view of his apparent failures in Paris, Orlando suddenly resigned on June 19. This action unexpectedly removed Orlando and Sonnino from the peace conference, less than ten days before the signing of the Treaty of Versailles.

Woodrow Wilson had hoped to resolve the Adriatic question simultaneously with the conclusion of the German settlement. Orlando's and Sonnino's fall now made this impossible. Their successors, Francesco Nitti and Tommaso Tittoni, would require some time before negotiations could be resumed. But Wilson had decided to return home right after the signing of the German treaty.

For the Yugoslavs the situation was unclear. Faced with the prospect of Wilson's departure and a fresh start with a new Italian team, they took fright and after much debate decided to send Pašić and Trumbić to Wilson.[108] But the President, for lack of time, could no longer receive them. They then frantically set to work on the letter to Wilson (first proposed on June 19), which Trumbić drafted and the others took apart. In it the Yugoslavs tried to define the *absolute minimum* they could accept, but such a policy statement could not be advanced without express government sanction. Failing to reach agreement, between June 24 and 27,[109] they decided to fall back on Belgrade. On the 27th, however, word arrived that Premier Protić and several members of the cabinet had decided to come to Paris [110] to explore the whole range of Yugoslav political and economic questions (mainly in connection with the Austrian treaty), and this temporarily shelved the "Wilson memorandum" project.

Sonnino's disappearance from the scene brought a whole era to an end. But Wilson's departure from Paris, after the signing of the Treaty of Versailles on June 28, 1919, marked an even more significant turning point. For the Yugoslav problem at the peace conference was not merely unresolved—it was only just beginning to unfold.

108. Ibid., p. 129 (K&H, p. 154).
109. Ibid., pp. 127–40 (K&H, pp. 154–58).
110. Ibid., p. 140 (K&H, p. 158).

8. The Making of St. Germain

FOR THE United States, Great Britain, and France the signing of the German treaty brought the main business of the peace conference to an end. Not so for Italy and Yugoslavia, whose chief interests revolved around the Austrian settlement. The Yugoslavs, moreover, had a vital stake in the Hungarian and Bulgarian settlements as well.

In its broadest context the peace of Versailles was conceived and designed mainly to keep Germany in tow by demolishing its power structure and, in the second place, to give expression to the universal right of national self-determination. Both objectives involved, in part at least, the dismantling of the Central Powers' empires and the creation of a new system of national states in Eastern Europe. (The break-up of the Russian empire was of course not expected, though temporarily it too served the interests of self-determination.) With the German treaty out of the way, the attention of the powers logically focused on Eastern Europe. This region now became the main political battleground of the peace conference.

Woodrow Wilson, Treaty and League in hand, returned home to face congressional warfare and physical calamity, both of which effectively barred his continuing intervention in peace conference affairs. Lloyd George, though present or close to the scene, gave himself largely to the problem of implementing the German terms, as well as to other fields of interest to Great Britain, of which Eastern Europe was not the main. It remained for France, with her historic continental concepts and her fear of a revived Germany, to take the most active part in casting the states of the Balkans and northeast Europe into a system of power designed to further her security. Italy tried to exploit the new postwar situation by replacing Austria-Hungary as the dominant factor in the Balkans, but ran afoul of French plans for the area. This became especially evident in the making of the Austrian and Bulgarian treaties. For as Italian policy sought to enhance its position by containment of the Yugoslavs and selective bolstering of their antagonists, French policy developed along opposite lines. Indeed, with regard to the territorial problems of Austria and Bulgaria in particular, the French gradually replaced Woodrow Wilson as champions of the Yugoslav cause.

The Yugoslavs, for their part, quickly became sensitive to this trend, encouraging it in every possible way. But partly because full French support did not extend to the Adriatic—due to the Treaty of London and French determination not to provoke Italy into open rivalry—and partly in the (correct) belief that American support was still decisive, they continued to portray themselves and act as protégés of the absent Wilson. They maintained close contact with the American delegation, while at the same time cultivating the French. Despite the limited possibilities for initiative, in this regard Yugoslav diplomacy met with some success in the months that followed the signing of the German peace.

Absorbed by their own affairs almost to the exclusion of more general peace conference problems, the Yugoslavs had little cause to rejoice as they faced the summer of 1919. Not only the Adriatic, but all of their frontier problems were as yet unresolved. As details of the territorial committee recommendations (of April 6) gradually became known, the Yugoslavs became increasingly alarmed. By the beginning of May they discovered that some of their claims along Bulgaria, Austria, and Hungary had been rejected. This prompted a re-examination of the claims within the delegation and a decision to stand by the original demands.[1]

In the late spring and early summer the diplomatic game that was being played in Paris assumed a new urgency as a recurrence of violence broke out in Carinthia, Albania, Fiume, and all along the Adriatic coast. Carinthia in particular developed into a major crisis, threatening to result in large-scale war. During the month of May so much fighting took place between Austrian and Yugoslav units in the Klagenfurt basin that the Council of Foreign Ministers in Paris was forced to intervene. Neither side had respected the poorly defined armistice line of November 1918, or

1. Zap., 2, 48 ff. (K&H, pp. 120 ff.).

the revised line suggested by the American investigating team of January 1919. The Yugoslav territorial committee, in its report of April 6, left the Klagenfurt problem in the hands of the Council of Four. The Council in turn, instead of dealing with it promptly, reassigned it to the expert committee for further study. In view of the uncertain state of affairs, the Yugoslavs and Austrians took things into their own hands in the field.

The main diplomatic problem revolved around economic issues, particularly the disposition of the railway complex connecting the Danubian plain with Italy and the Adriatic.[2] The Yugoslavs claimed both the Tarvis and Assling triangles as well as the entire Klagenfurt basin, arguing that the region as a whole was predominantly Slovene and economically vital to them. But while the majority of the population (except in the cities) was indeed Slav, there was some question as to whether it desired union with Yugoslavia. As much was (privately) admitted even by Trumbić.[3]

The American investigating team sent into the region in January and February 1919 failed to reach definite conclusions on this score, mainly as a result of deep divisions of opinion among the local inhabitants. Only one member of the team, Professor Robert J. Kerner, submitted two reports completely favorable to the Yugoslavs, but even he concluded that a line conforming at the same time to an ethnic division, to the wishes of local inhabitants, to natural geography, and to economic common sense was impossible to draw.[4] Kerner recommended the line of the River Drava as the only suitable frontier between Yugoslavia and Austria. His argument was based on a population tabulation that took into account the sentiments of local women as well as men, the women being more favorable to a union with Yugoslavia. On the basis of woman suffrage, which his colleagues did not admit, officially at least, the picture would thus shift in favor of the Yugoslavs. Economically, Kerner admitted that the whole basin constituted an inseparable unit, but unlike his colleagues, he argued that its

2. For a summary of the technical aspects involved, see Temperley, *Peace Conference, 4,* 368–71.

3. Trumbić to Ministry of Foreign Affairs, Paris, June 9, 1919 (TP, F66).

4. Report dated Feb. 10, 1919 (184.01102/80, Dept. of State, Washington). This and a subsequent report dated Feb. 12, 1919 (184.01102/91) were not included for publication in *FRUS-PPC.*

assignment to Yugoslavia would not impair its future viability. The line of the Drava, moreover, represented in his view the closest approximation to an ethnic as well as a natural frontier and should be adopted in preference to the more southern line of the Karawanken.

On May 9 the problem of the Yugoslav-Austrian frontier was taken up simultaneously in the Council of Foreign Ministers and in the Committee on Yugoslav Affairs. In both forums Italy again opposed a settlement in the north favorable to the Yugoslavs. Since the report of April 6 was limited to the line east of the Klagenfurt-Ljubljana road, and since west of it direct Italian interests were involved, the Council of Foreign Ministers delved into the dual problems of the Yugoslav-Austrian as well as the Italo-Austrian frontiers.[5]

With respect to Yugoslavia, American, British, and French opinion concurred on the desirability of assigning Maribor to the Yugoslavs. Sonnino in the Council and De Martino on the Committee, however, opposed this plan on the grounds that Maribor belonged properly to the Austrian economic system and that it would suffer under Yugoslav control.[6] As for Klagenfurt, the Italians insisted that the region be left to Austria on economic as well as strategic grounds, involving "the defense of the eastern frontier of Italy."[7] They therefore urged adoption of the Karawanken line, which would keep not only Klagenfurt but the whole of Gorizia, the Assling and Tarvis triangles, and Villach from Yugoslavia.

In the expert committee the other Allies challenged this argument. But they too favored the Karawanken line so as to preserve the economic unity of the region with Austria. In the Council, however, the United States, Great Britain, and France favored a plebiscite in the region as the best long-range solution to the problem. To this Sonnino vehemently objected, fearing any scheme that would place the Assling triangle in Yugoslav hands because it would interrupt, on that railway route, the direct connection between Italy and Austria. The discussion of May 9 was

5. See Council minutes for May 9–10, *FRUS-PPC, 4,* 680–84, 697–703.
6. CRYA-PV 21, May 9, 1919 (181.21601/21).
7. Ibid.

thus inconclusive and the Council of Foreign Ministers asked for a special report from the experts, to be submitted the following day.

The experts now (May 10) tried a compromise, supported by all save the Italians, proposing special arrangements to govern customs regulations in the Assling sector. Their committee also agreed on a line assigning 50,000 Slovenes to Austria and leaving the eventual disposition of Tarvis and Assling in the hands of the great powers. This report was adopted with minor modifications, and so far as the foreign ministers were concerned, the problem was thought to have been solved. But in the committee the Italians, seeing that the Karawanken line was in principle not opposed, pressed further in an effort to have the southern Karawanken slope assigned to Austria. This move met with strenuous American objections—similar to those concerning Bulgaria—because it would eliminate the natural frontier of the watershed and favor the Austrians strategically. After two fruitless sessions on May 10, the committee again referred the whole issue to the Council of Four, as it had done in April.[8] And the Council, true to its own precedent, postponed a final decision by creating a special investigating commission.

The Yugoslavs, meanwhile, decided to appeal to Clemenceau, Wilson, and Lloyd George for support in regard to Carinthia.[9] They were received by Clemenceau on May 18, but the interview only persuaded them to modify their claims and drop the demand for the German areas of Klagenfurt and Villach.[10] Otherwise the Allies would not support them. On the 19th, Pašić informed the territorial committee of the Yugoslav decision, which involved leaving some 20,000 Slovenes in Austria. The American and British experts approved immediately, provided the rest of the Klagenfurt basin were disposed of by plebiscite.[11] De Martino, for Italy, rejected both the new line and the idea of a plebiscite, and when the others proposed to invite the Yugoslavs, stipulated that he could agree only if the discussion were limited to the area

8. CRYA-PV 22–23, May 10, 1919 (181.21601/22–23).
9. On May 14. Zap., 2, 66 (K&H, p. 128).
10. Ibid., p. 70 (K&H, p. 129).
11. CRYA-PV 24, May 19, 1919 (181.21601/24).

east of Klagenfurt-Ljubljana. The Yugoslavs were nonetheless invited and, since they asked for a review of frontiers on all sides, they were told to submit proposals for other areas as well.

On May 20, four days after the ill-fated Crillon talks, Trumbić, Vesnić, Žolger, Cvijić, Vošnjak, and General Pešić appeared before the committee. Trumbić outlined the new Yugoslav line in Carinthia and Prekomurje. In both regions, he pointed out, the Yugoslavs were willing to reduce their claims. In addition to giving up Klagenfurt and Villach, he proposed a new line for Prekomurje following the watershed between the Raab and the Mur, thus renouncing an area of 366 square kilometers and 7,000 Slovenes. In Carinthia, Trumbić opposed the idea of a plebiscite on the shaky argument that plebiscites should only be held among allies, and not between ally and enemy. Actually, Trumbić was convinced the Yugoslavs would lose if the basin vote were taken as a unit.[12]

Following Trumbić, Cvijić detailed the Yugoslav claims in Bačka and Baranja, where no significant modifications were proposed. In the Banat, however, Vesnić offered to reduce Yugoslav claims in the Serb-occupied region of central Banat, thus giving up an area inhabited by 60,000 Serbs. But he insisted on retaining control over the Nagy Kikinda (Velika Kikinda)–Versecz railway as economically vital to northern Yugoslavia. He ended with a review of the Serbo-Bulgarian frontier, where again no important modifications were proposed, save in the region of Vidin, where Yugoslav demands were now limited to a strip six kilometers wide on the right bank of the Timok (from Zaječar to the Danube), in order to protect the railway along the opposite bank.

The overall Yugoslav proposal was still substantially out of line with the committee report of April 6. Yet, it represented a reasonable political compromise, particularly in view of the losses already incurred in Istria. These concessions were made mainly in order to influence the top-level talks then in progress over the Adriatic. As such, the gesture was largely wasted, for it neither influenced the question of Fiume in the Council, nor did it sway the territorial committee. The latter indeed, after a brief review of the Yugoslav proposal, promptly decided to stand by its April 6 line along Bul-

12. Trumbić to Ministry of Foreign Affairs, Paris, June 9, 919 (TP, F66).

garia, the Banat, and Baranja. As to Prekomurje, Clive Day of the United States, though still unhappy about shifting the frontier north of the Mur for reasons of strategy and geography, now agreed to the Yugoslav line (supported by the French) on ethnic grounds. De Martino objected to a change, but agreed in the end so as to maintain "allied unity." [13] But no agreement could be reached about Carinthia.

On May 26 Tardieu informed Trumbić that the committee would grant the Yugoslavs Prekomurje and a larger share of Baranja, but no increases along Bulgaria and in the Banat. In Carinthia, Tardieu said, France and Great Britain favored granting them the Slovene-inhabited southern zone, to which Italy was opposed. The United States still wavered, however, and this led Trumbić to wire home: "Outlook not bad, as we hope to win USA experts to our side in this regard." [14]

On the same day, however, military action in Carinthia upset the diplomatic applecart. Following a particularly ferocious military clash, Yugoslav units launched a general offensive, occupying within a week most of the basin, including the city of Klagenfurt, where they captured important stocks of war matériel. Since Austrian matériel belonged technically to the Allies, the Council of Four intervened on May 31, ordering immediate cease-fire and withdrawal from the basin on both sides. It took a week before an armistice was signed (June 6), only to be broken within two days by an Austrian offensive. On June 13, Italian forces—and according to Yugoslav information, the Italians had not only supplied the Austrians with arms, but directed their operation as well [15]— sprang into action and occupied the Villach-St. Veit railway. The Yugoslav army thereupon remained in Klagenfurt and most of the basin.

The military conflict naturally complicated things in Paris, where the Yugoslav delegation sought to persuade the Allies 1) to partition the basin, and 2) not to hold a plebiscite. The last days

13. CRYA-PV 26, May 20, 1919 (181.21601/26).

14. Trumbić to Ministry of Foreign Affairs, Paris, May 27, 1919 (TP, F66). In this message he also noted with pleasure that all Greek claims against Bulgaria had been approved, thus keeping the latter within pre-Balkan War boundaries and without an exit to the Aegean Sea.

15. Zap., 2 (May 27), 78, (June 19) 121 (K&H, pp. 134, 151).

of May and the first days of June saw much Yugoslav activity in this sense, particularly among the Americans.[16] Wilson was not persuaded that the basin should be divided, though Johnson actively backed the Yugoslav position.[17] And when on May 31 the Supreme Council informed the smaller states about the details of the preliminary peace with Austria and invited them to St. Germain on June 2 for the formal meeting with the Austrians, the Yugoslavs reacted sharply. They not only objected to approving the draft treaty before the Klagenfurt issue was resolved, but took strong exception to Article 59, pertaining to the protection of minorities.

The Allies designed Article 59 as a series of reciprocal arrangements to safeguard the rights of all the former Austro-Hungarian nationalities, binding on all the successor states. In the case of Yugoslavia, Trumbić pointed out to the Council on May 31, this provision could not be applied to Serbia, formerly a sovereign state (and not a part of the Dual Monarchy), whose sovereign rights would now be encroached on by Article 59.[18] As the Big Four refused to concede the point, the Yugoslav delegation thought of abstaining from the plenary session at St. Germain. After several hours of discussion on June 1, however, the delegation decided that in regard to Article 59 it would act in the same way as other interested states (Czechoslovakia, Poland, Rumania), but unless satisfaction were obtained in Carinthia, it would not go to St. Germain.[19] Late that evening Vošnjak was dispatched to see Colonel House, who earlier in the day had promised to speak with Wilson.

At about 10:30 P.M., House (who had summoned Johnson) received Vošnjak. Wilson still had reservations about partitioning the basin (as did Great Britian and France, he said) and thought the population should settle its own fate by plebiscite. The President also thought it a mistake for the Yugoslavs to stay away from St. Germain. The Italians had played such a game with very poor

16. Trumbić, Vesnić, Žolger, and Vošnjak were in constant communication with Johnson, White, and House.

17. Zap., 2, 97 (K&H, p. 141).

18. Ibid., p. 92 (K&H, p. 140).

19. Ibid., p. 94 (K&H, p. 140).

results. Instead, why did the Yugoslavs not attend and submit their reservations regarding Klagenfurt and Article 59 in writing to the President of the peace conference? Tomorrow's meeting, concluded House, would deal only with preliminaries and positions which could still be changed.[20] Next morning, the Yugoslav delegation voted unanimously to heed this advice and to attend the St. Germain session in the afternoon.

In the following days the Carinthian problem absorbed the attention of the Yugoslav delegation, the government in Belgrade,[21] and the Supreme Council. On the 5th, Vesnić appeared before the Council to elaborate on Yugoslav objections to the Austrian draft treaty, and as a result, the matter was referred to the territorial committee. The experts now finally agreed to divide the Klagenfurt basin into two zones, with Zone A (the larger southern part) allotted to Yugoslavia, and Zone B to Austria. A plebiscite would be held first in the Yugoslav and then in the Austrian zone to ascertain the desires of the population. After much bargaining,[22] the Council adopted this formula on the 21st and, over Italian objections, permitted Yugoslav troops to remain in Zone A.[23] A plebiscite was to be held in the Yugoslav zone three months after the Austrian treaty went into effect,[24] to be followed (in the event of a pro-Yugoslav vote) within three weeks by one in the Austrian zone.

20. Ibid., pp. 97–99 (K&H, pp. 141–42).

21. At an emergency session on June 5 the cabinet approved the idea of a plebiscite, if necessary. It also decided, with the Regent's approval, to make another effort in Paris to obtain Klagenfurt proper, which the delegation promptly voted not to do. (Protić to Trumbić, Very Urgent, Personal, No. 7030, Belgrade, June 5, 1919, received in Paris on June 7, 11:45 A.M., TP, F66).

22. The bargaining was complicated by continued military operations. Trumbić repeatedly urged Belgrade to discontinue the operations in Carinthia and to "treat [the] local population with great care" (Trumbić to Ministry of Foreign Affairs, Paris, June 9, 1919, TP, F66). On the 10th he warned: "Our military offensive has created a bad impression, all the more as it is asserted that our government has failed to keep its June 4 promise to stop the offensive" (Trumbić to Ministry of Foreign Affairs, Paris, June 10, 1919, TP, F66).

23. *Résolutions* 749, June 21, 1919; Trumbić to Ministry of Foreign Affairs, Paris, June 20, 1919 (TP, F66).

24. Vesnić tried to have Zone A assigned to Yugoslavia with the inhabitants given the right, within 3 or 6 months, to "express their desires, in writing, as to whether they wish to see the region transferred to Austrian sovereignty" (*Résolutions* 634, June 7, 1919).

Considering this arrangement to be the Allies' final decision, the Yugoslav delegation voted its acceptance on June 26.[25]

The Austrian peace treaty (of September 10, 1919) was ratified on July 16, 1920. In accordance with Article 50, a plebiscite was held in Zone A on October 10, 1920. It resulted in a vote favoring union with Austria by 22,025 to 15,279.[26] By this action the Klagenfurt basin reverted to Austria.

In the face of inevitable Slovene sacrifices in Carinthia as well as in Istria, Ivan Žolger became increasingly restive about signing either the German or the Austrian peace treaty. At the end of May —in agreement with Ribarž—he again declared that he would not sign. Trumbić then angrily announced: if Žolger did not sign, he would not sign either.[27] The others protested that this would lead to grave consequences and decided to consult Belgrade. Within five days Protić fired back: any delegate refusing to sign the peace treaty as instructed by the government should resign well in advance. Žolger should promptly inform the cabinet of the reasons behind his stand. What, moreover, "does he propose to do to prevent something from happening which neither he nor any of us wants?" [28]

Žolger took his time, but Trumbić meanwhile informed Belgrade that the non-Slovene delegates agreed on the following formula: Pašić, Trumbić, and Vesnić would sign the German and Bulgarian treaties, and Pašić, Trumbić and Žolger the Austrian and Hungarian treaties. Since the treaties would involve an "amputation" of the national territory, "a Serb, a Croat and a Slovene [must] bear the responsibility in solidarity with the government . . . each delegate represents not one-third of the nation but the nation as a whole, same as the government that gave us our mandate." If a Slovene did not sign, the Slovenes could claim that they were *not* represented in the treaty making, and accuse the Serbs and

25. Zap., 2, 136 (K&H, p. 157).
26. Temperley, *Peace Conference, 4,* 379. See also S. Wambaugh, *Plebiscites since the World War, 1* (2 vols. Washington, 1933), 163–205; 2, 124–59.
27. Zap., 2 (May 28) 82 (K&H, p. 136).
28. Protić to Delegation, No. 6888, Belgrade, June 2, 1919 (TP, F66).

Croats of selling them out. The facts spoke for themselves: all three groups would suffer "amputation." [29]

On June 15 Žolger finally cabled Protić, asking to be absolved of the duty to sign. In his view his signature was not necessary (as two Serbs and a Croat could legally sign), nor would it be wise. If he signed, Italy could claim that the Slovenes had agreed to mutilate their own territory, and irredentism would be stifled. At the same time, if he did not sign, the Slovenes could not accuse the Serbs and Croats of betraying their interests since Slovene delegates took part in all delegation decisions.[30]

To Trumbić, Protić replied thus: "The cabinet is fully aware of the great importance and immense responsibility it carries . . . before the Crown, before the people and before History." Whether to sign or not is a decision for the government to make, not the delegation. Žolger's position is wrong and "if you make your own signature conditional on that of Žolger . . . you are only adding importance to [his] position." But then in a weaker tone, Protić asked for a prompt report "about the attitude of each delegate." [31] To the delegation he sent instructions for Žolger to sign.[32]

A day after this telegram arrived, Žolger again refused to budge. Ribarž suggested that Žolger be given a free hand in the eventuality that the Slovenes left the government coalition (!) in preference to approving the cession of Slovene lands to Italy.[33]

In the end, Žolger (with Pašić and Trumbić) signed the German treaty. But he did so only because boundaries with Italy had not yet been officially set.

The arrival in Paris at the end of June of Premier Protić and three members of the cabinet—Trifković, Marinković, and Kramer —reflected the government's anxiety about the fate of Yugoslav interests at the peace conference. Political as well as economic issues were at stake.

Since mid-April, Yugoslav financial and economic experts had

29. Trumbić to Ministry of Foreign Affairs, Paris, June 13, 1919 (TP, F66).
30. Žolger to Protić, Paris, June 15 (TP, F66).
31. Protić to Trumbić, Very Urgent, No. 7688, Belgrade, June 17, 1919 (TP, F66).
32. Zap., 2, 123 (K&H, p. 152).
33. Ibid.

been working in coordination with their Polish, Czechoslovak, Rumanian, and Greek counterparts, in order to hammer out a joint economic front with regard to the Austrian and Bulgarian reparations settlements. This effort, though buffeted by much political bickering, especially between Yugoslavs and Rumanians, resulted in a joint declaration to the Allied reparations commission on May 6. In it the East European states called for the establishment of a joint Allied fund to be made up of German, Austrian, Hungarian, Bulgarian, and Turkish reparations. The intent was to prevent German reparations from being used to pay only England, France, and Belgium, with the rest used for Italy and the eastern states. The declaration also demanded the outright inheritance by the successor states of all former Austro-Hungarian state property and rejected the principle that the successor states should assume part of former enemy financial obligations, as they were not responsible for the outbreak of the war.[34]

These demands were not accepted by the great powers.[35] Instead, they decided to apportion part of the former enemy obligations among the successor states. In the Yugoslav case this meant that Serbia and Montenegro would receive reparations, while Croatia and Slovenia (and possibly Bosnia-Hercegovina) would have to pay. Since this formula was not likely to be abandoned, everything hinged on the ratio of payments the Allies would adopt. And as the final figures were not likely to be fixed until *after* the peace treaties were signed, Protić—faced with economic chaos at home—decided to come to Paris to influence the Allies.

His intervention did not lead to the desired results. But after two special delegation sessions,[36] Yugoslav economic policy was more firmly set. The government's main concern was to receive as much as possible, as soon as possible.[37] The delegation was instructed to work toward this end, with a view to keeping the maximum liability of the former Austro-Hungarian provinces to 200 million francs and increasing the *balance* of reparations to Yugo-

34. "Expose dr. Trumbića Narodnim Poslanicima," n.d. (TP, F60).

35. For general background on reparations, see Philip M. Burnett, *Reparation at the Paris Peace Conference* (2 vols. New York, 1940), and Borko Nikolajević, *Reparacije* (Sarajevo, 1956), Pt. II.

36. On June 30 and July 7. Zap., 2, 142–46, 156–59 (K&H, pp. 159–60, pp. 163–64).

37. Ibid., p. 145 (K&H, p. 160).

slavia to "five–six" billion francs.[38] Next, the main task would be to obtain a cash advance (as had been granted Belgium), without which the Yugoslav economy would remain in dire straits.

In the political sphere too, the cabinet ministers' presence prompted a detailed examination of the Yugoslav position. At a plenary meeting on July 1 Pašić reviewed all the problems the delegation had faced thus far, including the issues that had caused the delegates to split. Protić agreed with the principle that, beyond the establishment of an independent Fiuman state, no further concessions should be made. But then he declared, ambiguously, that in the final analysis only the government could decide whether to yield any more or not.[39] This prompted Trumbić to complain: "We feel the uncertainty of the ground on which we tread. . . . In regard to the Adriatic question we must determine the final concession." [40] Tittoni was coming and negotiations could be resumed at any moment; the delegation could not move so as to show that the government had still to pass on its actions. But Protić would not be swayed, declaring: "We must not here anticipate the government's judgment." The delegation should not act so as to make refusal to sign the Austrian treaty the only recourse left.[41]

Discussion was resumed next day. It would certainly have developed into an open contest had accident not intervened. Between the two sessions, Vesnić happened to have been visited by Johnson who, on Lansing's instructions, came to ask: will the Yugoslavs make their signature on the Austrian treaty conditional on a prior settlement with Italy, or will they sign the treaty and then negotiate with the Italians? Vesnić answered that he would have to consult the delegation; but when Johnson pressed for a personal opinion, the minister replied that he saw no reason to tie the Austrian treaty to a settlement with Italy.[42] In view of this development all discussion now centered on this question. Everyone agreed with Protić's analysis to the effect that the Yugoslav position

38. Ibid. With regard to the successor states' liability, the cabinet ministers and peace delegates decided to accept the same formula for Yugoslavia as for the other states.

39. Ibid., p. 148 (K&H, p. 161).

40. Ibid.

41. Ibid., p. 149 (K&H, p. 161).

42. Ibid., p. 150 (K&H, p. 162).

would only be strengthened by signing the Austrian treaty. The treaty, after all, would involve an Austrian renunciation of the provinces now incorporated into Yugoslavia, and this would prevent Italy from treating them in the future as enemy territory. Furthermore, Protić wisely noted, "our position improves as soon as we have peace, no matter on which side." [43] It was agreed to so inform Johnson.

Protić and the cabinet members left Paris several days later, without having resolved the question of Yugoslav minimum demands in the west. This was soon to complicate matters for the peace delegates, as the dispute with Italy moved into a new phase.

Nitti and Tittoni came to Paris at the end of June without a new Adriatic policy. They were greeted, however, by a joint Anglo-French memorandum, drawn up by Balfour and submitted to Tittoni on June 28.[44] On the surface, the document represented a momentous step: for the first time, Italy's partners formally challenged the validity of the Treaty of London. Two main arguments were given: first, that international conditions had changed radically since 1915—America's entry into the war, Russia's collapse, the creation of the Yugoslav state, none of these had been foreseen —and second, that for a full year, contrary to treaty terms, Italy had delayed declaring war upon Germany—the very argument Balfour had refused to use two months earlier.

If the memorandum was designed to shake Italian confidence in the treaty and in Sonnino's policy, it misfired.[45] On July 7 Tittoni replied at length, refuting the Anglo-French arguments point by point.[46] By the letter of the London treaty, he pointed out, Italy received no deadline for declaring war on Germany. The delay was merely due to military unpreparedness. As for the rest, changed international conditions did not absolve Italy's allies from their treaty obligations. The British and French decided not to press

43. Ibid., p. 151 (K&H, p. 162).
44. For the text of the Balfour memorandum, see E. L. Woodward and R. Butler, eds., *Documents on British Foreign Policy, 1919–1939, 4* (1st Ser. London, 1952), 4–6 (hereafter cited as *DBFP*).
45. Before long, Anglo-French confidence in their own memorandum gave way and the 2 partners again came to admit the validity of the embarrassing treaty.
46. Tittoni's note is sumarized in Albrecht-Carrié, *Italy*, pp. 238–42.

the issue, and so the fruitless debate about the 1915 treaty was once more allowed to lapse.

But simultaneous with his reply to the Anglo-French memorandum, Tittoni—on the verge of leaving for Rome for several days—sought out Johnson with a new idea to be conveyed to the Yugoslavs. If the latter granted Italy full sovereignty over Boka Kotorska and Mount Lovčen in Montenegro (for an Italian naval base), Italy would give up *all* the Dalmatian and Quarnero islands, all claims on the Dalmatian mainland, and accept the Wilson line as the eastern boundary of Italy and the western boundary of the buffer state of Fiume (where the Yugoslavs would enjoy the same rights as the Poles in Danzig). Johnson immediately took the proposal to Trumbić, but not before discouraging Tittoni about his chances of success. According to Trumbić's report to Belgrade, the Italian foreign minister agreed with the American, noting, however, that he had to deliver something new in return for renouncing Italian claims.[47]

Tittoni's motivation is not entirely clear. Lovčen dominates strategically both Montenegro and northern Albania, while Boka Kotorska holds the key to the southern Adriatic. An Italian naval base in Montenegro, while doubtless an attractive prospect to the Italian Admiralty, would become a center of political intrigue for the entire region. Surely Tittoni did not expect the Yugoslavs to accept such a proposal. Was it therefore mainly an empty gesture, designed to obfuscate the issue and display some initiative of action? Or was it a clever maneuver calculated to reopen the troublous Montenegrin issue and thus throw the Yugoslavs off balance?

Whatever the case, the Yugoslavs took it seriously. Within the hour after Johnson's departure Trumbić summoned an emergency meeting. Protić, scheduled to leave for Belgrade that same evening, also attended. To a man, the seven delegates and the Premier rejected Tittoni's proposal.[48] Trumbić promptly took the news to Johnson at the Crillon, explaining at length why the Yugoslavs would not accept an Italian base in Montenegro. The American evidently concurred.

47. Trumbić's notes of the conversation with Johnson, Paris, July 8, 1919 (TP, F112).

48. Leading Smodlaka to exclaim exultantly that the vote showed how Serbo-Croat-Slovene solidarity worked in matters of vital national interest!

Thus the first—tentative—round with Sonnino's successor produced no concrete result. Both sides, particularly the Italian, now needed time to prepare for the next. Five full weeks were to elapse before a new, and more formal, effort would be launched.

The interval, however, did not provide a respite. Aside from the oncoming duel with Tittoni, the delegation had to contend with pressures on all fronts. The powers were working on a peace settlement not only for Austria but for Hungary and Bulgaria as well. Then, too, Carinthia was but one of the battlegrounds where military arms had clashed. Fiume, Montenegro, northern Albania, and the Banat were all aflame with fighting. And as though this were not enough, the government coalition in Belgrade began to fall apart under the relentless pressure of economic disorder, political discord, and—perhaps most important—personal animosities within the cabinet.

The Allied force in Fiume—composed originally of American, British, French, Italian, and Serbian contingents—proved unable to maintain local order. With the withdrawal of the Serbs in November 1918 and the Americans in February 1919, there remained a predominantly Italian force, hardly checked by the presence of one British and two French battalions. The overall military command, headed by General Grazioli, and the civil government, taken over by the Italian National Council, closed their eyes to, and even facilitated, Italian annexationist activities.

In late spring countless incidents occurred between the Italians, French, and Yugoslavs. The Italian youth began to recruit a private volunteer corps to drive the Allies out. On the night of June 29 they attacked French troops in the city, following this three days later by an attack on the Croat Club. Within a week nine French soldiers lay dead and a French officer wounded.[49] The Supreme Council finally intervened on July 7,[50] appointing a four-power generals' commission to investigate the Fiume riots. It took the generals a month to submit their report. It called for the dissolution of the Italian National Council and the "private" volunteer corps, a drastic reduction of Italian forces, the replacement of Grazioli, and the election of a new municipal government under

49. Temperley, *Peace Conference, 4,* 307.
50. *Résolutions* 860, July 7, 1919, and 870, July 8, 1919.

Allied supervision.[51] The report was adopted on August 25, but its implementation was delayed. By the time a British force was to take over in Fiume, on September 12, it was too late. For on that very day the poet-condottiere, Gabriele D'Annunzio, launched his great adventure: the invasion and occupation of Fiume, with himself proclaimed as Fiuman Dictator.[52]

Northern Albania, meanwhile, had been a hotbed of Italian intrigue ever since the armistice. Promised as a sphere of influence to Italy in the Treaty of London, Albania was reserved for final disposition to the Supreme Council. With the Italians determined to gain control over the country and the Yugoslavs equally determined to restrict Italian control to Valona—and keep the Italians from Montenegrin borders—both sides took advantage of local anarchy to press their cause in the field. In the summer of 1919, Serbian troops still occupied parts of northern Albania, and Italian troops the rest. The Italians promoted constant ferment among the Albanians, and by arming and directing pro-royalist Montenegrin groups, sought to undermine the political stability of Montenegro itself. Thus the Montenegrin-Albanian border was continually involved in incidents of various sorts. During June and July the number of incidents increased, involving several attacks launched by Italian commanders against Yugoslav units.[53]

Even more serious than that, however, was the situation in the Banat. Hungary, where frustrated nationalism and incipient communism combined to produce a Bolshevik regime in March 1919,[54] had become a critical problem not only for its neighbors but for the peacemakers in Paris as well. Faced with this dangerous spread of Bolshevism, the Allies decided to put an end to the Hungarian Soviet Republic of Béla Kun. The Rumanians, worried by Bolshevism and seeing an opportunity to advance their territorial in-

51. Ibid. 1132, Aug. 25, 1919.

52. For greater detail, see the accounts by Alatri, Benedetti, and Giurati; also, F. Čulinović, *Riječka Država* (Zagreb, 1953).

53. On June 19, for example, Dodge reported a conversation with the Italian chargé d'affaires in Belgrade in which the latter admitted that Italian troops had launched an offensive to drive the Yugoslavs out (Dodge to Lansing, Belgrade, June 19, 1919, 763.72119/5411, Dept. of State, Washington).

54. On this subject see Oscar Jászi, *Revolution and Counter-Revolution in Hungary* (London, 1924).

terests in the Banat and Transylvania, became particularly active in the cause of undoing Béla Kun. With Allied, and especially French, approval, the Rumanian army invaded Hungary, and crossing the line established for them by the Allies, marched on Budapest, occupying the capital from early summer to mid-November.

When the Allies decided on military intervention, they solicited the help of the Rumanians and Czechs, as well as the Yugoslavs.[55] But the Yugoslavs wavered because of their own dispute with Rumania and because, beleaguered on all sides, they could ill afford to contribute a substantial military contingent. Rumanian successes in Hungary, meanwhile, which were indeed impressive, emboldened Bucharest into contemplating a military solution in the Banat, by driving out the Serbs. Intelligence to this effect reached the Yugoslavs in August through Beneš and other quarters.[56] Both the government and delegation became sufficiently alarmed to seek military and diplomatic assistance from Greece and Czechoslovakia.[57]

Greek help was needed to keep the Bulgarians in check, as they might exploit a war over the Banat to launch an action of their own. Thus Pašić broached Venizelos and the latter promised to intervene militarily in case of a Bulgarian attack. But Greece could not apply force against Rumania, though it would do everything possible diplomatically.[58] Beneš, who was approached by Trumbić, promised *limited* military aid in Hungary—he would not promise more, fearing a Polish attack in Teschen—as well as full diplomatic support.[59] This satisfied the Yugoslavs, though full re-

55. On July 11 Pašić and Vesnić were summoned to Pichon's office together with the Czechs and Rumanians. Pichon suggested that the Rumanians contribute 8 divisions for the offensive, the Czechs 2 divisions, and the Yugoslavs 8,000 men. Zap., 2, 163 (K&H, p. 166).

56. Trumbić to Ministry of Foreign Affairs, Paris, Aug. 18, 1919 (TP, F66).

57. On Aug. 21 the government asked Trumbić to inform Venizelos about Rumanian preparations and ask him to strengthen Greek forces along the Bulgarian frontier (Davidović, Personal and Strictly Confidential, Belgrade, Aug. 21, 1919, TP, F66). A second telegram (No. 10263) asked him to seek French help. A little later, a third telegram (No. 10276) arrived, informing Trumbić that the Yugoslav ambassador in Prague had been instructed to ask for Czech aid in case of a Rumanian attack. (TP, F66.)

58. Zap., 2, 194 (K&H, p. 178).

59. Trumbić to Ministry of Foreign Affairs, Strictly Confidential, Paris, Aug. 28, 1919 (TP, F66).

assurance came only after the Supreme Council (and the French government) informed Bratianu that it would not tolerate the use of force in the Banat.[60] The Rumanians now calmed down and a major conflict was averted. But the entire affair left a bitter after-taste.

In the midst of these events, word arrived from Belgrade that Protić had resigned. Trumbić, as a member of the cabinet, was the first to receive the message on August 2. In it Protić cited policy differences with Pribičević, the Minister of Interior, as the main reason for his decision to resign.[61] The government crisis—the first major coalition crisis of the young state—lasted ten days, until the Regent asked Ljuba Davidović to form a new coalition. And on August 13 Davidović asked Trumbić whether he would join the new cabinet in the same post. Since it would be "a mistake" to change foreign ministers at this time, the new Premier urged Trumbić not only to remain but to do so regardless of future coalition shifts at home.[62] Trumbić agreed.

Several days later the delegates met to consider whether to hand in a *pro forma* resignation.[63] The idea was opposed by Bošković and Žolger on the ground that the government could always revoke their mandates and the collective gesture would mean nothing. Vesnić, however, favored submitting a resignation, both as an act of courtesy and to make any desired changes easier for the new government. Pašić, Smodlaka, and Ribarž shared the same view. Trumbić was not present, but sent word through Smodlaka that he too favored such a move. The delegates then agreed to draft a letter of resignation, which was forwarded to Belgrade. Davidović decided to leave the Yugoslav delegation intact. The decision was wise, since negotiations over the Adriatic had just resumed in Paris and any change of the leading figures would likely be misinterpreted by the Italians. In fact, to bolster the delegates' morale, as

60. Zap., 2, 194 (K&H, p. 178). Pichon told Trumbić of the French action on Aug. 30, (Trumbić to Ministry of Foreign Affairs, Paris, Aug. 31, 1919, TP, F66).

61. He also cited differences in the cabinet over agrarian reform; parliamentary squabbles; the government's inability to improve the transportation system and national commerce; and personal attacks against him and the Vatican (!) in the press, etc. (Protić to Trumbić, Belgrade, Aug. 2, 1919, TP, F64).

62. Davidović to Trumbić, Very Urgent, Belgrade, Aug. 13, 1919 (TP, F66).

63. Zap., 2 (Aug. 19), 186–87 (K&H, p. 175).

well as to strengthen their hand, the new premier offered them special support in his maiden speech to the Skupština. Following a detailed review of Yugoslav foreign policy problems, Davidović warmly praised the peace delegation and vigorously promised to support its future work.[64] Yugoslav policy in Paris was clearly to remain unchanged.

A rumor reached Trumbić at the beginning of August to the effect that Tittoni had reached an agreement on the Adriatic with the French. Anxious, he went to see Tardieu on the 6th. The latter assured him the rumor was false and that, in any event, no decision would be made without consulting the Yugoslavs.[65] But something was definitely in the wind and Tardieu asked whether the Yugoslavs had had any contact with the Italians. Trumbić replied not with Tittoni, but one high official had informed them that Italy would now insist on making the Fiuman state *permanent*. The idea meant keeping the buffer territory permanently from Yugoslavia which, said Trumbić, could never be accepted. To his consternation, however, Tardieu urged exactly that, adding ominously that the Adriatic question must be settled by August 25, when the French Parliament would begin debate on the German treaty. A day or two later, Johnson warned that a final solution must not be delayed as the whole issue was dragging on too long and beginning to lose importance in general.[66]

The formal contest began on August 12. On that day Tittoni presented a new proposal to Clemenceau, Balfour, and Polk (now head of the American delegation, replacing Lansing) including: a free Fiuman state (including Krk) under League protection; eastern Istria with Cres and Lošinj to Italy; Italian sovereignty in Zara, and a mandate over Albania within the frontiers of 1913.[67] No mention was made of any plebiscite, thus indicating the permanence of the Fiuman state. After some discussion—and Clemenceau seemed to favor the proposal—the plan was forwarded to Washington for Wilson's approval.

64. "Pressburo Telegram," Belgrade, Aug. 24, 1919 (TP, F64).
65. "Razgovor Trumbić–Tardieu," Paris, Aug. 6, 1919 (TP, F90).
66. Trumbić to Ministry of Foreign Affairs, Paris, Aug. 9, 1919 (TP, F66).
67. Albrecht-Carrié, *Italy*, p. 244.

The President, with other pressing matters on his mind, delayed replying for several weeks. Opposed in principle to any scheme excluding a plebiscite in Fiume, he was not likely to approve it. But events made a veto unnecessary. D'Annunzio's coup on September 12 pushed Tittoni's project into the background. The "rape of Fiume," as Lloyd George put it, worked Wilson to "such a pitch of indignation" that he was furious with Italy for months.[68] He never replied to the note of August 12.

Tittoni had evidently seized on the idea of a permanent Fiuman state both as a palliative to Italian nationalists—for the city would thus never go to Yugoslavia—and as a lever for wresting alternate concessions from the Yugoslavs. Skillfully playing on Lloyd George's and Clemenceau's impatience to close the books on the entire affair, he obtained their agreement on most of his program. Trumbić learned this confidentially from Johnson, who visited him on September 2.[69] According to Johnson, an Italian-French-British agreement had already been reached, but Polk was not authorized to give American adherence. Therefore, Wilson would be asked directly. Tittoni insisted on eastern Istria; Zara; the islands of Vis, Lošinj, and Lastovo; Valona, and a mandate over the rest of Albania; as well as a permanent Fiuman state. If the Yugoslavs rejected the last point, he would agree to getting Fiume for Italy and assign the remaining free state territory to Yugoslavia.

Three days later, on the fifth, Trumbić again saw Johnson, this time at the Crillon.[70] Clemenceau and Tardieu, the American said, had apparently agreed to Tittoni's plan. But Balfour, whom Johnson saw the day before, did not. The Foreign Secretary rather appeared to agree with Johnson, who favored assigning Zara to the Yugoslavs—with adequate provisions for the rights of Italians—and leasing the *port* of Fiume to them for ninety-nine years.

Trumbić was not averse to such a plan, though the details had still to be worked out. What worried him was that Clemenceau and Lloyd George had already approved Tittoni's program. And at this very moment, the Yugoslavs were particularly vulnerable to Anglo-French pressure, for the Austrian treaty that was about to be

68. Lloyd George, *Truth about the Peace Treaties,* 2, 809.
69. Trumbić to Davidović, Paris, Sept. 2, 1919 (TP, F63/61).
70. "Razgovor Trumbić–Johnson," Paris, Sept. 5, 1919 (TP, F112).

signed contained some dangerous provisions for the Serbo-Croat-Slovene state.

Given the impossibility of drawing sound ethnic frontiers throughout Eastern Europe, the great powers hoped to forestall irredentism and future territorial revisions by a system of "minorities conventions." These were to be applied to all the successor states and were intended to guarantee, under League protection, the freedoms of speech, press, religion, etc., to all the minorities. The plan was bitterly resented by the Czechs, Poles, Rumanians, and Yugoslavs as an infringement on their national sovereignty.

The question of guaranteeing the cultural and political rights of minorities arose early at the peace conference. Several of the territorial committees had recommended a system of reciprocal guarantees among the new states of Eastern Europe, but not the great powers, and the idea was incorporated into the terms of the Austrian draft treaty. Specific responsibility for working out the details was vested in the Commission on New States and Minorities on May 1. By mid-summer, however, the Allied plan encountered major difficulties.

All the successor states complained at being forced to sign minorities conventions to which the great powers would not adhere. The Yugoslavs insisted that Italy undertake reciprocal obligations toward its Slavic minorities. This was to no avail, as in the end neither Italy nor the other great powers would accept the principle of reciprocity. A second, and still more objectionable, provision was the clause affording minority protection to pre- and postwar areas alike. In the case of Yugoslavia—and Rumania's position was quite similar—this would extend to Macedonian regions acquired by Serbia in the Balkan Wars and earlier, even though minority treatment in Macedonia was already regulated by the Treaties of Berlin (1878) and Bucharest (1913).

The Yugoslavs and Rumanians were willing to accept special provisions for territories acquired after 1918, but not for those held before 1914. On this score the Yugoslav delegation was in complete agreement. (Serbian emotions on the subject of Macedonia ran very deep.) Throughout June and July the delegation fought the proposed provisions. Pašić justly argued with the Allies that Serbia's prewar obligations were juridically inherited by the new state, as expounded in the declaration of union in December 1918. Hence, new contractual arrangements for Macedonia were unnecessary and would only appear as a lack of confidence in prewar Serbia as well as the Yugoslav state.

The Allies, however, pressed for a clarification of whether or not the Yugoslav state had "automatically" inherited Serbian obligations. If they had, the point should be spelled out. If not, a new set of commitments should be drawn up.[71] All agreed that Serbia had "fully carried out both the letter and the spirit" of the Treaty of Berlin.[72] But the part of Macedonia annexed in 1913 involved such mixed minorities that their cultural, political, and religious rights had to be spelled out anew.

Dissatisfied with the Allies' position, both the government and the delegation would not yield an inch. On August 1 Pašić submitted a restrained statement to the Commission on Minorities. The Yugoslav Kingdom, he pointed out, combined three peoples, three religions, and diverse political traditions and juridical and social systems. The nation could flourish only by insuring conditions of equality for all. The Macedonians had always been regarded as Serbs—rather than a minority—with full and equal rights. This in itself obviated the need for special guarantees. As to the Albanian minority, and Moslems in general, their rights were guaranteed by the Serbian-Turkish treaty of March 14, 1914.[73] Despite some sophistry, the plea was rather persuasive. The Commission, however, decided to ignore it and to stand by the original Allied demands.

On August 21 the Yugoslav delegates began to consider whether to sign the Austrian treaty at all and decided to ask Belgrade for instructions. Bošković wanted to urge the cabinet not to sign if the minority provisions (Article 59) remained unchanged. If it decided to sign anyway, Bošković warned, he would resign in protest.[74] Next day he appeared with a letter addressed to the

71. For the legal arguments in question, see K. Marek, *Identity and Continuity of States in Public International Law* (Geneva, 1954), Pt. II, chap. 3.

72. Temperley, *Peace Conference*, 5, 147.

73. "Commission des nouveaux États et des minorités," in *La Paix de Versailles*, Vol. 10, *PV* 40, Aug. 1, 1919.

74. Zap., 2, 188–89 (K&H, p.176).

cabinet, spelling out his objections to Article 59. In it, to the dismay of his colleagues, Bošković declared that the real danger lay not in a refusal to sign the Austrian or Bulgarian treaties; rather, Yugoslav difficulties stemmed from the fact that the Adriatic issue had not yet been solved. If the dispute with Italy were settled "our position would quickly improve on all sides; meanwhile, no concessions in the east will improve our position in the west . . ."[75]

The other delegates were thunderstruck. What did he mean by concessions in the east? By what right did Bošković indulge in such general considerations without consulting the entire delegation? If this letter was to be sent, a second letter expressing the majority view should go along with it. After bitter charges and countercharges, Bošković agreed to wait—but only until the next meeting.[76] That meeting took place on the 25th. All of his six colleagues urged Bošković to limit his observations to Article 59. After much discussion, he finally agreed to do so, though he thought that a "catastrophe" might soon overtake the Yugoslavs, and his conscience and duty required warning the government.[77] Nonetheless, he sent a revised letter. But within three days he changed his mind again, and on the 29th showed Pašić a new letter for Davidović. "We should come to terms with the Italians," Bošković wrote, because the Yugoslav state is isolated, unable to wage war against Italy, its political position in Paris is precarious, Wilson is no longer here to help, there is danger of an Italo-Rumanian military consortium, and only an agreement with Italy can lead to "the successful defence of our interests on all other sides."[78] But no concrete formula for compromise with Italy was offered.

Pašić relayed the text to the full delegation. The others disagreed sharply with Bošković's analysis, arguing that it would be a strategic blunder to modify their policy and to yield any more to Italy. The United States was still "our protector" and if Bošković insisted on forwarding this letter, the other delegates would send one of their own.[79] On August 31 Pašić and Smodlaka read drafts they had pre-

75. Ibid., p. 191 (K&H, p. 177).
76. Ibid.
77. Ibid., p. 193 (K&H, p. 177).
78. Bošković to Davidović, Strictly Confidential, Paris, Aug. 29, 1919 (TP, F48).
79. Zap., 2, 197 (K&H, p. 179).

pared refuting Bošković's arguments, and since the latter would not budge, all three texts were forwarded to Belgrade.

In the capital, meanwhile, oppostion to the minorities convention mounted, as was happening in Bucharest, Prague, and elsewhere. Feelings ran so high that at the end of August, Davidović informed the delegation in Paris that unless Article 59 were changed so as to exclude Macedonia, the treaty would not be signed. But before a definite decision was reached, the government would study the final treaty text. The delegation did not challenge this delay. It resolved to appeal urgently to Clemenceau, as President of the peace conference, to exempt pre-1914 Serbian territory from Article 59. General Pešić was alone in urging that the treaty be signed. His reason, however, was military, not political. The army was in "a terrible state" and it would be a godsend to "remove at least one enemy from our shoulders." [80]

The Austrian peace treaty was scheduled to be signed on Wednesday, September 10. On the preceding weekend the peace delegates tried frantically—and in vain—to persuade the Allies to change their stand. Pašić visited Balfour; with Vesnić he went to see Polk; and Vesnić twice went to Philippe Berthelot (the Secretary-General of the Quai d'Orsay). Balfour merely declared that it was difficult to divide a country into its pre- and postwar parts. Polk urged the Yugoslavs to sign and trust in the League. Wilson was very keen on the Minority Conventions, he said, and a refusal to sign would weaken his position. Besides, the American delegation would soon leave Paris and it might prove difficult to help the Yugoslavs! Berthelot was even more blunt. The Supreme Council had now made a final decision: to apply the Convention to the whole Yugoslav territory. The French government urged the Yugoslavs to sign. Refusal to do so might lead to *other* changes in the Austrian treaty, and the issue of Montenegro might have to be reopened.[81]

Such pressure was too much, and after a painful night session on the 8th,[82] Trumbić, Vesnić, Žolger, Ribarž, and Smodlaka voted to advise the government to sign. Bošković was opposed to giving in.

80. Ibid. (Sept. 3), p. 201 (K&H, p. 181).
81. Ibid., pp. 203–05 (K&H, pp. 182–83).
82. Lasting from 9 in the evening till 1 o'clock in the morning.

So was Pašić, though he agreed to carry out whatever instructions the government sent. As head of the delegation, he immediately cabled Davidović, asking for a reply before 10 A.M. on Wednesday, the time scheduled for the ceremonies at St. Germain.[83]

On Tuesday, the 9th, no instructions were received. When the delegates convened at 6 P.M., Ribarž urged that they sign the treaty on the following day. "We are," he said, "plenipotentiaries of the government, not its servants. We are convinced that a refusal to sign will bring more injury than to go ahead and sign. Hence the delegation should sign the peace, even contrary to governmental orders. If the government doesn't approve our action, it can dismiss us." [84] General Pešić seconded this view. But Pašić pointed out that the government had expressly forbidden signing (if Article 59 remained unchanged), and in the absence of final instructions the delegation did not have a choice. Vesnić and Trumbić (because he was a member of the cabinet, he said) were of the same opinion. Smodlaka and Žolger disagreed. In the end, the majority voted that unless specific instructions to sign arrived from Belgrade, the plenipotentiaries would not go to St. Germain next day. After the vote was taken, Pašić calmly announced that he would have to withdraw from the delegation and resign.[85]

In Belgrade, meantime, the cabinet had been pondering over what to do. The emergency over the Austrian treaty weighed oppressively on top of countless other problems. Party strife had continued unabated. On coming to power, Davidović had wanted to call early elections for a constitutional assembly, but Alexander had refused to do so in the face of the international crisis. On September 9, unable to decide on a course of action in Paris, the coalition cabinet decided to resign. This would enable the delegation to temporize while a new government was being formed and perhaps gain concessions from the Allies. But Pašić's urgent demand for instructions, and warning about possible consequences, arrived at 6 P.M. on the 9th, before the resignation had been handed in. This forced

---

83. Pašić to Davidović, Paris, Sept. 9, 1919 (TP, F66).
84. Zap., 2, 206 (K&H, p. 183).
85. Ibid., p. 207 (K&H, p. 183). The threat did not make much sense, was not taken seriously, and was not carried out.

Davidović to act. He sent a prompt, and masterfully equivocal, reply
—which arrived in Paris too late. Then, next morning, the cabinet
resigned.[86]

The ceremonies at St. Germain took place on schedule on the
morning of September 10. Since no word had been received from
Belgrade, Pašić informed Clemenceau that, for lack of instructions,
the Serbo-Croat-Slovene delegation could not sign the treaty.[87] At
2 P.M. Davidović's telegram arrived:

> We are overwhelmed [by your message] because your earlier
> telegram indicated an improvement in the situation. Had this
> improvement not been expected, the government would al-
> ready have resigned. . . . if delaying signature will not be
> regarded as not a refusal [sic], if that is by delaying we do not
> incur the dangers outlined in your telegram that would be in-
> curred by a refusal to sign, then postpone signing, in order to
> receive necessary instructions from the new government.
> Otherwise sign. Explain to Americans the problem is not the
> rights of minorities [which we accept and recognize] and there
> is no need to push us on this and dictate to us. The question
> is our sovereignty which is being violated without reason. We
> are not consoled by praise for our past stand towards minor-
> ities.[88]

The delegation now tried to decide what to do. Pašić, Trumbić,
and Bošković felt they should wait for instructions from the new
government. The others wanted to sign immediately, a course permitted by Davidović's telegram. But since Pašić's and Trumbić's
signatures were required, their view prevailed. The plenipotentiaries would not sign, and Pašić would inform Clemenceau that
the government in Belgrade had resigned.[89] When this was done,
Pašić cabled Davidović asking for immediate new instructions, and
also to be absolved from putting his own signature to a treaty he
did not "like." [90]

Davidović, however, did not send new instructions. On the 12th

---

86. Within 3 days it was reshuffled, with Davidović again at the helm.
87. The Rumanians also did not sign. The Poles, Czechs, and Greeks did.
88. The full text is given in the delegation minutes, Zap., 2, 208 (K&H, p. 184).
89. Ibid., p. 209 (K&H, p. 184).
90. Pašić to Davidović, Urgent and Confidential, Paris, Sept. 10, 1919 (TP, F63/80).

he asked Pašić to explain to Clemenceau why the government had resigned and to tell him that the Yugoslavs were willing to guarantee all minority rights through domestic legislation. But they would not submit to a limitation on their sovereignty from outside.[91]

The Allies responded by giving the Yugoslavs until the 17th to sign. On the 15th, Davidović ordered Pašić, Trumbić, Smodlaka, and Ribarž to Belgrade to confer about Article 59.[92] Clemenceau was to be told that Yugoslavia was *not* withdrawing from the peace conference. Vesnić, Žolger, and Bošković were empowered to sign the treaty—if and when Belgrade gave the word.

91. Davidović to Delegation, No. 11209, Belgrade, Sept. 12, 1919 (TP, F63/81).

92. Davidović to Delegation, Belgrade, Sept. 15, 1919 (TP, F66). They left on Sept. 17 and returned to Paris on Oct. 20.

9. Progress without Result: September 1919–February 1920

IN THE LONG RUN, the Yugoslavs gained little by refusing to sign the Austrian peace treaty. Their action, moreover, was not devoid of irony. For, having chosen at the very start to rest their whole case on Wilsonian principles, they now appeared to defy one of its central features: the protection of national minorities. It was also an anomaly to see them react so violently—out of wounded *amour propre*—to the minorities issue when they might, more plausibly, have rebelled against the territorial provisions of the settlement.

Yugoslav policies in this regard can be understood only in terms of the interplay of certain internal and external forces. The Treaty of St. Germain entailed a considerable "sacrifice" for the Slovenes, particularly as a last-minute decision of the conference deprived them of the important sector of Radgona.[1] But it confirmed Yugoslav possession of Carniola, southern Styria, Dalmatia, and Bosnia-Hercegovina. Austria also renounced any claim to Istria, and at the same time, formally recognized the Kingdom of Serbs, Croats, and Slovenes, as did the other signatory powers. In view of Italian hostility and the Allies' desire to assure to the fledgling Austrian republic minimum conditions for independent national existence —independent mainly from Germany—it is hardly likely that the Yugoslavs could have obtained more. Despite regrets and misgivings, they recognized as much. Furthermore, with the Adriatic problem unresolved, to reject the Austrian-territorial terms would only infuriate the Western powers and strengthen Tittoni's hand. Some "amputation" of national territory was unavoidable on every side and neither the Slovenes nor the Croats and the Serbs would be entirely satisfied. Where territorial failures were concerned—

1. During the last days of August, Tittoni maneuvered to have Maribor assigned to Austria. The Allies at first agreed, but after strong Yugoslav protests, they compromised by assigning Maribor to Yugoslavia and Radgona to Austria.

so long as these were not too unreasonable—*force majeure* could always be invoked, with the blame thrust on the Allies rather than on Belgrade.

The problem of minorities, however, involved considerations of a different order. Yugoslavia, from its inception on, was a complex mosaic of nationalities and minorities—more so than any other successor state. Its future would largely depend on the relationships that would evolve between the various ethnic groups. For over a decade, the underlying premise of Yugoslav nationalism (and, one may add, romanticism) had been the ethnic unity and identity of Serbs, Croats, and Slovenes, finding expression in the slogan "one people with three names." Yet though this premise was formalized by the act of union in December 1918 and the first constitution in 1921, it did not go unchallenged.[2] From the Corfu Declaration (1917) on, the Serbs and Croats engaged in a struggle for power that was to plague—and in 1941 to expedite the collapse —of the new state. In the second half of 1919 the contest had not yet developed far, being paradoxically both stimulated and kept in check by the critical international situation. Yet premonitory symptoms of political malaise began to appear at many turns. The growing debate over centralization versus decentralization, the parliamentary strife, the tension within the ruling coalition, and the personal clash of leading political figures, all revolved in varying degrees around the basic "national question."

The government in Belgrade was not opposed to guaranteeing minority rights. But it had reason to fear a system of international obligations and League controls that could in the future lead to foreign interference. Once the definitive frontiers were set, Yugoslavia would absorb some foreign elements on every side. These could be manipulated from the outside and the Italian, German, Magyar, and Albanian minorities might become a source of major trouble. Given the potential dangers of Serbo-Croat discord, the government was anxious to gain absolute control over the borderland minorities. In advancing the argument of *sovereignty* to the Allies, it was thus not merely arguing a technicality and acting out of misplaced vanity. Vital political motives were at stake.

2. See Slobodan Jovanović, *Ustavno Pravo Kraljevine Srba, Hrvata i Slovenaca* (Belgrade, 1924), pp. 55 ff. and passim.

To this must be added the factor of Macedonia. For the Serbs, Macedonia symbolized their historic destiny in the Balkans. They had gained it after generations of bloody fighting, and for many Serbs, Macedonia meant more than all western Yugoslav territory combined. To submit it to international supervision now, as the Serbs began to strive for political supremacy in the new state, would be tantamount to equating Serbia with the former Austro-Hungarian provinces. That would indeed be a psychological blow.

In September 1919, however, the government made one miscalculation. By refusing to sign the treaty, it thought, the Allies could be pressured into changing the minorities provision for Macedonia. In reality, of course, its position became greatly weakened. For the Allies could—and did—logically argue that the Austrian peace treaty had now been formally signed and could no longer be changed. No matter how much the Yugoslavs objected, this was to remain the Allied stand.

The day the Austrian treaty was signed at St. Germain, Johnson visited Trumbić at Yugoslav headquarters. The Adriatic problem, he said, was coming to a head, and Balfour and Tardieu were now prone to accept Tittoni's program. With Polk's approval, Johnson was preparing to cable Wilson, urging: 1) that a temporary buffer state be created, with a plebiscite in five years; 2) that if this idea were rejected, then Fiume in the old *corpus separatum* borders would become independent under League guarantee (and under no circumstances to go to Italy), with the port leased to Yugoslavia for ninety-nine years; and 3) that some limitation be made of Italian mandate in Albania.[3] Johnson's ideas were rather favorable to the Yugoslavs, and Trumbić indicated approval. But the American, who in a few days was to leave for Washington, warned that Wilson faced grave problems at home and might be prevented from intervening in the matter right away, if at all.

Trumbić continued to see Johnson during the remaining days, and on the 13th, at the latter's request, submitted a memorandum for American use. This note assumed special urgency, following by one day the jolting news of D'Annunzio's coup in Fiume. Yugoslav "conditions" for solving the Adriatic problem, wrote Trumbić,

3. "Razgovor Trumbić–Johnson," Paris, Sept. 10, 1919 (TP, F112).

involved: 1) the creation of a buffer state with Fiume (but excluding Porto Baroš and Sušak) up to the river Raša, with a plebiscite as soon as possible; 2) if this were rejected, then that the old corpus separatum, without Fiume, be given right away to Yugoslavia, with Porto Baroš assigned to Sušak; 3) Fiume as a free city under the League, with the harbor leased to the S.C.S. state; 4) Italian frontiers not beyond the Raša; 5) giving Lošinj and Vis to Yugoslavia; 6) giving Zara to Yugoslavia with guaranteed autonomy for Italians; and 7) Albanian independence within the borders of 1913, but if a mandate is given to Italy then, and only then, the Yugoslavs demand a mandate over northern Albania.[4] With this document Johnson left for home.

Meantime, of course, D'Annunzio's action changed the situation. After landing in Fiume, he immediately began to talk about annexing the city to Italy. The Yugoslavs promptly asked the Supreme Council to intervene, which the peacemakers refused to do with arms and, instead, asked the Italians to do. Nitti's government appeared genuinely embarrassed, disavowed D'Annunzio, and promised to restore the status quo ante. This, however, was easier said than done and it took a year and a half before D'Annunzio was finally expelled.

Undaunted by the crisis in the field, the diplomats in Paris returned to their customary labors on September 15. Tittoni appeared before the Council with the following proposal: doing away altogether with the buffer state; giving the corpus separatum to Italy, with the rest to Yugoslavia and the port administered by the League; Zara to be a free city represented diplomatically by Italy; giving Lošinj, Vis, and Palagruža, as well as Valona with hinterland, to Italy; neutralization of the coast and islands; and a mandate over "independent" Albania.[5]

Clemenceau was agreeable. Indeed, by this time he was ready to assign Fiume to Italy outright. Lloyd George would accept any plan worked out by the Italians with Wilson. But Polk, after noting that Wilson had not even replied to the proposal of August 12,

4. "Glavni Uslovi Za Rešenje Jadranskog Problema No Koje Bi Mogla Pristati Jugoslavenska Delegacija Uz Rezervu Odobrenja Vlade," Paris, Sept. 13, 1919 (TP, F112).

5. *Résolutions* 1226, Sept. 15, 1919.

asked the Italian how this plan differed from the earlier one. It eliminated the need for a plebiscite, replied Tittoni, but if Wilson insisted, he could choose either one (though the Italians favored the latter).[6]

Wilson's agreement, however, was not forthcoming. Not only was the President opposed to any scheme that would forestall a plebiscite, but his involvement in the Adriatic dispute was cut short by physical collapse. After twenty-two days of grueling speech-making in favor of the League and the Treaty of Versailles across the United States, his strength gave way in Pueblo, Colorado, on September 26. Two days later, he suffered a paralytic stroke that kept him an invalid for several months. At the end of September, in his stead, Polk informed the peace conference that the proposed formula for Fiume was not acceptable, thus shelving the Tittoni plan.

By this time the Americans had also become annoyed over Nitti's failure to remove D'Annunzio from Fiume. When the Italians complained in Paris that Yugoslav provocations were making this task impossible, Polk countered that Italy was provoking disorders in Zara, Split, and Kotor, and said flatly that the United States would do nothing "under the pressure of the facts in Fiume." [7] To continued Italian insistence that the Yugoslavs were mobilizing and preparing to attack Italian occupation forces, all three Western Allies replied that the Yugoslavs intended no such thing.[8] To the contrary, they were impressed with Yugoslav forbearance and Belgrade's strict orders to all civil and military authorities to prevent incidents.

Having gotten nowhere with this approach, the Italians in mid-October renewed diplomatic efforts to break the Fiume deadlock.

6. See Albrecht-Carrié, *Italy*, p. 248.

7. Scialoja to Ministry of Foreign Affairs (Rome), Paris, Sept. 23, 1919 (Tel. 434, Gab. 6207, MFA, Rome).

8. De Martino to Ministry of Foreign Affairs (Rome), Paris, Oct. 1, 1919 (Tel. 504, Gab. 6308); De Martino to Ministry of Foreign Affairs, Paris, Oct. 2, 1919 (Tel. 1307), in which De Martino reports that Crowe, Pichon, and Berthelot had all praised the Yugoslavs for being so patient and warned the Italians against any provocations in the Adriatic (MFA, Rome); Athelstan-Johnson to Curzon, Belgrade, Sept. 30, 1919 (*DBFP*, p. 90), reporting strongest assurances from the Yugoslav government that it would follow a policy of restraint.

On the 13th, Tittoni proposed a new plan, involving mainly two variations on the theme of his earlier projects: 1) the city of Fiume wholly independent, with the coast from the Wilson line to Fiume annexed to Italy; and 2) a free state without the city proper but with control of the port and railway, to be established under League control. As for the rest: Zara independent under the League, with Italian diplomatic representation; the entire Dalmatian coast neutralized, and Italy to receive Lošinj, Vis, and Palagruža.[9]

This plan was immediately rejected by the Yugoslavs, who continued to insist both on the Wilson line and the principle of a plebiscite for the entire free state, including Fiume.[10] On October 27 Lansing sent Tittoni a note (through Polk) rejecting the Italian proposal on similar grounds. The American government, wrote Lansing, insisted on the establishment of a free state including the city of Fiume, and favored a plebiscite after five years. The tough language of Lansing's memorandum was reinforced on November 13 by a "personal" note from Wilson to Nitti—a note actually composed by Lansing and worthy of fuller quotation—stating that

> any solution of the problem of Fiume at variance with the one which I have advocated, would run counter to the foreign policy which I have pursued. I firmly believe that your doubts in regard to the reaction of the Italian people to a solution of the problem of Fiume other than that advocated by an imperialistic minority have no foundation in fact. The Italian people are not seriously interested in the question of Fiume, but rather in the solution of their major social and economic problems. In any case I regret to have to say that our attitude is not susceptible of any change. I should rather ask of you and your colleagues of the Peace Conference that, for the good of mankind, the Adriatic problem be resolved without delay. The need of a European readjustment is felt by all the peoples of the world and that country which would prevent this readjustment would compel my country to take unsympathetic

9. Albrecht-Carrié, pp. 250–51.
10. Athelstan-Johnson to Curzon, Belgrade, Oct. 14, 1919 (*DBFP*, pp. 126–27).

measures dictated solely by the irrevocable decision of the
Government of my country to assist in the task of economic
reconstruction only those countries which adhere to its program.[11]

Under this assault, Tittoni's project caved in. The American
President, infuriated by the D'Annunzio coup and annoyed by
Lloyd George's and Clemenceau's acquiescence in Tittoni's designs, again blocked Italy's way. Caught in the crossfire of American and growing Italian opposition to his policies, Tittoni resigned at the end of November—ostensibly for reasons of poor
health—and passed the foreign ministry on to Vittorio Scialoja. His
resignation, however, was as much brought on by D'Annunzio's
actions as by American pressure. For in the face of the events in
Fiume, Italian nationalist circles resumed clamoring for the annexation of the city. At the end of September, after Tittoni informed the Chamber of Deputies that the Treaty of London would
have to be modified, a veritable political storm broke out. The
government took fright, dissolved parliament, and called for a general election in November. As may well be imagined, the electoral
campaign that ensued was anything but dull.

Nitti's cabinet, meanwhile, tried to talk D'Annunzio into quit-
ting Fiume. Of all people, it appointed General Badoglio—now
military commandant of Venezia Giulia—to conduct talks with
the poet-condottiere. The two maintained contact in Abbazia
(Opatija) all through October,[12] but nothing came of it. It is worth
noting, however, that in the months that followed, D'Annunzio
and his lieutenants established contact with dissident Croat groups,
whom they encouraged to conduct anti-Serbian activities in Yugoslavia.[13] This is not to suggest that the government in Rome was
lending itself to these nefarious schemes, for both Nitti and Tittoni
acted in good faith in their endeavors to remove D'Annunzio from

11. Quoted in Albrecht-Carrié, pp. 254–55. The note was dated Nov. 13. Ten
days earlier Polk told Trumbić in Paris that Wilson's illness prevented the President's personal intervention in Adriatic affairs, but that Lansing and he (Polk) were
dealing with the Italians "in accordance with the known views of the President"
("Razgovor Trumbić–Polk," Paris, Nov. 3, 1919, TP, F63/71).

12. Alatri, *Nitti, d'Annunzio,* pp. 271 ff.

13. Giurati, *Con d'Annunzio e Millo,* pp. 151 ff. and passim.

Fiume. But some collusion existed between D'Annunzio and Italian military and naval authorities. Without their tolerance and, as was claimed by Belgrade, secret support and supplies,[14] the Fiuman enterprise would quickly have collapsed. Moreover, the cordiality of tone used between Badoglio and D'Annunzio, while in itself evidence of little value, is nonetheless suggestive of considerable mutual sympathy [15] and the undermining of Nitti's policy.

On October 30 D'Annunzio's regime sponsored a "plebiscite" in Fiume, resulting in an overwhelming vote to annex the city to Italy. This action had little bearing on the course of events in Paris, but it further inflamed the electoral campaign in Italy. The analysis contained in Wilson's note to Nitti was—perhaps surprisingly—close to being right. For when the elections were finally held on November 16, and despite the great frenzy over Fiume, the nationalists suffered a grievous blow. Concerned much more with the economic aftermath of the war and the spreading industrial strikes than with Fiume, the Italian electorate tripled the Socialist membership in parliament from 52 to 155 and gave 101 seats to the Catholic *Partito Popolare,* now the two strongest political parties. Fiume had indeed proved a secondary issue and ultranationalism a sterile theme. Under these circumstances, and in the face of adamant American opposition to his plans, Tittoni could no longer hope to break the Adriatic deadlock. His successor was to be similarly plagued.

During most of the autumn the Yugoslavs remained absorbed by the issues of Fiume and the minorities conventions. While continuing to protest D'Annunzio's presence in Fiume and to ask for Allied intervention, they decided against military countermeasures of their own for fear of alienating the Allies as well as risking possible war with Italy. On the whole, they displayed remarkable restraint.

During their five-week stay in Belgrade, Pašić and Trumbić reviewed all of the peace conference problems with the government. They took part in five separate cabinet meetings between September 21 and October 20. The thorniest question discussed was that

14. See *DBFP,* p. 127.
15. See Alatri, pp. 276–77.

of the unsigned Austrian treaty, though the issues of the Adriatic and other frontiers, the Bulgarian and Hungarian treaties, reparations, and the merchant fleet were thoroughly explored as well. By mid-October, continued refusal to accommodate the Allies on the subject of minorities conventions began to appear futile, particularly in the face of the dangerous situation in Fiume. Trumbić, worried lest Yugoslav intransigence lead to a loss of American support in the Adriatic, argued that the time had come to give in on the Austrian treaty. After much soul-searching, both Pašić and Davidović came to share this view, and on October 20, at the final joint session of the cabinet and the peace delegates, the previous stand was officially reversed. The government decided that one more effort should be made to exclude from the minorities convention all Serbian territory held before 1914. If the Allies again refused to concede this point, the delegation would be authorized to sign both the Austrian and Bulgarian treaties in their present form. This decision, Davidović wrote to Paris on October 21, was taken in the context of the overall Yugoslav situation and as a result of a "written declaration by the French chargé d'affaires from which it appears that continued refusal to sign the treaty might bring into question the very existence of our state." [16] With this decision Pašić, Trumbić, Smodlaka, and Ribarž returned to Paris.

However, very soon new complications arose. Davidović's letter of October 21 included excerpts of the cabinet decision which, he said, should be "regarded" as new instructions. But they were not official instructions as such. And after the return of the peace delegates to Paris, there were second thoughts on the subject in Belgrade, and for the time being, no definitive *instructions* were sent. Pursuant to the cabinet decision, however, the delegation did ask the Allies to exclude all Serbian territory from the convention. But on October 29, rather than yield, the Allies went a step further, and to apply even greater pressure, resolved that the Yugoslavs would not be permitted to sign the Bulgarian treaty until after they adhered to the Austrian.[17] In the week that followed, Trumbić was informed by Pichon, Berthelot, Polk, and Eyre Crowe that there was no hope for an Allied change of mind.[18]

16. Davidović to Delegation, Belgrade, Oct. 21, 1919 (TP, F69).
17. *La Paix de Versailles*, Vol. 10, *PV* 56, Nov. 3, 1919.
18. Zap., 2, 214–15, 217 (K&H, pp. 186–87, 188).

More important still, Trumbić learned from Polk that the American delegation was planning to leave Paris at the beginning of December and was pressing for completion of the Bulgarian and Hungarian treaties by then, as well as for a solution of the Adriatic question. The American government would stand by its earlier position in regard to Fiume and a plebiscite, seek a "fair agreement," and support only proposals "acceptable to the Yugoslavs." [19] Henry White was even more forceful and on November 6 assured Trumbić that the United States would not give in to Italy and would never abandon the Yugoslavs. If need be, economic pressure would be applied against Rome to bring about a just solution.[20] But neither American gave any encouragement in regard to the minorities convention.

On November 5 Pašić sent a formal note to Clemenceau asking again for the exclusion of Serbian territory. The request was turned down on the 12th with a demand for a final decision: will the Yugoslavs sign the treaty or not in its present form? Next day Pašić summoned the delegation to make such a decision.[21] In view of the October 20 cabinet directive, he thought the treaty should be signed. But a final letter had to be sent to Clemenceau, indicating Yugoslav disappointment with the Allied decision, especially since other states had not yet accepted similar restrictions on their own sovereignty. Trumbić agreed, save for the reference to other states. A final decision was not reached, but later in the day a telegram arrived from Davidović authorizing the delegation to sign the *Bulgarian* treaty and, for the time being, not the Austrian.[22] Forty-eight hours later the Prime Minister also informed the delegation that the Rumanians had definitely decided to adhere to the Austrian treaty in its present form and proposed to act jointly with the Yugoslavs in Paris.[23]

What followed was a series of incredible maneuvers and counter-maneuvers within the delegation, between the delegation and Belgrade, and between the delegation and the Allies. First, Bošković

---

19. "Razgovor Trumbić–Polk," Paris, Nov. 3, 1919 (TP, F63/71). If the Adriatic issue were not resolved, Polk said, the American side would deal with it from Washington and through the U.S. ambassador in Rome.

20. "Razgovor Trumbić–White," Paris, Nov. 6, 1919 (TP, F63/83).

21. Zap., 2, 223 (K&H, p. 190).

22. Davidović to Delegation, Urgent No. 13399, Belgrade, Nov. 13, 1919 (TP, F66).

23. Davidović to Delegation, Belgrade, Nov. 15, 1919 (TP, F66).

handed in his resignation, which Davidović accepted. Next, the Allies informed Pašić that the Bulgarian peace treaty was scheduled to be signed on November 27 at Neuilly, and that all outstanding issues had to be resolved by the 25th. On the 24th the delegation resolved to sign both the Austrian and Bulgarian treaties.[24] On that day, however, Davidović cabled objections to the proposed compensation for Serbia and forbade signing the *financial* protocols of either treaty.[25] At the last minute the cabinet had decided to oppose the assessment of one and a half billion francs against the former Austro-Hungarian provinces to be assumed by all of Yugoslavia as its share of the Dual Monarchy's debt. For this was interpreted as a penalty against Serbia.

Trumbić felt personally stung by this decision, for the issue had been settled in his presence on October 20, and he now raised a storm. After an explosive debate on November 25, the whole delegation decided to resign.[26] Next day Trumbić cabled the Prime Minister that the government's decision jeopardized the whole Yugoslav position at the peace conference; that the Americans had warned him the day before that the consequences of further delays might be grave; that the only choice left might be to withdraw altogether from Paris; and that so far as financial arrangements were concerned, if need be a public loan could be floated in Yugoslavia for the exclusive use of Serbia, to be repaid not by Serbs but exclusively by the former Austro-Hungarian provinces! [27]

Having informed the Allies that they would sign the Bulgarian settlement, and the Allies having dropped the threat that the Austrian treaty would have to be signed first, the Yugoslavs appeared at Neuilly on November 27, duly signed the Bulgarian peace treaty, and accepted the minorities provisions embodied in that document. The fact that the delegation had resigned two days before did not interfere; that action was meant for internal purposes only. The Treaty of Neuilly assigned to the Serbo-Croat-Slovene state several strategic salients—in the Strumica valley and

24. Zap., 2, 233 (K&H, p. 194).

25. Davidović to Delegation, Very Urgent No. 13989, Belgrade, Nov. 24, 1919 (TP, F66).

26. Pašić to Davidović, Urgent and Strictly Confidential, Paris [Nov. 25, 1919] (TP, F66).

27. Trumbić to Davidović, Paris, Nov. 26, 1919 (TP, F63/68).

in the districts of Vranje, Tsaribrod, and Negotin—of some 960 square miles and a population, much of it Bulgarian, of 100,000. Vidin and the surrounding region claimed in the north, however, was left to Bulgaria.[28]

After signing the Bulgarian treaty, it became illogical to make further difficulties about the Austrian. The financial aspects of the several treaties were still to be worked out by the reparations commission, and the government in Belgrade decided to send the Regent and two cabinet members—Drašković and Kosta Stojanović—to Paris to work out the details with the Allies. As for the rest, faced with the Rumanian decision to sign, with Trumbić's bitter warning, and with the earlier disposition of the cabinet to give way on the minorities issue, Davidović finally brought the drawn-out affair to an end. On December 5, after refusing to accept the delegation's resignation—save for Žolger's, but only *after* his signature was placed on the Austrian treaty[29]—he announced Yugoslav adherence to the Treaty of St. Germain.[30] Together with the Rumanians, the Yugoslavs thus bowed to the inevitable.

The Yugoslav decision at first seemed to clear the air with the Allies. But by the beginning of December a new trend had set in that was to spell a turning point in regard to Yugoslav affairs. In the first place, the Allies had become generally anxious to bring the peace conference to an end. Following the signing of the Versailles treaty back in June, public opinion in the Western countries became increasingly concerned with the problems of Germany and Bolshevism, and with the domestic issues of postwar development and policy. The remaining work before the peacemakers seemed almost anticlimactic after June, and many statesmen in Paris were anxious to return home. By late November, Lloyd George was particularly determined to adjourn the conference, hoping to transfer it to London to settle the remaining work on the Russian, Hungarian, and Turkish problems. The Americans

28. The treaty also limited Bulgaria's armed forces to 33,000 men, forbade compulsory military service, and placed severe limits on the manufacture of munitions. These provisions were sought by the Serbs, as well as by the Rumanians and Greeks.

29. Davidović to Pašić, No. 14121, Belgrade, Dec. 5, 1919 (TP, F66).

30. See N. Almond and R. H. Lutz, eds., *The Treaty of St. Germain: A Documentary History of Its Territorial and Political Clauses* (Stanford, 1935), p. 502.

too, especially in view of the mounting opposition to the League at home, wanted to adjourn. Polk was preparing to return to Washington at the beginning of December and to leave the conduct of American peace conference policy in the hands of the United States ambassador in Paris.

Much of the impatience to adjourn reflected discouragement at the course of events in America. News of Republican opposition to the League of Nations and indications that Wilson was losing political ground at home produced inevitable rumors that the United States might refuse to ratify the German treaty and the League Covenant and thus deal a severe blow to the whole peacemaking enterprise. And the greater the uncertainty about America, the greater also became Allied impatience with the problem children in Paris—Italy and Yugoslavia—who appeared to complicate matters unduly. For in fact, the endless Adriatic imbroglio was no nearer to a solution now than it had been six months earlier.

In this general atmosphere the Americans decided to make another effort before leaving Paris. At their instigation, Allied unity —broken over Anglo-French support for, and American opposition to, Tittoni's various plans—was to be restored through a joint Anglo-French-American statement to the Italians.[31] The idea was to synchronize Allied positions and present Italy with a unified front to which the British and French, having failed to reconcile Washington and Rome, now acceded. The result was the joint memorandum of December 9, handed to the Italians following a meeting of Lord Curzon and Scialoja, Tittoni's successor, in London, at which both agreed to keep the memorandum secret so as to keep it from appearing as an ultimatum.[32] The document in effect signified a substantial victory for the Americans, for it now formally associated Great Britain and France with the ideas expressed in Lansing's note of October 27.

In Istria the Allies decided to stick by the Wilson line, assigning some 300,000 Yugoslavs to Italy only in order to cater to Italian strategic and economic sensitivities. As for Fiume, the memorandum proposed establishing a buffer state, including the city proper,

31. See Crowe to Curzon, Paris, Nov. 1, 1919 (*DBFP*, p. 153).
32. See Šišić, *Jadransko Pitanje*, pp. 41–51, and *DBFP*, p. 238.

of some 200,000 Yugoslavs and 40,000 Italians. Given Italy's natural antipathy for a plebiscite, it was agreed to leave the fate of the entire free state to the League of Nations. Zara would become self-governing under the League, but within the Yugoslav customs system. For strategic reasons, Italy could have the island groups of Palagruža, Vis, Lošinj, provided they were demilitarized and local Yugoslavs received autonomy. Italy would also receive in sovereignty the city of Valona with the necessary hinterland, and a mandate over the rest of Albania within the frontiers of 1913, save in the south where the borders remained to be worked out.

The memorandum spelled out these points in detail, ending with a full review of the problem of Albania. The Italian mandate, as all mandates under the League, was to be temporary. The Albanian state was to work out the northern frontiers with Yugoslavia. The Yugoslavs were to construct and operate a railway in northern Albania and to have a voice in the development of the river Bojana.

On the whole, the memorandum of December 9 (which was not communicated to the Yugoslavs) represented a rejection of the Italian position on Fiume, as maintained all during the fall. It also put heavy pressure on Rome, because it signified a change of policy by the British and the French. The Italians, under the circumstances, delayed their reply for a month and used the intervening time in efforts to modify the Allies' position. They also explored the possibility of resuming direct Italo-Yugoslav talks, as a way of reaching quick agreement and at the same time circumventing the December 9 proposals.

For the Yugoslavs, of course, the general outlook at the moment seemed favorable. There was no immediate reason to sit down with the Italians and risk having to make concessions. They knew the Allies had sent a joint note to Scialoja, and though the text was kept secret, there was no reason to expect the Americans to go back on their word. Furthermore, the Yugoslav position had been strengthened by the conclusion of peace with Austria and Bulgaria. Yet they became uneasy when the Italians suddenly made separate inquiries about direct talks: in Paris (through Professor Victor Bérard), in Rome (through Antonijević), and in Belgrade (through the French chargé d'affaires).[33] The cabinet's immediate reaction was to advise the French chargé that the Italians should approach the peace delegation in Paris, hoping in effect to avoid direct talks for the time being.[34] But the delegation, after much debate on December 24, took the view that if the Italians were seriously interested in direct talks, the Yugoslavs could not in good faith turn them down.[35] Trumbić cabled this view to Davidović on Christmas Day,[36] and three days later the Premier informed the delegation that the government agreed to hold direct talks in Paris, provided the initiative came from Nitti and the Allies were informed and approved.[37] Davidović would have preferred having the talks held personally with Nitti, fearing that otherwise the Italians would be merely exploring rather than negotiating.

The talks did not come to pass immediately, however, due to a series of new maneuvers in the Allied camp. While in London on a brief trip at the beginning of January, Nitti discussed the Adriatic issue with Lloyd George. On the 6th he submitted a memorandum asking first the implementation of the Treaty of London and then offering the following "compromise": a free Fiuman state, with the "Italianity" of Fiume fully guaranteed within the framework of the corpus separatum; territorial contiguity of the Fiuman state with Italy; Cres, Lošinj, Vis, Palagruža, and Lastovo to Italy; the whole coast with the islands neutralized; and Zara a free city.[38]

On the 9th, Lloyd George and Clemenceau replied that if Italy insisted, Great Britain and France would abide by the London pact, implying there would be difficulty about Fiume. But if Italy agreed to set the Treaty of London aside, the British and French leaders—who now took things into their own hands, without reference to Wilson—would try to promote a solution midway be-

33. Davidović to Delegation, No. 14891, Belgrade, Dec. 14, 1919; Davidović to Pašić, Strictly Confidential No. 15149, Belgrade, Dec. 19, 1919; Trumbić to Ministry of Foreign Affairs, Strictly Confidential, Paris, Dec. 22, 1919; Trumbić to Ministry of Foreign Affairs, Paris, Dec. 25, 1919 (TP, F66).

34. Davidović to Delegation, No. 15094, Belgrade, Dec. 19, 1919 (TP, F66).

35. Zap., 2, 283 (K&H, p. 214).

36. Trumbić to Ministry of Foreign Affairs (for the Prime Minister), Paris, Dec. 25, 1919 (TP, F66).

37. Davidović to Pašić, Strictly Confidential No. 15448, Belgrade, Dec. 28, 1919 (TP, F66).

38. Alatri, *Nitti, d'Annunzio*, pp. 372–73.

tween the Allied proposals of December 9 and Nitti's "compromise" offer of January 6. They also offered to accept the contiguity of the Fiuman state with Italy and to press this on the Yugoslavs.[39] Lloyd George and Clemenceau clearly thought that Belgrade could be forced to accept and that Washington would not oppose the conclusion of a quick agreement.[40]

That same day (January 9) Trumbić received an urgent message from Nitti suggesting a meeting between their aides. When Trumbić sent word back that such a meeting was not likely to yield results, Nitti concurred and within the hour suggested a direct meeting between the two, "if possible still today." [41] Trumbić and his colleagues wondered what this was all about, for earlier in the day Nitti had met with Lloyd George and Clemenceau behind closed doors. His motivation now was unclear. Nevertheless, such a high-level contact could not be turned down, and at 6:00 P.M., with the approval of the other delegates, Trumbić set out for the appointed meeting, at the home of Baroness Grazioli, 1 Rue de Buenos Aires.

The meeting, attended as well by Scialoja and the Marchese della Torretta, was cordial though inconclusive.[42] Nitti began by emphasizing the need for good relations, with which Trumbić fully agreed. But the Yugoslav immediately pointed out that though

> we look upon the situation realistically [and] know that we
> have to make many concessions to Italy, we make these sacri-
> fices with a heavy heart and they too have to have their limits.
> With Istria and the hinterland you receive over 400,000 of
> our compatriots. By this we are showing great courage. But
> you, Italians, must realize that you cannot defend Trieste
> without us . . . Germany is resigned for the moment, but
> awaits the time when it can raise its head. You will defend

39. See Albrecht-Carrié, *Italy*, pp. 269–70.

40. On Jan. 10 Scialoja released the official Italian reply to the Allied memorandum of Dec. 9, rejecting the Wilson line and any geographic separation between Italy and Fiume.

41. Zap., *3*, 45 (K&H, p. 233).

42. Trumbić's full report is recorded in Zap., *3*, 46–49 (K&H, pp. 234–35). Scialoja and Della Torretta took little part in the exchange. Nitti asked to keep the meeting secret.

Trieste only if you stand together with us. Take Trieste, therefore, but everything over the Wilson line must remain to us as purely ours. Beyond that line significant Italian groups remain only in Fiume and Zara.[43]

Unimpressed, Nitti countered by proposing four alternatives from which the Yugoslavs could choose any one: 1) implementation of the Treaty of London, with Fiume to the Yugoslavs; 2) Istria with Fiume to Italy, and Dalmatia with all the islands to Yugoslavia; 3) Julian Alps and the Raša as the boundary, with a buffer state of Fiume; 4) Julian Alps and the Raša as the boundary, no buffer state, the town of Fiume to Italy, and Zara independent with Italian diplomatic representation.[44] Trumbić rejected all four, saying each was unfortunate for both sides. He put forth, as the only possible solution, a frontier along the Wilson line, and Fiume to Yugoslavia with wide internal autonomy. Only such a frontier embodied principles, he implied, that would create a durable basis for future amity and cooperation. Nitti did not reject this argument, but merely pointed out that if he went home empty-handed, his ministry would immediately fall and he would doubtless be lynched. The same, replied Trumbić, would be true in the opposite case; hence internal considerations should not dominate their work.

Nitti tried a different approach: "The Fiumans don't want to be trampled by the Croats, there is an anti-Croat mood." Replied Trumbić: "This anti-Croat spirit was artificially created, it is in reality Magyar." All in all, Nitti did not *reject* the Yugoslav's arguments. As Trumbić noted, he rather showed great anxiety about reactions at home. He asked whether demilitarization of the coast and islands would be accepted. Trumbić said no, because this would expose Yugoslavia to great danger.

> *Nitti:*   But your coast with the islands represents an immense danger to us, as was the case under Austria.

> *Trumbić:* The advance of modern technology equalizes all that. But in the fear for your security you forget our own vulnerability.

43. Ibid., p. 46 (K&H, p. 234).
44. Ibid., p. 47 (K&H, p. 234).

Only brief exchanges followed. At one point Trumbić stated his opposition to an Italian mandate over Albania, only to have Nitti reply: "Let's leave that question aside for now." Both men agreed that the merchant fleet problem could be speedily settled. But when Trumbić, making his final point, asked for sufficient guarantees to assure national development for the Slovenes in Italy, Nitti only said. "Of this there can be no discussion," adding that these talks had to be continued, since he could "not return to Italy without a solution of the Adriatic question." [45] The meeting ended on this note.

Trumbić was pleased by the friendly atmosphere that prevailed. Little did he know that this meeting was but the prelude to a storm.

On January 10, 1920, the ratification ceremony for the German peace treaty was held at the Quai d'Orsay. Only two days earlier —the day before the Trumbić–Nitti meeting—the Yugoslavs sent Clemenceau a note, in effect rejecting the Allied proposals of December 9 in regard to Fiume, Zara, and Albania, insisting instead on the Wilson line, and on obtaining both Fiume and Zara with wide internal autonomy. As for Albania, they sought only frontier rectifications, but if the Allies did not agree to its independence, they proposed outright partition of the country.[46]

Now on the 10th, during the tea following the Quai d'Orsay ceremony, Clemenceau unexpectedly approached Trumbić and invited him into Pichon's *cabinet*. Already present were Lloyd George, Nitti, Scialoja, and various members of the three Allied governments. In a moment Pašić, Žolger, and Radović were also asked to come in, and when the door closed behind them, the

45. Ibid., p. 48 K&H, p. 234).
46. For the text of the Yugoslav note see Šišić, *Jadransko Pitanje*, pp. 52–60. The decision to ask for a partition of Albania was taken, after much debate within the delegation, between Dec. 17 and Jan. 6 (Zap., 2, 266 ff.; 3, 1 ff. [K&H, pp. 20 ff.]). Cabinet members Drašković and Stojanović took part in the discussions of Dec. 17, 24, 29, 30, and 31 but not in the final and crucial meetings of Jan. 4 and 5. Nonetheless, they shared the majority view that Italy's presence in Albania, particularly in the north, would jeopardize Yugoslav security as well as regional Balkan stability. The concrete idea of partition, and of extending the Yugoslav frontier to the Drim in the event that Italy received Valona plus a mandate in Central Albania, was most vigorously advocated by Andrija Radović.

unwarned Yugoslavs found themselves before a grand session over
the Adriatic. When Clemenceau asked for a review of the Yugoslav position, Trumbić felt, as he later wrote Smodlaka, that
"though I am familiar with the question, the surprise was most
unpleasant." [47] Still, he launched into a detailed analysis that
wore his listeners out, so that after two hours Trumbić himself
suggested an adjournment. A new meeting was set for the 12th.
Yet a new and alarming trend of thought among the Allies was already evident on the 10th. For all during Trumbić's exposé, Lloyd
George, flanked by his expert Leeper and armed with maps, kept
interrupting with pointed questions about the Slovenes, Zara, and
Albania.[48] His intent, and that of his colleagues, soon became
quite clear. On the 12th, Trumbić concluded his review before
the Allies, and a few hours later Lloyd George—who was rapidly
emerging as the decisive figure in this round of talks—called him
on the telephone, suggesting a meeting *à deux* next day.

Trumbić went. Lloyd George now sprang the following formula
on him: Italy is to receive Fiume proper as well as eastern Istria,
while Yugoslavia, in return for the loss of Fiume, is to be com-
pensated in northern Albania. With that he handed Trumbić a
pencil and a map, suggesting the latter mark the extent of Yugoslav desires in northern Albania.[49] Trumbić declined, observing
he could not improvise the national frontier. Lloyd George went
on. In the Adriatic he offered Cres and the demilitarization of all
islands but not of the coast. Lošinj, Vis, and Palagruža, however,
would have to go to Italy. At about this point he was handed a

47. Trumbić to Smodlaka, Paris, Jan. 23, 1919 (TP, F112).

48. In regard to Albania, Trumbić argued thus: "We are convinced that the
best solution for this question lies in maintaining the arrangements worked out in
London in 1913, that is to say, to leave the Albanian state as it was when created,
with an autonomous administration . . . We are indeed convinced that a foreign
administration, of whatever nature, [would be unwise] . . . From all that we
know of the Albanians, they have adequate elements for the establishment of an
administration capable of governing the country." Albanian national unity, Trumbić
further argued, would be in the best interests of all the Allies, not only the Yugoslavs. He disputed Italy's juridical right to a mandate, since the League of Nations
Covenant envisaged mandates only for territories and colonies that had never enjoyed independence. ("Extraits de l'exposé de M. Trumbitch; notes du secrétaire
prises au cours d'une réunion dans le cabinet de M. Pichon au Quai d'Orsay, le
10 Janvier 1920, à 16:30," TP, F73.)

49. Trumbić to Smodlaka, Paris, Jan. 23, 1919 (TP, F112).

message informing him that Nitti had arrived. Lloyd George immediately left the room. Returning shortly, he added that Lastovo island would have to go to Italy too and the city of Šibenik would have to be demilitarized! "I told him my opinion," wrote Trumbić to Smodlaka, "whereupon we both went to see the Heir Apparent, who had invited him [Lloyd George] to lunch." [50] There the discussion continued, with the Yugoslavs [51] adamant on Fiume, and Lloyd George increasingly annoyed. "It was clear what he wanted," wrote Trumbić. "To the Italians the bay of Fiume and Scutari to us!" [52]

Having got nowhere with the Yugoslavs, Lloyd George immediately after lunch hurried to a meeting with Clemenceau and Nitti at the Quai d'Orsay. After a while, the three premiers sent a message to Pašić and Trumbić, asking them to come to the Quai d'Orsay right away. When the Yugoslavs arrived, Nitti, à la Orlando, retired from the room. Speaking "energetically, heatedly and sometimes as though carried away," [53] Clemenceau *announced* the formula agreed upon by himself, Lloyd George, and Nitti, who was "listening behind the open door." [54]

The Yugoslav delegation stayed up most of the night drafting

50. Ibid. Regent Alexander was in Paris at this time. As Krizman rightly notes, he did considerable harm by promoting the notion among the Allies that the Serbs were more inclined toward compromise than the Croats. Alexander even remarked to Trumbić that Fiume was not too important, but that Scutari was vital. See B. Krizman, "Saveznički Ultimatum u Jadranskom Pitanju Siječnja 1920 godine," *Jadranski Zbornik*, 2 (Rijeka-Pula, 1957), p. 212, n. 40.

51. Pašić and the other peace delegates were present as well.

52. Trumbić to Smodlaka, Paris, Jan. 23, 1920.

53. Ibid.

54. Ibid. The formula: (1) The city of Fiume to Italy, Sušak to Yugoslavia, Fiuman port and railroad facilities to the League for the use of Yugoslavia and other Danubian states; (2) no buffer state, instead the Istrian coast as far as Fiume to Italy, while railroad lines north of Fiume would be made Yugoslav national territory; (3) the municipality of Zara a free state under League protection, with the right of choosing its own diplomatic representation; (4) Valona under Italian sovereignty with the rest of Albania under an Italian mandate; rectification of the Yugoslav-Albanian frontier, but Albanian districts assigned to Yugoslavia to enjoy special autonomous regime; Argyrokastro and Korča to Greece; (5) Lošinj, Palagruža, and Vis island groups to Italy, all others to Yugoslavia; (6) all islands demilitarized; (7) Italians in Dalmatia to opt between Yugoslav and Italian citizenship, with no obligation to leave the territory; (8) security of existing economic enterprises in Dalmatia guaranteed by an international convention (Trumbić to Ministry of Foreign Affairs, Paris, Jan. 13, 1920, TP., F85).

its reply, rejecting the latest formula.[55] This was submitted to Clemenceau next morning, January 14, and in the afternoon Pašić and Trumbić were again invited to meet with Lloyd George and Clemenceau. And again, Nitti was next door. In angry and threatening tones, Clemenceau now attacked the Yugoslavs, claiming among other things that two currents existed in their midst—a Croat and a Serbian. He said that the Serbs were reasonable and would accept the proposed arrangement, and that the Croats were the intransigent ones. After praising Serbia's role in the war, he even blurted out that the Croats after all fought against the Allies. His final proposal, worked out with Lloyd George, modified only the first point of the January 13 formula: the Fiume corpus separatum would now become an independent state under League guarantee, with the right to choose its own diplomatic representation. To all this the Yugoslavs, he said, were now to reply simply "yes" or "no." If the answer was "no," Nitti would be authorized to implement the Treaty of London.[56]

Trumbić replied that there were no divergent currents among the Yugoslavs. The reply sent earlier that morning represented the view of the entire delegation and was within the sense of the government's instructions. As for the Croat role in the war, Trumbić felt provoked enough to make a whole speech on the subject, rejecting the old Sonnino line that had now evidently found a response with the irritated and impatient premiers of France and Great Britain. In conclusion, Trumbić also refused to answer "yes"

55. Pašić, Trumbić, Žolger, Radović, Ribarž, and Drašković worked from 10:00 P.M. to 3:30 A.M. Trumbić, whose views prevailed in the end, was certain that Wilson would never approve Clemenceau's project. He also argued that the Italians would never apply the London treaty without American concurrence. In their reply, the Yugoslavs (a) rejected Italian sovereignty over Fiume (even Tittoni never went this far); (b) rejected contiguity between Italy and Fiume; (c) rejected Zara as an independent town (they offered local autonomy under Yugoslav sovereignty, guaranteed by an international convention and the League); (d) demanded northern Albania and a rectification of the Serbo-Albanian frontier *if* Italy were to receive Valona and a mandate over the rest of the country, and *if* Greece were to receive Argyrokastro and Korča; moreover, any Italian mandate should be of short duration and all of Albanian territory should be neutralized; (e) would agree to the demilitarization of Adriatic islands, but only if all were assigned to the S.C.S. state. Zap., III, 52–58 (K&H, 236–38).

56. For a transcript of the talks between Pašić, Trumbić, Clemenceau, and Lloyd George, see Šišić, *Jadransko Pitanje*, pp. 89–102.

or "no" to the Allied proposition, stating that the matter would be submitted to the government for a decision.[57]

The delegation immediately cabled Belgrade. So did the French government, in an attempt to press Davidović into acceptance.[58] But on the 17th, Davidović instructed the delegation to inform Clemenceau, in the name of the government, that it would be a tragic error to think for a moment that Serbs and Croats differed in their views on this question.[59] The following day the government voted its reply to the proposals of January 14 and decided: 1) to ask that the Fiume corpus separatum, without railroads or port, be made independent, *without* the right to choose its representation but rather under League of Nations representation and sovereignty; and that Sušak with Porto Baroš go to Yugoslavia; 2) to insist on the Wilson line as the definitive boundary between Italy and Yugoslavia; 3) to have Zara, *if possible,* go to Yugoslavia, with local autonomy; 4) to accept the suggested frontier in northern Albania but oppose the division of the country, and to insist on the rectification of the eastern Serbo-Albanian line; 5) to make a further effort to obtain Lošinj, Vis, and Palagruža, but since Wilson had already granted these islands to Italy, not to make an issue of them; and finally, 6) to accept demilitarization of all the islands.[60]

The delegation prepared the formal note incorporating this reply between 10:00 P.M. and 5:00 A.M. of January 19–20, submitting it to Clemenceau several hours later. At 2:00 P.M. an invitation arrived for Pašić and Trumbić to meet with the "Supreme Council" at 8:15 that evening. When they arrived at the Quai d'Orsay, Clemenceau and Lloyd George were waiting. Hugh Campbell Wallace, the American ambassador, was present too.[61] So was Alexandre Millerand, who had just replaced Clemenceau as head of the French government. The atmosphere was tense. Clemenceau

57. Zap., 3, 60–61 (K&H, p. 240).

58. Davidović to Delegation, Belgrade, Jan. 16, 1920 (TP, F85).

59. See Krizman, "Saveznički Ultimatum," *Jadranski Zbornik*, 2, 216.

60. Davidović to Delegation, Most Urgent No. 575, Belgrade, Jan. 18, 1920, 11:00 P.M. (TP, F85). The message was received in Paris on Jan. 19 at 8:00 P.M.

61. His presence was unexpected. Three days earlier, it should be pointed out, Trumbić cabled Davidović that he was keeping the Americans informed about all developments and was in constant contact with them. "Please maintain the highest discretion about this," he added. (Trumbić to Davidović, Most Confidential, Paris, Jan. 17, 1920, TP, F85).

lost no time and began by telling the Yugoslavs that their reply was unsatisfactory. The Supreme Council would not change its proposal of January 14 and the Yugoslavs were to declare whether they would accept it—*in its entirety*—or not. If the answer were "no," the London treaty would be put into effect.

It was Pašić who replied. The Yugoslav note already envisaged important concessions, he said. But Clemenceau pressed him as to whether the note represented the government's definitive reply, or Pašić and Trumbić reserved the right to consult with Belgrade. Pašić pointed out that they could not give a final word on the spot and would submit the matter to the government. Thereupon, as Pašić cabled Davidović, "Clemenceau took note of this and gave a limit of four days for the reply. He stressed that the reply must be 'yes' or 'no' and that there is no more room for discussion or proposals. If no answer is given [within the time limit], the reply will be regarded as being negative." [62]

This ultimatum came as a heavy blow and Pašić immediately cabled Belgrade for instructions. While awaiting the reply, Trumbić went to see Wallace (on January 21) to sound out the American position. Wallace, it turned out, was present as an observer only; he came in effect to attend a session dealing with other matters. Was Clemenceau's declaration made in the name of the United States as well? No, only in the name of the Entente. What was the American position regarding Clemenceau's declaration? This Wallace could not answer without specific instruction from the government, but he promised to cable Washington that very evening and immediately inform the Yugoslavs.[63] Needless to say, Trumbić felt much relieved.

Nevertheless, a real crisis was at hand. Nitti had succeeded in winning Clemenceau and Lloyd George entirely to his side. The two premiers were now acting on their own, without reference to Wilson or even to earlier French and British positions. Woodrow Wilson, aside from being far away, had been inactive in this affair due to his own problems at home. The Yugoslavs were eager not

62. See Krizman, "Saveznički Ultimatum," *Jadranski Zbornik*, 2, 218. Pašić interpreted Wallace's presence as signifying American concurrence with Clemenceau and Lloyd George.

63. "Razgovor Trumbić–Wallace," Paris, Jan. 21, 1920 (TP, F67).

to forfeit French and British good will and support. Reliance on the Entente was a keystone of Belgrade's foreign policy. But how far would the United States go? Would Wilson stop the Entente? Faced by these uncertainties, the delegation chose to follow a well-tested course: it decided in effect to leave matters up to the government.

In Belgrade, however, there was little inclination to make the difficult decision. A stormy cabinet meeting took place on January 22.[64] Several ministers favored a straight "no"; some suggested temporizing, trying for modifications of one point or another, holding direct talks with Nitti (Marinković), to reply first "no" and then, if no modifications were possible, "yes"; Pribičević in desperation suggested leaving the final decision to Trumbić; Drašković voted "yes" so long as the Supreme Council was told this decision was made under duress; Stojanović, "yes" under protest. . . . Then the Prime Minister, Davidović, suddenly announced that he had just cabled Paris asking for an extension of the deadline and asking the delegation: 1) is the moment decisive or is there time and a possibility to maneuver; 2) if the moment is decisive, which answer "in the view of the Delegation is more harmful for our state organism and national conception: 'yes' or 'no?' " What has been the result of consultations with the Americans? In any event, "try to gain an extension of three days." [65] Following the dispatch of this message, the cabinet authorized Davidović to cable a second one, specifying neither "yes" nor "no," but asking Trumbić whether direct talks could be resumed with Nitti—not knowing that the latter had returned to Rome on January 20—or failing that, to give in gradually "point by point." [66] Seized by paralysis, the cabinet clearly did not want the responsibility for reaching a decision, expecting the delegation to perform last-minute mira-

64. For a partial transcript of the discussion see Krizman, in *Jadranski Zbornik, 2,* 219–21. In the midst of the meeting the French ambassador appeared with a note demanding acceptance of the Supreme Council's program or the Treaty of London would be put into effect.

65. Davidović to Delegation, Belgrade, Jan. 22, 1920 (6:00 P.M), Confidential and Most Urgent No. 689 (TP, F85). Received in Paris on Jan. 23 at 10:00 A.M.

66. Davidović to Delegation, Belgrade, Jan. 22, 1920, Confidential and Most Urgent No. 699 TP, F85). Received in Paris on Jan. 23 at 10:00 A.M.

cles. Clemenceau's words had been very clear; to give in "point by point," hoping for a concession here or there, represented at this critical moment an abdication of political will.

Pašić and Trumbić did what was asked. They applied to Millerand (Clemenceau now having vanished from the stage) for a three-day extension, and on January 23 called a delegation session to make a joint recommendation to the government.[67] The discussion, at first dominated by a feeling of revulsion against the manner in which the ultimatum was made, soon gave way to a sober appraisal of the Yugoslav position. There was agreement that Clemenceau's action represented an ultimatum, not mere pressure, and concurrence with Trumbić that direct talks with Italy, as a way of circumventing the Entente, were not immediately possible. No one was certain about the extent of support that could be expected from the United States, nor whether Italy would *or could* in fact implement the Treaty of London. But unanimity prevailed on the necessity of keeping the treaty from coming into force. At half past noon word arrived that Millerand would receive the Yugoslavs, whereupon Pašić and Trumbić went immediately to the Quai d'Orsay. They did not see the French Premier —who had to leave for a session of his cabinet—but Maurice Paléologue spoke to them in friendly tones, indicating that the time limit would most likely be extended.

When the Yugoslav delegation reconvened at 5:15 P.M., Ribarž announced a significant item of news. He had just learned from the publicist Gauvain that Nitti had promised Lloyd George Italian support in all matters relating to Russia, in return for which the Italian and British premiers had worked out the fateful formulas of January 13 and 14. Lloyd George had promised to "impose it first on Clemenceau and then, together with the latter, on us. Clemenceau resisted at first, but in the end gave in." [68] When Ribarž finished, Prince George (the Regent's brother) came into the room to relay the following: "From a leading French political figure, one very close to the ministry, I have just learned that our

67. Present were Pašić, Trumbić, Žolger, Ribarž, Radović, and Major Marinković, the military representative. The sessions began at 11:00 A.M. and lasted, with several interruptions, until 7:45 P.M. Zap., *3*, 78–88 (K&H, pp. 246–50).

68. Ibid., p. 81 (K&H, p. 247).

affairs stand very well not only in America but in the relevant French circles. The same personage advises us not to yield under any circumstances beyond the Wilson line." [69]

The two reports, as well as Paléologue's encouraging words, ironically only further contributed to the uncertainty that prevailed. Major Marinković gave a pessimistic report about Yugoslav military capabilities. Though the Treaty of London was "unfulfillable," as Radović put it with probable accuracy, (could Rome "expel" D'Annunzio from Fiume?), no one could predict the consequences of a straight "no" answer to the Supreme Council. Pašić in particular argued that only the cabinet could decide on questions of war or peace and assume the responsibility for immediate or long-range consequences stemming from Yugoslav actions in the present conflict. After much debate the delegation could only decide to have each member formulate his own views in writing by the following day.

On the 24th, two lines of thought emerged. One was that of Trumbić, to which Žolger, Ribarž, and Radović came finally to adhere. The other was that of Pašić. Trumbić expressed his view as follows: 1) in answer to Davidović's question as to whether the moment was decisive, he would reply with a categorical "no"; the Allied threat cannot be implemented; 2) the government has every right not to reply "yes" or "no," but instead to pose certain questions concerning possible Allied guarantees that Italian troops would be withdrawn from those regions assigned to the Yugoslavs, that D'Annunzio and Millo would cooperate, etc.; 3) the government's reply should be evasive since the Allies would have to think twice before carrying out their threats; moreover, the government's reply should insist that if the Treaty of London is to be implemented, the concurrence of the United States, still a member of the peace conference, must be indicated.[70] In short, Trumbić was dead set against bowing to the ultimatum.

Pašić's view was wholly different. He was convinced that defy-

69. Ibid.

70. Ibid., pp. 89–91 (K&H, pp. 250–51). Characteristically, Trumbić also advised Belgrade to insist on receiving an official text of the London treaty, which had never been given to the Yugoslavs. The tactic was calculated to add to French and British discomfiture.

ing the Allies would lead to grave consequences which the Yugoslavs could not afford to risk. Though a straight "no" need not
lead to an immediate conflict with Italy, it would create dangerous tension for an unforeseeable period of time and involve forfeiting French and British military (in case of need) or diplomatic
support. Ultimately, a solution could be found only through direct dealings with Italy. An evasive reply to the Entente at this
point would not lead to concessions, and under the circumstances,
"I think we would incur less harm for our young state, if we decided to accept the lesser evil, which is involved in the proposal
of the Entente . . ." This should be done on the condition that
Porto Baroš and Sušak be assigned to Yugoslavia, that no change
"to our detriment" be made in the Wilson line, that Italy declare
its disinterest in the question of Montenegro, and that the Entente
guarantee the agreement and insure the withdrawal of all volunteer troops from Dalmatia, Fiume, and those parts of Albania outside the Italian sphere.[71]

Both views were communicated to Belgrade. Trumbić also sent
a separate message urging the government to resign.[72] Meanwhile,
the Quai d'Orsay sent word extending the time limit by four
days, which too was immediately relayed to Belgrade.

On the 25th an urgent message arrived from Slavko Grujić, the
Yugoslav minister in Washington. Polk, with whom he had just
spoken at great length, declared that the United States had not
approved the proposals of January 14; that the United States government had protested against it, demanding also an explanation
for the French and British action; that the Anglo-French proposals
were shown to Wilson, who had not yet officially reacted but would
certainly oppose them; and that the threat of implementing the
London pact made no sense, since it had been decided long ago
that the secret treaty was not valid.[73] Next day Trumbić, in a top

71. Ibid., 91 (K&H, p. 251); Pašić to Davidović, Paris, Jan. 24, 1920 (TP, F85);
Krizman, "Saveznički Ultimatum," *Jadranski Zbornik, 2,* 225.
72. Trumbić to Ministry of Foreign Affairs, Paris, Jan. 25, 1920, Highly Confidential (TP, F85).
73. See Krizman, "Saveznički Ultimatum," *Jadranski Zbornik, 2,* 226. Also, Zap.,
3, 93–94. It turned out, in fact, that on Jan. 20 Lansing instructed Wallace to obtain
an explanation from Clemenceau and Lloyd George concerning their action. On
Jan. 22 the two premiers tried to justify themselves to Wilson by claiming that
they had no intention of bypassing the President; in his absence from Paris, they

priority cable, asked the government again not to give in and to insist on a solution jointly agreed upon by France, Great Britain, and the United States, which was even advised by highly placed French sources.[74] Greatly heartened by the news from Washington, Trumbić also relayed Grujić's message with the observation that now a rift had developed between the United States and the Entente (and Italy) and, consequently, the Yugoslav position had much improved.

In Belgrade the cabinet met on the 27th to take final action. It decided, first of all, to heed Trumbić's advice and resign—a measure designed to forestall Allied sanctions, in case of need—but in view of all the information from Washington and Paris, it also agreed on issuing the following instructions to the delegation: 1) the government approves Pašić's proposal for accepting the ultimatum if the Allies fulfill the conditions specified by Pašić; 2) failing that, the government accepts Trumbić's suggestion to propose a joint American, British, and French decision; 3) it accepts Trumbić's proposal to inform the Allies that they had brought the Yugoslavs into an impossible situation, and that the Yugoslavs could hardly choose between the Allied offer which was known and the Treaty of London which was unknown to them. Hence, the Allies should first communicate the official text of the treaty and then set a new deadline. In this case, too, if the Entente were set upon acting in defiance of the American protest, the delegation was to seek guarantees for the evacuation of Fiume and the other regions, as well as for the status of Montenegro.[75]

Upon receipt of these instructions the delegation met to draft the formal note. Meanwhile, a follow-up cable had arrived from Grujić. Polk had further declared that the United States government would never agree to assigning Fiume to Italy, that an Italian mandate in Albania would be difficult to avoid, that Italy would never accept a plebiscite in any buffer state, and that Washington did not accept a corridor between Italy and Fiume.[76] After some

---

were merely trying to find a formula that would work. See Šišić, *Jadransko Pitanje*, pp. 105–07.

74. Trumbić to Ministry of Foreign Affairs, Paris, Jan. 25, 1920, Most Urgent and Strictly Confidential (TP, F85).

75. Davidović to Delegation, Belgrade, Jan. 27, 1920, Confidential No. 57 (TP, F85).

76. See Krizman, "Saveznički Ultimatum," *Jadranski Zbornik*, 2, 227.

discussion—in which Pašić first objected to the dilatory tactics proposed by Trumbić and accepted by the government, since he favored an immediate and final solution—the delegation carried through with Davidović's instructions. On the 28th, Pašić and Trumbić took the Yugoslav note to the Quai d'Orsay. A skillfully worded and succinct document,[77] it noted that the Allied communication was taken as a friendly proposal rather than a threat; that it was not in keeping with the principles of self-determination as enunciated by the peace conference, or with geographic or economic realities; that the Yugoslav government was still prepared to resolve all issues through arbitration or a plebiscite and wished to continue inter-Allied discussion of all issues. As for the Treaty of London, the Yugoslav government did not understand the intimations concerning the application of a pact concluded between third parties, whose contents still remained unknown. The proposals of January 20 could not be accepted in their entirety and the government hoped that it would be allowed to put forth certain suggestions for changes such as would assure peace on the Adriatic.

That this tactic worked had, of course, little to do with clever semantics. It succeeded rather because of the unexpected American intervention and also because Millerand, a newcomer to the scene who faced a multitude of other problems, was far less inclined to push matters to a head than his predecessor, Clemenceau. In the days that followed, there was considerable discussion in Paris concerning the Yugoslav note—which was generally regarded as a rejection of the January 20 plan—but from the moment of its transmission the danger of prompt Franco-British-Italian counteraction had waned. The Italians evidently were in no mood to make experiments with the London pact, nor were the French (and to a lesser extent the British) prepared to lend them the necessary support. On February 4 Trumbić felt sufficiently confident to declare to the delegation: "We have successfully overcome the critical moment, the ultimatum; now our position is good and Italy is in a pickle [*škripcu*]." [78]

Great Britain and France still continued to press for Yugoslav

77. For the text, see Šišić, *Jadransko Pitanje*, pp. 107–08.
78. Zap., *3*, 109 (K&H, p. 258).

acceptance, and on February 6 their ministers in Belgrade informed Davidović that they had been instructed to transmit the text of the London treaty to him (although they did not have a copy available right then). They also urged the Premier to accept the Allied proposal, "which is more favorable, they say, than the treaty." [79] And in London, where the Allied prime ministers had convened on February 12 and where, in fact, the "peace conference" had now been transferred, Lloyd George made another effort to obtain Yugoslav adherence to the January 20 program. But on February 13 Wilson intervened, accusing London and Paris of unilateral action contrary to the lines agreed upon in the joint memorandum of December 9, 1919. He objected strongly to the ultimatum and program of January 20.[80] On the 17th, Lloyd George and Millerand replied, asking the President in effect to adhere to their program which, a week later, Wilson again refused to do.[81] But Wilson advanced one final idea: he would subscribe to any solution mutually acceptable to Belgrade and to Rome. This had the effect, of course, of burying the Treaty of London, as well as the ultimatum of January 20. It also offered a way out for Lloyd George and Millerand, whose position could no longer be maintained. Bowing to what now became inevitable, they responded within twenty-four hours that they too were willing to leave the whole problem to the Yugoslavs and Italians and were, consequently, prepared to withdraw the proposals of December 9 and January 20.[82] On March 4 Wilson, in his final communication on the subject, observed that the proposals of December 9 could not be withdrawn since they represented the joint Allied agreement in regard to the entire Adriatic. And he again stressed his desire for the conclusion of a direct Italo-Yugoslav agreement.

In effect, the final exchange between Lloyd George, Millerand, and Wilson removed the Allies from the center of the stage they had so long dominated. It brought to a close a critical phase of the Adriatic question, but the decisive one was yet to come.

79. Davidović to Delegation, Belgrade, Feb. 6, 1920, Urgent and Strictly Confidential No. 81 (TP, F85).

80. For the text of Wilson's note, see Šišić, *Jadransko Pitanje*, pp. 108–13.

81. Ibid., pp. 113–23.

82. Ibid., pp. 123–25.

10. The Road to Rapallo

THE GOVERNMENT CRISIS caused by the resignation of the Davidović cabinet on January 27 had almost no effect on Yugoslav foreign policy or events in Paris and London. Neither did the appointment of a Radical cabinet, under Protić, on February 19.[1]
The interim period only placed a heavier burden on the delegation, which was briefly left to its own resources. One of the questions to be decided was whether the delegates should go to London
for the meeting of the Allied prime ministers on February 12. As
no official invitation was received, Trumbić was at first loath to
go, but at a private luncheon with Nicolson and Leeper, the latter
strongly urged him to attend the London session. Venizelos would
be there, and though Leeper's invitation was not official, Trumbić
changed his mind and decided to go. The delegation concurred [2]
and on February 11 he crossed the Channel to England.[3] A few
days later, however, following Wilson's timely intervention, he
returned to Paris.

The several talks he had had with Lloyd George, Curzon, and
Millerand had yielded little result, but the American action immediately changed the whole situation. For one thing, it prompted
the Italians to renew feelers for direct talks with the Yugoslavs.
On February 24 Nitti sent word urging Trumbić to return to
London right away to meet with him.[4] This time Trumbić did not
go alone; Pašić, Radović, Žolger, and Ribarž went as well. Immediately upon their arrival they learned that Nitti had indeed

1. Trumbić retained the foreign ministry, but was not consulted about the cabinet's composition. Without his consent, Spalajković was appointed as his alternate
in Belgrade. (Protić to Trumbić, Belgrade, Feb. 20, 1920, TP, F64.)

2. Zap., 3, 115–20 (K&H, pp. 260–62); Trumbić to Ministry of Foreign Affairs,
Paris, Feb. 9, 1920 (TP, F66).

3. Nitti happened to cross on the same boat, but the two did not meet "due to
the unruly sea" (Trumbić to Ministry of Foreign Affairs, London, Feb. 12, 1920,
TP, F66).

4. Zap., 3, 153 (K&H, p. 274).

announced to the conference his intention of dealing directly with the Yugoslavs.[5]

Before that phase opened, however, the Yugoslav delegation was to experience another jolt within its own ranks. Pašić's reasons for coming to London—for Trumbić, as foreign minister in the Protić cabinet, was the man charged with conducting the talks —were not entirely clear. On the morning of February 27 Pašić informed his colleagues that he would see Lloyd George at 3:30 that afternoon and would tell him "that we certainly cannot agree to a corridor [between Italy and Fiume]; that we demand Baroš and an independent Albania, but if Italy receives Valona and the Greeks Argyrokastro, we demand a strategic frontier on the Drim, while about everything else we can hold friendly talks." [6] The others, according to Trumbić, all became convinced that Pašić was planning to yield to Lloyd George—in order to reach a quick agreement and strengthen the position of the Radical Protić government, thought Trumbić—and protested that he *had* to hold to the joint delegation stand of January 14. After much and bitter debate before and during lunch, Pašić agreed, but not before observing that in his view the formula of January 20, 1920, was more favorable than that of December 9, 1919. After lunch Pašić went to see Lloyd George, while the others anxiously awaited his return. They did not have to wait long, for before an hour was up, Pašić came back with the message that Lloyd George would like him [Pašić] as well as Trumbić to return for tea. Nitti was to come too so that an agreement could be worked out, as Lloyd George put it, "on the basis of Italian sovereignty over Fiume." [7]

Pašić and Trumbić went. Nitti arrived together with Scialoja, whereupon Lloyd George retired, stressing that he would be in the next room in case of need; and before Trumbić could react, the direct Italo-Yugoslav session got under way. Nitti began by pointing to the difficulties of the general situation and to the need and his desire to reach an agreement, territorial as well as commercial. Though scheduled to leave on Sunday, he would gladly postpone his departure by a few days. He then tried to draw out

5. Trumbić to Ministry of Foreign Affairs, London, Feb. 26, 1920 (TP, F66).
6. Note by Trumbić, London, Feb. 26, 1920 (TP, F90).
7. Ibid.

the Yugoslavs' views, intimating that he might accept the Wilson line in return for Italian sovereignty in Fiume. This both Pašić and Trumbić immediately turned down. In regard to Zara, he did not seem unwilling to consider a formula whereby the city would choose between independence and Yugoslav sovereignty. To Trumbić's proposal of a plebiscite for the islands of Lošinj and Vis he gave a noncommittal reply. As for Albania, when Trumbić spoke in favor of that country's independence and territorial integrity, Nitti observed that he cared very little about a mandate—from which, he said, Italy would gain no advantage, as "billions" had already been spent there—but the military insisted on Valona and Wilson had agreed on this as well.

With the question of Albania the explorations came to an end. The tone had been quite friendly and Nitti now suggested another meeting, on Sunday morning at 10 (February 29), asking only that it be kept secret because "the press could spoil things." [8] Trumbić proposed the quarters of the Yugoslav Committee on Ashburn Place, to which Nitti agreed, asking at the same time for a written draft of proposals. It was evident that he was anxious to bring the whole issue to a head and return home with a final agreement. On leaving, he asked Pašić and Trumbić, if they did not have *pleins pouvoirs* from the government, to cable Belgrade right away so that everything could be settled promptly.

In anticipation of the scheduled meeting with Nitti, the Yugoslav delegation met on the 28th at Claridge's to decide on a joint line and discuss the position paper Trumbić had drafted during the night. Pašić, unusually nervous and contrary-minded according to Trumbić, "which happens whenever he sees things won't go his way," [9] raised numerous objections over details. What he really wanted seemed unclear, but early next morning, just prior to the meeting with the Italians, he gave Trumbić a brief note asking him to stress that the Albanian clans on the right bank of the Drim were eager to join Yugoslavia. Pašić's heart, Trumbić bitterly noted in his record, was set on northern Albania; on "everything else he is ready to give in, so long as we receive some little

8. Ibid.

9. Trumbić's notes on the meeting, Feb. 28, 1920 (TP, F90). The official delegation minutes contain no record of meetings held between Feb. 24 and March 8.

satisfaction with Port Baroš and Opatija [Abbazia], so he can justify himself and show some new success." [10]

At the appointed hour on Sunday morning, February 29, Pašić and Trumbić prepared to receive Nitti and Scialoja in the Yugoslav Committee building. They had heeded Nitti's urgent request and cabled Protić for pleins pouvoirs. Protić's reply had arrived the night before, granting the request "in the hope and belief that it [the delegation] will in unity defend our national interests, involved in this question, to the end." [11] The stage was thus set for a possible finale. But three hours of intensive discussion showed plainly that the time for this had not yet come.

The discussion was more detailed than that of February 27. Nitti, accompanied by De Martino as well as by Scialoja, did not ask for any written statement. He was willing to give up the corridor, but then for strategic reasons Italy would need modifications of the Wilson line. The Premier also seemed willing to accept Trumbić's formula to allow Zara a choice between independence and Yugoslav sovereignty, and to leave Baroš to Sušak. Furthermore, he seemed willing to trade the island of Vis for Lastovo or Cres.

Now Pašić turned to the subject of Albania,[12] whose independence, he emphasized, would be acceptable only if Italy gave up Valona. Otherwise, the Yugoslavs would insist on the Drim as a strategic frontier. The Italians refused to relinquish Valona, but Nitti was willing to give up the mandate. In Istria he was also willing to grant Volosko and Opatija to the Yugoslavs, but only in return for Fiume. He saw Italian sovereignty over Fiume as a way of resolving the D'Annunzio problem. Trumbić, however, did not feel that the Italians would insist on this. But they would insist on Valona, on Učka as protection for Pola, and probably on Vis.

Nitti correctly described this exchange of views as inconclusive. He was planning to remain in London until Tuesday evening.

10. Ibid.

11. For the text of this exchange, see Krizman, "Saveznički Ultimatum," *Jadranski Zbornik*, 2, 232.

12. At "great length and very insistently," wrote Trumbić, whose notes during these days display much irritation with Pašić ("Meeting with Nitti, Scialoja and De Martino," Feb. 29, 1920, TP, F90).

The next Allied conference, he said, would be held in Rome. If the issue were not resolved in London, it would not likely be solved in Rome, where all manner of pressure would affect the atmosphere. Moreover, he warned, he still had two ways out: he could apply the Treaty of London or the inter-Allied position of December 9, 1919. Pašić returned to the question of Albania, urging Italy to give up Valona. Otherwise, he would insist on the Drim. Nitti and De Martino refused to budge. Then Trumbić spoke up in support of Pašić, arguing that Italy's entry into Albania would mean Austria in Bosnia-Hercegovina. Nitti protested that though Italy entered the war overestimating the Adriatic issue, it could not now give up all that even Wilson had promised. Retorted Trumbić: "That which Wilson, or anyone else, has recognized to you is worth less than that to which we would agree. Our agreement would be your greatest success, since it's our skin that is at stake. Only our agreement can create peaceful relations in the Adriatic." To that Nitti gave this final word: "I cannot agree to what will not be accepted at home. You must keep in mind our internal condition as well." [13] And on that uncertain note the meeting closed.

Two days later, Pašić again visited Lloyd George. The occasion provoked one of the bitterest clashes between himself and Trumbić during a delegation session. The latter demanded to know at whose initiative the meeting had taken place, and after much verbal sparring, Pašić would only say: "Well, I went as a friend . . ." [14] Yet the initiative was clearly his and he now reported that, according to Lloyd George, Nitti had now given up the idea of a corridor, but in return had demanded Fiume for Italy. Lloyd George also "energetically stressed that England and France would not interfere with Nitti's efforts, in the absence of an agreement, to implement the Treaty of London." [15] Trumbić demanded to know why Pašić had not immediately and as energetically rejected Italian sovereignty over Fiume. That, Pašić replied, was for the government to do—even though the delegation had pleins pou-

13. Ibid.
14. Note by Trumbić, March 2, 1920 (TP, F90).
15. Ibid.

voirs. Acrimony grew until in the end it was agreed that Pašić would tell Lloyd George that he would cable Belgrade and wait for a reply. Pašić doubted that the government would agree but did as he was asked.

A full week passed, in the course of which Wilson sent his final message to the British and French premiers.[16] On the 10th, Trumbić impatiently sought out Pašić to ask whether any instructions had arrived from Protić. When Pašić answered in the negative. Trumbić, suspecting the old Serb of suppressing information, particularly if the information were not agreeable, asked again whether the government had replied to Pašić's cable of March 2. "No answer has arrived." "How can it be," asked Trumbić, "that no answer has arrived in response to such an urgent and important dispatch?" "Well, they probably have other worries," was Pašić's reply.[17] The mutual antipathy ran very deep indeed and a rupture between the two men seemed very near at hand.

The following day a message arrived from Belgrade, but it was not a reply to the cable of March 2. Protić suggested that the peace delegation consider ending its work and returning home, where urgent domestic matters required immediate attention.[18] This Trumbić was not inclined to do and the idea was dropped. Then nearly two weeks passed and still no instructions arrived from Belgrade. The cabinet was having difficulty making up its mind

16. On March 3 Trumbić received word from Steed that Nitti was about to leave for Paris and would like to meet with Trumbić there, in complete privacy. The Yugoslav decided to go, and on the 5th met with Nitti in Paris. After exacting a promise of secrecy, the Italian Premier told Trumbić candidly that his present dilemma stemmed from Sonnino's short-sightedness. Describing his position at home as "weak," he went on to threaten Trumbić with the Treaty of London unless the Yugoslavs allowed Fiume to go to Italy. In return, the Italians would concede Porto Baroš and agree to demilitarization of the Adriatic. But he also wanted Lošinj and Palagruža, as well as an independent Zara, Valona, and an Italian mandate over the rest of Albania. Trumbić naturally rejected the whole package. Nitti then threatened to make difficulties over the "Montenegrin question," but also raised the bait of an agreement over the merchant fleet. If he hoped to frighten Trumbić or soften the Yugoslav stand, the effort was a total failure. The record of this meeting is preserved in a 17-page handwritten memorandum by Trumbić, dated March 5, 1920 (TP, F90).

17. Note by Trumbić, March 10, 1920 (TP, F85).

18. Protić to Pašić, Belgrade, March 11, 1920 TP, F85).

and on March 23 Protić asked Pašić and Trumbić to return to Belgrade immediately. Before elaborating a final position on the Adriatic, the cabinet wanted to hear both their views.[19] Pašić agreed, but Trumbić was in no mood to go to Belgrade. He had not been feeling well, and on doctor's advice, decided to enter a hospital in Neuilly at this time, with a possibility of surgery not excluded. He informed Protić of this, adding the comment, "Pašić can tell you everything . . ."[20] Protić persisted—"In the name of the government I have the honor to ask you to come anyway . . ."[21]—but Trumbić again refused. As chance would have it, Pašić suddenly fell ill, and so in the end it was Andrija Radović who reported to the cabinet in Belgrade on the views of the principal peace delegates. The report did not alter very much.

During his confinement in the sanatorium at Neuilly, Trumbić received one important visitor. En route from London to San Remo, where a forthcoming inter-Allied conference was about to convene, Scialoja interrupted his trip in Paris, partly to have a talk with Trumbić. The two met for an hour on April 13 and for two hours the following day.[22] Scialoja wanted to know whether the Yugoslavs were coming to San Remo. Not unless officially invited, replied Trumbić, in line with a previous decision of the Yugoslav delegation. Nitti, as president of the Allied conference, would immediately issue an invitation, said Scialoja, if an agreement in broad lines were reached beforehand, leaving only details to be worked out at San Remo. His purpose at the moment, the Italian foreign minister then revealed, was to conclude an agreement "in broad lines." [23]

19. Protić to Pašić, Belgrade, March 23, 1920, Highly Confidential No. 157 (TP, F66).

20. Trumbić to Protić, March 26, 1920 (TP, F66). Having learned that the cabinet was about to resign, Trumbić warned Protić on the same day that, while he favored a coalition government, he would serve only in the same post as before. (Trumbić to Protić, March 26, 1920, TP, F66.) Two days later Protić replied that Smodlaka had proposed Trumbić as premier, but that the idea of a nonparty neutral premier had been abandoned. And he again urged Trumbić to return to Belgrade, where they could discuss the matter at length. (Protić to Trumbić, March 28, 1920, TP, F66.)

21. Protić to Trumbić, Belgrade, March 28, 1920, Very Urgent (TP, F85).

22. "Conversation Scialoja–Trumbić," Neuilly, April 13–14, 1920 (TP, F90).

23. Trumbić to Protić, Neuilly, April 15, 1920 (TP, F85).

Trumbić was disturbed by their exchange. Scialoja insisted on modifying the Wilson line, on gaining Italian sovereignty over Fiume, and on treating Montenegro as an open question. And neatly twisting the political tourniquet, the Italian pointed out that Woodrow Wilson had been effectively removed from the scene and that American protests would have only academic value if the other powers accepted a special Italo-Yugoslav arrangement in regard to Albania and the Adriatic Sea.[24] Trumbić refrained from making official replies, and in two separate dispatches informed Protić of what had transpired. The day following Scialoja's second visit, he also warned the Prime Minister that a wave of pro-Nicholas Montenegrin propaganda was mounting in England, where indeed for some time Nicholas' partisans in the House of Commons and elsewhere were becoming increasingly vociferous. Since the issue, at this delicate juncture, might be exploited by Nitti and Scialoja, Trumbić in unison with all the peace delegates urged Belgrade to again publicize the facts of Montenegro's union with the rest of the new state.[25]

The cabinet, meanwhile, sent new instructions to the delegation on April 14, which crossed paths with Trumbić's report on the Scialoja talks. After a thorough review of the entire problem and the testimony of delegate Radović, the instructions read, the government had concluded that "now is the decisive moment to solve the Adriatic Question and bring it to an end." The delegation already had full powers to negotiate and to agree "to everything which it [the Delegation] finds ought to be agreed to." Nonetheless the government wished to specify the following as the most important points:

1. The Adriatic question should be treated as an entity and all its aspects should be resolved at the same time.

2. Every effort should be made to reject the idea of a corridor, to retain the Wilson line, and to reject the principle of diplomatic representation for Fiume. Porto Baroš must go to Yugoslavia.

24. "Conversation Scialoja–Trumbić" (TP, F90).

25. Trumbić to Protić, April 15, 1920 (TP, F66). The cabinet, however, failed to share this view and Protić quickly replied that Montenegrin affairs were strictly an internal matter. No special action would be taken. (Protić to Trumbić, April 18, 1920, TP, F66.)

3. Zara should be autonomous, without diplomatic representation.

4. There should be demilitarization of Yugoslav as well as of Italian islands, with those islands specified by the December 9 memorandum to Italy.

5. Rectification of frontiers with northern Albania to the west and south of Lake Ohrid should be insured, and the Black and the Great Drim rivers as the Yugoslav frontiers be obtained.

6. If direct negotiations develop unfavorably or too slowly, the delegation is to speed them up and bring them to an end, announcing to "the other side" that no further concessions can be made and "the only thing left" would be to seek the arbitration of "England, France and America."

7. The government is to be kept informed, through dispatches and if necessary special couriers.[26]

Protić, too, had now become as anxious as Nitti to arrive at a quick settlement. His position at home—for economic disorder was resulting in serious political strife—was becoming increasingly difficult, and a dramatic diplomatic success might save the life of the Radical ministry. On April 23 he asked Trumbić (and Vesnić) to go to San Remo. But Trumbić was in no hurry to go and, in effect, played for time. When Nitti, through various channels, indicated that he was anxious for Trumbić to come to San Remo, the latter used the lack of an "official invitation" as an excuse not to go. He even learned that Nitti would now accept the memorandum of December 9, 1919, as a solution, but the idea of a Fiuman buffer-state, which had been abandoned with much difficulty, made him even more recalcitrant. At the end of April he suddenly decided to visit Belgrade for a few days, informing Nitti a) that Italo-Yugoslav talks should not be considered broken off, and b) that en route back from Belgrade he would gladly meet with Scialoja. Protić was furious that the Sam Remo opportunity had been missed, but aside from reproaching Trumbić in Belgrade, there was not much he could really do.

With the Italians it was agreed to meet in Pallanza, on Trumbić's way back to Paris. Pašić would come from Evian-les-Bains.

26. The above is summarized from Protić to Delegation, Belgrade, April 14, 1920, Strictly Confidential No. 176 (TP, F90).

Both sides expected this to be the decisive and, hopefully, final meeting. Before Trumbić left Belgrade, the cabinet drew up the following instructions for Pašić and Trumbić:

I) The Adriatic question, with all its parts, is to be treated as an entity.

II) The government desires to achieve an agreement through direct talks with the Italian government. In the event a direct agreement is not possible and the United States, Great Britain, and France remain by the memorandum of December 9, 1919, the government "will have to submit to their collective will."

III) In the talks with Italy, the Yugoslav delegates are to make the following counterproposals to Scialoja's proposals of April 13 and 14, 1920:

1. The villages around Fiume to Yugoslavia.

2. The city of Fiume and suburbs "demilitarized and neutralized."

3. The port and railroad station of Fiume to Yugoslavia, which will make special arrangements for their use, under League control, with Czechoslovakia, Hungary, and Rumania, as well as with the city of Fiume.

4. Porto Baroš with Sušak to Yugoslavia.

5. The Wilson line as the Italo-Yugoslav frontier, with territory running along *both* sides demilitarized.

6. The disposition of Lošinj and Vis to be decided by local populations through plebiscite.

7. The city of Zara to Yugoslavia, but with wide internal autonomy, internationally guaranteed.

8. All islands to be demilitarized.

9. The Italian government to agree that Montenegro is an integral part of the S.C.S. Kingdom.

10. Albania to be independent—and demilitarized—in the frontiers of 1913, with no mandates. If Italy and Greece, however, receive parts of that country, and if Italy receives a mandate, northern Albania to the river Drim is to go to Yugoslavia as an autonomous province.[27]

27. Summarized from "Instructions to Messrs. Nikola Pašić and Ante Trumbić, Plenipotentiary Delegates for Negotiations with the Italian Delegation Concerning

Pašić and Trumbić were also asked to conclude a final agreement concerning the Austro-Hungarian merchant fleet. The instructions then ended with these remarkable words:

> Inasmuch as His Royal Highness the Heir Apparent and His Government have full confidence in the delegates Messrs. N. Pašić and A. Trumbić, the plenipotentiaries for negotiating with the Italian delegates, and have complete trust in their patriotic spirit and their statesmanlike wisdom, they are allowed complete freedom in their work, if necessary even to the point of departing from the above points, and the Royal Government will regard itself bound by everything they agree upon with the Italian delegates, in its name, in the conviction that the result attained represents the best success attainable.
>
> It is particularly emphasized that the delegates are authorized, if they deem it absolutely indispensable, to make extreme concessions in regard to Fiume and to allow to Italy sovereignty over Fiume. If it were to come to that, the Royal Government will be convinced that its delegates were forced into this sacrifice only in order to forestall another solution, representing a greater evil for our people.[28]

The Radical government wanted agreement at all costs and now Fiume was the price it was willing to pay. For Trumbić the pill must have been a bitter one to swallow, but he carried through as ordered, no doubt still hoping to salvage what he could. Studying the government's instructions en route to Pallanza, little did he suspect that chance would again intervene and, at least for a while, postpone the surrender that was becoming increasingly inevitable.

At 11:00 A.M. on Tuesday, May 11, Pašić and Trumbić met with Scialoja (and Carlo Garbasso, his *chef du cabinet*) at the Villa Casanova in Pallanza. The meeting had not been publicized, yet the little town was filled with Italian journalists, twelve of whom even stayed in the same hotel with the Yugoslavs. Scialoja and Garbasso were hospitable and friendly. They complimented Trum-

---

an Agreement on the Adriatic Question," Belgrade, May 7, 1920, Strictly Confidential No. 204 (TP, F119).

28. Ibid.

bić on the clarity and eloquence of his opening remarks and on his faultless Italian.[29] But when matters of substance were taken up, little progress was achieved.

In reply to Scialoja's inquiry, the Yugoslavs said they were willing to remain in Pallanza for a while if an agreement could be worked out. The rest of the morning was taken up by Trumbić's exposé, which was strictly in accordance with the government's instructions. When at one point he observed that in the case of failure the Yugoslavs would agree to the Allied memorandum of December 9, 1919, the Italians were, in his words, "obviously shocked," [30] but did not interrupt. What interested them most was Trumbić's remark, made also in accordance with the instructions, that "we are willing to take into consideration the difficulties of the Italian government" in regard to Fiume, though he said nothing about granting Italian sovereignty and insisted that the Italians in turn take into account Yugoslav realities and problems.

Scialoja took the floor in the afternoon, at the beginning of the second session. Point by point he rejected the Yugoslavs' central demands. Italy would insist on Fiume, Lošinj, Vis, and Palagruža; but since Mr. Trumbić, "as a good citizen of Split, has special regard for Vis . . . we now want to recognize [it] as a Yugoslav island"—in return for Lastovo and Cres. Scialoja rejected Trumbić's assertion that the issue of Montenegro had been settled, and insisted on Valona and an Italian mandate over Albania. At this Pašić interjected, "We place tremendous importance on this question," but the Italians passed over his remark. Too much Italian money had been invested in Albania, particularly in Valona; the military were determined to obtain a naval base in the eastern Adriatic, and though "Albania is a stone and a swamp," Italy's security demanded her presence there and only Italy could help develop that country's economy.[31]

Scialoja offered meager concessions: small changes in the corpus separatum that would place more Slavs in the Serbo–Croat–Slovene

29. Official minutes were not kept, but Trumbić took copious notes which are preserved in his handwriting in TP, F90, under the heading "Pašić, Trumbić–Scialoja, Garbasso Meeting," Pallanza, May 11, 1920.
30. Ibid.
31. Ibid.

state; *perhaps* the island of Lastovo; possible acceptance of the Yugoslav solution for Zara; and favorable commercial arrangements. None of these, however, amounted to a basis for agreement. Scialoja then informed the Yugoslavs that in view of the mass of technical problems connected with Istria, Albania, and demilitarization, he had invited General Badoglio (now Chief of Staff of the Italian Army) and Admiral Acton, head of the navy. Both were due in Pallanza the following day. Since an impasse had been reached, both sides decided to resume the discussion next day, with the military experts present.

The intervening night, however, brought a sharp turn of events. Early on the morning of the 12th, Scialoja and Garbasso came to Pašić and Trumbić with the news that the Nitti government had resigned. Scialoja had to leave for Rome immediately, though he hoped their talks would not be broken off. He asked whether the Yugoslavs could remain in Pallanza. Pašić and Trumbić agreed to stay for a "short time." [32] They stayed on for three days. But as it became apparent that the Italian political crisis would not quickly be resolved, they decided to leave. Pašić departed for Evian to continue his cure, while Trumbić went on to Paris. Thus "Pallanza," too, was not destined to mark the final act.

The government crisis in Rome was followed shortly by a similar, though unconnected, development in Belgrade. Failing to keep his parliamentary majority over domestic issues, Protić resigned at the beginning of May. After two weeks of difficult bargaining, Milenko Vesnić was chosen as a compromise candidate, and on May 17 this professional diplomat took over the reins of government. At Vesnić's invitation, Trumbić remained foreign minister.[33]

In both Italy and Yugoslavia internal politics dominated most of May and June, leaving little time for sustained efforts on Adriatic negotiations. The first half of June, nevertheless, brought two important developments for the Yugoslavs. On June 4 the much delayed signature of the Hungarian peace treaty took place at Trianon, stabilizing Yugoslavia's frontier in the north. Though the Yugoslav-Hungarian line had already been determined in the

32. Trumbić to Vesnić, May 20, 1920 (TP, F90).
33. Vesnić to Trumbić, Belgrade, May 17, 1920 (TP, F66).

autumn of 1919, the Treaty of Trianon formalized the new status quo.[34] The second development was the conclusion of the Italian crisis, on June 12–13. After one last effort by Nitti to salvage his position, the government passed into the hands of Giovanni Giolitti, who appointed Count Sforza as his foreign minister. On the surface, the combination of Giolitti and Sforza augured a shift in Italian orientation. Giolitti, the "grand old man" of Italian politics, had never placed much stock in the Treaty of London and had even admitted that Italy failed to live up to its terms.[35] Sforza, a close friend of the Serbs and especially of Pašić, with whom he developed close ties at Corfu,[36] had always maintained that Italian policy had to be based on an understanding with the Yugoslavs. Both men were eager to settle the Adriatic problem. But would they, too, not succumb to nationalist pressures? Would they succeed in overcoming the suspicion and mistrust that beclouded the relations of the two nations? More important, given the grave economic and social conditions in Italy, would they not strive for a "triumph" in foreign policy, at the expense of the Yugoslavs? The immediate prospects were imponderable.

Trumbić was optimistic and Pašić pessimistic. Neither believed the new Italian government would be more reasonable and conciliatory. But Trumbić felt that the Yugoslavs should adopt a tougher line, believing that toughness coupled with Italy's domestic problems would force Giolitti into retreat. Pašić disagreed. He preferred dealing with Nitti to Giolitti, for whom he nurtured much distrust. A new Pašić-Trumbić conflict now developed, which the old man felt he could not carry on. His health had been giving way and he now decided to resign—in earnest. The difficulties with Trumbić, his prolonged absence from the political scene at home, and ill health all contributed to this decision. On June 21 Vesnić and the cabinet accepted Pašić's resignation. On the same day the entire peace delegation was formally dissolved. Trumbić was asked to remain in Paris to maintain contact with what remained of the peace conference.[37] But before long, he too was expected to return

34. See Deák, *Hungary at the Peace Conference*, pp. 30–56, 305–06.
35. See Albrecht-Carrié, *Italy*, p. 293.
36. See Sforza, *Nikola Pašić*, a biography as well as personal tribute.
37. See B. Krizman, "Predigra Konferenciji u Rapallu," *Zadarska Revija*, 7 (1958),

home to assume his regular duties as foreign minister and member of the cabinet.

Trumbić and Sforza were brought together at the beginning of July during the inter-Allied conference at Spa. The encounter was informal and in no way a continuation of Pallanza. Sforza used the opportunity to declare that the present Italian government would maintain the same position on the Adriatic as Nitti and Scialoja had and that it wished to continue holding direct talks. Trumbić indicated he too wanted to reach a direct agreement and that Belgrade regarded the Pallanza meeting as only temporarily interrupted.[38] But Sforza was not ready to resume formal talks quite yet.

During the next two weeks at Spa the two men conversed seriously only twice, the last time—for over an hour—on July 17, immediately prior to Sforza's departure for Rome. Sforza stressed that he had no mandate to discuss the Adriatic, and that the talk was purely private and should be treated as such. Nonetheless, he probed the Yugoslav position. He assured Trumbić that Italy wanted good relations with Yugoslavia, that he disapproved of the militant factions in Rome and opposed implementing the London pact, that Giolitti shared his views, that final Italian policy would soon be worked out in Rome, and that he would promptly inform Trumbić of the result.[39] But things did not move so fast.

Sforza and Giolitti were in no hurry to resume direct negotiations. Belgrade was diplomatically isolated and the new Italian government counted on this isolation and on internal Yugoslav difficulties to aid its cause. But it also decided on other means to break the general impasse. In a stroke as bold as it was imaginative, the Giolitti government decided during July to withdraw completely from Albania, evacuate Valona, and recognize the country's independence in the framework of 1913. On August 2 Rome and Tirana concluded a formal convention by which Italy re-

---

38–39. It should be noted that at this particular juncture Trumbić was not in favor of having Pašić resign and he so informed Vesnić. No doubt he would have preferred to have Pašić share responsibility for any final agreement.

38. Trumbić to Vesnić, Spa, July 5, 1920 (TP, F66).

39. Trumbić to Vesnić, July 19, 1920 (TP, F94).

linquished all its claims in Albania and agreed to immediate with-drawal of all Italian forces. It received in sovereign possession only the island of Saseno off Valona. Henceforth, word was passed from Rome, Italy would seek security in the Adriatic through close co-operation with Albania.[40]

The Italo-Albanian convention indeed laid the foundations of a policy that was to become a significant element of European poli-tics in the following two decades. In July 1920 Giolitti's dramatic action was in part prompted by internal considerations, for at the moment Italy lacked the wherewithal for a sustained economic and political effort of the kind that would have been involved in a mandate and in prolonged military tension along the southern Adriatic. More important, however, was the desire to embark on a political course that in the long run offered greater likelihood of success, and one that at the moment promised a tangible im-provement in Italy's diplomatic position abroad. Giolitti and Sforza were not disappointed. Their action was welcomed every-where and their position became strengthened in inter-Allied councils.

For Albania, too, the Rome decision was momentous, and on December 17, 1920, this troubled nation was admitted to the League of Nations.[41] For the Yugoslavs this development entailed two important results. For the time being at least, they would not face the Italians along their southern frontier. Their proclaimed desire for an independent Albania within the frontiers of 1913 now unexpectedly materialized. An independent Albania, how-ever, also meant giving up Scutari, the cherished objective of Montenegrins as well as of many Serbs. Nevertheless, in the cir-cumstances of 1920 the removal of the Italian "threat" in the south overshadowed, or at least should have overshadowed, the "loss" of Scutari. (The final Yugoslav-Albanian frontier was not stabi-lized until 1924, at which time some modifications of the 1913 frontier were agreed upon.[42]) In the last analysis, an Italian pres-

40. See Temperley, *Peace Conference, 4,* 343–45, and Albrecht-Carrié, *Italy,* pp. 294–97.

41. For the background, see Albert Mousset, *L'Albanie devant l'Europe (1912–1929)* (Paris, 1930), pp. 22–34.

42. See *Dokumenti o Pitanju Granice sa Arbanijom* (Belgrade, 1924); H. Baerlein, *A Difficult Frontier* (London, 1922).

ence to the south in the immediate postwar years would likely have impaired the stability of Montenegro as well as of northern Albania.

After adopting the new policy toward Albania, the Italians had little reason to resume immediate contact with the Yugoslavs. Their calculated passivity made both Vesnić and Trumbić nervous. In August another government crisis broke out in Belgrade and it was only with the greatest difficulty that Vesnić succeeded in forming another cabinet.[43] He retained Trumbić in the foreign ministry and again urged him strongly to come home. Trumbić was undecided. By now he too was anxious to return to Belgrade, yet he felt his presence was needed in Western Europe.[44] There was much important business to look after: complications in regard to the forthcoming Klagenfurt plebiscite, discussions between Yugoslav and Italian experts concerning the Austro-Hungarian fleet, the question of reparations, the Turkish peace settlement, pro-Nicholas propaganda in Great Britain, British complaints that Yugoslav units were crossing into Albania,[45] and various reports indicating that D'Annunzio was planning to proclaim the "independence" of Fiume on September 12, the first anniversary of his coup. On balance, it seemed even imperative to him to remain in the west, and for two weeks Trumbić disregarded repeated and urgent requests for his return home. He tried, with little success, to enlist French and British support against D'Annunzio's planned proclamation. But the main reason for Trumbić's having postponed his return to Belgrade had to do with the Austro-Hungarian merchant fleet.

In the first half of 1920 almost no progress was made on this vital issue. Despite the Crespi-Trumbić agreement of April 1919 assigning 250,000 tons of shipping to Yugoslavia, the Italians used the question of the fleet as an instrument of political pressure,

43. Vesnić to Trumbić, Belgrade, Aug. 16, 1920, Strictly Confidential No. 257 (TP, F66).

44. Trumbić to Vesnić, London, Aug. 23, 1920, No. 81 (TP, F66).

45. The British seemed quite upset over this and Harold Nicolson conveyed to Trumbić Lord Curzon's great concern. Trumbić could only reassure the British that the Yugoslavs were not planning a fait accompli in northern Albania. (Trumbić to Vesnić, London, Aug. 20, 1920, No. 78; Trumbić to Vesnić, London, Aug. 23, No. 82; TP, F66.)

making a final agreement contingent on a territorial settlement. As late as January 1920, Nitti told Trumbić that the fleet problem would be resolved the minute a general agreement was concluded. The direct Italo-Yugoslav talks in the spring of 1920 brought little change in the situation. Nitti and Scialoja were in no hurry. Trumbić repeatedly asked for French and British intervention, but it was not until July that Lloyd George promised to urge Rome to conclude a final agreement in this regard.[46] Meanwhile, as reparations discussions proceeded at successive inter-Allied conferences, Italy became increasingly interested in having this issue settled. Thus at the Spa Conference an inter-Allied agreement was reached, by which France and Great Britain relinquished their share of the Austro-Hungarian merchant fleet, with the understanding that Italian and Yugoslav experts would negotiate directly a final division of the fleet between the two Adriatic states.

Assured of French and British support and of a division that would heavily favor them, the Italians toward the end of August sat down with Yugoslav maritime experts to work out details of the agreement. Trumbić, anxious to settle this issue once and for all, proposed as a basis that the property of shipping companies having a majority Yugoslav interest be assigned to Yugoslavia, and that of companies with a majority Italian interest to Italy.[47] This formula was accepted and by September 5 the two sides completed work on the final protocols. Two days later, in Paris, Trumbić and Pietro Bertolini signed the formal documents, thereby bringing to a close one of the thorniest issues in Italo-Yugoslav relations since the armistice. By the Trumbić-Bertolini agreement,[48] the division was as follows: out of a total tonnage of 797,000, Yugoslavia received 117,000 and Italy 680,000 tons. The division was less favorable to the Yugoslavs than that of the Trumbić-Crespi formula, due mainly to changes in the ownership structure of shipping companies and the heavy Italian investments in shipping stocks since the armistice. Nevertheless, there was good reason for both sides to welcome the end of this dispute, as a stimulus to economic normal-

46. Kojić, "Postanak Jugoslavenske Trgovačke Mornarice," p. 36.
47. Ibid., p. 37.
48. "Sporazum Izmedju Kraljevine Srba, Hrvata i Slovenaca i Kraljevine Italije o Razdiobi Austro-Ugarske Trgovačke Mornarice," Paris, Sept. 7, 1920 (TP, F63).

ization and a prelude to further diplomatic negotiation. Trumbić was pleased, and so was a wide segment of Yugoslav opinion.[49]

With the conclusion of the agreement, Trumbić resolved to leave Paris, and at long last he entrained for home.

Trumbić left Paris believing that Yugoslav affairs, on the whole, stood rather well. He also felt that the merchant fleet convention with Italy augured well for the conclusion of a territorial agreement. Further initiative would have to come from Rome, but the Allies, he thought, would now facilitate a reasonable settlement. Little did he, or anyone else in Belgrade, foresee how rapidly Yugoslav affairs would deteriorate and what role the Allies would soon come to play.

The initiative, indeed, did come from Rome. On September 20 Sforza sent word through Vincenzo Galanti, Italy's chargé d'affaires in Belgrade, that negotiations could be resumed *in Italy* by the end of the month, if Yugoslav delegates came with pleins pouvoirs and were prepared to reach an agreement quickly.[50] He hoped "Trumbić and Pašić" would be sent. At the same time, it was learned in Belgrade, Sforza had assured the Italian Parliamentary Commission for Foreign Affairs, where considerable opposition developed to the prospect of holding direct talks with the Yugoslavs, that Italy would obtain the most favorable frontier in Istria in return for giving up Dalmatia! [51] Was this information deliberately leaked out to indicate Italian terms for holding the promised talks? While the Belgrade government pondered this item of news, a disturbing note was sounded from Paris. On September 21 the French chargé in Belgrade visited Tihomir Popović, Trumbić's senior aide at the Foreign Ministry, and in confidence read him a telegram from Millerand. Giolitti had informed the French Pre-

49. It may be noted that Italy began turning over the required vessels to Yugoslavia in mid-December 1920, shortly after the signing of the Treaty of Rapallo, but months before the formal ratification of the Trumbić-Bertolini agreement on July 28, 1921.

50. Vojislav M. Jovanović, ed., *Rapallski Ugovor 12 November 1920. Zbirka Dokumenata* (Zagreb, 1950), p. 8.

51. Antonijević to Cabinet, Rome, Sept. 20, 1920, No. 743 (TP, F119). The Yugoslav minister in Rome received this information from "sources close to the Foreign Minister."

mier that Italy 1) would insist on the independence of Fiume; 2) would insist on Monte Nevoso (Snežnik) in Istria; 3) could not "disinterest herself" in the destiny of the Italians in Zara; and 4) would insist on the independence of Albania within the frontiers of 1913.[52] A second telegram from Millerand made clear the official attitude in Paris:

> The French Government attaches great importance to the prompt and satisfactory conclusion of the Adriatic question, not only from the point of view of pacification in general and in Central Europe, but also in regard to the interest of the young Serbo–Croat–Slovene State as well as that of Italy.
>
> It is desirable that the government in Belgrade envisage a solution of this problem and that it approach [the forthcoming negotiations] with the desire of reaching a speedy agreement, in conditions that will finally inaugurate normal relations between Italy and the State of Serbs, Croats and Slovenes.[53]

This message caused much gloom. The Yugoslavs could expect little help from Paris; they would meet the Italians without Allied support, for the prevailing mood in London was not noticeably warmer, while Washington was too deeply concerned with the oncoming presidential electoral campaign to intervene decisively in Adriatic affairs. Trumbić was willing to meet Sforza in Italy, where the interrupted negotiations had taken place; he, too, hoped Pašić would be a delegate, though that would depend on the latter, not on him. However, due to Italian insistence on the Monte Nevoso line in Istria and the new situation in Albania, the Yugoslav government was in no position to enter a final round of talks by the end of the month. Too many imponderables had to be considered; too many conflicting positions within the cabinet ironed out. But there was no question that Belgrade, too, wanted to bring the whole affair to an end and that it would welcome the conclusion of peace with Italy.

---

52. Ironically, the Italians now came to insist on the solution—first propounded by the Yugoslavs—of forestalling Montenegrin and Serbian efforts to gain northern Albania.

53. Memorandum by Tihomir A. Popović, Belgrade, Sept. 21, 1920 (TP, F119).

Sensing the trend of events in Yugoslavia as well as abroad, Sforza sent to Belgrade, on September 28, an unofficial emissary, Giuseppe Volpi, a former honorary Serbian consul in Venice and an old friend with whom Vesnić was *per tu*. Volpi's mission was to explore the Yugoslav position and to elaborate in broad lines the agreement that would then be formalized in Italy.[54] In separate meetings with Vesnić, with Vesnić and Trumbić, and a final one with Trumbić on October 1, Volpi argued that Italy must receive a strategic frontier at Monte Nevoso; that Fiume should be an independent state, an admittedly temporary solution; that Italy would not insist on contiguity with Fiume (the Istrian coast around Abbazia would thus remain in Yugoslav hands); that Zara as an *independent* city could be in a customs union with Yugoslavia; that Albania must be independent within the frontiers of 1913; and that in case of agreement, Italy would "disinterest herself" in the issue of Montenegro and cease pro-Nicholas activities. While observing that his was not a "formal" mission and the Yugoslavs could not therefore refer themselves to these talks when they met with Sforza, Volpi further argued that internal conditions in Italy were difficult and that Giolitti alone had sufficient stature to resolve the Adriatic problem.

Neither Vesnić nor Trumbić would engage in much detail; both pointed out that Yugoslav conditions were difficult too and that Belgrade could never accept the Monte Nevoso line; and though the atmosphere was always friendly, Trumbić even implied that Volpi's entire program offered no basis for an amicable settlement. Yet they concurred on the necessity of reaching an agreement and the Yugoslavs indicated a willingness to meet Sforza before long. Volpi therefore left Belgrade fully believing that an agreement could be reached.

Having ascertained what he wanted to hear, Sforza, however, did not rush into precipitate action. Rather, he used the next three weeks to prepare his ground. Sudden aid to his cause came from unexpected quarters. On Sunday, October 10, the critical plebiscite in Klagenfurt was held that resulted in a resounding defeat for the Yugoslavs, demoralizing spirits from Slovenia to Montenegro. The Yugoslav army in Ljubljana reacted by march-

54. "Conversation Vesnić, Trumbić–Volpi," Belgrade, Sept. 30, 1920 (TP, F119).

ing into the plebiscite zone and occupying the region militarily. The action only added to Yugoslav frustrations, since it was promptly followed by a Franco-British-Italian ultimatum to withdraw within two days, with which Belgrade meekly complied.[55] The episode contributed to French and British impatience with the Yugoslavs, which Sforza was quick to exploit. Within a week he instructed Bonin Longare in Paris and Imperiali in London to suggest renewed Anglo-French pressure on Belgrade in the interests of resolving the Adriatic question. The British government temporized, but the French government promptly agreed.[56]

In Belgrade, meanwhile, the cabinet was having difficulty in deciding on the plenipotentiaries. As early as October 8, Pašić's name was hardly mentioned, whether or not by his choice unfortunately remains unclear. Trumbić would definitely go, but who else could be sent with him? Momčilo Ninčić (Trumbić's choice), Bošković, and Spalajković were considered. Lazar Marković proposed Vesnić, but the Premier would go only if Giolitti went with Sforza. Ninčić, when asked, refused. The cabinet was unanimous only on another subject—on refusing to accept the Monte Nevoso line, which would place additional ten-thousands of Slavs in Italy and afford the Italian army commanding strategic superiority over the Yugoslavs.

At the same time, the government decided to formulate anew its position on the questions of Montenegro and Albania, which the Italians were doubtless going to raise. By special commission from the cabinet, Andrija Radović prepared two memoranda on the subject. The fact is significant because Radović's maximalist policy, supported by wide Montenegrin segments, exerted great influence within the government, particularly in Radical circles.

55. Though the inner story behind the Yugoslav action still remains obscure, it has been suggested that the orders for this knowingly futile gesture were issued in Belgrade to show the Slovenes that all means to secure Carinthia had been tried and that, contrary to some Slovene opinion, Belgrade was not oblivious to Slovene national sentiments. There may be good reason for this view. Certainly, and despite official Yugoslav protests to the contrary, the Klagenfurt plebiscite represented a fair reading of popular feelings in the region, while Belgrade's protestations reflected internal strains rather than disbelief in the plebiscite's results. See Thomas M. Barker, *The Slovenes of Carinthia—A National Minority Problem* (New York, 1960), p. 193.

56. V. Jovanović, *Rapallski Ugovor*, pp. 22–23, 25–26.

The first memorandum, dated October 5, repeated in regard to Montenegro the oft-propounded line that the issue of Montenegro's union with the rest of the Serbo–Croat–Slovene state had been settled by popular will, as expressed in the vote of the Podgorica Assembly. The dynastic question was thereby settled as well. If the Italians brought up Nicholas' private interests, the former king could be referred directly to the Yugoslav government or the forthcoming Constituent Assembly, which would include full Montenegrin representation. This was nothing new, and as Radović and the government knew, "the question of Montenegro" was a political weapon that Italy would wield only up to a point and drop as soon as agreement on main issues was reached.

Radović's proposals regarding Albania are of greater interest. He approved the principle of Albania's independence. However, he urged that the possibility of neutralizing that country through the abolition of a national army be considered. A declaration of neutrality "in a country like Albania" would not suffice; it would only be used against Yugoslavia. Moreover, if the Albanian people opted for a monarchy, the Yugoslavs should make certain that the king be a native, not a foreigner. And since, as he put it, "it is in the interest of our state to have as great an influence in Albania as possible, and exclude or at least minimize Italian influence," he urged the government to demand autonomy for the Albanian region adjacent to Yugoslavia, a customs union with that region, and perhaps even a federation between the two states.[57] As to actual frontiers, Radović proposed, under any circumstances, to ask for the Drim valley ("the only natural entry from the Adriatic to the heart of the Balkan Peninsula"), as offered by England and France in January 1920. That would assign Scutari and both banks of the Drim to Yugoslavia. If the United States objected as it had done in the past, Radović continued, Debar (north of Ohrid) could be turned over to Albania. In any case, the Yugoslavs should obtain the right of "completely" building a railroad from the Adriatic to the Danube along the Drim. Should the Drim remain in Albanian hands, the Italians would most likely build the railroad

57. Radović to the Cabinet Committee for Foreign Affairs, Belgrade, Oct. 5, 1920 (TP, F73).

from the Adriatic to the Yugoslav frontier, and the Yugoslavs should build the rest.

At this late hour, this plan for obtaining northern Albania was illusory as well as fatuous. In a way Radović even recognized as much, for he next argued that "if the above is not realizable," the Yugoslavs should ask for rectification of the 1913 frontiers, in keeping with their declaration of January 1920. That would mean the line of the river Bojana, though the western periphery of the city of Scutari, with the city and surroundings to become an autonomous Albanian province, joined in a customs union with Yugoslavia. Belgrade, however, should receive exclusive rights of building railroads along the Bojana as well as the Drim.

Radović's entire project evidently encountered opposition within the cabinet, for on October 19 he sent a second memorandum, this time to Trumbić. In it he made no mention of obtaining northern Albania to the river Drim. Rather, he elaborated the arguments in favor of gaining the Bojana-Scutari line, along with the Klementis clan south of Lake Scutari. The arguments were economic and political, and as a concession to Albania, Radović proposed to trade Debar, not only the town but a whole territory twenty-five kilometers long and eight kilometers wide. Thus, in effect, Serbia's loss (in Macedonia) would pay for Montenegro's gain, a fact again reflecting the competitive character of intranational relations in the young state. The Bojana, Radović pleaded, was the natural and commercial outlet of Montenegro which that state was assigned by the San Stefano treaty in 1878! Economic and political preponderance in northern Albania was indispensable to the security and development of the Yugoslav state, while Montenegrin preponderance around Scutari would, in effect, fulfill historic rights and commercial requirements. The Catholic Klementis clan (numbering around 8,000) were needed, because the valley they inhabited formed a natural line of communication with Montenegro, which they often entered to graze their herds and which they had to cross to get to the town of Scutari. Yet, Radović frankly admitted, the Yugoslavs should not ask for a plebiscite of the Klementis, who would prefer entering the Albanian state, despite various declarations from a number of their elders indicating a desire for union with Yugoslavia.[58] What counted most in his view was insuring conditions for the extension of Yugoslav influence in Albania. Following Giolitti's Albanian coup, however, Radović's plans, in reality, stood little chance of being fulfilled. They met with sympathy but with little hope.

The cabinet, at the moment, was preoccupied with a variety of affairs. Sforza had sent word on October 13 that Giolitti would, after all, be one of the Italian delegates, and though he could personally attend only the concluding session of the conference, Vesnić's nomination as a Yugoslav delegate would be greatly welcomed in Rome. In consequence, on October 16 the Yugoslav cabinet voted to send as its delegation Vesnić, Trumbić, and Kosta Stojanović, the Minister of Finance. The Italians were pleased. In a gesture of appreciation Galanti informed Trumbić (on October 19) that, in deference to Yugoslav sensitivities about undue publicity, the meeting would not be held in Florence as originally intended but in a smaller neighboring locality. That, however, would necessitate a brief delay. Still, the Italian invitation was expected momentarily in Belgrade.

What arrived instead was an urgent message from Fotić in Vienna. Baron Aprato, who had just arrived in Vienna from Rome, called on the Yugoslav minister with what appeared to be a message from Sforza. Italy, sincerely desirous of reaching an amicable agreement, had relinquished all claims to Albania and to sovereignty over Fiume. In return, however, the Yugoslavs would have to agree to the Monte Nevoso line for the strategic protection of Pola and Trieste. Fotić had the impression that Sforza was making this a precondition to holding the talks.[59] The war of nerves thus mounted and Yugoslav anxieties increased.

Vesnić and Trumbić were ready to go at a moment's notice when further word arrived (on October 21) that Sforza was traveling to Piedmont to visit Giolitti, with whom he would set a date for the Italo-Yugoslav talks. When Sforza returned to Rome, he informed Antonijević that Giolitti and he had agreed on the desirability of opening the talks right away. But in view of internal

58. Radović to Trumbić, Belgrade, Oct. 19, 1920 (TP, F73).
59. Fotić to Trumbić, Vienna, Oct. 19, 1920, Confidential No. 773 (TP, F119).

Italian political conditions it would be best to hold the conference on the eve of the new session of Parliament, scheduled to open in Rome on November 10. Italy would be represented by Sforza, Ivanoe Bonomi—the Minister of War—and Giolitti who, however, would not attend until later. The conference would most likely begin between November 5 and 8; the precise date and place would shortly be set. On October 29 Sforza informed Antonijević that Santa Margherita, near Rapallo, had been selected and that the Hotel Imperial would serve as conference headquarters and residence for the Yugoslavs. In the interests of security Sforza asked for maximum secrecy. Next day, Sforza informed Trumbić that the Italian delegation would arrive in Santa Margherita early on November 5 and hoped the meetings could begin that same day. Trumbić immediately replied that, due to pressing government business and the temporary absence from Belgrade of the Regent, the Yugoslavs could not take the Simplon Orient-Express until the night of November 4, so that the conference could begin only on November 7. Vesnić, he added, could remain in Santa Margherita no longer than three days. Sforza agreed on the date. A last-minute decision delayed the Yugoslavs' departure until the night of November 5, postponing the opening until the 8th. But that had no effect on the events that had now been set in motion.

As the Yugoslavs prepared to leave for Italy, several inescapable facts stood out clearly. They knew the decisive moment had arrived. They also knew they could expect no help from Paris or from London; on the contrary, France and Great Britain were relentlessly driving them toward surrender. In America, Woodrow Wilson stood on the eve of his supreme test. His cause was not likely to triumph on election day, nor was there reason to expect American support at this late stage. The prospects thus were gloomy and the three plenipotentiaries felt downcast.

Indulging in a final futile gesture, the cabinet armed the delegates with a set of ambitious and uncompromising instructions based on a review of "the current international and internal situation"—and the ideas "of delegate Radović." Vesnić, Trumbić, and Stojanović were given full powers to negotiate and "to agree to everything [the delegation] finds necessary . . ." However, the delegates were instructed to obtain the Wilson line in Istria, secure Porto Baroš, reject contiguity between Fiume and Italy, insure self-government for Zara but without separate diplomatic representation, work for demilitarization of Yugoslav as well as Italian Adriatic islands (granting to Italy only those islands assigned to it in the memorandum of December 9, 1919), and effect an extension of the Yugoslav frontier in Albania west and south of Lake Ohrid and down to the Black and Great Drim rivers. If negotiations on this basis floundered, the Yugoslavs were empowered to bring them to an end with a notice to the Italians that no further concessions could be made and that the whole dispute should be submitted to the arbitration of Great Britain, France, and the United States.[60]

Such a threat, however, could hardly be carried out. For even as the Simplon was preparing to depart from Belgrade, the French minister, Joseph de Fontenay, boarded the train to inform Trumbić that the Yugoslavs *had* to come to an agreement with Sforza. The French government's hands were still tied by the Treaty of London and if no agreement were reached, said Fontenay, Italy would be free to implement the treaty. So far as Italian demands were concerned, the French approved the Monte Nevoso line. When the train pulled out and Fontenay had left, Trumbić went to inform Vesnić. The Premier in turn told him that earlier in the day the British minister, Sir Alban Young, read him a cable from London in the same general sense.[61]

Sforza had prepared his ground well. He had made no preconditions for holding the talks with the Yugoslavs. Instead, in a series of urgent exchanges with Paris and London [62] he persuaded the two governments that the only chance of ending the Adriatic imbroglio lay in decisive intervention on their part in Belgrade. Italian demands, he argued, were reasonable, for Italy after all was prepared to relinquish the Treaty of London and had already given up all claims in Albania. The Monte Nevoso line in Istria was indispensable to the protection of Trieste and Pola, and also

60. For the full text, see Krizman, in *Zadarska Revija, 1,* 51.
61. V. Jovanović, *Rapallski Ugovor,* pp. 30–31.
62. See ibid., pp. 23–30.

to quell nationalist passions at home. Above all, Sforza emphasized his and Giolitti's desire for peace in the Adriatic and throughout Central Europe, their intention of establishing normal Italo-Yugoslav relations, and the need for stabilizing internal conditions in both countries. The approach was both intelligent and skillful. Due to French anxiety over Germany and their desire for stability in Eastern Europe, Sforza's arguments struck a responsive chord in Paris and Millerand agreed to do as he was asked. Lord Curzon and Lloyd George were not quite as willing to grant Italy carte blanche, without examining Sforza's program in detail. In the end, however, Lloyd George, too, concluded that unless Belgrade were pushed—by threatening the application of the London treaty and other implied sanctions—the Adriatic problem would likely drag on. Neither the British nor the French appear to have considered promoting a solution that would have involved dissuading Rome from insisting on Monte Nevoso, or in any way placing restraints on the Italians.

For their part, the Italians had reason to expect success. With the approval of the entire cabinet, Sforza, Giolitti, and Bonomi resolved to obtain the Monte Nevoso line—thus in effect substituting the Treaty of London for the Wilson line in Istria and claiming 100,000 more Slavs than asked for in January 1920; to make Fiume (the corpus separatum) an independent state in contiguity with Italy; and to obtain the islands of Cres, Vis, and Lošinj, as well as Zara. If the Yugoslavs refused to agree, Giolitti was prepared to break off the talks and annex the above territories, and to occupy part of Dalmatia with a notice of willingness to discuss its future in return for international recognition of Fiume's independence.[63] Yet chances that such action would become necessary were not considered to be great.

Considering the overall circumstances, the final act of the drawn-out Adriatic drama was anticlimactic, though the occasion was fraught with political hazards. The Italo-Yugoslav conference opened on the morning of November 8 with an address by Sforza. After observing that Italy genuinely desired agreement, political as well as economic, he outlined the Italian terms: the Monte Nevoso line, contiguity with independent Fiume, and sovereignty

63. Krizman, "Predigra Rapallu," *Zadarska Revija*, 7, 50.

over Zara. Bonomi elaborated on the "defensive" nature of the proposed Istrian frontier and on why the Wilson line could not be accepted.[64] Vesnić and Trumbić then outlined the Yugoslav position, indicating they could not accept the Italian program and insisting on the Wilson line. However, they offered demilitarization of specified zones on both sides of the Wilson line, guaranteed by an international convention so as to meet Italian security needs. This the Italians would not accept and by the end of the opening session Vesnić had already concluded that it "appears they will not give in on [Monte Nevoso]." [65] In fact, after the session ended, Sforza drew Trumbić aside and, according to the latter's notes, said: "Mr. Trumbić, I swear to you on my only son, that if I returned to Rome without 'Nevoso' . . . I would not remain alive an hour in Italy; I would have to expatriate. 'Nevoso,' as a symbol, has bewitched all Italians; the army will not even hear about giving up this claim." [66] Thus Nevoso, affecting the strategic balance of the entire region as well as the destiny of 100,000 Slavs, developed into the main stumbling block.

Sforza also offered to sign a joint anti-Habsburg convention and made vague allusions to favorable economic agreements. But he passed over the subject of Albania. When Vesnić brought up the Yugoslav demands, the Italian spoke in favor of Albania's independence. He added, however, that Italy would accept any collective decision by the Allies and would certainly not go to war over this issue. A bait was thus tentatively cast.

When the meeting resumed in the afternoon, it was apparent that neither side would yield. Next morning Sforza reiterated the Italian stand, and since the Yugoslavs would not alter theirs, the conference was recessed for the day. A critical juncture had been reached, with no prospect that the Italians would relent on the central points: Monte Nevoso, independent Fiume contiguous with Italy, and Italian Zara. They offered to end once and for all the issue of Montenegro, but that was evidently of secondary import now. As the pressure mounted, all mention of Albania was dropped.

---

64. V. Jovanović, *Rapallski Ugovor*, pp. 32–33.

65. Vesnić to Ninčić, Confidential No. 5, Santa Margherita, Nov. 8, 1920, in V. Jovanović, *Rapallski Ugovor*, p. 33.

66. Ibid., p. 34.

On the 10th, Yugoslav resistance suddenly collapsed. Early in the day Vesnić still informed Belgrade and the Yugoslav missions in Paris, London, and Washington that, due to Italian intransigence, the situation was critical and the talks might be broken off. Should this happen, he added, "our Delegation disclaims any responsibility." [67] Later in the day, however, after Sforza again refused to yield—except for granting the island of Vis to Yugoslavia and adding to the territory of the Fiuman state part of the area demanded by Italy—the Yugoslavs agreed. Vesnić wired Belgrade: "As there is no prospect of receiving better terms, and we consider an agreement indispensable with respect to external as well as internal conditions, we have decided unanimously and in the full solidarity of our responsibility to accept after a long struggle [that] which we could not alter." [68] Italy would receive the Monte Nevoso line, contiguity with the independent Fiuman state, the islands of Cres, Lošinj, Palagruža, and Lastovo, and sovereignty over Zara. The Yugoslavs accepted these "heavy sacrifices," as Vesnić put it in a second telegram to Belgrade, "to avoid a rupture and further bad consequences for these and other territories, and for the nation as a whole." [69]

In reality, they had little choice. They knew Giolitti and Sforza were prepared to take unilateral action should the conference break down. The Treaty of London, which ironically no one wanted to see applied, was still a reserve weapon that could be used. To their dismay, the Yugoslavs learned of Woodrow Wilson's utter defeat in America. The shock was compounded by the knowledge that France and England were formally arrayed on the side of Italy. To make matters worse, they learned on November 9, four days after the French and British intervention in Belgrade, that the French government had reiterated its support of the Italian position and again urged the Yugoslavs to give in.[70] After weighing all the factors, therefore, Vesnić, Trumbić, and Stojanović concluded that acceptance of the Italian terms was their only

67. Ibid., p. 37.
68. Ibid., p. 38.
69. Ibid., p. 39.
70. On Nov. 11 Bonin Longare cabled Sforza that Millerand had personally intervened with the Yugoslav chargé in Paris, saying it would be "a very serious matter" if the Yugoslavs assumed responsibility for a breakdown of the Santa Margherita talks. See V. Jovanović, *Rapallski Ugovor*, p. 39.

course.[71] By agreeing to the Monte Nevoso line, they would accept strategic exposure in the west and northwest, and would sign over an additional 100,000 Slavs to Italy. But the advantages of concluding the peace—even if it meant accepting a "temporary" solution for Fiume and learning to live with an Italian enclave in Dalmatia—and thus nullifying once and for all the odious Treaty of London, overshadowed the risks involved in continuing the conflict with Italy and the alienation of France and England. The decision required and reflected considerable courage,[72] for as Vesnić rightly pointed out to the Italians, the Yugoslav delegation was clearly acting "against the current and public opinion." Nevertheless, he added, "what we have accepted we will uphold." [73]

The signatures of peace were affixed on November 12, 1920—two years and one day after the armistice ending World War I. Giolitti rushed to Rapallo for the final ceremony and at the last minute the Italians granted Porto Baroš to the town of Sušak. But Sforza kept this concession out of the text of the Treaty of Rapallo. Instead, he effected it on November 12 through a secret letter to Trumbić, which the latter formally acknowledged the same day.[74] Sforza chose this method so as not to commit future Italian governments to this solution for Porto Baroš; as he later admitted, the exchange of letters had no juridically binding character, except for the Giolitti cabinet.[75] The Yugoslavs, nevertheless, were pleased, and Porto Baroš, as it turned out, has remained in their possession ever since.

With the signing of the Treaty of Rapallo, Sforza could triumphantly, and justly, cable all Italian embassies and missions

71. According to a recent biography of Trumbić, Vesnić and Stojanović left the difficult choice to him. The two Serbs favored accepting Sforza's terms, but since Croat and Slovene sacrifices were involved, they insisted Trumbić make the final decision. Faced with such awesome responsibility, Trumbić is said to have agonized over every detail. In the end, however, he felt he had no choice but to accept a far from perfect solution in the interests of broader national and international considerations. See Pavelić, *Dr. Ante Trumbić*, pp. 274–76.

72. Apart from all else, it was also taken without consultation with the rest of the cabinet. Due to poor communications, Belgrade learned of all developments at least 24 hours late.

73. V. Jovanović, *Rapallski Ugovor*, p. 40.

74. For the texts of this exchange, see ibid., pp. 49–50.

75. Ibid., pp. 58–60.

abroad that national unity was now consummated in its most complete form.[76] The Treaty of London line was achieved in the north; Zara, with a district encompassing a radius of seven kilometers, became an Italian enclave in Dalmatia; the island groups of Cherso (Cres), Lussin (Lošinj), Lagosta (Lastovo), and Pelagosa (Palagruža), Italian outposts off the Yugoslav coast. The Fiuman state, embracing mainly the old corpus separatum, became independent "in perpetuity," but territorially linked to Italy. The interests of Italian economic concerns in Dalmatia received protection under a provision that also granted Italians in Yugoslavia special cultural privileges as well as the right to opt, within one year, for Italian citizenship, without having to leave Yugoslav territory. No reciprocity was given to the Slavs assigned to Italy. Both governments undertook to uphold the Treaties of St. Germain and Trianon, and in a separate anti-Habsburg convention, pledged to prevent a Habsburg restoration in Austria and Hungary. Italy recognized the integrity of the Kingdom of Serbs, Croats, and Slovenes, thereby ending the issue of Montenegro. However, the Treaty of Rapallo made no mention of Albania, and thus Serbo-Montenegrin hopes in that regard failed to bear any fruit.

Once signed, the treaty was quickly ratified: by Yugoslavia on November 22, 1920, and by Italy on February 2, 1921. Italian evacuation of all Yugoslav territory also followed promptly, as did the return of the remaining Yugoslav prisoners of war from Italy. The Allied world hailed the end of the Adriatic struggle and congratulatory messages flowed in from all quarters—mainly to Giolitti and Sforza. Understandably, the moods in Rome and Belgrade contrasted sharply. Instead of enthusiasm, soberness prevailed in Belgrade, reflecting a sense of relief, weariness, and considerable apprehension. For *Rapallo* completed the national frontier, and henceforth the nation's energies could be directed to vital internal tasks; but it also opened a festering wound that was to cause bitter dissension at home and promote Yugoslav *irredentism*.

Vesnić and Trumbić had no illusions on this score. Trumbić in particular returned home with a heavy heart, but ready to face his critics, assume personal responsibility for the final decision,

76. Ibid., p. 40. For the text of the Treaty of Rapallo, see pp. 41–47.

and defend the necessity of the Rapallo settlement.[77] True to his word, given in December 1918, he resigned from the cabinet on November 22, 1920, to devote himself to internal affairs, now that the peacemaking task was done.

Yet the Rapallo treaty did not spell the complete end. There remained the anomaly of independent Fiume which could hardly survive in the long run. There was also D'Annunzio, who still hoped to thwart the decision of Rapallo. In a final flamboyant gesture the poet-condottiere declared war on Italy on December 1, 1920. However, in the face of a determined ultimatum from Rome and the appearance of the Italian army, he retired from the city within a month.[78]

The free state of Fiume led an artificial existence for two years. In March 1922 a Fascist coup overthrew its government, an action that led to the city's immediate occupation by Italian troops. On October 23, 1922, Yugoslavia and Italy signed a convention reaffirming the Treaty of Rapallo and the independence of Fiume. Five days later, however, Mussolini overthrew Premier Facta and took over the reins of government. Given the relation of power between Italy and Yugoslavia and the prevailing and general international indifference, Fiume's annexation to Italy was now only a matter of time. A façade of independence was maintained for another year, while Mussolini's diplomatic pressures on Belgrade mounted. The Yugoslav government of the day was both ill-equipped and disinclined to resist. By the Treaty of Rome of January 27, 1924, it agreed to the formal annexation of Fiume to Italy, recognizing in reality an accomplished fact. Yet the event was not devoid of irony. For the man who signed as premier of the Kingdom of Serbs, Croats, and Slovenes was the aged Pašić who, not long after Rapallo, returned to the political forefront to guide the destinies of the young state.

77. See Pavelić, p. 280.
78. For the final phases of D'Annunzio's adventure, see Benedetti, *La Pace di Fiume*, pp. 71–140, and Čulinović, *Riječka Država*, pp. 160–208.

11. Epilogue

THE TERRITORIAL SETTLEMENTS OF 1919–20—as effected through the Treaties of St. Germain, Neuilly, Trianon, and Rapallo—spelled the final victory of the nationalist struggle that resulted in the foundation of the Yugoslav state. But it was an ambiguous victory, giving cause both for satisfaction and for grievance. Looking back on the troubled years just passed, the Yugoslavs had much reason to feel gratified. When World War I began, the prospects for the union of all Southern Slavs seemed indeed remote, as remote as the prospects for the total collapse of the great eastern empires. Yet within four years the Yugoslav union became reality; within six it had imperfect but viable frontiers. In conferring general international recognition on the new state, the peace treaties also provided it with a sense of psychological security indispensable to a healthy national existence.

At the same time, however, the territorial settlements suffered from grave defects. By leaving some 720,000 Yugoslavs beyond the national frontiers—no less than 480,000 in Italy alone—they clearly contravened the principles of nationality and self-determination.[1] This promoted a natural feeling of grievance among the Yugoslavs. It also stimulated nationalist passions which, in an age of nationalist abandon throughout Europe, were not likely to serve constructive ends. The settlements, moreover, created problems of another sort. A country of nearly twelve million inhabitants, according to the census of 1921, and half the size of France, Yugoslavia was assigned some 231,000 Rumanians, 467,000 Magyars, and 505,000 Germans,[2] also in contravention of the na-

1. Both figures are probably conservative. See Temperley, *Peace Conference*, 5, 150–54; and C. A. Macartney, *National States and National Minorities* (London, 1934), p. 525.

2. Of the total population, about two million inhabitants were non-Slavs. Of these, the largest group consisted of Albanians who, over the centuries, concentrated in the Kosovo-Metohija region, but also filtered farther north and east. The Italian minority was negligible, amounting to 12,553. See *Definitivni Rezultati Popisa Stanovništva od 31 Januara 1921 god.* (Sarajevo, 1932), pp. 2–3.

tionality and self-determination principles. The special conditions that obtained along Yugoslavia's northern frontiers left the peacemakers little choice. However, these national minorities became a political liability for the new state and, in the 1930s, a source of considerable weakness.

Except on the side of Italy, Yugoslavia's frontiers represented a reasonable compromise between considerations of nationality, geography, economic expedience, and strategic security. Writing not long after Rapallo, Jovan Cvijić pointed out that the frontiers with Albania, Bulgaria, Rumania (along the Danube), and Austria (along the Karawanken) were geographically sound.[3] The line from Prekomurje to the Banat, however, was geographically artificial, since the complex of rivers and meandering streams, subject to frequent floods, often rendered the barrier indistinguishable. While geographically imperfect, this line nevertheless approximated an ethnic partition. Of some 54,000 Yugoslavs remaining in Hungary,[4] many were Bunjevci and Šokci who had spilled over so far into Magyar territory that they could not reasonably be joined to Yugoslavia.

Yugoslavia's northwest frontier, determined by the Klagenfurt plebiscite in October 1920, left some 30,000 Slovenes in Austria, but provided an effective geographic division. The partition of the Banat, while satisfying neither the Yugoslavs nor the Rumanians, nevertheless represented a tangible gain in view of the secret Treaty of Bucharest, by which the Allies had promised the entire Banat to Rumania. The partition provided vital strategic security for Belgrade and ethnically it favored the Yugoslavs. On the Bulgarian side, where mainly strategic considerations were at stake, the Yugoslavs obtained the Strumica salient and frontier rectifications along the Timok valley, Caribrod, and Vranje, assuring them sufficient protection for the Morava valley, the Niš-Salonika, and the Negotin-Zaječar railway lines. The settlement also gave special satisfaction to the Serbs, whose Macedonian gains in the Balkan wars were now reconfirmed. No changes were ef-

3. J. Cvijić, "Granice i Sklop Naše Zemlje," in *Cvijićeva Knjiga* (Belgrade, 1937), pp. 1–23.

4. See Macartney, *National States*, p. 521, and his *Hungary and her Successors* (London, 1937), pp. 390–402.

fected along the Greek frontier, where none were actually sought. As for Albania, where the final outcome fell far short of Yugoslav hopes, the result did not prove to be a liability.[5] All in all, the Yugoslavs fared rather well.

From the strategic point of view, the territorial settlements provided Yugoslavia with sound defensive lines everywhere except in the Bačka, the western Banat, and, of course, along Italy. Nevertheless, Yugoslav military leaders were not unduly alarmed, and for at least a decade after Versailles, they regarded the nation's strategic position as reasonably secure.[6] This view, in retrospect, failed to take into consideration two vital elements: 1) the possibility of concerted military action against Yugoslavia from several sides at once, and 2) the extent to which internal political and economic strains, coupled with complacent military planning, would weaken the nation's strategic security. For in reality, the territorial settlements, while affording the new state a viable basis for national existence, did not—perhaps inevitably—bring stability to Southeast Europe as a whole. Inherent in the order established at Versailles was a confrontation between "beneficiary" and "victim" states. As one of the principal beneficiary states, Yugoslavia, facing an array of disaffected neighbors—Austria, Hungary, and Bulgaria—had good reason to uphold the status quo and seek international security through the Little Entente and close association with France. Yet Yugoslavia was in the anomalous position of also nurturing irredentist aspirations and thus hoping for a future modification of the status quo.

The Rapallo settlement between Italy and Yugoslavia, and Italy's subsequent annexation of Fiume, could hardly bring long-run stability to this troubled zone of Europe. Responsibility for this situation, however, cannot be laid entirely at the door of the two Adriatic rivals. The peacemakers of Versailles, and in particular the

5. See S. Tchirkovitch, "Règlement des questions de frontières entre le Royaume de Yougoslavie et ses voisins balkaniques: Albanie, Grèce, Bulgarie, et Roumanie," *Annuaire de l'Association yougoslave de droit international*, 2, (Belgrade, 1934), 136–55. Also, G. Andrassy, "Règlement des questions de frontières entre la Yougoslavie d'une part et l'Italie, l'Autriche et la Hongrie, d'autre part," ibid., 2, 115–35.

6. For a more detailed survey of the military factors involved see K. R. Djordjević and D. I. Živanović, *Vojna Geografija—Osnovni Deo Balkanskog Poluostrva* [Belgrade, 1931], pp. 25–34.

authors of the Treaty of London, contributed heavily to the final result. Yugoslav diplomacy—often buffetted by personal animosities, regional politics, and divergencies between the peace delegation and the government in Belgrade—contributed its share. Still, the Yugoslavs had limited possibilities for influencing the great powers and the broader issues that arose at Paris. Because of the piecemeal approach adopted toward their problems, the Yugoslavs systematically reduced their claims—in Istria, Carinthia, the Banat, and Bulgaria—without materially strengthening their bargaining position. The great powers, on the other hand, by failing to resolve the Italo-Yugoslav controversy at the collective peace conference table, compounded the general problem and paved the way for Rapallo.

In November 1920 the Yugoslavs had little choice but to accept Italian terms. Faced with Wilson's electoral defeat, concerted French and British pressure, and the economic disarray and mounting political strife at home, they recognized that a stabilization of their international position was as imperative as a military conflict with Italy was unthinkable. The decision to accept Italian terms was also wise. The Treaty of London was forever buried at Rapallo. Future Italian governments—and it may be imagined how Mussolini might have proceeded—would have no recourse to it. Dalmatia, except for Zara, and most of the Dalmatian archipelago were securely gained. Adriatic peace also led to an immediate improvement in relations with France and Great Britain, whose freedom of action in regard to Italy was now fully restored.

Yet the inescapable fact that half a million Croats and Slovenes were assigned to Italy remained. In this respect the Rapallo settlement sowed the seeds of future conflict. It is not unlikely that a more moderate solution—such as adoption of the Wilson line in Istria—designed to sharply reduce the size of the Slav component assigned to Italy, would have brought greater long-range stability to the region. For the failure to effect a reasonable solution of the ethnic problem perpetuated a grievance that could be eliminated, a generation later, only by reopening the entire territorial problem in the west.

Appendix

The Yugoslav Delegation at the Paris Peace Conference *

Plenipotentiaries:
  Nikola P. Pašić, former Prime Minister.
  Ante Trumbić, Minister of Foreign Affairs.
  Milenko Vesnić, Minister in Paris.
  Ivan Žolger, University Professor.

Delegates:
  Mata Bošković, former Minister in London.
  Otokar Rybař, Lawyer, Representative.
  Smodlaka, Lawyer, Representative.

Secretary General (of the Yugoslav Delegation) at the Peace Conference:
  B. Vošnjak, University Professor.

General Secretariat of the Mission:
  Chief—Jovan T. Marković, Minister Plenipotentiary.

Secretariat:
  Jovan Vučković, Consul-General.
  Stevan Pavlović, First Secretary of Legation.
  Ljubomir Nešić, Secretary in the Ministry of Foreign Affairs.
  Dragutin Kojić, Secretary of Legation.
  Ninko Perić, Secretary in the Ministry of Foreign Affairs.
  Pavle Karović, Secretary in the Ministry of Foreign Affairs.
  Petar M. Jovanović, Secretary in the Ministry of Foreign Affairs.
  Dragomir Kasidolac, Secretary in the Ministry of Foreign Affairs.
  Vasilije Protić, Secretary in the Ministry of Foreign Affairs
  Aleksandar Cincar Marković, Secretary in the Ministry of Foreign Affairs.
  Radomir N. Pašić, Attaché of Legation.
  Vladislav Kojić, Attaché of Legation.

Assigned to Secretariat:
  M. M. Petronijević, former Chef de Cabinet.

* Given as listed in Act No. 72 of the Military Mission, March 13, 1919, K&H, pp. 10–11. The translation of titles is mine.

Marcel Guiesse, former Vice-Prefect.
Ivo Šubelj, Lawyer, Counselor.
Franja Juvančić, Professor.
Živko Barlovac, former Honorary Consul-General.
Bruno Hugo Stare, Secretary.

Ethnographic and Historical Section:
Jovan Cvijić, former Rector of Belgrade University.
Tihomir Djordjević, University Professor.
Lujo Vojnović.
Aleksandar Belić, Professor at Belgrade University.
Jovan Radonić.
Gazzari, Lawyer.
Stanoje Stanojević, Professor at Belgrade University.
Pavle Popović, Professor at Belgrade University.
Niko Županíc, Vice-Director of Ethnographic Museum.
Boža Marković, Professor of Belgrade University.
Janko Mačkovšek, Engineer.
Tomaš Šorli, Recording Secretary.
Franja Vesel, Director of Surveys.
Fran Kovačić, Doctor of Philosophy, Professor.
J. Slavić, Doctor of Theology, Professor.
Janko Pretnar, Doctor of Literature, Professor.
J. Ribarič, Professor.
Ivan-Marija Čok, Doctor of Law, Lawyer.
M. Krmpotić, Doctor of Law.

International Law Section:
Slobodan Jovanović, Rector of Belgrade University.
Kosta Kumanudi, Professor at Belgrade University.
M. Novaković, Professor at Belgrade University.
Leonid Pitamic, Professor at Ljubljana University.

Section of Experts for Different Provinces:
Aleksandar (sic) Radović, former Prime Minister of Montenegro.
D. Vasiljević, Deputy.
N. Stojanović, Deputy.
Tresić-Pavičić, Deputy.

Press Section:
Žujović, former Minister.
Janko Spasojević, former Minister of Montenegro.
Lazar Marković, Professor at Belgrade University.

Cvjetiša, Publicist.
L. Savadžijan, Journalist.
Grgur Jakšić, Consul.
Milan Grol, Director of the National Theatre in Belgrade.
D. Tomić, Journalist.
J. Čelović.
Pavle Stefanović, Professor.
Ivan Švegelj, Consul-General.
Pavle Popović, University Professor.

Military Mission. Delegates:
General Pešić.
Admiral V. Šuteršić.
Colonel D. Kalafatović.

Experts:
Major Marinković.
Major K. Stojanović.
Lieutenant V. Budisavljević.
Lieutenant S. Tobolar.
Lieutenant Andrić.

Financial and Economic Section. Delegates:
Milorad Drašković, former Minister.
Kosta Stojanović, former Minister.
Velizar Janković, former Minister.

Experts:
Milan Todorović, Inspector in the Ministry of Agriculture.
M. Stanarević, Bank Director.
V. Bajkić, Bank Director.
D. Dučić, Secretary in the Ministry of Finance.
K. Jovanović, Secretary.
Mirko Brezigar.
Mirko Kramer, Industrialist.
Vekoslav Kisovac.
Fran Golouh, Journalist and Publicist.

Railroads and Communications Section. Delegates:
Andra Stanić, former Minister.
B. Vuković, Chief of Services in the Serbian Directorate of Railroads.
Milos Savčić, former Minister.

Experts:

D. Dimitrijević, Chief of Section in the Ministry of P.T.T. (Posts, Telegraph, and Telephone).

Radisav Avramović, Engineer.

B. Pajević, Engineer.

M. Pujić, Inspector in the Ministry of Public Works.

Bibliography

The following listing is selective and includes mainly titles central to this study. Certain unpublished sources consulted—such as the diary of Colonel Edward M. House, located at Yale; the confidential memoranda and notes of Robert Lansing, at the Library of Congress; the prewar notes and correspondence of Nikola Pašić, at the Serbian Academy—are not listed because they did not materially contribute to the study. In some instances, however, special use is referred to in the footnotes.

UNPUBLISHED DOCUMENTARY SOURCES

France: Dossiers Klotz, the papers of Louis-Lucien Klotz, French Minister of Finance and Delegate Plenipotentiary at the Peace Conference, deposited at the Bibliothèque de Documentation Internationale Contemporaine, Paris. Dossiers: "The Banat," "Hungary," "Italy," "Roumania," "Yugoslavia," and "Status of the Balkan Peoples: Bulgarian frontiers, Serbia, Bulgaria, Montenegro."

Italy: Ministero degli Affari Esteri. Commissione per la Pubblicazione dei Documenti Diplomatici Italiani, Rome.
  1. Archivio di Gabinetto: Serbian files for 1916, 1918, 1919; Recognition of the New Serbian State files for 1918–19.
  2. Archivio della Direzione degli Affari Politici: Serbian files for 1916, 1918, 1919; Yugoslav files for 1918, 1919.
  3. Telegrammi Ordinari: miscellaneous pertaining to Serbia and the Yugoslavs.

Paris Peace Conference:
  1. Confidentiel. Recueil des Actes de la Conférence. Partie I. *Actes du Conseil Suprême. Recueil des résolutions* (en quatre fascicules). (Paris, Imprimerie Nationale, 1934–35). At the BDIC.
  2. Papers of the American Commission to Negotiate the Peace, National Archives, Washington, D.C.:
      a. "Committee on Rumanian and Yugoslav Affairs."
      b. "Central Territorial Committee."

    c. "Commission of Inquiry on Fiume Incidents (July 7, 1919)."
    d. "Klagenfurt Mission (June 6, 1919)."
    e. "Commission on Issues of Laibach (March 8, 1919)."

United States: Department of State (National Archives), Washington, D.C.

1. Correspondence between the Department of State and the United States Legation at Corfu/Belgrade, 1915–19; between the Department of State and the Serbian/Yugoslav Legation in Washington. Decimal classifications: 763.72/; 701.0072/; 860H.01/.
2. Papers of the American Commission to Negotiate the Peace, 1918–19. Decimal classification: 184.01102/.

Yugoslavia:

1. The Trumbić Papers (Arhiv. Istorijski Institut Jugoslavenske Akademije Znanosti i Nauka, Zagreb). The collection includes the archive of the Yugoslav Committee and Trumbić's official correspondence as Minister of Foreign Affairs, 1919–20.
2. "Zapisnik Delegacije S.H.S. na Mirovnoj Konferenciji u Parizu, 1919–1920," Manuscript Division, Library of the University of Zagreb (MS No. R 5271).

PUBLISHED DOCUMENTARY SOURCES

Almond, N., and Lutz, R. H., eds., *The Treaty of St. Germain: A Documentary History of its Territorial and Political Clauses,* Stanford, Stanford University Press, 1935.

Great Britain: Foreign Office. *Documents on British Foreign Policy 1919–1939,* E. L. Woodward and R. Butler, eds., Vol. 4, 1st. Ser. London, H. M. Stationery Office, 1952.

Italy: Ministero degli Affari Esteri. *I Documenti diplomatici italiani,* R. Mosca, ed., Vol. 1, 6th Ser. Rome, Istituto poligrafico dello stato, 1956.

—— *The Italian Claims on the Alps and in the Adriatic,* Paris, 1919.

Jovanović, V. M., ed., *Rapallski Ugovor 12 Novembra 1920. Zbirka Dokumenata,* Zagreb, Jadranski Institut Jugoslavenske Akademije, 1950.

Krizman, Bogdan, and Hrabak, Bogumil, eds., *Zapisnici sa Sednica Delegacije Kraljevine SHS na Mirovnoj Konferenciji u Parizu 1919–1920,* Belgrade, Institut Društvenih Nauka, 1960.

Mantoux, P., ed., *Les Délibérations du Conseil des Quatre (24 Mars–28 Juin 1919)*, 2 vols. Paris, Centre national de la recherche scientifique, 1955.

Michel, P. H., ed., *La Question de l'Adriatique (1914–1918) (1914–1918)—recueil de documents,* Paris, Alfred Costes, 1938.

Paris Peace Conference: "Commission des nouveaux États et des minorités," Procès-Verbaux, *La Paix de Versailles,* Vol. 10, Paris, Éditions Internationales, 1932.

Plamenac, J., *Montenegro before the Peace Conference* (Paris, 1919). Three memoranda submitted to the Peace Conference on March 5, 1919.

Rumania: *Roumania before the Peace Conference. The Banat of Temeshvar,* Paris, 1919.

—— *La Roumanie devant le Congrès de la Paix. Ses Revendications territoriales,* Paris, 1919.

Russia: Commission for the Publication of Documents in the Age of Imperialism. *Die Internationale Beziehungen im Zeitalter des Imperialismus,* O. Hoetzsch, ed., 8 vols. Berlin, Verlag von Reimar Hobbing, 1931–36.

Šišić, F., ed., *Dokumenti o Postanku Kraljevine Srba, Hrvata i Slovenaca, 1914–1919,* Zagreb, Matica Hrvatska, 1920.

—— *Jadransko Pitanje na Konferenciji Mira u Parizu, Zbirka Akata i Dokumenata,* Zagreb, Matica Hrvatska 1920.

Stojanović, N., *Jugoslovenski Odbor: Članci i Dokumenti,* Zagreb, Nova Evropa, 1927.

United States: Department of State. *The Adriatic Question, Papers Relating to the Italian-Jugoslav Boundary,* Division of Foreign Intelligence, Ser. M. 167, Washington, Government Printing Office, 1920.

—— *Papers Relating to the Foreign Relations of the United States, 1918–1919,* 4 vols. Washington, Government Printing Office, 1930–34.

—— *Papers Relating to the Foreign Relations of the United States. The Lansing Papers, 1914–1920,* 2 vols. Washington, Government Printing Office, 1939–40.

—— *Papers Relating to the Foreign Relations of the United States. The Paris Peace Conference, 1919,* 13 vols. Washington, Government Printing Office, 1942–47.

Yugoslavia: Memoranda submitted to the Peace Conference:
Delimitations between Serbians and Magyars in the Batchka, Paris, 1919.

Delimitation between the Serbians and the Roumanians in the Banat, Paris, 1919.

Delimitations between the Serbians, Croatians and Slovenes and the Hungarians in Baranya and Somogy, Paris, 1919.

Frontier between the Kingdom of the Serbians, Croatians and Slovenes and German-Austria and Hungary, Paris, 1919.

Frontiers between the Kingdom of the Serbians, Croatians and Slovenes and the Kingdom of Italy, Paris, 1919.

Memorandum Presented to the Peace Conference, in Paris, concerning the Claims of the Kingdom of the Serbians, Croatians and Slovenes, Paris, 1919.

The Serbo-Bulgarian Relations and the Question of the Rectification of the Frontier, Paris, 1919.

The Territories of Goritza and Gradiska and the Town of Trieste, Paris, 1919.

The Town of Riyeka (Fiume), Paris, 1919.

The Town of Trieste, Paris, 1919.

Yugoslavia. *Definitivni Rezultati Popisa Stanovištva od 31 Januara 1921 god.,* Sarajevo, 1932.

—— *Dokumenti o Pitanju Granice sa Arbanijom,* Belgrade, 1924.

—— *Stenografske Beleške Privremenog Narodnog Pretstavništva Srba, Hrvata i Slovenaca, 1919–1920,* 5 fascs. Belgrade, 1920.

GENERAL

A.E., *La Question de Fiume,* Paris, 1919.

Adams, J. C., *Flight in Winter,* Princeton, Princeton University Press, 1942.

Alatri, P., *Nitti, d'Annunzio e la Questione Adriatica,* Milan, Feltrinelli, 1959.

Albania, Paris, 1919.

Albertini, L., *Venti Anni di vita politica,* 5 vols. Bologna, Zanichelli, 1950–53.

Albrecht-Carrié, R., *Italy at the Paris Peace Conference,* New York, Columbia University Press, 1938.

Aldrovandi Marescotti, Luigi, *Guerra Diplomatica: Ricordi e frammenti di diario, 1914–1919,* Milan, Mondadori, 1938.

—— *Nuovi Ricordi e frammenti di diario per far séguito a "Guerra Diplomatica,"* Milan, Mondadori, 1938.

Annuaire de l'Association yougoslave de droit international, 3 vols. Belgrade-Paris, Éditions Internationales, 1931–37.

Auerbach, B., *L'Autriche et la Hongrie pendant la guerre,* Paris, Alcan, 1925.

—— *Les Races et les nationalités en Autriche-Hongrie,* Paris, Alcan, 1917.

Baerlein, H. P., *The Birth of Yugoslavia,* 2 vols. London, Parsons, 1922.

Baker, R. S., *Woodrow Wilson and World Settlement,* 3 vols. Garden City, N.Y., Doubleday, Page, 1922.

—— *Woodrow Wilson: Life and Letters,* 8 vols. Garden City, N.Y., Doubleday, Page, 1927–39.

Barac, F., *Croats and Slovenes, Friends of the Entente,* Paris, 1919.

Barker, T. M., *The Slovenes of Carinthia—A National Minority Problem,* New York, League of C.S.A., 1960.

Belić, A., and Mihaldjić, S., *La Question du Banat, de la Batchka et de la Baranya. La Baranya,* Paris, 1919.

—— *La Question du Banat, de la Batchka et de la Baranya. De la Statistique de la Baranya,* Paris, 1919.

Benedetti, G., *La Pace di Fiume dalla conferenza a Parigi al Trattato di Roma,* Bologna, Zanichelli, 1924.

Beneš, É., *Souvenirs de guerre et de révolution, 1914–1918,* 2 vols. Paris, Leroux, 1928.

Bernardy, A. A., and Falorsi, V., *La Questione Adriatica vista d'oltre Atlantico, 1917–1919,* Bologna, Zanichelli, 1923.

Bogdanov, Vaso, "Bunjevci," in *Živa Prošlost,* Zagreb, Zora, 1957.

—— *Historijska uloga društvenih klasa u rješavanju južnoslovenskog nacionalnog pitanja,* Zagreb, Jugoslavenska Akademija, 1954.

Bonsal, S., *Suitors and Suppliants: the Little Nations at Versailles,* New York, Prentice-Hall, 1946.

Borgese, G. A., *Goliath: the March of Fascism,* New York, Viking, 1937.

Bratianu, G. I., *Origines et formation de l'unité roumaine,* Bucharest, Institut d'Histoire Universelle "N. Iorga," 1943.

Budisavljević, S., *Stvaranje Države Srba, Hrvata i Slovenaca,* Zagreb, Jugoslavenska Akademija, 1958.

Burnett, P. M., *Reparation at the Paris Peace Conference,* 2 vols., New York, Columbia University Press, 1940.

Chopin, J., *Les Yougoslaves et l'Entente,* Paris, 1918.

Comité Monténégrin pour l'Union Nationale, Geneva, 1917.

Crespi, S., *Alla Difesa d'Italia in guerra e a Versailles. (Diario 1917–1919),* Milan, Mondadori, 1937.

Čulinović, Ferdo, *Državnopravna Historija Jugoslavenskih Zemalja XIX i XX vijeka. (Druga Knjiga: Srbija-Crna Gora-Makedonija. Jugoslavija, 1918–1945.),* Zagreb, Školska Knjiga, 1954.

—— *Nacionalno Pitanje u Jugoslavenskim Zemljama*, Zagreb, Novi List, 1955.

—— *Odjeci Oktobra u Jugoslavenskim Krajevima*, Zagreb, "27 Srpanj," 1957.

—— *Razvitak Jugoslavenskog Federalizma*, Zagreb, Školska Knjiga, 1952.

—— *Riječka Država,* Zagreb, 1953.

Cvijetiša, F., *Les Problèmes nationaux de l'Autriche-Hongrie—les Yougoslaves,* Paris, 1918.

Cvijić, J., *Cvijičeva Knjiga*, Belgrade, 1927.

—— *La Frontière septentrionale des Yougoslaves,* Paris, 1919.

—— *Iz Uspomena i Života,* Novi Sad, 1923.

—— *La Péninsule balkanique. Géographie humaine,* Paris, Colin, 1918.

—— *Unité ethnique et nationale des Yougoslaves,* Bologna, 1918.

Cvijić, J., Radonić, J., et al., *La Question du Banat, de la Batchka et de la Baranya. Le Banat,* Paris, 1919.

—— *La Question du Banat, de la Batchka et de la Baranya. La Batchka,* Paris, 1919.

—— *La Question du Banat, de la Batchka et de la Baranya. La Baranya,* Paris, 1919.

Deák, F., *Hungary at the Paris Peace Conference,* New York, Columbia University Press, 1942.

Denis, E., "Du Vardar à l'Istrie," *Revue yougoslave, 1,* (1919), 13–37.

Digović, P., *La Dalmatie et les problèmes de l'Adriatique,* Lausanne, F. Rouge, 1944.

Dinčić, K. M., "Le Fédéralisme chez les Slaves du Sud, 1804–1954," MS (1955), used by permission of the author.

Djonović, N., *Crna Gora pre i posle Ujedinjenja,* Belgrade, 1939.

Djordjević, K. R., and Živanović, D. I., *Vojna Geografija–Osnovni Deo Balkanskog Poluostrva* [Belgrade, 1931].

Djordjević, M., *Srbija i Jugosloveni za Vreme Rata, 1914–1918,* Belgrade, Sveslovenska Knjižara, 1922.

Dominian, L., *The Frontiers of Language and Nationality in Europe,* New York, Holt, 1917.

Eisenman, L., *Le Compromis austro-hongrois,* Paris, 1904.

Errera, C., *Italiani e Slavi nella Venezia Giulia,* Rome, 1919.

Gelfand, Lawrence E., *The Inquiry: American Preparations for Peace, 1917–1919,* New Haven, Yale University Press, 1963.

Ghisleri, A., *Italia e Jugoslavia,* Rome, 1945.

Giurati, G., *Con d'Annunzio e Millo in difesa dell'Adriatico,* Florence, Sansoni, 1954.

Glaise-Horstenau, Edmund von, *The Collapse of the Austro-Hungarian Empire,* London and Toronto, Dent, 1930.

Gmajner, I., *Savremeni Pokret za Narodno Ujedinjenje,* Geneva, 1918.

Gottlieb, W. W., *Studies in Secret Diplomacy during the First World War,* London, Allen and Unwin, 1957.

Grey, Sir Edward, *Twenty-five Years, 1892–1916,* 2 vols. New York, Stokes, 1925.

Grigosono, P., *Ujedinjena Jugoslavija,* Ljubljana, Narodna Tiskara, 1938.

Hanak, H., *Great Britain and Austria-Hungary during the First World War. A Study in the Formation of Public Opinion,* London, Oxford University Press, 1962.

Haumant, É., *La Frontière septentrionale de l'Etat yougo-slave,* Paris, 1919.

Hauptmann, F., *Rijeka od Rimske tarsatike do Hrvatsko-Ugarske Nagodbe,* Zagreb, Matica Hrvatska, 1951.

Hautecoeur, L., *L'Italie sous le ministère Orlando, 1917–1919,* Paris, Bossard, 1919.

Helmreich, E. C., *The Diplomacy of the Balkan Wars, 1912–1913,* Cambridge, Mass., Harvard University Press, 1938.

Hinković, H., *Iz Velikog Doba,* Zagreb, 1927.

Holborn, H., *The Political Collapse of Europe,* New York, Alfred A. Knopf, 1951.

Horn, G., *Le Compromis de 1868 entre la Hongrie et la Croatie,* Paris, 1907.

Howard, Harry N., *The Partition of Turkey: A Diplomatic History, 1913–1923,* Norman, University of Oklahoma Press, 1931.

L'Istrie, Paris, 1919.

L'Istrie, terre yougoslave, Ljubljana, 1919.

Ivanović, I., *O Bunjevcima. Povjesničko-narodnopisna rasprava,* Subotica, 1894.

Iz Istorije Jugoslavije, 1918–1945. Zbornik Predavanja, Belgrad, Nolit, 1958.

Jaquin, P., *La Question des minorités entre l'Italie et la Yougoslavie,* Paris, 1929.

Jareb, J., ed., *Leroy King's Reports from Croatia, March to May 1919,* New York, Journal of Croatian Studies (Reprint-booklet), 1960.

Jászi, O., *The Dissolution of the Habsburg Monarchy,* Chicago, University of Chicago Press, 1929.

—— *Revolution and Counter-Revolution in Hungary,* London, King and Son, 1924.

Jelavich, C., "Nikola P. Pašić: Greater Serbia or Jugoslavia?" *Journal of Central European Affairs, 11* (1951), 133–52.

Johnson, D. W., "Fiume and the Adriatic Problem," in E. M. House and C. Seymour, *What Really Happened at Paris,* New York, Charles Scribner's, 1921.

Jovanović, Jovan, *Borba za Narodno Ujedinjenje, 1914–1918,* Belgrade, Srpska Književna Zadruga, 1934.

—— *Stvaranje Zajedničke Države Srba, Hrvata i Slovenaca,* 3 vols. Belgrade, Srpska Književna Zadruga, 1929.

Jovanović, Slobodan, *Moji Savremenici: Nikola Pašić,* Windsor, Can., Avala, 1962.

—— *Ustavno Pravo Kraljevine Srba, Hrvata i Slovenaca,* Belgrade, Geca Kon, 1924.

Kann, R. A., *The Multinational Empire: Nationalism and National Reform in the Habsburg Monarchy, 1848–1918,* 2 vols. New York, Columbia University Press, 1950.

Karolyi, M., *Faith without Illusion,* New York, Dutton, 1957.

Kerner, R. J., *The Yugoslav Movement,* Cambridge, Mass., 1918.

Kojić, B., "Postanak Jugoslavenske Trgovačke Mornarice," MS (1956), used by permission of the author.

Kovačić, F., *La Question du Prekmurje, de la Styrie et de la Carinthie. La Styrie,* Paris, 1919.

Kratchounov, K., *La Politique extérieure de la Bulgarie, 1880–1920,* Sofia, 1932.

Krizman, Bogdan, "Kako je Dr. Ante Trumbić Postao Prvi Jugoslavenski Ministar Vanjskih Poslova," *Slobodna Dalmacija* (April 17, 1956).

—— "Pred Početak Konferencije Mira 1919 godine," *Slobodna Dalmacija,* April 19, 1956.

—— "Iza Kulisa Vijećanja Naše Delegacije," *Slobodna Dalmacija,* April 26, 1956.

—— "Pitanje Medjunarodnog Priznanja Nove Države," *Slobodna Dalmacija,* May 16, 1956.

—— "Saveznički Ultimatum u Jadranskom Pitanju Siječnja 1920 godine," *Jadranski Zbornik,* 2 (Rijeka-Pula, 1957), 199–236.

—— "Predigra Konferenciji u Rapallu," *Zadarska Revija,* 7, March 1958.

Lansing, Robert, *The Peace Negotiations. A Personal Narrative,* Boston, Houghton Mifflin, 1921.

—— *War Memoirs,* Indianapolis, 1935.

Lazić, A., *Frontière ethnographique italo-yougoslavo-allemande,* Paris [1918]. A map.

Léger, L., *La Liquidation de l'Autriche-Hongrie,* Paris, 1915.

Lloyd George, D., *The Truth about the Peace Treaties,* 2 vols. London, Gollancz, 1938.

Logio, G. C., *Bulgaria Past and Present,* Manchester, Sherratt and Hughes, 1936.

Maček, V., *In the Struggle for Freedom,* New York, Robert Speller, 1957.

Macartney, C. A., *Hungary and Her Successors, 1919–1937,* London, Oxford University Press, 1937.

—— *National States and National Minorities,* London, Oxford University Press, 1934.

Mamatey, V. S., "The United States and the Dissolution of Austria-Hungary," *Journal of Central European Affairs, 10* (1950), 256–70.

—— *The United States and East Central Europe, 1914–1918. A Study in Wilsonian Diplomacy and Propaganda,* Princeton, Princeton University Press, 1957.

Mandić, A., *Fragmenti za Historiju Ujedinjenja,* Zagreb, Jugoslavenska Akademija, 1956.

Marek, K., *Identity and Continuity of States in Public International Law,* Geneva, Droz, 1954.

Marjanović, M., *Londonski Ugovor iz Godine 1915,* Zagreb, Jugoslavenska Akademija, 1960.

Marston, F. S., *The Peace Conference of 1919,* London, Oxford University Press, 1944.

May, A. J., *The Hapsburg Monarchy, 1867–1914,* Cambridge, Mass., Harvard University Press, 1951.

Mazzini, G., *Scritti editi e inediti di Giuseppe Mazzini,* Vol. 14, 3rd ed. Rome, 1885.

Mémoire sur la Question Dalmate, Paris, 1919.

Meštrović, I., *Uspomene na političke ljude i dogadjaje,* Buenos Aires, Knjižnica Hrvatske Revije, 1961.

Miller, D. H., *My Diary at the Conference of Paris,* 20 vols., privately printed, 1928.

Mitrinović, C., and Brašić, M. N., *Jugoslavenske Narodne Skupštine i Sabori,* Belgrade, Narodna Skupština, 1937.

Moodie, A. E., *The Italo-Yugoslav Boundary,* London, Philip and Son, 1945.

Mousset, A., *L'Albanie devant l'Europe (1912–1929),* Paris, 1930.

—— *La Royaume des Serbes, Croates et Slovènes,* Paris, 1921.

Le Mouvement yougo-slave en Autriche-Hongrie pendant la guerre, Paris, 1919.

The National Claims of the Serbians, Croatians and Slovenes. (Presented to the Brothers of Allied Countries by the Serbian Brothers), Paris, 1919.

Nicolson, H., *Peacemaking, 1919,* New York, Harcourt, Brace and Company, 1939.

Niederle, L., *La Race slave. Statistique-démographie-anthropologie,* Paris, 1916.

Nikolajević, B., *Reparacije,* Sarajevo, Veselin Masleša, 1956.

Nitti, Francesco Saverio, *Rivelazioni. Dramatis Personae,* Naples, Edizioni Scientifiche Italiane, 1948.

Orlando, Vittorio Emanuele, *Memorie, 1915–1919,* Milan, 1960.

La Paix de Versailles (Questions territoriales), 2 vols. Paris, Éditions Internationales, 1939.

Paresce, G., *Italia e Jugoslavia dal 1915 al 1929,* Florence, 1935.

Nikola P. Pašić, Belgrade, Samouprava, 1937.

Nikola Pašić u Novoj Evropi, Zagreb, Nova Evropa, 1926.

Paulova, M., *Jugoslavenski Odbor,* Zagreb, Prosvjetna Nakladna Zadruga, 1925.

Pavelić, A. S., *Dr. Ante Trumbić: Problemi Hrvatsko-Srpskih Odnosa,* Munich, Knjižnica Hrvatske Revije, 1959.

Pekić, P., *Propast Austro-Ugarske Monarhije i Postanak Nasljednih Država,* Subotica, Globus, 1937.

Picot, E., *Les Serbes de Hongrie,* Prague, 1873.

Potočnjak, F., *Iz Emigracije,* 2 vols. Zagreb, 1919.

—— *Kobne smjernice naše politike spram Italije,* Zagreb, 1925.

Prezzolini, G., *La Dalmatie,* Paris, 1917.

Prodanović, G., "Nikola Pašić," *Srpski Književni Glasnik,* 20 (1927), 123–34.

Protić, S., "A Serbian Protests," *New Europe,* 8 (1918), 258–59.

Purić, B., "Nacionalna Politika Nikole Pašića," *Sloboda,* Chicago, 1952–54.

The Question of Scutari, Paris, 1919.

Radović, A., et al., *The Question of Montenegro,* Paris, 1919.

Randi, O., *Nicola P. Pašić,* Rome, 1927.

Redlich, J., *Austrian War Government,* New Haven, Yale University Press, 1929.

Roglić, J., *Le Recensement de 1910. Ses Méthodes et son application dans la Marche Julienne,* Sušak, Jadranski Institut, 1946.

Rojnić, M., *Istrie. Aperçu historique*, Sušak, Jadranski Institut, 1945.

Roncagli, G., *Il Problema militare adriatico spiegato a tutti*, Rome, Reale Società Geografica Italiana, 1918.

Salandra, A., *L'Intervento*, Milan, Mondadori, 1931.

—— *La Neutralità italiana*, Milan, Mondadori, 1928.

Salvemini, G., *Dal Patto di Roma alla Pace di Roma*, Turin, Gobetti, 1925.

Šepić, D., *Supilo Diplomat. Rad Frana Supila u Emigraciji, 1914–1917 godina*, Zagreb, 1961.

Seton-Watson, R. W., *The Balkans, Italy and the Adriatic*, London, Nisbet, 1916.

—— *A History of the Roumanians*, Cambridge, Eng., Cambridge University Press, 1934.

—— "Serbia's Choice," *New Europe, 8*, (1919), 121–28.

—— *The Southern Slav Question and the Hapsburg Monarchy*, London, Constable, 1911.

—— "Supilo u Rusiji," *Nova Evropa, 14*, (1926), 348–63.

—— *Treaty Revision and the Hungarian Frontiers*, London, Eyre and Spottiswoode, 1934.

Seymour, C., *The Intimate Papers of Colonel House*, 4 vols. Boston, Houghton Mifflin, 1926–28.

Sforza, C., *L'Italia dal 1914 al 1944 quale io la vidi*, Rome, Mondadori, 1946.

—— *Jugoslavia, storia e ricordi*, Milan, 1948.

—— *Nikola Pašić*, Belgrade, Kosmos, 1937.

Šišić, F., *Abrégé de l'histoire politique de Riéka-Fiume*, Paris, 1919.

—— *Predratna politika Italije i postanak Londonskog pakta*, Split, 1933.

—— *Jugoslavenska Misao. Istorija ideje Jugoslavenskog narodnog ujedinjenja i oslobodjenja od 1790–1918*, Belgrade, Balkanski Institut, 1937.

Slavić, M., *La Question du Prekmurje, de la Styrie et de la Carinthie. De la Statistique du Prekmurje*, Paris, 1919.

Slepčević, P., *Jovan Cvijić*, Sarajevo, 1927.

Slipičević, F., *Prvi svjetski rat i stvaranje države Jugoslovenskih naroda*, Sarajevo, Veselin Masleša, 1957.

Slivensky, I., *La Bulgarie depuis le Traité de Berlin et la paix dans les Balkans*, Paris, Jouve, 1927.

Smodlaka, J., *Jugoslav Territorial Claims*, Paris, 1919.

The Southern Slav Programme, London, 1915.

Spasojević, J., *Ujedinjenje Crne Gore sa Srbijom*, Geneva, 1917.

Spector, Sherman D., *Rumania at the Paris Peace Conference: A Study of the Diplomacy of Ioan I. C. Brătianu,* New York, Bookman, 1962.

Steed, H. Wickham, "R. W. Seton-Watson," MS, used by permission of the author.

—— *Through Thirty Years, 1892–1922,* 2 vols. Garden City, N.Y., Doubleday, Page, 1925.

Tamaro, A., *L'Adriatico—golfo d'Italia; l'Italianità di Trieste,* Milan, 1915.

—— *Il Patto di Roma,* Rome, 1923.

—— *Il Trattato di Londra,* Milan, Treves, 1918.

Tardieu, A., *The Truth about the Treaty,* Indianapolis, Bobbs-Merrill, 1921.

Taylor, A. J. P., *The Habsburg Monarchy, 1809–1918,* London, Hamilton, 1951.

Tchoubinski, M. P., *L'Idée de l'unité serbo-croate,* Paris, 1918.

Temperley, H. W. V., ed., *A History of the Peace Conference of Paris,* 6 vols. London, Henry Frowdy, Hodder and Stoughton, 1920–24.

Thompson, C. T., *The Peace Conference Day by Day,* New York, Brentano's, 1920.

Toscano, M., *Il Patto di Londra,* Bologna, Zanichelli, 1934.

—— *La Serbia e l'intervento in guerra dell'Italia,* Milan, 1939.

Trieste et la Yougoslavie, Ljubljana, 1919.

Trifunović, M., "Nikola Pašić," *Srpski Književni Glasnik,* 20 (1927), 197–206.

Vojnoistoriski Institut J.N.A., *Jugoslovenski Dobrovoljački Korpus u Rusiji,* Belgrade, 1954.

Vojnović, L., *La Dalmatie, l'Italie et l'unité yougoslave, 1797–1917,* Geneva, Georg et Co., 1917.

—— *Histoire de la Dalmatie,* 2 vols. Paris, Hachette, 1934.

Vojnović, L., Šišić, F., et. al., *The Question of the Adriatic. Fiume (Rieka),* Paris, 1919.

Vošnjak, B., *A Bulwark against Germany: The Fight of the Slovenes for National Existence,* London, 1917.

—— *U borbi za ujedinjenu narodnu državu,* Belgrade-Zagreb, 1928.

—— *Yugoslav Nationalism,* London, 1916.

Wambaugh, S., *Plebiscites since the World War,* 2 vols. Washington, Carnegie Endowment for International Peace, 1933.

Wendel, H., *Der Kampf der Südslawen um Freiheit und Einheit,* Frankfurt-am-Main, 1925.

Wilder (Vilder), V., *Dva Smjera u Hrvatskoj Politici*, Zagreb, 1918.

Woodhouse, E. J., and Woodhouse, C. G., *Italy and the Jugoslavs*, Boston, Badger, 1920.

Zelenica, M., *Rat Srbije i Crne Gore 1915*, Belgrade, Vojno Delo, 1954.

Zeman, Z. A. B., *The Break-up of the Habsburg Empire, 1914–1918. A Study in National and Social Revolution*, London, Oxford University Press, 1961.

Žolger, I., et al., *La Question du Prekmurje, de la Styrie et de la Carinthie. La Carinthie*, Paris, 1919.

Index

Index 341

ported by Clemenceau and Lloyd
George, 263–68; with Trumbić and
Pašić in London, 277–78; resigns, 288
Novosti (Zagreb), 74

Obzor (Zagreb), 74, 198 n.
Orlando, Vittorio Emanuele, Italian
Prime Minister: and the Fourteen
Points, 27–28; and Trumbić, 29; and
Pact of Rome, 30; opposes recognition
of Narodno Vijeće (Zagreb), 54; authorizes occupation of Fiume, 63; and the
Badoglio Plan, 75; on French disem-
barkation at Fiume, 77; on Wilson and
the League, 118; free city "west of
Fiume," 187; with Wilson, 195, 199;
and on "Regarding the Disposition of
Fiume," 201; walks out of Conference,
201; and the Tardieu Plan, 214; resigns, 217

Pact of Rome (1918): and legitimacy of
Yugoslav aspirations, 30; no lasting ef-
fect on Italian policy, 32; subject of
controversy between Serbian government and Yugoslav Committee, 36
Paderewski, Ignacy, 91
Page, Nelson, American ambassador to
Italy, 45
Palagruža (Pelagosa), 7, 209, 212, 214,
216, 249, 251, 259, 260, 264, 265 n., 267,
287, 305, 307
Paléologue, Maurice, 270, 271
Pan-Serbianism, 4; in Pašić's view on national self-determination, 41–42; in
Pašić's attitudes, 93; and the Yugoslav
delegation at Paris Conference, 160,
198 n.
Paris Peace Conference, x, 81, 82; transferred to London, 275; Committee on
the Banat (also called Committee on
Rumanian and Yugoslav Affairs, and
Rumanian-Yugoslav Territorial Committee), a microcosm of the Council of
Ten, 172, Italy opposed to U.S., Britain, and France, 174–75, split into factions, 179; Council of Ten, and Yugoslav territorial claims, 143, 154–55, the
"double standard," 158, investigation
of Italian occupation of Fiume and
Dalmatia, 167, becomes Council of

Four, 185; Council of Four (Supreme
Council), and Austro-Hungarian fleet,
190, and Wilson memorandum on
Fiuman state, 216, policy on successor
states, 229–30
Pašić, Nikola P., Serbian Prime Minister,
4; and Treaty of London, 10–12; and
Treaty of Bucharest, 14–19; "success"
in Western Europe, 20–21; assesses
British and French attitudes toward
Yugoslav unification, 24; and Yugoslav
Committee, 24; relations with Com-
mittee improve, 25; favors centralized
government, 26; asks interpretation of
Fourteen Points, 28; resents Pact of
Rome, 30; term "Yugoslav," 36; charges
parliamentary opposition conspires
with Yugoslav Committee, 37, 43; states
Serbian policy on national self-determination, 41–42; opposes Trumbić in
Geneva negotiations, 46–49; sabotages
Geneva Declaration, 49–50; forms new
Serbian coalition government, 50; dismissed as Prime Minister by Alexander, 52; appointed head of Yugoslav
delegation to Paris Peace Conference,
53; reacts to Bolshevik Revolution, 83;
personal qualifications, 84; refuses to
serve with Trumbić in Conference
delegation, 85; the enigma of the delegation, 91–92; favors Yugoslav-Greek
liaison, 92; with Take Ionescu on
Banat, 100; opposes Trumbić, 110; on
"ethnic frontiers," 121–23, 124–28, 130,
133; presents Yugoslav case on Banat
to Council of Ten, 143–44; memorandum to Protić on arbitration for
Trieste and western Istria, 150–51;
presents Yugoslav territorial claims to
Council of Ten, 157; dispute over listing of territories, 160; and Borghese
incident, 163; and Smodlaka plebiscite
proposal, 164; before territorial commission, 174; asks abolition of Treaty
of London, 186; in dispute over Trumbić démenti, 207; designated to sign
German, Bulgarian, and Austrian
treaties, 227; moves to thwart Rumanian threat, 235; protests minorities
convention of Austrian Treaty, 239–